KV-470-197

European Economic Integration and South-East Europe

European Economic Integration and South-East Europe

Challenges and Prospects

Edited by

Klaus Liebscher

Governor of the Oesterreichische Nationalbank, Austria

Josef Christl

Member of the Governing Board of the Oesterreichische Nationalbank, Austria

Peter Mooslechner

Director of Economic Analysis and Research at the Oesterreichische Nationalbank, Austria

Doris Ritzberger-Grünwald

Head of Foreign Research at the Oesterreichische Nationalbank, Austria

Edward Elgar

Cheltenham, UK • Northampton, MA, USA

Published by
Edward Elgar Publishing Limited
Glensanda House
Montpellier Parade
Cheltenham
Glos GL50 1UA
UK

Edward Elgar Publishing, Inc.
136 West Street
Suite 202
Northampton
Massachusetts 01060
USA

A catalogue record for this book
is available from the British Library

Library of Congress Cataloguing in Publication Data

Conference on European Economic Integration (1st: 2004: Vienna, Austria)
European economic integration and South-East Europe: challenges and prospects/edited by Klaus Liebscher . . . [et al.].
p. cm.
'This book contains contributions made to the Oesterreichische Nationalbank's first Conference on European Economic Integration, which took place in November 2004' – Preface.
Includes bibliographical references and index.
1. Europe—Economic integration—Congresses. 2. European Union countries—Economic policy—Congresses. 3. European Union—Europe, Southern—Congresses. 4. European Union—Europe, Eastern—Congresses. 5. Europe, Southern—Economic conditions—21st century—Congresses. 6. Europe, Southern—Economic policy—21st century—Congresses. 7. Europe, Eastern—Economic conditions—21st century—Congresses. 8. Europe, Eastern—Economic policy—21st century—Congresses. I. Title.
HC241.C63 2004
332.4'566'09496—dc22 2005047802

ISBN 1 84542 517 0

Printed and bound in Great Britain by MPG Books Ltd, Bodmin, Cornwall

Contents

List of contributors ix

Preface
Klaus Liebscher, Josef Christl, Peter Mooslechner and Doris Ritzberger-Grünwald xi

Navigating the road to Europe 1
Klaus Liebscher

South-East European challenges and prospects 6
Jean-Claude Trichet

Changes in the focus of European economic integration 12
Axel A. Weber

PART I SOUTH-EAST EUROPE: WHERE DO INSTITUTIONS AND THE ECONOMY STAND?

1 South-East Europe: signs of catching up 21
Michael A. Landesmann

2 South-East Europe on the way to Euro–Atlantic integration 30
Erhard Busek

3 The Western Balkans' European perspective 39
Reinhard Priebe

4 South-East Europe: opportunities and potential for investment and growth 47
Elisabetta Falcetti, Peter Sanfey and Sladjana Tepic

PART II THE CASE OF DOLLARIZATION AND EUROIZATION

5 The euro in Central and Eastern European countries: some introductory remarks 65
Josef Christl

6 *De jure* dollarization and euroization 69
Eduardo Levy Yeyati

7 Lessons from sustained cases of official dollarization/euroization 77
Adalbert Winkler

PART III MONETARY AND EXCHANGE RATE POLICIES: CIRCUMSTANCES AND CHOICE IN SOUTH-EAST EUROPE

8 Monetary policy in a euro-dominated environment: challenges for central banks in South-East Europe 99
Peter Mooslechner and Doris Ritzberger-Grünwald

9 Disinflation and monetary policy arrangements in Romania 119
Daniel Daianu and Ella Kallai

10 Choice of exchange rate regime: implications for South-East Europe 145
Julius Horvath

11 Euroization in Montenegro: benefits, weaknesses and economic implications 155
Ljubiša Krgović

12 Exchange rate and monetary policies in Bulgaria since 1990 176
Mariella Nenova

PART IV FDI AND TRADE AS PIVOTAL ELEMENTS FOR CATCHING UP AND COMPETITIVENESS

13 FDI and trade as pivotal elements for catching up and competitiveness 201
Ewald Nowotny

14 Foreign direct investment in South-East Europe: what do the data tell us? 209
Dimitri G. Demekas, Balázs Horváth, Elina Ribakova and Yi Wu

15 Trade integration of the new EU member states and selected South-East European countries: lessons from a gravity model 242
Matthieu Bussière, Jarko Fidrmuc and Bernd Schnatz

16 Foreign direct investment and trade as pivotal elements for catching up and competitiveness in CEE 269
Boris Nemsic

PART V CONFRONTING SERIOUS CHALLENGES: HIGH UNEMPLOYMENT, POVERTY, BRAIN DRAIN

17 Poverty, migration and employment in South-East Europe: what can the data tell us? 281
Robert Holzmann

18 Jobless growth in South-East Europe, migration and the role of the EU 305
Tito Boeri

19 Unemployment in the Western Balkans: a synoptic diagnosis 312
Kalman Mizsei and Nicholas Maddock

20 Unemployment, poverty and brain drain: summing up 331
Thomas Wieser

PART VI BANKING IN SOUTH-EAST EUROPE AND THE LEADING ROLE OF AUSTRIAN BANKS

21 Estimating the gap in banking efficiency between Eastern and Western European economies 335
Laurent Weill

22 Banking reform in South-East Europe: accomplishments and challenges 350
Evan Kraft

23 Banking in South-East Europe: *status quo* and the way forward 368
Norbert Walter

24 Banking in South-East Europe: the case of the Raiffeisen Group 382
Heinz Wiedner

25 Banking in South-East Europe: the case of Erste Bank 386
Manfred Wimmer

Index 391

Contributors

Tito Boeri, Professor, Università Bocconi, Milan, and Fondazione Rodolfo Debenedetti, Milan.

Erhard Busek, Special Coordinator of the Stability Pact for South Eastern Europe, and coordinator of the Southeast European Cooperative Initiative.

Matthieu Bussière, Economist, External Developments Division, European Central Bank.

Josef Christl, Executive Director, Oesterreichische Nationalbank.

Daniel Daianu, Professor, The National School of Political and Administrative Studies (SNSPA), Bucharest, and former Finance Minister.

Dimitri G. Demekas, Chief, Southeastern I Division, European Department, International Monetary Fund.

Elisabetta Falcetti, Principal Economist, EBRD.

Jarko Fidrmuc, Economist, Foreign Research Division, Oesterreichische Nationalbank.

Robert Holzmann, Director for Social Protection, The World Bank Group.

Balázs Horváth, Deputy Division Chief, Northeastern Division, European Department, International Monetary Fund.

Julius Horvath, Professor, Central European University Budapest and Comenius University Bratislava.

Ella Kallai, Head of Research Department, Alpha Bank Romania.

Evan Kraft, Director, Research Department, Hrvatska Narodna Banka.

Ljubiša Krgović, President, Centralna Banka Crne Gore (Central Bank of Montenegro).

Michael A. Landesmann, Scientific Director, The Vienna Institute for International Economic Studies, and Professor, Johannes Kepler University, Linz.

Eduardo Levy Yeyati, Director, Centre for Financial Research, Business School, Universidad Torcuato Di Tella, and Research Associate, Office of the Chief Economist, Inter-American Development Bank.

Klaus Liebscher, Governor, Oesterreichische Nationalbank.

Nicholas Maddock, Western Balkans Economist, United Nations Development Programme.

Kalman Mizsei, Director, Regional Bureau for Europe and the CIS, United Nations Development Programme.

Peter Mooslechner, Director of the Economic Analysis and Research Section, Oesterreichische Nationalbank.

Boris Nemsic, CEO, mobilkom austria, and COO Wireless Telekom Austria.

Mariella Nenova, Director, Economic Research and Projections, Bălgarska Narodna Banka.

Ewald Nowotny, Professor, University of Economics and Business Administration, Vienna, former Vice-President of the European Investment Bank.

Reinhard Priebe, Director Western Balkans, DG Enlargement, European Commission.

Elina Ribakova, Economist, Systemic Issues Division, Monetary and Financial Systems Department, International Monetary Fund.

Doris Ritzberger-Grünwald, Head of the Foreign Research Division, Oesterreichische Nationalbank.

Peter Sanfey, Lead Economist, Transition Strategy and Country Analysis, European Bank for Reconstruction and Development.

Bernd Schnatz, Principal Economist, External Developments Division, European Central Bank.

Sladjana Tepic, Economic Analyst, EBRD.

Jean-Claude Trichet, President, European Central Bank.

Norbert Walter, Chief Economist, Deutsche Bank Group and Managing Director of Deutsche Bank Research, Frankfurt.

Axel A. Weber, President, Deutsche Bundesbank.

Laurent Weill, Professor, Université Robert Schuman, Institut d'Etudes Politiques, Strasbourg.

Heinz Wiedner, Member of the Board, Raiffeisen International Bank-Holding AG, Vienna.

Thomas Wieser, Director General, Austrian Federal Ministry of Finance.

Manfred Wimmer, General Manager, Strategic Group Development, Erste Bank, Vienna.

Adalbert Winkler, Deputy Head of the EU Neighbouring Regions Division, European Central Bank.

Yi Wu, Economist, Trade Policy Division, Policy Development and Review Department, International Monetary Fund.

Preface

Klaus Liebscher, Josef Christl, Peter Mooslechner and Doris Ritzberger-Grünwald

South-East Europe promises to be the next major focal region of European integration dynamics and modernization efforts. While not much research has been devoted to it so far, South-East Europe is now among the fastest-growing regions on the continent and possesses large potential yet to be tapped for further expansion. South-East Europe as we understand it and as it is generally defined in contemporary political geography comprises the following countries: Albania, Bosnia and Herzegovina, Bulgaria, Croatia, FYR of Macedonia, Romania, Serbia and Montenegro. Since Central Europe joined the EU in May 2004, the focus of the integration process has clearly shifted south-east. Apart from Romania, Bulgaria and Croatia, which are the candidates for the next accession rounds, all other countries of the region now have an accession perspective. Moreover, the Stability Pact for South-Eastern Europe has been assisting the difficult catching-up process of this region through various initiatives for years. Austria is a neighbour and intimately linked to South-East Europe by the Danube, by geography and by history. Today, economic links play a prime role, with trade volumes developing on a dynamic trajectory and Austrian investors being in the forefront of the microeconomic re-integration process of the region with the rest of Europe.

This book contains contributions made to the Oesterreichische Nationalbank's first Conference on European Economic Integration, which took place in November 2004. This event continued the tradition of our East–West Conferences, but with a new name chosen to reflect the growing-together of Europe that we have witnessed and the challenges we will have to meet in the future. After decades of Cold War and separation, we were recently able to welcome ten new member countries to the EU. But, as mentioned, the re-unification of our continent is not yet over. Further deepening and widening of the Union promises to be the focal point of efforts of economic policies in the next quarter of a century. The title of the conference, South Eastern EUROPEAN Challenges and Prospects, on which this book is based, highlights important regional issues as well as the integration dimension. High-ranking representatives from government and international organizations, central and commercial banks, as well as universities and research institutes contribute their expertise to several key topics related to macroeconomic, structural and external economic and institutional relations of South-East European countries.

To single out a few topics, taking stock of where South-East Europe stands as a point of departure yields a fascinating variety of positions in a number of fields: while major catching-up efforts are necessary virtually everywhere, some countries seem to have already embarked on a path of steady economic expansion, whereas others have apparently not yet reached the point of take-off. Some countries are in the acceding process to the European Union, while others still have quite a way to go. Some have already been reaping benefits of industrial restructuring whereas others have yet to develop viable export sectors. Challenges include the necessity to overcome problems of corruption, weak judiciary systems and to improve the investment climate. Does the region more or less correspond to what Central Europe was ten years ago? What is the current state of relations between the EU and the individual countries of the region? How has the Stability Pact for South-Eastern Europe piloted and assisted modernization efforts? On this range of issues, this book compiles first-hand evidence and background information from authors from the region and experts on the region.

The heterogeneity of traits resurfaces in the domain of monetary and exchange rate policies. Most types of exchange rate regimes can be found in the region: the solutions adopted range from a majority of hard pegs (even including cases of unilateral euroization) to a loosely managed float. Heterogeneity notwithstanding, the broad picture of anti-inflationary performance has been quite bright in recent years, although further progress is needed. There appear to be various paths to a common goal. Whereas one may assume that overall monetary policy credibility and perseverance are the decisive ingredients, one may doubt whether this is sufficient to sustain performance in the long run, if monetary policy commitment is not flanked by fiscal awareness and structural reform. In any case, euro holdings and bank deposits of the populations of South-East Europe remain high, which underlines the attractiveness of the common European currency throughout the region.

All is not bright in South-East Europe. Macroeconomic imbalances, particularly current account deficits, seem to have become entrenched across the region. While the fiscal situation has improved recently in some countries, most of them continue to be plagued by 'twin deficits'. The majority of economies remain dependent on foreign grants and financial assistance.

But this support is on a declining trend. Perhaps the most serious challenges are high unemployment, poverty and brain drain. Despite the robust average growth rates of recent years, sluggish reforms, economic mismanagement and in some cases even armed conflicts, ethnic separations and political disruptions affecting the whole region imply that most countries have still not recovered far enough to have re-attained the GDP level of 20 years ago. As a reaction to the impoverishment, migration has increased. But is migration unequivocally bad for the countries of origin? What are the main causes for the stubbornly high joblessness?

For South-East European countries saddled with deep-seated structural problems and opting for a catching-up strategy that should be as swift as possible, opening up to trade and foreign direct investment constitute pivotal steps to boost economic expansion, competitiveness and real convergence. While contributing to the reduction of external disequilibria and aid dependency, FDI and its role in enhancing know-how and creating access to international markets can be considered a 'key to success' in modernizing the economies of the region and fully 'attaching' them to the world economy. In doing this, FDI can make an important contribution to alleviating joblessness, although this seems to be an extended and not painless process. Featuring among the region's leading investors, Austrian enterprises are strongly engaged in these endeavours. However, FDI still falls well short from what it could be in most countries of the region. What would be needed to attract more foreign business into the south-east of Europe?

Shaping up banking and financial intermediation is another crucial area for harnessing South-East European economic expansion. And it is particularly the banking sector where foreign investors, among them Austrian ones, are prominently positioned in the modernization drive. They have raised the quality of services and contributed to restoring confidence in financial systems. Since the fall of the Iron Curtain, Austrian bankers have acted as pioneers not only in Central Europe, but have also been among the first to take risks and venture south-east. Today, Austrian banks together account for no less than a quarter of total banking sector assets in South-East Europe. The earlier referred to integration dynamics, the strong economic links as well as the involvement of our credit institutions in the region and its impact on the financial stability of the Austrian banking sector explain why it is essential for the Oesterreichische Nationalbank to monitor and analyse South-East Europe closely. Given multiplying cross-border links, to what degree is increased supervisory coordination on the European level necessary? Are there sizeable risks connected to the current lending booms in the region? These are just a few of the questions that are dealt with in the following pages.

Summing up, we do hope that this book will offer some fresh insights into and a better understanding of this new focus of emerging Europe which, for all its variety, possesses one overriding prospect – as Jean-Claude Trichet put it in a nutshell: progress toward EU membership.

Navigating the road to Europe

Klaus Liebscher

In 2003 the Oesterreichische Nationalbank (OeNB) hosted its last 'East–West Conference'. At the time, we had come together to debate 'The economic potential of a larger Europe – keys to success' and thus revisited the most important topics of previous East–West conferences, such as human capital formation, financial stability, and the specification of a suitable policy mix for structural reforms. I am very proud to be able to say that the OeNB has been following the transition process very closely from the very beginning. Already in 1989, the Oesterreichische Nationalbank started to build up an international platform – comprising seminars, workshops and conferences – to discuss questions that are related to the transition process and to European integration. By 1995, the East–West Conference was established as an annual event of the OeNB in Vienna that highlighted numerous aspects of mutual interest year after year. Finally, in the setting of the 2003 East–West Conference, we pre-celebrated the historic event of the enlargement of the European Union (EU) towards the East in May 2004 – truly a major milestone in the European integration process. Up to today, the European Union has reached a high degree of stability and prosperity. One may safely assume that in the first half of the last century people would not have dared to dream of this period of peaceful convergence across Europe.

Despite the successes, one has to acknowledge that much remains to be done for strengthening and advancing European integration. To single out just one of these major challenges, the so-called Lisbon strategy, there is a lack of clear and decisive progress in achieving the objectives, as recently pointed out by a report written on behalf of the European Commission (European Commission, 2004). The subdued pace of economic recovery in the euro area puts the spotlight on its structural inefficiencies with frictions both in the labour and in the product market. The EU single market has to be fully implemented in order to enhance productivity and employment, and, above all, economic growth and prosperity. The new European Commission, the European Council and the governments of the individual member states should now clearly embrace the Lisbon strategy and speed up their structural reforms in order to strengthen their international competitiveness, foster economic growth and support employment.

The EU, the Economic and Monetary Union (EMU) and the euro are Europe's strategic responses to global competition and challenges that globalization poses. The EMU represents a key step in completing the Single European Market. Today, the euro area has already established itself as a stable monetary anchor in the global economy. However, it is essential not to rest on our laurels. It has to be acknowledged that we have to work hard to keep and assure the success of EMU in the future. Several governments of euro area member states have repeatedly had difficulties to fulfil their responsibilities and obligations with regard to fiscal rules. For the stability of the euro and the credibility of the monetary union, it is essential to comply with the fiscal rules set by the Stability and Growth Pact (SGP), which provides a clear, transparent and simple framework.

Today's discussion about making the SGP rules more flexible as a short-term remedy to the fiscal problems occurring in some member states is counterproductive and at odds with the Maastricht consensus. In my mind, the SGP works as it is. The problem has been in its implementation. It is not the Pact itself which has disadvantages or which has failed. It is the missing will of several governments to fulfil their responsibilities and obligations – they failed. Thus, should the rules be made exceedingly complex and contingent on too many exceptional economic circumstances, this will clearly weaken the SGP in its implementation and credibility. Therefore, I would like to stress that a return to a path of long-term sustainable public finances is necessary in order to foster public trust in this pillar of the EMU stability architecture and to cushion possible effects of the Lisbon structural reform agenda as well as to moderate the challenges of ageing societies in Europe.

Where and how do Central and Eastern Europe and South-East Europe enter this picture? The deepening of the European Union came along with the widening of the European Union. Since the fall of the Iron Curtain in 1989, the Central and Eastern European countries have made impressive and successful, and often painful, experiences of transition to market economies; efforts there have been crowned by their accession to the EU. Membership includes the commitment to the eventual adoption of the euro.

The creation of the euro area was based on the sustainable fulfilment of the Maastricht convergence criteria, and they will be applied to future euro area entrants in the same way. These criteria form a coherent package based on a set of economic indicators that is neither negotiable nor subject to change. From a legal perspective, this ensures continuity and equal treatment; from an economic perspective, the logic of lasting convergence has not changed and is all the more important when countries are at different stages of economic development.

As was pointed out in the Convergence Report 2004 by the European Central Bank, new member states still have some way to go, and nominal and real convergence with the euro area differs considerably in some of the new member states. Therefore, reform efforts and implementation of sound policies, especially in the fiscal field, are still required on the way to monetary union. In this light, a weakening of the Stability and Growth Pact would certainly send a wrong signal to any new EU country.

As mentioned before, the OeNB very closely tracks and analyses the process of European integration of Central and Eastern European countries. To keep the interested public informed about economic topics pertaining to this region, we hosted the 'East–West Conference' year after year and published a 'Focus on Transition' twice a year. Since the process of European integration has permanently closed the divide that used to run across Europe and since the new Central and Eastern European EU member states have successfully completed most of the transition steps – and therefore can no longer be labelled transition economies – we had good reasons to update the names of two of our most important products. Our conference and our publication are complementary products. Therefore we decided to choose a common name.

The conference in 2004, on which this book is based, was the first to take place under the new name: 'Conference on European Economic Integration (CEEI)', a name which reflects the growing-together of Europe. In parallel, the OeNB relaunched the 'Focus on Transition' as 'Focus on European Economic Integration'. We will continue to investigate economic topics relevant to the new Central and Eastern European EU countries, such as the adoption of the euro. Furthermore, we used the opportunity to extend our geographical focus to the region of South-East Europe.

The 2004 'Conference on European Economic Integration' entitled 'South Eastern EUROPEAN Challenges and Prospects' was dedicated especially to this part of Europe; which comprises, as we understand it, the countries Albania, Bosnia and Herzegovina, Bulgaria, Croatia, Macedonia, Romania, Serbia and Montenegro. Since the eight Central and Eastern European countries joined the EU, the EU integration process has clearly shifted South-East. Apart from Romania, Bulgaria and Croatia, which are the next candidates for accession, all other South-East European countries now have an accession perspective, as recently stated by the European Commission. The Stability Pact for South Eastern Europe has been assisting the difficult catching-up process of this region. For the sake of completeness, let me briefly mention the case of Turkey.

Let me perhaps briefly illustrate why the OeNB has such a pronounced interest in the countries of Central and Eastern Europe, and more and more in the region of South-East Europe.

With the recent enlargement round, Austria moved closer to the geographic centre of the European Union. EU integration comes along with economic integration. Economic and financial relations between Austria and the Central and Eastern European countries have substantially deepened since the end of the Cold War.

Central and Eastern European countries have developed into one of the prime destinations of Austria's foreign direct investments. Austria is the main foreign investor in Slovenia and the third-largest in the Czech Republic and in Slovakia. Austrian companies situated in the EU's new Central European member states employ more than 220 000 persons. At the same time, Austrian companies are doing more and more business in South-East Europe.

Austrian banks, in particular, play a major role in the banking sector in this part of Europe. In Albania, the Austrian share of total banking assets reaches an impressive 51 per cent; in Bosnia and Herzegovina almost 50 per cent; in Croatia the share amounts to around 40 per cent. Due to strong involvement of Austrian commercial banks in South-East Europe and its impact on the financial stability of the Austrian banking sector, it is essential for the OeNB to monitor and analyse this region more closely. At the same time, we aim at providing a better understanding of this region, which for some people – even for some experts from Central and Eastern Europe – is still *terra incognita*. So far, not much research has been devoted to this region. However, South-East Europe promises not only to be the major focus of European integration dynamics in the coming years but it is already among the fastest-growing regions on the continent.

We very much hope that the contributions we have put together for this book will offer new insights into, and a better understanding of this region, whose political and economic perspectives are most heterogeneous. I hope that this book will make an important contribution to setting the stage for future interest in, research into and public awareness of this focus of emerging Europe.

REFERENCES

European Commission (2004), *Economic Forecasts: Autumn 2004*, Brussels: European Commission.

South-East European challenges and prospects

Jean-Claude Trichet

I am delighted to contribute to the book on the 2004 conference on South-East Europe, the first of its kind, organized by the Oesterreichische Nationalbank (OeNB). Let me also warmly congratulate the OeNB and Governor Liebscher for the initiative.

When I think of the recent enlargement of the EU in central banking terms I cannot do so without thinking of the contribution of the OeNB, which has been involved in enlargement issues from the very beginning. This was thanks to its long-standing expertise on Central and Eastern Europe. With this event, the OeNB clearly demonstrated once more that it is, inside the Eurosystem, at the forefront of the analysis of European integration.

The topic of South-East European challenges and prospects is indeed a broad one.[1] Challenges refer mainly to those that arise in the process of transition from a centrally planned to a market economy. In this respect, they are similar to the ones that those eight countries faced that joined the EU in 2004. But for countries in the former Yugoslavia there are also two other transitions with their own particular challenges: the transition from being part of a larger state to being independent democratic countries, and the transition from war to peace. I do not intend to dwell on these issues but they are indeed important when thinking about South-East Europe.

In setting the stage for the following chapters, I will focus my remarks on three aspects. I will first make some remarks on the economic and monetary performance of the region; I will then touch upon the process of economic and financial integration into the EU and, lastly, I will briefly discuss the use of the euro in the region. As I will explain in more detail, economic and monetary performance has improved over the last years, although much remains to be done. Economic links with the EU have been strengthening. These links are also based on a widespread use of the euro.

ECONOMIC AND MONETARY PERFORMANCE IN SOUTH-EAST EUROPE

South-East Europe is a diverse and complex region, characterized by a relatively low level of income compared to that of Western Europe. The seven countries considered here as South-East Europe have a combined population of around 53 million people, while the combined GDP in 2003, at nominal exchange rates, amounted to around 120 billion euros. This gives an average GDP per capita of around EUR 2300. Even when one adjusts for purchasing power standards, income per capita across the region stood in 2003 at only 26 per cent of the EU average (compared to the equivalent figure for the new member states of around 48 per cent of the EU average).

Another feature common to the countries in the region is the relatively fast growth that has been experienced in recent years. Annual real GDP growth in the region has been above 4 per cent since 2001 and catching up in real incomes is taking place. In 2003, for a third year in a row, the economies of the countries of South-East Europe grew faster, on average, than the countries in Central Eastern Europe and the Baltics that joined the EU in May 2004.

However, estimates suggest that, in real GDP terms, the economies from South-East European countries are still below where they stood 15 years ago, reflecting slow progress in transition in the early 1990s and economic disruptions due to wars and political turmoil. Thus, in order to catch up with living standards in the EU, strong growth is needed to foster real convergence.

Monetary performance across the region has also seen significant improvements in the recent past. Up until 1998 no fewer than four countries in the region (out of seven) had inflation rates that exceeded 20 per cent annually. After 1998, disinflation has proceeded and the median inflation rate among the countries in the region has remained in single digits ever since. This is not to say that there are no challenges ahead on the disinflation front. In some cases inflation remains high and the challenge remains to continue bringing inflation down. In other cases, adjustments to administered prices and indirect prices may still cause a pick-up in inflation. In those circumstances, the challenge is to avoid temporary spikes in the inflation rate translating into increases in inflationary expectations.

Progress in bringing inflation down is being accomplished through a variety of monetary and exchange rate frameworks. One can classify the regimes in place in three different groups: (i) euro-based currency boards (Bosnia and Herzegovina and Bulgaria); (ii) pegs or managed floating with the euro as a reference currency (Croatia, FYR of Macedonia, Romania and Serbia); and, (iii) independent floating (Albania). In addition, there are two territories within Serbia and Montenegro (Kosovo and Montenegro) where the monetary and exchange rate policy is determined by their unilateral euroization. As other chapters in this book highlight, country-specific circumstances have called for different choices of monetary and exchange rate policy, and changing circumstances may have called for changes in the approaches to be followed. I will not expand on this issue further than to emphasize that regardless of the actual monetary and exchange rate framework chosen, it is crucial to consolidate a culture of price stability, buttressed by independent central banks.

Outside the realm of monetary and exchange rate policy I would like to touch briefly upon fiscal and external developments. In the area of fiscal developments, it is fair to recognize that the fiscal deficit for the region as a whole stands at its lowest level, in terms of GDP, since the beginning of transition. Nevertheless, this should be interpreted with caution, particularly in light of the very positive output developments that have been observed recently. The more positive side of the economic cycle provides in fact a fitting opportunity to proceed further with fiscal consolidation, as well as with the necessary reforms of the structure of fiscal expenditures and revenues.

Developments in the external balances of the countries in the region provide sobering reading. Current account deficits have increased over the last three years and stood, for the region as a whole, above 8 per cent of GDP in 2003. While these deficits may partly stem from a natural and welcome recapitalization of the economies in the region, fast credit growth may have contributed to exacerbate the current account deficits in a number of countries. Of course, given the low levels of financial intermediation that characterize the economies in the region, the increase in lending activity is to some extent a welcome sign of a financial sector that is performing its role within the economy as a whole. However, given the links that have often been identified between lending booms and banking and currency crisis, it is clear that authorities in the region have in a number of cases to take steps to avoid credit growth that may be too fast.

More broadly, countries in the region still lag behind those in Central Eastern Europe and the Baltics, as measured by indicators such as the European Bank for Reconstruction and Development (EBRD)'s transition indicators. Improvements in the quality of the judiciary, the overall business environment and, generally, institutional reform are needed. On the positive side, it is noteworthy that, among all transition countries, it is precisely in the South-East European region where one has seen most progress in the last year or so. One cannot help but to associate this progress with the pull that enlargement of the EU may provide.

ECONOMIC AND FINANCIAL INTEGRATION WITH THE EU

In recent years we have observed a number of developments that are testament of the ongoing process of economic and financial integration between the South-East European region and the EU.

The EU is by far the most important trading partner for the countries in the region, accounting for between half and three quarters of the foreign trade of the countries in the region. Moreover, export performance of these countries has remained positive regardless of economic conditions in their main export markets. At the same time, the old trading patterns within the regions are long gone, leaving trading integration among South-East European countries at a very low level. More needs to be done, for example through the implementation of bilateral free trade agreements already signed, in this area.

Another element pointing towards economic and financial integration between the region and the EU is the recent increase in inflows of foreign direct investment (FDI). While precise figures are hard to come by, such FDI inflows often come from the euro area. Austria, for instance, ranks among the top five leading investors in no less than four countries in the region. In addition to the financial sector, FDI has typically been concentrated in the manufacturing industry as well as transport and telecommunications. Often, manufacturing activity in the region is well integrated into the production structures of Western European economies, which have been attracted by the comparatively low costs in South-East Europe and a relative geographic proximity. For the region as a whole, FDI as a percentage of GDP was close to 5 per cent in 2003. It is to be noted that this level is low compared to Central Eastern Europe and the Baltic countries. The cumulative FDI inflows into the countries of South-East Europe over the period 1989 to 2003 has been on average less than USD 700 per capita, approximately one-third of the comparable figure for Central Eastern European and Baltic countries.

I mentioned briefly investment in financial intermediaries as an area where euro area investors have been particularly active. In fact, euro area banks and financial institutions have been the most important investors in the respective banking sectors, contributing to financial development in the region. Let me now turn my attention to the use of the euro in the region.

USE OF THE EURO IN SOUTH-EAST EUROPE

South-East Europe is a region where one can see the use of the euro as an international currency in all its dimensions. The ECB regularly monitors developments in the international role of the euro, including its use in South-East Europe.

The Eurosystem takes a neutral position regarding the internationalization of the euro. In this regard, it is also worth recalling the position adopted, already by the Ecofin in November 2000, that countries aiming at EU accession cannot use unilateral euroization as a way of circumventing the stages foreseen by the treaty establishing the European Community for the adoption of the euro.[2]

As a financing currency, euro-denominated debt is regularly issued by the countries of the region, which also, as I noted above, often make use of the euro as an anchor, reserve and intervention currency for their monetary and exchange rate frameworks. The euro is also being increasingly used as an invoicing currency in the international trade of the countries in the region. In the case of Bulgaria, for which a longer span of data is available, we have seen that while 37 per cent of Bulgarian exports were invoiced in euros in 2000, the figure had risen to 61 per cent in 2003. The increase is particularly notable given the fact that Bulgarian exports to the euro area accounted for only 51 per cent of total Bulgarian exports in 2003, compared to 42 per cent back in 2000. That is, while in 2000 Bulgarian exports to the euro area were greater than its exports invoiced in euros, by 2003 the opposite was true.

Euro cash inherited the role of a store of value that some legacy currencies, principally the Deutsche mark and also the Austrian schilling, had played in some countries in the region. But the introduction of the euro also coincided with an interesting development in the region. In a nutshell, the euro cash changeover was accompanied in many South-East European countries by a strong increase in euro-denominated deposits. In many countries, particularly in the former Yugoslav republics, households deposited cash in legacy currencies – previously kept 'under the mattress' – with banks, rather than exchange them directly for new euro banknotes, reflecting increased confidence in the respective banking systems.

CONCLUDING REMARKS

Let me conclude by focusing on the prospects. To a large extent, these prospects can be summarized in just a few words: progress towards EU membership. Of course, countries in the region are at very different stages in their path towards EU membership. Indeed, Bulgaria and Romania signed the accession treaty in 2005 whereas other countries are still preparing negotiations on stabilization and association agreements. Moreover, there are not only economic, but also political criteria countries have to pass to transform the current EU perspective into real progress towards association or accession.

Let me also emphasize that the ECB and the Eurosystem as a whole is a contributor to this process, not least through the provision of technical assistance. Cooperation among central banks has involved twinning projects – led by some Eurosystem central banks, in particular Banque de France, Banca d'Italia and De Nederlandsche Bank – with the Bulgarian National Bank and the National Bank of Romania, as well as visits and training, all geared towards sharing information and know-how. It has taken place in a large number of areas, such as payment systems, supervision and financial stability, statistics, central bank operations, and so on. Looking ahead, such technical assistance will continue to intensify as countries progress towards aligning themselves with EU regulations and directives.

The recent enlargement to ten new member states, as well as the progress in the accession of Bulgaria and Romania and the decision to begin negotiations with Croatia serve as powerful reminders that the enlargement of the EU remains an ongoing process.

However, for all countries in the region, no matter how far they have already travelled on the road towards the EU, there is no time for complacency. Clearly, the speed at which South-East European countries progress towards accession to the EU depends on the policies followed. It is the culture of stability and the exercise of responsibility in economic policy making that are the crucial ingredients to achieve the bright prospects that lie ahead for the region.

NOTES

1. Within the context of this book, South-East Europe is understood to comprise the following countries: Albania, Bosnia and Herzegovina, Bulgaria, Croatia, FYR of Macedonia, Romania and Serbia and Montenegro.
2. Report by the (Ecofin) Council to the European Council in Nice on the exchange rate aspects of enlargement, Brussels, 8 November 2000, Council of the European Union press release No. 13055/00. Also reiterated in 'Policy position of the Governing Council of the European Central Bank on exchange rate issues relating to the acceding countries', Frankfurt, 18 December 2003, www.ecb.int.

Changes in the focus of European economic integration

Axel A. Weber

In the process of European integration, 2004 was undoubtedly one of the most memorable years. In May 2004 ten new member states joined the European Union. The eastward enlargement of the EU presents major political, institutional and economic challenges. Moreover, there is a very high probability that the process of eastward enlargement has not yet come to an end.

Does the enlargement of the EU imply a new shift in the focus of economic integration in Europe? At this juncture, it is difficult to give a clear answer to that question. The history of the EU has seen several such shifts. While in the early years of European integration the focus was on the goods markets, financial market integration has received more attention of late.

1. EARLY STEPS TO EUROPEAN ECONOMIC INTEGRATION

Some fifty years ago, a quite ordinary, yet pressing, cause gave rise to European economic integration. In the midst of reconstruction efforts, steelmakers – representing the backbone of several European economies – were heading for a crisis of overproduction. The danger of competition being restricted by the re-erection of cartels was looming large, when Robert Schuman, then French Minister of Foreign Affairs, proposed the establishment of a European Coal and Steel Community.[1] His proposal not only aimed at creating a unified market for coal and steel products; it also encompassed the bold idea that member states should surrender control over the coal and steel industry, which was still deemed strategically important, to a supranational body, the 'High Authority', later called the 'Commission'. Indeed, the transfer of sovereignty in specific areas from member states to newly created supranational institutions was to become a prominent feature of European integration.

The idea of a single market for coal and steel was quickly extended to encompass the free movement of all products as well as free access to the means of production. The realization of a common market of this kind (i.e. an 'extended customs union') was the primary goal envisaged in the treaty establishing the European Economic Community (EEC), one of the Treaties of Rome.

By contrast, economic and monetary policy were considered merely a 'matter of common interest' and did not play a major role in the early years of European economic integration. In particular, monetary and exchange rate policies seemed to be sufficiently aligned by the Bretton Woods arrangements.

This assessment proved to be wrong, however. By the end of the 1960s, the Bretton Woods system, once characterized by Robert Mundell as the 'international disequilibrium system',[2] started to creak under the strain of permanent external imbalances and speculative capital movements. Recurring balance of payments crises also posed a threat to the liberalization efforts in goods and capital markets, triggering calls for higher tariffs and stricter capital controls.

During those difficult times and after the customs union between EEC member countries had become fully effective in 1968, European governments acknowledged the need to gradually move towards a genuine economic and monetary union. As a first step recommended in the so-called Werner Report, European countries tried to stabilize the exchange rate movements between their currencies within a band narrower than the fluctuation margins established by the Bretton Woods system. As we all know, this effort – the 'snake in the tunnel' as well as its successor, the snake – eventually failed due to a lack of willingness to align economic and monetary policies within Europe.

In 1979, a new start was made through the establishment of the European Monetary System (EMS). Although the European Monetary System was intended to promote macroeconomic stability among participating countries, the original aim of the Werner Plan – the introduction of economic and monetary union (EMU) by 1980 – had to be abandoned.

In the mid-1980s fresh impetus for the process of European economic integration came from the White Paper in which the Commission proposed the creation of a single European market, allowing the free movements of goods, services, people and capital by the end of 1992. This final implementation of the common market originally envisioned in the Treaties of Rome was subsequently codified in the Single European Act.

However, in a setting where capital markets are completely integrated and, in addition, exchange rates are pegged but adjustable – as was basically the case in the EMS – individual countries cannot pursue independent monetary policies. (Unfortunately, Europeans had to learn this lesson the hard way during the crisis of the EMS). Thus, along with the realization of the single market, monetary integration was revived as well. Indeed, based on the seminal Delors Report, a roadmap to EMU was eventually enshrined in the Maastricht Treaty.

The prominence that financial market integration received after the adoption of the Single European Act reflects technological progress as well as market and policy developments in this field. Financial market deregulation and the liberalization of cross-border capital movements featured prominently on the international agenda during the 1980s and 1990s as the virtues of integrated financial markets became widely accepted.

Market integration is the precondition for efficient risk-sharing across countries as well as across market segments; in fact, standard economic theory tells us that only complete markets allow for a perfect hedge. A second gain is the superior allocation of capital in integrated financial markets, creating the potential for enhanced growth. Moreover, barrier-free markets promote competition, giving a further boost to welfare. In addition, debtors – governments as well as the corporate sector – can gain in an integrated market from reduced bond spreads, while investors gain from the expanded choice of assets.

Several Directives aimed at promoting competition and creating a level playing field in the market for financial services have come into effect. More recently, the Financial Services Action Plan (FSAP) was adopted in 1999. It is to date the most ambitious initiative for integrating capital markets and achieving a single market for financial services in the EU. Meanwhile almost all 42 FSAP measures have been converted into Directives and Communications. Nonetheless, implementation in national legal systems is still outstanding in many areas.[3]

2. ESTABLISHMENT OF MONETARY UNION

The launch of EMU had repercussions on the international financial markets in general and on the integration of European financial markets in particular. Indeed, the final stage of the establishment of EMU in 1999 saw the creation of a new currency, which, if only because of the economic weight of the currency area concerned, had far greater significance than the event itself might lead one to expect. As an investment and reserve currency, the euro now ranks just after the dollar.

The new currency regime has brought about noticeable changes in the level and pattern of cross-border capital flows. In the case of Germany, the importance of portfolio investment in other euro area countries, for example, has seen a particular increase while, conversely, large amounts of capital have flowed into Germany from countries not participating in monetary union. Particularly at the start of monetary union there was a remarkably strong momentum among German investors towards the internationalization and diversification of their portfolios. Since the start of EMU their net purchases of foreign securities have amounted to nearly EUR 700 billion. Parallel to the increase in German investment abroad, non-residents have invested about EUR 650 billion in German securities. These trends have contributed significantly to the integration of financial markets in Europe.

From the central bank's point of view, the money market is of vital importance. Only in sufficiently integrated money markets can the central bank manage the money supply in an efficient manner, that is without having to analyse liquidity separately for each market and being able to auction off money without regard to the counterpart.

Fortunately, we can observe near-perfect integration in the overnight unsecured market, where the dispersion of spreads oscillates around two basis points. The repo market exhibits fewer signs of integration, though significant progress has been made over the past few years. The remaining discrepancies are mainly due to differences in market practices, legislation, regulation and the fragmentation of the infrastructure in the euro area, all of which are currently in the process of being harmonized.

With regard to the market for short-term debt derivatives we observe a large, liquid and well-integrated market. Rates converged quickly after the introduction of the euro and since mid-1999 their cross-sectional standard deviation for either one-year or ten-year swaps has not exceeded a single basis point on any one day.

Other financial markets also exhibit strong integration tendencies, although they remain less integrated than the money market. As one would expect, retail banking reveals the most pronounced home bias, largely due to non-regulatory barriers and cultural differences, such as diverse preferences for types of credit. The euro area government bond market has shown a distinct trend towards unification, that is yields can be observed to be driven increasingly by common news, rather than by purely local risk factors.

An enlightening example of the introduction of the euro fostering integration is provided by the portfolio structure of mutual funds in Germany. Traditionally exhibiting a strong home bias, they reveal evidence of a trend towards diversification prior to the introduction of the euro. In December 1998, German mutual funds for the first time held more stocks of foreign provenance than of domestic issuers. A similar pattern can be observed in the composition of bond holdings. The share of securities issued by foreign entities has been rising steadily since 1996.

The observed assimilation in different financial markets needs to be analysed in greater detail, since convergence effects are not due to enhanced integration only. Account needs to be taken of at least three other factors. First, the exchange rate premium has vanished by definition in the single currency area. Furthermore, economic and monetary policies have converged throughout the euro area and, finally, governments face similar restrictions in their fiscal policies as a consequence of the Stability and Growth Pact.

The concluding message is bright: financial markets within the euro area are already widely integrated, albeit to varying degrees. The money market – in particular the unsecured overnight lending market – is almost perfectly integrated, allowing the European System of Central Banks (ESCB) to conduct an efficient monetary policy. Further integration in other financial markets can be expected when all the FSAP measures have been fully implemented.[4]

3. EU ENLARGEMENT

European economic integration not only entails the deepening of economic relationships between a given set of countries but has at the same time a regional component. The first group of Central and Eastern European countries acceded (together with Cyprus and Malta) to the European Union on 1 May 2004. Other countries will follow in the years to come.

This so-called eastern enlargement is of special interest, since the new member countries (with the exception of Cyprus and Malta) have gone through a fundamental social and economic transformation. Within a decade they have caught up with the process of economic integration which in Western Europe started more than fifty years ago with the European Coal and Steel Community.

Orientation to and integration into the European Union has been the key element of economic transformation from the very beginning. In the first half of the 1990s political concern focused on macroeconomic stabilization and the timing and sequencing of external liberalization. The eight countries which now participate in the European single market quickly removed the impediments to current account transactions and redirected their trade to Western Europe. Today their share of intra-EU trade exceeds 50 per cent and is thus comparable with or even exceeds the ratio in the older EU countries.

In contrast to current account convertibility, a greater variation can be observed in the approaches to capital liberalization. Some countries opted for a gradual procedure and initially only removed restrictions on inflows of foreign direct investment and other long-term capital. Controls on short term capital inflows which are considered to be more speculative in nature and are more susceptible to speculative attacks were relaxed at a later stage. Other countries deregulated the entire capital account in a 'big bang' and thereby increased the pressure on the domestic economy to adjust to a highly competitive environment.

Despite these differences in the intermediate period, all the new member states have now introduced the *acquis communautaire* of the European Union with, at most, marginal temporary arrangements. This contrasts with former enlargements when far-reaching exceptions, especially in capital account liberalization, were granted to countries such as Greece, Portugal or Spain.

Today, the focus of economic integration in the new member states is more or less the same as in the rest of the European Union – the development and integration of the financial markets and further progress in monetary integration. Markets apparently expect most of the Central and Eastern European 'pre-ins' to adopt the euro within the next decade. This is underlined by the convergence of long-term interest rates vis-à-vis the average euro-area rate. Three countries, namely Estonia, Lithuania and Slovenia, have already joined ERM II, which is an important instrument for the coordination of the exchange rate policy within the Eurosystem.

Despite the economic convergence achieved so far, however, there are still major differences between the new and the old member states. The present income differences – which are still considerable – indicate that real convergence is not yet complete and will entail further adjustments in relative prices and real exchange rates. Their development will need to be observed closely and reviewed carefully. However, the key issue in Central and Eastern Europe is the need to develop and strengthen further the financial sector. Especially with regard to the single financial market, it is essential to further financial intermediation and to establish the efficiency of capital markets which are at the moment only at an early stage of development.

Let me conclude this review of enlargement with some remarks on future prospects. European integration is a process which will not be terminated in the foreseeable future. The next challenge is already waiting in the wings: Bulgaria and Romania are negotiating with a view to acceding in 2007, Turkey has the official status of an accession candidate and other countries, especially from the Western Balkans, have expressed their wish to accede to the European Union.

This is not the place to discuss the likely future shape of the European Union nor to assess the current progress in political and economic reform by individual countries. Without doubt, however, further enlargement will at the same time make the European Union more heterogeneous, and constant efforts will be needed to ensure that it continues to function smoothly. This said, however, the process of integration can be expected to benefit all European countries and thus enhance welfare across the entire continent.

NOTES

1. See Fontaine (2000).
2. See Mundell (1961).
3. See Deutsche Bundesbank (2004).
4. See European Central Bank (2004).

REFERENCES

Deutsche Bundesbank (2004), 'Regulation of the European securities markets', *Monthly Report*, July, pp. 33–48.

European Central Bank (2004), 'Developments in the EU framework for financial regulation, supervision and stability', *Monthly Bulletin*, November, 81–93.

Fontaine, Pascal (2000), *A New Idea for Europe – The Schuman Declaration – 1950–2000*, European Commission.

Mundell, Robert A. (1961), 'The International Disequilibrium System', *Kyklos*, **14**, pp. 153–72.

PART I

South-East Europe: Where Do Institutions and the Economy Stand?

1. South-East Europe: signs of catching up

Michael A. Landesmann

INTRODUCTION

The 1990s was a decade in which South-East Europe (SEE)[1] fell dramatically behind the more advanced transition economies of Central and Eastern Europe (Czech Republic, Hungary, Poland, Slovakia, Slovenia – we shall call them the CEE-5). The cause was, of course, the disintegration of former Yugoslavia, which included a succession of wars, regional conflicts and economic and political disintegration. Even the countries of the region which were not directly involved in these conflicts, such as Bulgaria and Romania, suffered significantly in terms of interrupted trade routes and the disintegration and collapse of a neighbouring economic region.

Since 2000 things have improved. The growth of GDP in SEE over the most recent period (2000–2004) has even been higher than in the CEE-5; and in quite a few of the countries the most recent growth rates have been in the region of 5–7 per cent (Table 1.1). There has even been some significant improvement in industrial production in SEE with the exception of Macedonia and Serbia over that period (see Table 1.2). Hence a catching-up process has started, and in all the contributions to this book on this issue, a positive tone as to the prospects of the SEE region has been adopted. Table 1.1 provides the information regarding GDP levels in the years 2000 and 2004 in relation to 1990 (= 100). It shows that with the exception of Albania, only some of the SEE economies had rebounded to their 1990 GDP levels by 2004, and quite a few of them (Serbia and Montenegro, Macedonia and Bosnia and Herzegovina) are still way below that level. However, the growth over the period 2000 to 2004 was substantial with the exception of Macedonia.

In the following we shall discuss some of the factors which make the growth process still vulnerable and which therefore require further attention in terms of economic policy-making both from within the region and from outside the region (the latter would mainly refer to EU policy towards the region).

Table 1.1 Gross Domestic Product (real change in per cent against preceding year)

	1995	1996	1997	1998	1999	2000	2001	2002	2003	2004[1]	2005 forecast	2006 forecast	Index 1990 = 100 2000	Index 1990 = 100 2004	Index 2000 = 100 2004
Albania	8.9	9.1	−10.2	12.7	10.1	7.3	7.6	4.7	6.0	6	6.5	6.5	117	144	126.6
Bosnia and Herzegovina	–	–	–	15.6	10.0	5.5	4.5	5.5	3.5	6	5	5	42	63	120.9
Bulgaria	2.9	−9.4	−5.6	4.0	2.3	5.4	4.1	4.9	4.3	5.6	5	5	78	98	120.3
Croatia	6.8	5.9	6.8	2.5	−0.9	2.9	4.4	5.2	4.3	3.7	3.5	3.5	84	102	118.3
Macedonia	−1.1	1.2	1.4	3.4	4.3	4.5	−4.5	0.9	3.4	2	4	4	91	93	101.6
Romania	7.1	3.9	−6.1	−4.8	−1.2	2.1	5.7	5.0	4.9	7.8	5	5.5	81	106	125.5
Serbia and Montenegro[2]	6.1	5.9	7.4	2.5	−18.0	5.2	5.3	3.8	2.0	7	5	5	39	58	119.3

Notes:
1. Preliminary.
2. Up to 1998 Gross Material Product.

Source: wiiw database incorporating national statistics, forecast: wiiw.

Table 1.2 Gross industrial production (real change in per cent against preceding year)

	1995	1996	1997	1998	1999	2000	2001	2002	2003	2004[1]	2005 forecast	2006 forecast	Index 1990 = 100 2004	Index 2000 = 100 2004
Albania[2]	6.0	13.6	−25.8	26.1	34.2	0.5	7.1	1.8	2.7	3.1	4	5	43.8	115.4
Bosnia and Herzegovina[3]	–	–	–	23.6	8.0	7.9	4.9	5.7	5.1	12	10	10	–	130.5
Bulgaria	4.5	5.1	−18.4	−8.5	−8.0	8.3	1.5	6.5	8.3	17.8	12	10	73.2	138.0
Croatia	0.3	3.1	6.8	3.7	−1.4	1.7	6.0	5.4	4.1	3.7	3.5	3.5	77.4	120.6
Macedonia	−10.7	3.2	1.6	4.5	−2.6	3.0	−3.1	−5.3	4.7	−12.7	3	5	44.3	83.9
Romania	9.4	6.3	−7.2	−13.8	−2.4	7.1	8.3	4.3	3.1	5.3	5	5	75.2	122.3
Serbia and Montenegro	3.8	7.6	9.5	3.6	−23.1	11.1	0.0	1.7	−2.7	8	5	5	47.0	106.8

Notes:
1. Preliminary.
2. According to gross value added.
3. wiiw estimates based on weighted averages for the two entities (Federation BH and Republika Srpska).

Source: wiiw database incorporating national statistics, forecast: wiiw.

DEINDUSTRIALIZATION AND THE NEED FOR RE-INDUSTRIALIZATION

What strikes one in a comparison of industrial production figures with GDP is that the downturn over the 1990s has taken a much bigger toll on industry than on the economy as a whole (see Tables 1.1 and 1.2, last but one columns). What the region experienced to a much greater extent than Central and Eastern Europe is a severe case of *deindustrialization*. The levels of industrial production remain substantially below those in 1990 (between 25–55 per cent below!); this is in contrast to the eight new EU member states (NMS) from Central and Eastern Europe (the NMS-8) which achieved a volume of industrial production in 2004 that was about 55 per cent above (!) the 1990 level; in these countries industrial recovery significantly exceeded the recovery in the overall economy.

In contrast, while the levels of GDP in SEE have just about reached 1990 levels (with the exceptions of Macedonia, Serbia and Bosnia and Herzegovina), the levels of industrial production remained way below these levels. Hence there is a big discrepancy here: the NMS show signs of a strong process of *re-industrialization* following the initial contraction of their economies in the early 1990s, while the SEE economies are still a long way from this situation.

We shall see below that some of the other persistent problems of SEE economies (current account deficits, the shares of the informal sectors and the associated low tax base, characteristics of the labour markets, and so on) are at least in part related to this persistent feature of de-industrialization.

EXPORT PERFORMANCE, SERVICES TRADE AND THE NEED FOR DIVERSIFICATION

Table 1.3 shows large discrepancies between exports and imports of goods as a percentage of GDP and, in many of the countries, big differences between the deficits in the current accounts and the deficits in goods trade. The much higher deficits in goods trade reflect the weaknesses of the manufacturing sectors in the SEEs mentioned above and these get partly compensated by some surpluses in services trade (in Croatia, Bulgaria and Bosnia and Herzegovina) or by high personal transfers/remittances (especially high in Albania, Macedonia and Serbia and Montenegro, but it is a general phenomenon across SEE) or aid flows (Bosnia and Herzegovina).

A comparison of the export and import goods-to-GDP ratios between the NMS-8 and the SEEs shows that import ratios in SEE are much more along NMS lines (with the exception of exorbitantly high import ratios in Bosnia-Herzegovina) while export-to-GDP ratios are generally very low in SEEs. This striking weakness on the export side is also a reflection of the fact that during the 1990s SEE missed out on the sharp increases in FDI flows into the CEE region, which have contributed substantially towards export capacities expanding over the years. Only recently has FDI picked up (in some countries very considerably), but, except for Bulgaria and Romania, not much went into industry.

CURRENT ACCOUNTS, INCOME TRANSFERS, AID AND FOREIGN DEBT

Consistently high current account deficits (significantly higher in the SEEs than in the NMS; see again Table 1.3) were a persistent feature of all transition economies and also, generally, a feature of catching-up economies which need to import technologically superior equipment to upgrade their production capacities; they also started off with a high backlog of consumer demand for imported items. The question of course is whether (and how quickly) the current account situation builds up into an unsustainable one. This depends upon three factors: the prospective trend growth rate of GDP, the addition to debt through persistent current account deficits (which translate into additional debt) and the current level of debt. There are a number of countries which seem to be moving in an unsustainable direction: Macedonia because of a low GDP growth rate, Serbia and Montenegro and Bosnia-Herzegovina because of very high current account deficits, and Croatia as a result of a combination of the two.

Of course, growth can improve and current account deficits can be reduced for a number of reasons – the above only pinpoints that a number of SEE countries are vulnerable in this direction. This may be because they rely on inflows (aid, remittances) which might not be that reliable in the medium- to longer-run, or that they rely on potentially volatile items in their services accounts (such as tourism income) or that financing current account deficits through privatization receipts without an effort to build up stronger export capacities is an insufficient strategy to provide for external equilibrium in the longer run.

Table 1.3 *South-East Europe: an overview of economic fundamentals, 2004*

	Albania	Bosnia and Herzegovina	Bulgaria	Croatia	Macedonia	Romania	Serbia	NMS-8[1]	EU-15	EU-25[2]
GDP in EUR at exchange rates, EUR billion	6.55	6.55	19.56	27.66	4.25	57.14	17.78	459.28	9 720.11	10 204.45
GDP in EUR at PPP, EUR billion	14.61	17.04	53.13	46.19	11.40	151.39	42.01	874.83	9306.40	10 204.45
GDP in EUR at PPP, EU-25 = 100	0.1	0.2	0.5	0.5	0.1	1.5	0.4	8.6	91.2	100.0
GDP in EUR at PPP, per capita	4 570	6 090	6 830	10 400	5 620	6 980	5 600	12 034	24 251	22 288
GDP in EUR at PPP per capita, EU-25 = 100	20	27	31	47	25	31	25	54	109	100
GDP at constant prices, 1990 = 100	144.0	63.0[3]	97.5	101.8	92.6	105.6	57.5	136.9	130.6	131.0
GDP at constant prices, 2000 = 100	126.6	120.9	120.3	118.8	101.6	125.5	119.3	114.5	105.9	106.2
Industrial production real, 1990 = 100	43.8	–	73.2	77.4	44.3	75.2	47.0[13]	154.8	119.8	121.4
Industrial production real, 2000 = 100	115.4	130.5	138.0	120.6	83.9	122.7	105.8	125.4	101.2	102.3
Population – thousands, average	3 200	3 850	7 780	4 440	2 030	21 700	7 500	72 965	383 759	457 847
Employed persons – LFS, thousands, average	925[4]	634[5]	2 923	1 583	540	9 180	3 000[6]	28 458	161 792[7]	190 225[7]
Public sector expenditures, nat. def., in % of GDP	27.5	42.6[8]	39.7	49.5[8]	22.3[8]	31.9[8]	56.8[13]	47.6	48.0	48.0
Public sector revenues, nat. def., in % of GDP	22.3	43.3[8]	41.5	44.9[8]	21.3[8]	29.8[8]	52.6[13]	42.8	45.3	45.1
Price level, EU-25 = 100 (PPP/exchange rate)	45	39	37	60	37	38	42	52	104	100
Average gross monthly wages, EUR at exchange rate	188[9]	380	153	799	200	204	190[10]	780[11]	2 900[11]	2 625[11]
Average gross monthly wages, EUR at PPP	420[9]	974	415	1 334	536	540	449[10]	1 485[11]	2 777[11]	2 625[11]
Exports of goods in % of GDP	7.5	24.5	40.9	23.9	31.8	33.1	17.5	46.1[12]	27.9[12]	28.7[12]

Imports of goods in % of GDP	26.0	79.5	53.7	48.5	55.0	42.5	46.6	49.8[12]	26.8[12]	27.8[12]
Exports of services in % of GDP	11.7	10.3	17.1	27.8	7.2	5.1	6.1	8.0[12]	8.1[12]	8.1[12]
Imports of services in % of GDP	11.6	5.7	13.3	10.8	8.2	5.5	4.6	7.4[12]	7.7[12]	7.7[12]
Current account in % of GDP	−4.3	−27.7	−7.2	−6.1	−7.1	−7.7	−14.0	−4.4	0.3	0.1
FDI stock per capita in EUR	440	390	740	2370	590	600	700	2280	–	–

Notes:
PPP: Purchasing power parity: wiiw estimates for Albania, Bosnia and Herzegovina, Serbia.
NMS-8: Czech Republic, Estonia, Hungary, Latvia, Lithuania, Poland, Slovak Republic, Slovenia. EU-15: EU up to 30 April 2004. EU-25: EU as of from 1 May 2004.
1. wiiw estimates. 2. wiiw estimates, except: employed persons, budget and compensation per employee. 3. wiiw estimate. 4. Employment total. 5. Employees, end of year 2003. 6. Data for 2002. 7. Employed persons aged 15–64, 2Q2004. 8. Year 2003; Croatia IMF-def. 9. Public sector. 10. Average net monthly wages, including various allowances. 11. Gross wages plus indirect labour costs, whole economy, national account concept. 12. NMS-8, EU-15 and EU-25 data include flows within the region. 13. Serbia.

Source: wiiw, AMECO, Eurostat.

UNEMPLOYMENT, THE INFORMAL SECTOR AND THE (MAL)FUNCTIONING OF THE LABOUR MARKETS

Unemployment rates in South-East Europe are very high with the exception of Romania. Even by standardized LFS (Labour Force Survey) methodology they range from a low in Romania of 7.5 per cent to a high of 37 per cent in Macedonia; in between are the rates for Croatia (14 per cent), Bulgaria (12 per cent), Serbia and Montenegro (15 per cent), with no LFS figures available for Albania and Bosnia-Herzegovina. With the exception of Bulgaria where the unemployment rate is falling, there is no significant dent in unemployment in spite of high GDP growth.

Many commentators remark that unemployment figures in SEE economies are not reliable because of a high share of the so-called 'informal economy', which may very well be the case (although LFS figures should take account of any sort of employment). Nonetheless, it is important to point out that the existence of such a high share of the informal sector reflects itself a number of deficiencies in SEE development which will not automatically go away: it reflects a failure of administrative control, but it also reflects the fact that (and this is important in comparison to the NMS where the informal sector is much smaller) opportunities for regular full-time employment opportunities have broken away. This brings us back to the major shrinkage that has happened to industry, where jobs are typically more regular and are also easier for the administrative authorities to account for (and easier to include in the formal social security system and the tax base).

FISCAL DEFICITS AND STATE EXPENDITURE

Fiscal deficits have improved substantially in a considerable number of SEE economies over the past few years. For one, this is the result of resumed growth over the past few years and, secondly, there were some important attempts to reign in fiscal expenditure in some countries such as Macedonia. Nonetheless, as Table 1.3 shows, the GDP shares of public spending are high in the follower states of the Federal Republic of Yugoslavia, and in some countries, Serbia in particular, public spending is currently spiralling out of control. In terms of the longer-run fiscal policy scenario, I would like again to emphasize that an increased tax base derived from the building up of a stronger goods producing sector will *ceteris paribus* allow fiscal consolidation to be achieved with less social hardship.

HUB AND SPOKE WITH THE EU AND TRADE REINTEGRATION OF SOUTH-EAST EUROPE

It is always emphasized that FDI will flow more massively only into an integrated South-East European region. Signs are much more promising now than they were even a few years back. A set of bilateral trade agreements have been achieved criss-crossing the region and it is envisaged that these would get multi-lateralized in the next phase. Now it is important to tackle the issue of non-tariff barriers, which are at present the more important barriers in the region. Further, major improvements in the infrastructure for cross-regional transport have to be made, as the current situation reflects the hub-and-spoke situation in trade with the EU, where the overwhelming part of good transport routes exist or are being built to link up with EU markets, with little attention being given to intra-regional connections. My opinion is that a real resumption of intra-regional trade flows will depend upon substantially more FDI activity in the region, which will build up cross-regional production networks. We are observing such developments in the NMS currently with a recent boost to intra-NMS trade flows.

THE PROSPECTS OF EU MEMBERSHIP AND PRE-ACCESSION PROGRAMMES

Of course, prospects of EU membership are vital for the region. As often said, EU membership is important for qualitative institutional development and provides a catalyst for a major shift in economic policy. But its most important impact is (or was) to shift the political economy within the individual countries towards new incentive structures for the political and economic elites which had vested all their powers in the past in a developmentally and regionally destructive direction. One hopes this phase is over – although not yet assured everywhere, viz. Serbia, Kosovo, Montenegro; it should not be taken for granted by the EU and it remains vital to adhere to clear timetables to resolve the outstanding difficult issues.

In the meantime, the wise and efficient use of pre-accession programmes is very important for institutional, infra-structural and political-economic development prior to EU membership.

NOTE

1. The following countries are included in our account of South-East Europe (SEE): The EU candidate countries: Bulgaria, Romania and Croatia; and then Albania, Bosnia-Herzegovina, Macedonia, and Serbia and Montenegro.

2. South-East Europe on the way to Euro–Atlantic integration

Erhard Busek

The Stability Pact for South Eastern Europe – which was established at the EU's initiative in Sarajevo in July 1999 – and the Southeast European Cooperative Initiative – which was launched in December 1996 as a regional initiative by the United States to back the implementation of the Dayton Agreement – have both been success stories.

Of course, there have been shortcomings, but what is more important is that we have achieved a lot. Following four wars in the region, the map of South-East Europe has been redrawn substantially and improvements have been brought about in a comparatively short time. Today, many ministerial meetings convene former opponents in war. I think this is an impressive development despite the fact that we still have to wait for full reconciliation to take place. That is of course the ultimate objective.

But I think things are moving in the right direction. My message is the following: Let's focus on the positive developments!

What has been achieved in South-East Europe over the past decade?

Firstly, the process of democratization is certainly irreversible. All the elections are monitored by the Organization for Security and Cooperation in Europe and are conducted in a free and fair manner. But some uncertainties still exist of course; for instance, the party landscape has not reached a consolidation phase, it is moving, similarly to other European countries.

Secondly, the region was given a clear European perspective at the Thessaloniki European Council in 2003, which is of high importance. The driving force for all transformation processes in these countries is the perspective to eventually join the EU and, in a way, also the perspective of joining NATO. However, at the same time, the countries are also realistic and understand the lightness of the current weight of this promise. The EU is plagued by an enlargement fatigue, and thus Europe's interest in the Western Balkans is limited. This is aptly symbolized by the length of the latest EU–Western Balkans Summit (November 2004). It was scheduled to last for 45 minutes, but in the end, the meeting was reduced to 25 minutes.

At the same time, there are difficulties regarding the image of the region. The expression 'Balkans' is not very helpful because it has a negative connotation. To counter that, the EU came up with the term 'Western Balkans', which you cannot find in any geography or history book. However, I think that the Western Balkans is ultimately just another way of saying 'countries of former Yugoslavia', which is again not very appropriate. But a widely accepted term is still out of reach. The Italians call the area the 'Eastern Adriatic region', while the outgoing Romanian state president Iliescu proposed the use of 'South-Central Europe', arguing that South-East Europe brings to mind the Caucases.

This reflects the difficulty we all have with European geography, and it is very revealing that 15 years after the events of 1989 we are still not able to say what Europe means both geographically and in terms of its identity.

Back to the question of what has been achieved. A third very positive point is the reduction of the military forces and a new focus on fighting organized crime. The threat by the military forces has been reduced. This is a significant achievement as all the armies were too big for the current situation. The only problem that remains is the continuing existence of military mercenaries, especially from the former Yugoslav People's Army.

Fourth, the economic and investment climate has improved significantly. South-East Europe's economies now grow on average by 4 and 5 per cent of GDP. The foreign capital inflow was EUR 8 billion in 2003, of which EUR 5 billion as foreign direct investment (FDI). European investors have been increasing their share of FDI in South-East Europe, particularly in some EU candidate countries, where EU countries account for 60 per cent of the FDI stock.

As is well known, geographic proximity and cultural links are important determinants of FDI. Italy for instance accounts for 48 per cent of Albania's FDI stock. Austria and Germany each account for 23 per cent of Croatia's FDI stock. Greece accounts for 25 per cent of the FDI stock in the former Yugoslav Republic of Macedonia. Today FDI is concentrated in the financial services area, reflecting a wave of bank privatizations in the region. In addition, trade and telecommunications are also important.

Generally speaking, the investors have also focused on the cement, beer, tobacco and soft drinks industries. The private sector's perception of the business climate has improved in the areas of finance, infrastructure, taxes, regulations, judicial efficiency, crime and corruption. But there are still major problems and gaps.

THE IMPORTANCE OF A EUROPEAN PERSPECTIVE

Because of the geographic proximity, the countries next in line for EU accession benefit from increased investor interest. Romania, Bulgaria and Croatia all show higher economic growth rates, a higher share of FDI, as well as lower rates of unemployment. Here, there is a clear link between the European perspective and the level of FDI. Without a tangible European perspective, there is less interest to invest.

Many of the countries are constitutionally complex and thus their economic organization is different. In Bosnia and Herzegovina, and Serbia and Montenegro there are several separate markets inside the national borders. This is also true in the case of Moldova. But coming onto Moldova, I also have to say that Moldova is an altogether different case for the Stability Pact than the Western Balkans. Currently, Moldova does not have an EU perspective and organized crime is endemic in Transnistria. I believe the EU should have a firmer and clearer strategy on this country.

LOOKING AHEAD

2005 is going to be a very difficult year because we have to start discussing the status of Kosovo. This is generally known, but at the moment nobody, especially not within the EU, knows what this solution might be. Without discussing the options for the solution, we have to remember that it is crucial for the international community to reach consensus. The fate of Kosovo cannot be settled through a unilateral decision from any one country. Another concern is the fate of Serbia and Montenegro; we still do not know whether we are dealing with one country or two. The approaching referendum should decide on this issue. Furthermore, the so-called Bonn powers cause great concern regarding Bosnia and Herzegovina, as the High Representative can still overrule domestic institutions, impose legislation and dismiss local officials.

On a positive note, the importance of regional cooperation is increasingly being recognized. Regional cooperation is not only a factor of stabilization but a key determinant of FDI-related decisions. Foreign investors perceive regional trade initiatives as encouraging. Or to put it more pragmatically, investors are looking at the region as one potential market. The evidence of regional cooperation in economic areas includes trade agreements, regional energy market initiatives, a Memorandum of Understanding on Core Transport Networks, as well as the annual Vienna declaration on investment promotion. Despite that, I often come across a certain reluctance to cooperate, and many governments promote their countries by saying that 'It is better to invest here; not there'.

But let us go back to the existing concerns. The legacy of the wars and conflicts continue to plague the region – economic decline and a high rate of unemployment are difficult to reverse in a post-war environment. Macedonia, for example, has an unemployment rate of 30 per cent, but this is topped by more than 50 per cent in Kosovo, where more than 50 per cent of the unemployed are under 25. Unemployment leads to disillusionment with the political and economic situation and makes people more susceptible to nationalist rhetoric and calls to take up weapons. Therefore, not only is the status of Kosovo an important issue – it is most important to invest in Kosovo. A stable Kosovo would have a stabilizing impact on the region as a whole, beyond its own borders.

Economic growth is greatly dependent on the level of FDI, but that is spread quite unevenly. In 2003, of the EUR 5 billion FDI attracted into the region, EUR 4 billion was absorbed by four countries: Bulgaria, Croatia, Romania and Serbia-Montenegro, whereas the four remaining countries accounted for only EUR 1 billion between them. This rift in the region reflects the absence or presence of a European region-wide perspective.

Serbia-Montenegro's development has been delayed for the obvious reasons – Milosevic's rule and the subsequent chaos and a series of fragile governments. We should keep in mind that the political situation and the future perspectives are extremely important for economic development. FDI is now decreasing given that the privatization process nears an end. At the same time, it is becoming increasingly important to attract greenfield investment, which is, however, much more difficult. This is why we are pressing so hard for 'one shop stop' FDI solutions for the region as a whole.

What is also important to consider is the extent of corruption and the weak efficiency of local governance structures. That means that the authorities of various autonomous areas of the region must be assisted to develop a higher efficiency. This is a focus area for us, as we understand the importance of local governments in attracting and keeping investment.

The reports carried out in the framework of the Investment Compact show that many countries have a weak record in designing investor-friendly legal and economic environments. Overall, the Investment Compact is aimed at improving the region's business and economic environment, and sets out the desired commitments for the region's governments to lay the structural policy foundations for sustainable reform and growth. Progress in policy reform is measured with the Investment Compact Monitoring Instruments and published on the website of the Stability Pact (www.stabilitypact.org/investment).

It is very important in this respect to have a political vision. This is something I often fight for. But creating a solid political vision is difficult at a time when the trade balance continues to remain negative despite the fact that exports from the region into the EU are rising. At the same time, the international community is currently redesigning its assistance portfolio, and will apply loans as opposed to grants. In terms of funds, accession countries are also benefiting from pre-accession assistance, and we are also doing our best to promote the establishment of public–private partnerships in cooperation with the EBRD and other financial institutions. While regional cooperation is evident in certain areas, international pressure is still required in many cases to drive regional cooperation and regional ownership.

CHALLENGES FOR THE FUTURE

What are the challenges? First, the need to ensure that the reform process will continue. In Serbia for example the reform process has stalled due to the volatility of the political landscape. No decisions are being agreed upon and we expect another election to be held in the spring of 2005. The international community needs to keep up the pressure if we want Belgrade to make a success out of its accession perspective and the stabilization and the association agreement.

The bilateral free trade agreements in the region have been difficult to negotiate and have proved particularly difficult between Serbia and Montenegro, which have separate trade regimes. This difficulty has been overcome through the adoption of a double track strategy for Serbia-Montenegro. It was a wise decision by the Commission and Chris Patten to create this strategy, but whether this is yet an additional push toward Montenegro's independence is of course an open question.

Evidence shows that countries which are most committed to reform have the highest growth rates and attract more foreign direct investment. The private sector's perception of the business environment has improved over the past few years. But there is still a need for improved private sector and public sector dialogue, which we are trying to enhance. The state tradition from the communist era is still strong, given the existence of the old boys' networks in all the countries. It seems that one can change state presidents and prime ministers but it is not that easy to enforce changes on the local level.

Another challenge for us is to continue enhancing regional cooperation. International experience shows that market size is a key determinant for FDI compatibility, and global and regional trade initiatives greatly influence FDI decisions. We are working on improving the infrastructure (transport, energy, environment) and we consider it vital to promote and sustain growth.

However, the region's demands are enormous. The European Commission has estimated that EUR 60 billion would be required between 2004 and 2015 to meet all railway infrastructure needs. Energy and environmental requirements will be even higher. Of the Quick Start projects launched within the Stability Pact framework to improve the quality of infrastructure services, 80 per cent are under construction while 20 per cent have yet to be started because decisions of the different governments are still pending.

As a case in point, Bulgaria and Romania agreed on the construction of a – second – bridge over their shared sector of the Danube between Vidin and Calafat back in 2000. Yet it took Romania and Bulgaria until November 2004 to work out how many highway tracks and how many railway tracks the bridge should have. This shows how long-winded the process is. We criticize the governments for this, as we believe such infrastructure projects are crucial. The same is true for the bridge at Novi Sad. The current pontoon bridge is blocking the transport on the Trans-European Corridor Number VII – that is the river Danube – and this avenue has basically been closed since 1991, since the disintegration of Yugoslavia.

As mentioned earlier, the initiatives of the Stability Pact include the facilitation of public–private partnerships and the establishment of the European Commission-led Infrastructure Steering Group. The latter brings together the Commission, the World Bank, European Investment Bank (EIB), EBRD, as well as the Council of Europe Development Bank. The message of the Infrastructure Steering Group has been that there is enough money available, but the governments' capacity to develop projects is limited. They all have good ideas: we need a highway from here to there. However, the projects are rarely elaborated and prepared well. In other words, funds would be available, but due to the capacity problems, they cannot be used.

This message is, of course, not very friendly. However, the region must understand that regional cooperation on infrastructure will facilitate better links between the countries themselves and will advance their integration into Europe. This is our priority. And it will also facilitate the identification and financing of key projects.

WHAT HAS BEEN THE CONTRIBUTION OF THE STABILITY PACT?

Several instruments are at our disposal to enhance regional cooperation in key sectors. These vary from bringing together key actors from South-East

Europe and the international community, to securing the political commitment and providing technical guidance. The process makes significant use of peer pressure. Our efforts complement the political processes such as EU accession, stabilization and association processes.

The examples of our initiatives include the Investment Compact, managed by the OECD, which has improved the overall business climate and boosted investment promotion activities. We have also encouraged the setting up of Foreign Investors Councils and to stimulate the development of small and medium-sized enterprises (SMEs). We have published a regional White Book on the investment climate in South-East Europe to create a platform for investors to communicate ideas to governments on how the business climate could be improved. The independent evaluation of the Investment Compact by a leading management consulting group, A.T. Kearney, concludes that the Investment Compact has directly and indirectly contributed to the improvement of the investment climate in South-East Europe. (For more details see www.investmentcompact.org.) In 2005 and 2006, we will focus on two main areas. First, the improvement of the business climate – particularly international institutional frameworks, legislation, regulation and promotion. That means capacity building, marketing, and a sectoral focus. The second point is enterprise and SME development.

Furthermore, a Business Advisory Council (BAC) for South-East Europe has been established to advise the Stability Pact on private business issues. The members are senior executives of South-East Europe and international companies, and they meet quarterly in the region, on a high level and in direct contact with the governments. The BAC strives to build viable partnerships between governments and the private sector in each country.

In addition, the Stability Pact Trade Working Group has achieved the signing of 28 bilateral trade agreements, of which 22 are already in force. Currently, the main problem is implementation, as some governments implemented protection measures the day after they signed the free trade agreements with a partner in the region. The long-term perspective is to build up a multilateral Free Trade Association, and the actual elimination of non-tariff barriers.

To continue, we are trying to implement the Memorandum of Understanding on the Core Transport Network for the Western Balkans, signed in June 2004. We have also created an informal task force to improve the environment for public–private partnership through the development and implementation of pilot projects and infrastructure. Finally, the so-called Athens process, aimed at creating a regional energy market, led to the establishment of the Energy Community of South-East Europe (ECSEE), which is basically built along the lines of the Coal and Steel

Community, a precursor of today's EU. Under the ECSEE framework, a legally binding agreement will be concluded with all the countries concerned in order to move the electricity companies in a European direction.

Just to give you an impression about the extent of the difficulties: the difficulties are not limited to regulators and transmission lines, in Bosnia for instance, there are three separate electricity companies: a Serbian one, a Croatian one and a Bosnian one. But is there a difference between the Serbian light, Croatian light and Bosnian light when you switch it on? I think we have to convince them that it is cheaper and more effective for the consumers to have a regional, and not an ethnic-based solution to these infrastructure questions.

This chapter was meant to give a brief overview of some of the activities that are conducted under the framework of the Stability Pact for South-East Europe. Let me conclude by emphasizing some of our additional concerns.

Today, everybody is talking about Turkey but nobody is talking about South-East Europe. In terms of its population, this region – and I mainly refer to the Western Balkans plus Albania – is minor compared to the recent enlargement area. Poland has twice the population of this region. Of course, unlike Poland, here you have different governments and different problems. But geographically speaking, the integration of this region should not be a problem. On the positive side, it is a big advantage that within the European Commission, Olli Rehn is responsible for the whole of South-East Europe, because responsibility used to be divided between Günter Verheugen and Chris Patten.

Overall, the problem is not the volume, it is more on the political level. But to be a little bit critical, I have to say that it is good that the EU is developing a global approach, but it is also necessary to come up with a European approach to address European problems. The negotiation talks for Croatia might be postponed because of the Hague criteria, which means that negotiations with Turkey might open even before Croatia. This would be a very bad political signal to the region. The other problem is that we have to start discussing the status of Kosovo, because otherwise it will remain a black spot on the map.

Thus, 2005 will be a critical year also for the international community. After having learnt how we get involved in post-conflict management, we also have to learn how we leave. As of now, no exit strategy has been devised for the office of the High Representative in Bosnia, or for the United Nations Mission in Kosovo (UNMIK), or for the Stability Pact. These initiatives should not be suddenly shut down one day, but it is extremely necessary that they are phased out because policy makers in the region have to assume responsibility.

Imagine that since 821 – when the revolutionary war of the Greeks against the Ottoman Empire started – every major decision has been taken by outsiders. In London, in Paris, in Berlin, in Vienna until the end of the First World War, in St Petersburg and afterwards in Moscow. The region has to learn to really assume regional ownership. We have to move the responsibility to the region step by step. This is how we approached the issue of organized crime. This is how we tackled legislation on organized crime, corruption, arms limitation, the collection of light arms and small weapons and, more recently, migration. A gradual approach is imperative.

To conclude, I am inviting you to see the glass as half full, not as half empty – because much has been achieved.

3. The Western Balkans' European perspective

Reinhard Priebe

This chapter discusses the key challenges facing the countries of the Western Balkans today: their economic development and their integration into the European Union (EU).

There can be no doubt about the European perspective of the five Western Balkan countries, Albania, Bosnia and Herzegovina, Croatia, the former Yugoslav Republic of Macedonia, and Serbia and Montenegro (including Kosovo[1]). We want them to become members of the EU one day, and they want it. The fact that accession negotiations will soon start with Croatia is proof of that. And we hope that this will inject some new energy into the reform processes in the other countries of the region. Our policy framework to lead the countries to EU membership is the Stabilisation and Association Process. The integration into European structures needs to be preceded by significant reforms in most policy areas. The economic revitalization is one of the major challenges the countries of the Western Balkans are facing today, and perhaps the most difficult one.

ECONOMIC DEVELOPMENT IN THE REGION: A MIXED PICTURE

The Western Balkans can take credit for some major achievements, made in a relatively short period of time, in terms of reform and economic recovery.

Economic stabilization continued in 2004, with output growth in the region reaching about 4.7 per cent of GDP. There are differences between the countries, of course. Albania, Bosnia and Herzegovina, Croatia, and Serbia and Montenegro have a comparatively high growth level while it is weak in the former Yugoslav Republic of Macedonia and sluggish in Kosovo.

Across the region, inflation is decreasing and exchange rates remain stable due to cautious monetary and exchange rate policies, which are supported by IMF arrangements. Fiscal consolidation has improved for several consecutive years, but stalled in 2004. The average government deficit is expected to have remained at about 3.5 per cent, the same as in 2003. Until recently, the countries in the region have relied on external grants to cover a large share of their public expenditures. The inevitable decline in donor assistance will put additional pressure on public finances. Further consolidation will be necessary and will need to be accompanied by an improvement in public administration efficiency, including in the collection of taxes and other revenues.

Progress has been achieved in terms of market-oriented reforms. The privatization of small and medium-sized enterprises (SMEs) is practically complete in most countries. This process started later in Serbia and Montenegro but is now progressing at a good pace. Privatization, restructuring and, where needed, the liquidation of large enterprises constitute a more lengthy process, however, and until the obstacles to bringing this forward have been removed – issues like clarity on liabilities, ownership rights and settlement of debt claims – large loss-making public enterprises will continue to put a strain on public finances. Given that job losses in this area in most cases are inevitable, procrastination may only delay structural change and increase public deficits.

Considering the size of the individual countries and their national markets, intra-regional trade is instrumental to economic recovery. Under the auspices of the Stability Pact, the countries of South-East Europe have signed free trade agreements with one another. To date, intra-regional trade has been rather limited but the new network of free trade agreements, as well as the rehabilitation of regional infrastructure networks in areas like transport and energy, should stimulate an increase in intra-regional trade. The European Commission welcomes the recent declaration by trade ministers from South East Europe envisaging the conclusion of a single free trade agreement for the region.

The region's main trading partner is the EU. Supporting their economies by facilitating trade has been a key element of our policy. The EU therefore introduced Autonomous Trade Measures in 2000. This means that the countries of the Western Balkans can export almost all their goods – including most agricultural products – to the EU market without duties or quotas. To date, the countries have had problems reaping the full benefits of this preferential treatment. There are several reasons for this: a lack of productive capacity and insufficient ability to comply with EU quality and health standards are major obstacles to increasing exports. Despite these problems, results are encouraging. Exports are increasing. The countries' exports to the EU are increasing at a faster pace than their exports to other parts of the world. The EU envisages extending the Autonomous Trade Measures beyond 2005. They will gradually be replaced by bilateral trade agreements.

Nevertheless, the trade deficit of the Western Balkan countries remains high and this represents a major challenge for them. The European Commission has allocated part of its assistance to sectors with potential for export (for example the agro-industry), developing laboratories and other systems to enable exports in compliance with European standards. The large trade deficits also reflect a growing demand for imports for domestic consumption and investment, a common feature of transition economies.

The EU supports World Trade Organization (WTO) membership of all countries in the region since this is a powerful driving force for wider economic and sectoral reforms.

While noting substantial progress in economic reform and recovery, huge challenges still remain.

Economic growth in this region is higher than the world average, but considering the starting level it is still too low. With the exception of Albania, the countries have not reached the GDP levels they had in the early 1990s. By European standards, the countries are poor, living standards are low and unemployment generally very high with social deprivation as a consequence. They need to attract a higher level of investment – particularly foreign direct investments (FDI). The high current account deficits need to be watched carefully. The existence of large informal economies deprives governments of much-needed tax revenues. The countries therefore need to pursue their structural reform agenda vigorously. More attention needs to be paid to local development in the countries. In the medium to longer term they also need to, progressively, incorporate the EU *acquis*.

Widespread corruption and organized crime negatively affect the countries' development, not only in economic terms. These problems are also holding back their political and institutional development. Unfortunately, most countries have so far failed to get sufficiently to grips with these problems.

Overcoming these issues and setting the countries firmly on the track towards full economic recovery and future EU membership poses major institutional challenges.

Strong administrative capacity will be crucial to deal with these challenges. Public administration reform should therefore be one of the main priorities ahead. For example, having fully functioning, competent, independent and sufficiently equipped judicial systems that can guarantee the rule of law is essential. Foreign investors need to know that they can obtain legal redress if contracts are not honoured; they need to know that their property rights will be clear and sufficiently protected; banks need their collateral rights to be enforced. Progress has been made in these areas but more needs to be done. The establishment of cadastres to ensure land ownership is important – this is currently a bottleneck in the whole region. The countries also need to establish sustainable social security systems and to reform the pension schemes.

The perspective of future EU membership serves as an incentive to reform. EU rapprochement and reform implementation go hand in hand. It is important that the countries understand that they have to carry out wide-ranging reforms, not because the EU asks them to do so, but because they have to do so to address the needs of their citizens, to raise their living standards. Therefore, the countries need to internalize the reform agenda.

The countries need to ensure that reforms are not only EU compatible but also that, at the same time, they address their particular needs, that legislation is enforceable and that they have the institutions required to implement reforms. There is sometimes a tendency to push through legislation and reform initiatives to satisfy EU criteria but without in-depth reflection on what the reforms mean. Profound structural and institutional reforms are required to cope with the challenges of EU membership and, even more importantly, the countries must associate themselves to the underlying European values, such as respect of human and minority rights. The whole integration process must be used to achieve genuine change.

INTEGRATING THE WESTERN BALKANS INTO EUROPE – THE STABILISATION AND ASSOCIATION PROCESS

As mentioned, the Stabilisation and Association Process (SAP) is the EU's policy frame to lead the Western Balkan countries to EU membership one day. Trade liberalization, financial assistance and the Stabilisation and Association Agreements are the three pillars of this process.

The EU has invested a tremendous amount of resources in helping the region. The current assistance programme amounts to almost EUR 5 billion (for 2000–2006), providing the Western Balkan countries with some of the highest per capita assistance in the world. The programme is tailored to their needs, that is from emergency post-conflict reconstruction to institution building and economic development. In addition, the European Commission provides macro-financial assistance, which finances exceptional balance of payment needs and supports reforms in the context of the IMF programmes; since 1992 we have committed about EUR 1 billion in macro-financial assistance. Our member states, as bilateral donors, are also heavily engaged in the Western Balkans.

The main aim of Community assistance today – as the reconstruction phase is more or less over – is to address challenges related to the countries' economic and social development. The assistance programmes include projects aimed at improving the business climate, at supporting SMEs and the privatization of large state-owned enterprises. Where relevant, we still have infrastructure projects as well as projects in the areas of transport, energy and education. Assistance in areas such as standards and legislation should enable the countries to take better advantage of the preferential treatment granted to them by the EU and to improve their productivity and competitiveness.

Justice and home affairs and institution building are other priorities for assistance. These are important in their own right and also in the light of economic regeneration. Building institutions and administrative capacity, developing the skills of civil servants and supporting the institutions guaranteeing the rule of law and accountability – to put it simply: ensuring good governance – are essential for the countries to fulfil the political, economic and *acquis*-related criteria for EU membership. They are also the basis for economic and social development.

The Stabilisation and Association Agreements (SAA) engage the countries and the EU in a wide-ranging contractual relationship. These are demanding agreements which oblige the countries to gradually align their legislation with that of the EU, to progressively introduce the four freedoms and to cooperate closely with the EU on a number of issues at the heart of the internal market. Through the institutional framework which is set up under an SAA, they will also be exposed to all parts of the *acquis*. Implementing an SAA is thereby an important preparation for future membership.

PROGRESS BY THE COUNTRIES IN THE SAP

The Commission is currently negotiating an SAA with Albania. The negotiations may be concluded during 2005. The EU's concerns at the moment are related to Albania's capacity to properly implement such an SAA. Albania needs to work harder to combat organized crime, corruption and the sizeable grey economy, and needs to ensure that the judicial system and public administration function properly. Furthermore, the customs services and tax administration need to perform better – customs collection here is the lowest in the region. The Parliamentary elections in June 2005 have to be carried out in accordance with international standards.

On Bosnia and Herzegovina the Commission last year presented a report on the feasibility of Bosnia negotiating, concluding and implementing an SAA. It then identified 16 priority reform areas where significant progress needs to be made before it would make any sense for the Commission to recommend the opening of negotiations to the Council. Progress has been made in terms of legislation. However, this needs to be backed up with solid implementation and there are still shortcomings. The Commission supports the introduction of VAT in Bosnia. This, combined with customs reform, should make a significant contribution to meeting the state's financial requirements. Bosnia and Herzegovina must become a viable, administrable and, last but not least, an affordable state. Constitutional reforms beyond Dayton are necessary for the country to be able to manage closer relations with the EU.

The SAA with Croatia has come into force on 1 February 2005. Croatia was granted candidate country status in June 2004. Subsequently, the Commission presented a proposal for a pre-accession strategy for Croatia. This means that it will start issuing Regular Reports on Croatia as from 2005, that Croatia should benefit from all three pre-accession financial instruments and be able to participate in Community programmes. The same criteria apply to Croatia as to all other candidates – the 1993 Copenhagen criteria. Whether we can start accession negotiations soon will depend on Croatia's readiness to fully cooperate with the Hague Tribunal. Croatia will remain in the Stabilisation and Association Process and must also continue to fulfil its obligations under the SAA, for example in terms of regional cooperation and other international obligations. The functioning of the judiciary is one of our main concerns as regards Croatia; it negatively affects the country's economic development. Property restitution is another issue which needs to be resolved.

After the entry into force of an SAA last spring, the next step for the former Yugoslav Republic of Macedonia on the ladder towards membership is the Commission's opinion on its application for membership. In February 2005, the country has replied to the Commission's questionnaire. It is essential that the Ohrid Framework Agreement is implemented and thus internal stability is maintained. Reform of the public administration, reducing the number of municipalities and transferring various competences from state to local level is one essential element in this context and is a key part of the Ohrid Framework Agreement. As far as economic development is concerned, the privatization process and the elimination of loss-making companies are almost completed. The crisis in 2001 interrupted economic development. The perception of instability, corruption and red tape is negatively affecting much-needed FDI.

For Serbia and Montenegro the Commission recently proposed a new approach, the so-called 'twin track approach' as a way to re-energize our relations with the state. This approach will in time lead to a single Stabilisation and Association Agreement with Serbia and Montenegro, with parts of the agreement negotiated with the republics covering those policy areas which fall under republican competence. The issues for the state level are political cooperation, compliance with international obligations (in particular cooperation with ICTY), respect for human and minority rights and regional cooperation; and the issues to be negotiated with the constituent republics would be trade and customs, economic issues and sectoral policies like agriculture, the police and judiciary – all within the framework of one single SAA for the state. Since all our interlocutors have explicitly agreed on this approach, the Commission has re-launched the Feasibility Study for an SAA with Serbia and Montenegro and hopes to publish it in early 2005. The Feasibility Study, published in April 2005, proposes the opening of association negotiations with Serbia and Montenegro. This should bring the country out of its isolation.

2005 will be a crucial year for Kosovo. The new Provisional Institutions of Self-Government (PISG) elected in October 2004 will begin work, and more competencies and responsibilities will be transferred to them from the United Nations Mission in Kosovo (UNMIK). Progress in standards implementation will be reviewed with a view to a decision on whether the process to define Kosovo's future status can start, and UNMIK will probably be restructured as a result of all these developments. Particular economic problems include privatization, which is made even more difficult by the unclear status, and the need for UNMIK/PISG to develop a comprehensive economic strategy.

Could we do more, should we do things differently or do different things?

The perspective of future membership and pre-accession strategy proved effective in the countries of Central and Eastern Europe. The enlargement methodology will be used for the Western Balkans, adjusted where necessary to the specific challenges of this region. The reorganization of the new Commission with the Western Balkans Directorate moving to DG Enlargement enables the Commission to better deal with the region of South-East Europe as a whole rather than dividing it between candidate and potential candidate countries. This is particularly appropriate when dealing with economic issues.

Community funds are significant but, as with all financial assistance, nevertheless limited and should be focused on areas where the EU can add most value. The World Bank, the IMF, the Stability Pact, the EU member states and the USA are also important actors. With a large number of actors in the region, coordination is essential in order to avoid conflicting advice and to work on a consistent strategy.

We all want the same for the Western Balkans – we want to see them as prosperous, democratic, fully functioning countries and market economies, on the road towards EU membership. Therefore, we carefully listen to the many ideas which are put forward to us, for example by excellent think tanks. We particularly welcome concrete and realistic proposals on what more we could do for the economic development of the region.

Appropriate answers need to be found to the following questions. Why do the countries not manage to fully benefit from our trade concessions and how can we help the countries to better understand the concepts of free trade and single economic space in the region? Given the size of the countries, how could we help increase their attractiveness to potential foreign investors? How can we help them think not in terms of their own markets, but rather as part of a region and a regional market? What is the basic level of security and stabilization needed to make the economies 'take off'? What is the required level of 'good governance' needed for domestic stability as a basis for sound economic development? How do the grey economy, organized crime and corruption negatively affect the region's economic development and what can we do to counteract it?

Today, we still talk too much about minimum standards and requirements. As the countries make progress towards the EU, this will not be enough; the rationale will become one of preparing them to be able to function successfully as future member states of the EU – to be able to apply its laws, to implement and to benefit from its policies.

NOTE

1. As defined by UN Security Council Resolution 1244.

4. South-East Europe: opportunities and potential for investment and growth[1]

Elisabetta Falcetti, Peter Sanfey and Sladjana Tepic

1. INTRODUCTION AND OVERVIEW

The year 2004 is a significant landmark in the transition process. Not only does it mark the 15th anniversary of the fall of the Berlin Wall, but it is also the year when eight countries of Central Europe and the Baltics (CEB) joined the European Union (EU).[2] For these countries, the transition to a market economy is not yet over, but full EU membership is a clear sign that many of the difficulties and hurdles associated with transition have been successfully overcome. Can this success be replicated in another part of the transition region – South-East Europe (SEE) – where the next wave of accession is expected in the coming years?

This chapter examines the prospects for eight transition countries in SEE: Albania, Bosnia and Herzegovina, Bulgaria, Croatia, FYR of Macedonia, Moldova, Romania, and Serbia and Montenegro. We argue that these countries have the potential over the medium-term to grow rapidly and to become an increasingly attractive investment destination in the run-up to further EU expansion. This chapter outlines several reasons for cautious optimism about the future of SEE. Overall, our judgement is based on the clear and unmistakeable progress that the region has made since the late 1990s. Notwithstanding difficulties and occasional setbacks, it is now a region of opportunity and potential.

Some of the recent progress in SEE has been remarkable. Politically, the most significant change has been the re-integration of Serbia and Montenegro (formerly the Federal Republic of Yugoslavia) into the international community after the fall of the Milosevic regime in October 2000. Elsewhere, three countries (Bulgaria, Croatia and Romania) are now candidates for EU accession. The current level of cooperation among countries in the region would have been hard to imagine five years ago. In terms of economic progress, all countries are growing, some quite strongly, inflation is generally low and structural reforms are proceeding steadily in each country. The foundations are largely in place for future growth and prosperity.

Some people remain sceptical about SEE's future. One legacy of the conflicts and civil unrest that affected much of the region during the 1990s is an image problem that is difficult to shake off. It is true that some key issues have yet to be resolved, most importantly the future status of the province of Kosovo.[3] The possibility of renewed tensions and conflict in parts of the region cannot be completely ruled out. But it is important not to exaggerate these threats. By and large, governments in the region are firmly focused on a medium-term agenda of sustainable growth and poverty reduction through economic reforms, increasing cooperation and enhanced domestic and foreign investment.

Historically, the links among these eight countries have been quite fragmented; even today, few people would see this grouping as a coherent regional entity. Nevertheless, under the aegis of the Stability Pact for South Eastern Europe, regional cooperation in selected areas has led to concrete results and achievements. For example, there is now a network of bilateral free trade agreements in SEE, and the establishment of a regional energy market is well under way. Both of these initiatives have been pushed and coordinated by the Stability Pact, along with international financial institutions (IFIs) and through bilateral agreements. As a result of these and other initiatives, investors are starting to view these diverse countries as part of a more unified whole. This trend is likely to continue in the future.

The chapter outlines recent progress, and the remaining challenges, in six areas vital for long-term prosperity: macroeconomic performance, structural reforms, business environment, access to capital, foreign investment, and international trade. The chapter then charts the way ahead for the region, pointing to the crucial role of eventual EU accession as an anchor for further reform.

2. PROGRESS AND CHALLENGES

Macroeconomic Performance

Although SEE economies are stable and growing, they all face a number of tough challenges over the medium-term. A 'snapshot' of macroeconomic indicators for the year 2003 is contained in Table 4.1.

Living standards vary widely in the region: column 1 shows that Croatia has a GDP per capita more than ten times that of Moldova. The other countries are bunched more closely together, averaging close to USD 2300

Table 4.1 *Macroeconomic indicators, 2003*

	Per capita GDP (in USD)	Per capita GDP[1] (at PPP exchange rate)	Real GDP growth (% change)	Consumer prices (end-year, % change)	Unemployment (end-year, % of labour force)	Consolidated general government balance (% of GDP)	Current account/GDP (in %)	External debt/GDP (in %)
Albania	1 942.0	4 830.0	6.0	3.3	15.0	−4.5	−7.6	23.1
Bosnia and Herzegovina	1 849.0	5 970.0	3.5	0.1	42.0	−0.2	−17.4	34.9
Bulgaria	2 531.0	7 130.0	4.3	5.6	12.7	−0.4	−8.4	65.6
Croatia	6 518.0	10 240.0	4.3	2.2	14.1	−6.3	−6.1	81.8
FYR of Macedonia	2 341.0	6 470.0	3.1	2.5	36.7	−1.6	−6.0	38.7
Moldova	451.0	1 470.0	6.3	15.8	7.9	0.1	−8.0	89.2
Romania	2 624.0	6 560.0	4.9	14.2	7.2	−2.4	−5.8	34.6
Serbia and Montenegro	2 492.0	n.a.	3.0	7.8	34.5	−4.2	−10.2	68.9
CEB	7 394.2	n.a.	3.8	3.2	11.3	−3.6	−5.8	56.4
SEE	2 593.6	n.a.	4.4	7.3	16.5	−2.4	−8.9	56.2
CIS	1 049.8	n.a.	7.6	10.0	5.9	−0.7	−1.8	51.0

Notes:
[1] Per capita GDP data from 2002, except for Bosnia and Herzegovina, which are from 2001.
All regional averages are unweighted except real GDP growth.

Source: EBRD staff estimates and World Bank.

per capita. When these estimates are adjusted for differences in purchasing power (see column 2), the picture is less bleak, but the gap with more prosperous EU members is still wide. On the positive side, this indicates a strong potential in SEE for catching up in the coming years.

Encouragingly, all economies in the region are growing, and inflation is broadly under control (see columns 3 and 4). Real GDP growth in 2003 averaged around 4.4 per cent, above that of either CEB or the euro area. This was the third year in a row where growth in SEE was higher than in CEB. Annual (end-year) inflation was in single figures in all countries except Moldova and Romania (see column 4). In both countries, inflation is on a downward trend.[4]

Policy makers in SEE face four major macroeconomic challenges: reducing unemployment, controlling spending, expanding exports, and managing debt. Turning to the first challenge, column 5 gives an idea of the extent of the unemployment problem in SEE. Some countries have official unemployment rates at around one-third of the labour force. One should caution that official rates of unemployment may be exaggerated. The measurement of unemployment in transition countries, where informal and casual labour is common, is problematic. For example, the World Bank estimates (based on household survey data) that the 'true' rate of unemployment in Bosnia and Herzegovina is about 16 per cent, rather than the 40-plus per cent recorded in official data. Nevertheless, the unemployment problem throughout the region is a pressing one. Many people are long-term unemployed with little prospect of ever getting work again. In some countries, ongoing public sector reforms and post-privatization restructuring are adding to the already high unemployment levels.

The fiscal accounts in most SEE countries are in reasonable shape. Most governments are either running a budget surplus or a small deficit (see column 6). However, the fiscal challenges for the medium-term are quite daunting. One lesson from the new EU members is that it is difficult to manage spending during the run-up to EU accession. The costs of meeting the standards and obligations of the *acquis communautaire* are substantial, although significant pre-accession funds are available from the EU for this purpose. For those countries not yet on the accession path, the main fiscal risk lies in declining sources of official aid. Over the medium-term, spending will have to fall unless new sources of revenue can be found.

Many SEE countries export less than expected, and most run substantial trade and current account deficits; the latter (see column 7) range from 5.8 per cent of GDP in Romania to 17.4 per cent in Bosnia and Herzegovina. These deficits partly reflect the difficulties exporters face in raising the standards of the products to a sufficient standard for external markets. While high current account deficits are common in transition countries, especially those with strong growth and major restructuring needs, deficits of these magnitudes cannot be sustained indefinitely. Trade and export opportunities are expanding, but more progress is required.

In most countries the scope for absorbing new foreign debt is limited. Some have no access to international capital markets and rely on official sources of finance, others are constrained by fairly high levels of existing debt. In general, as column 8 in Table 4.1 shows, the level of external debt, expressed as a percentage of GDP is relatively moderate, with the exception of Moldova which has a recent history of arrears and debt payment rescheduling. However, several countries face rising levels of debt servicing in the second half of this decade, as grace periods on concessional loans draw to a close. Managing this process correctly is crucial if credibility and investor confidence are to be maintained.

Structural Reforms

Transition in SEE has been a slow and sometimes painful process, but the pace of reform has increased sharply in recent years as countries make up for lost time. Figure 4.1 gives a 'snapshot' of where all transition countries stand now in the transition, based on the EBRD transition indicators (updated and published each year in the EBRD *Transition Report*). The most advanced countries are Croatia, Bulgaria and Romania, all of which made strong progress in 2003–04.[5] Croatia is at a stage of transition that is comparable to most EU accession countries, and even ahead of its neighbour, Slovenia. Bosnia and Herzegovina and Serbia and Montenegro lag behind. Both countries started their transition later than most and, despite some catching up, still have ground to make up. In both cases, progress over the past year has been limited.

In most SEE countries, the relatively 'easy' parts of transition – initial-phase reforms such as price, trade and foreign exchange liberalization, and small-scale privatization – are close to completion. What is left is much harder: institutional reforms such as large-scale privatization, reforms to corporate governance and competition policy, deepening of financial intermediation and infrastructure reform. Progress is being made but much more is needed to bring these countries to the standard necessary for EU membership. The accession countries – Bulgaria, Croatia and Romania – are leading the way, highlighting the beneficial impact of the EU 'carrot'.

Business Environment

Private sector growth is at the heart of the revival of economic fortunes in SEE. The private sector accounts for nearly two-thirds of economic

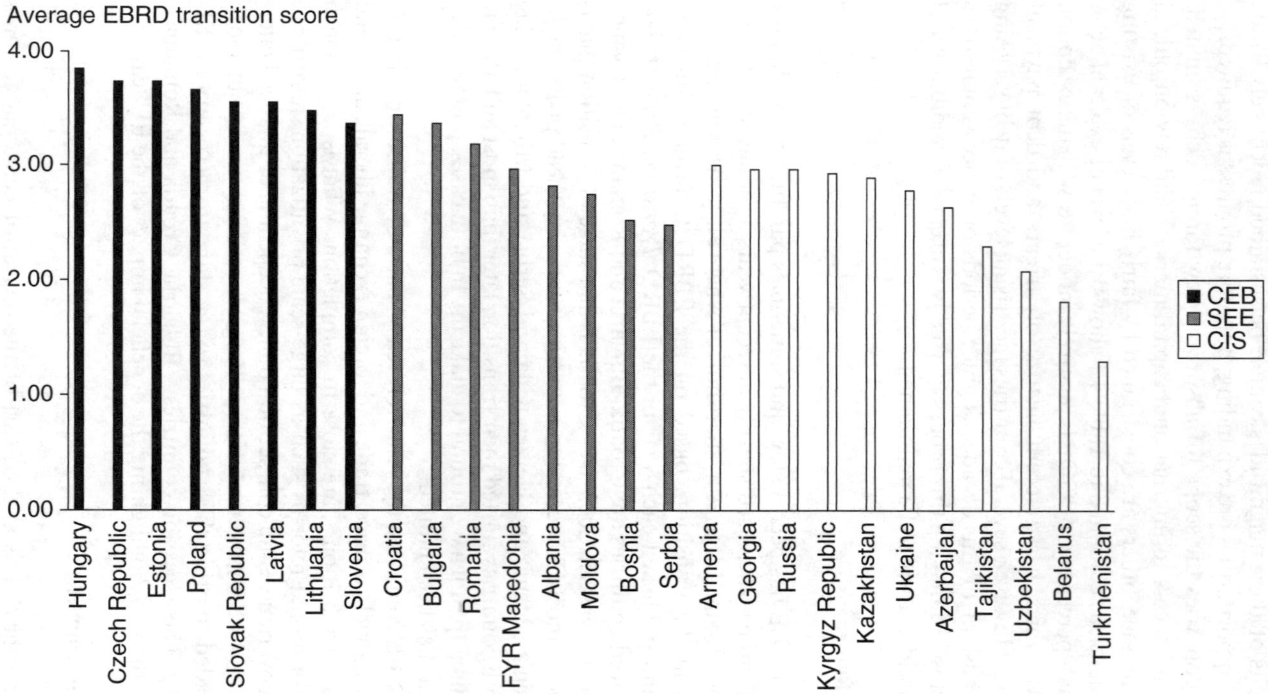

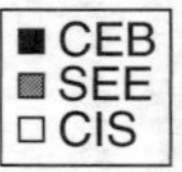

Source: EBRD Transition Report, 2004.

Figure 4.1 Progress in transition

activity in the region, according to EBRD estimates.[6] The privatization process, now at an advanced stage in SEE, has contributed to private sector growth, especially when it has been accompanied by fresh management and extra resources. But an equally important factor behind recent growth has been the improvement in the business environment.

Doing business is still difficult in SEE but less so than it used to be. One piece of evidence for this assertion is a comparison of the results of two waves (1999 and 2002) of a major survey, the EBRD–World Bank 'Business Environment and Enterprise Performance Survey' (BEEPS). Seven broad areas, directly or indirectly related to the functioning of the state and public administration, were assessed: taxation, business regulation, the judiciary, crime, corruption, finance and infrastructure. Managers of enterprises were asked to convert their subjective impressions of aspects of the investment climate to a numerical scale of 1 to 4. If an obstacle was seen as minor or insignificant it was given a score of 1, while a score of 4 indicated a major impediment to doing business.

On average, the business environment appears to have improved significantly across almost every category between 1999 and 2002, as Figure 4.2 shows. Areas that seem to show the largest improvement are infrastructure, access to finance, and crime. But there is little room for complacency. Taxation is a particular concern for enterprises and is seen as one of the three main barriers to investment in all countries of the region. Another pervasive problem is corruption, which is also a major deterrent for businesses in all countries. SEE countries generally score poorly in cross-country comparisons of corruption, including those published annually by Transparency International. Efforts are being made to tackle the problem, but evidence from other countries suggests that these efforts will take a long time to have any real effect.

Access to Finance

Access to finance is essential for private sector development. In SEE the most common source of finance, especially for SMEs, is internal funds, including retained earnings. But borrowing from commercial banks is becoming increasingly significant. In the more advanced countries – Bulgaria, Croatia and Romania – commercial banks (both domestic and foreign) are playing an important role, especially for large enterprises. In Croatia, for example, they provided in 2002 about 46 per cent of funds for new investments for large enterprises and 21 per cent for small and medium-sized enterprises (SMEs), according to BEEPS 2 estimates. In less advanced countries there is a heavy reliance on other internal funds, some of which come from emigrants' remittances which are a major source of

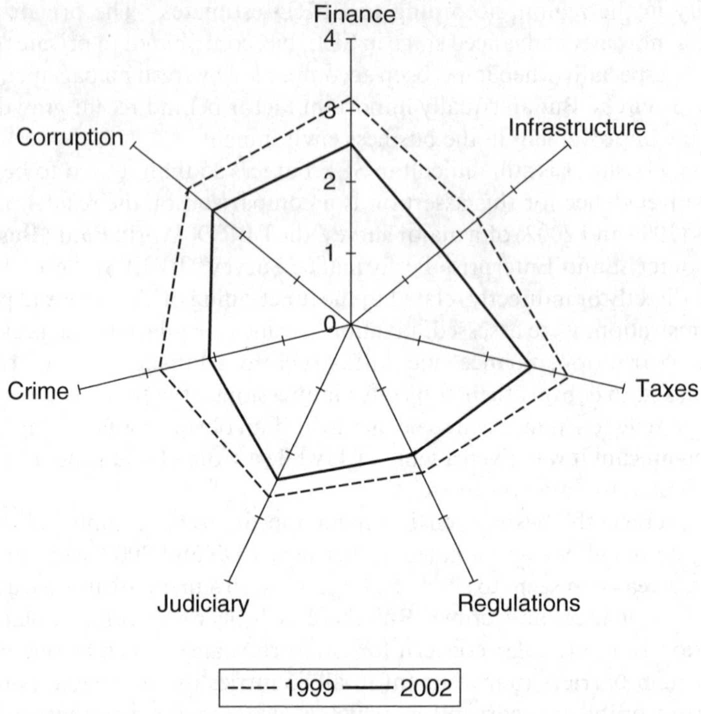

Note: The score along each dimension is the simple average across all firms in the sample in SEE. The values range from 1 to 4, with 1 indicating no obstacles to business growth and operations, and 4 indicating major obstacles. Data for 1999 exclude Serbia and Montenegro.

Source: Business Environment and Enterprise Performance Survey (BEEPS), 1999 and 2002.

Figure 4.2 Business environment in SEE: 1999 and 2002

income for several countries in the region. In addition, various SME programmes, supported by IFIs and other outside agencies, have emerged over time in the region, including dedicated micro-finance institutions (specializing in very small loans) and SME credit lines.

People in SEE are regaining confidence in local banks. One way to see this is to look at the significant increase, from a low base, in the deposit–GDP ratio during the previous two to three years. For example, the ratio increased from 21 per cent in 2000 to about 37 per cent in 2003 in Bosnia and Herzegovina, from 27 to 40 per cent in Bulgaria, and from 48 to 70 per cent in Croatia. Even in Moldova the ratio rose from 14 to 26 per cent over the same period. The changeover to the euro in the EU at the start of 2002 encouraged large sums of hoarded cash to be channelled into the financial system in many SEE countries. The fact that much of it has stayed in the banking sector implies a growing trust in banks.

In line with this growth in deposits, domestic credit to the private sector has also seen a significant increase across the region during 2002–2003. Figure 4.3 shows that the private sector, especially in the more advanced countries of the region, such as Bulgaria and Croatia, has substantial access to finance. However, significant real growth in lending to the private sector has also occurred in less advanced countries such as Albania, Bosnia and Herzegovina, FYR of Macedonia and Moldova. Bank credit to households (including consumer credit and mortgage loans) contributed in a major way to the growth of domestic credit to the private sector across the region during 2003.

Foreign Investment

SEE has become an increasingly attractive destination for foreign investors. This is crucial for long-term growth, as a successful transition cannot be financed solely from domestic sources. The integration of SEE into the international capital markets is a relatively recent phenomenon. However, since the late 1990s the region has increased its share of total capital inflows to emerging markets, indicating that increased political and macroeconomic stability, coupled with progress in reforms, are making the region more open to investors. Most inflows are private in origin, although some of the countries of the western Balkan region remain partly dependent on official inflows.

Foreign direct investment (FDI) is the most important type of capital inflow for SEE countries, both in size and in terms of impact on private sector development. Figure 4.4 shows that annual net FDI inflows have been stable between 1998 and 2002, typically around USD 3.5 to 4 billion. The year 2003 saw a notable increase to USD 6.66 billion, a record level for the region.[7] This impressive increase in net FDI inflows to SEE came not only from progress in large-scale privatization (especially in Croatia, with the partial privatization of the oil company, INA, and in Serbia, with lucrative privatizations in the tobacco and oil sectors) but also through increased greenfield investment in the region.

As privatization-related and official inflows to SEE are projected to decrease in the future, the key challenge ahead is to build on this momentum and attract increasing inflows of foreign private capital, preferably in the form of FDI into new enterprises. Whether the region meets this challenge successfully depends on a number of factors, including political stability, further progress in reforms, and deeper integration with the EU.

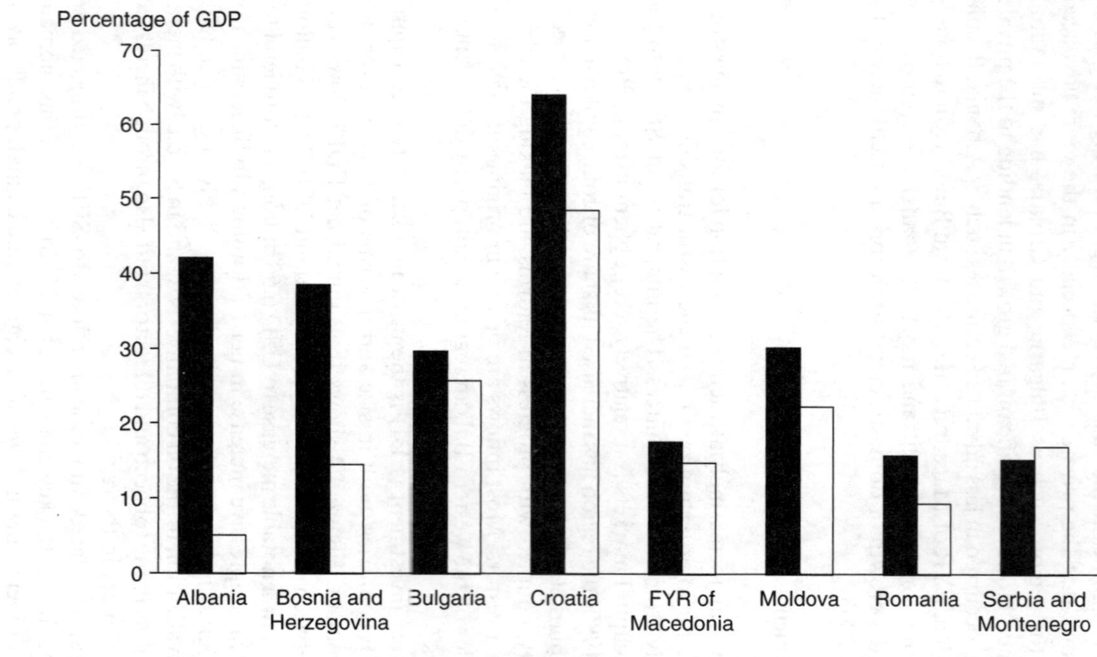

Source: EBRD and IMF-International Financial Statistics.

Figure 4.3 Domestic credit in SEE, 2003

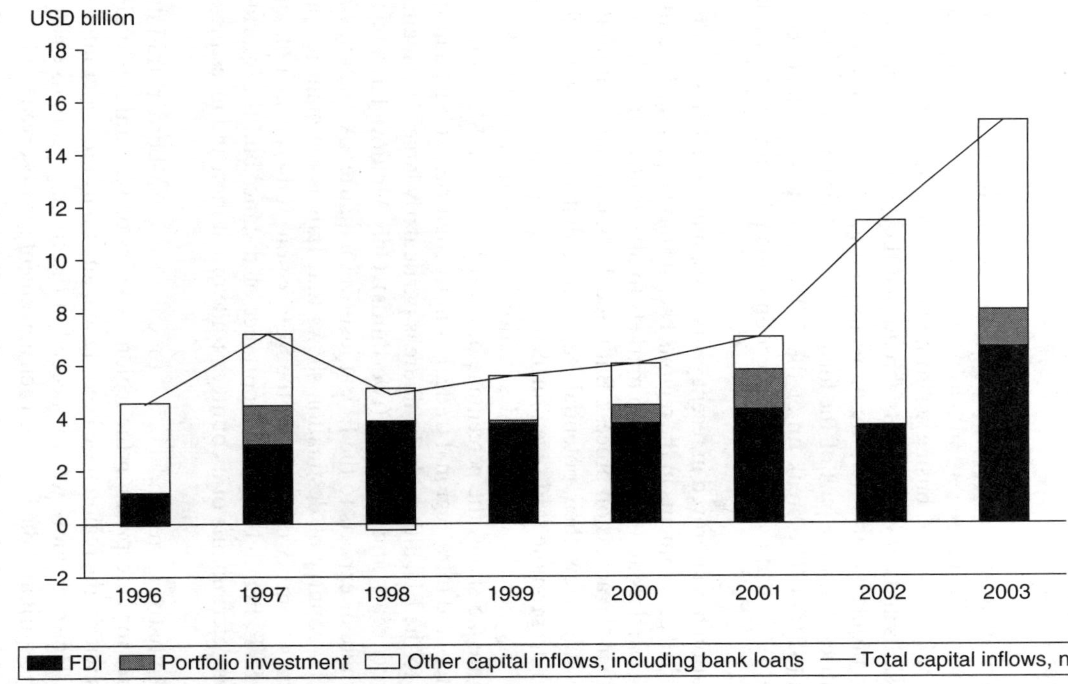

Source: World Economic Outlook database and EBRD staff estimates.

Figure 4.4 Total net capital flows to SEE by type, 1996–2003

The creation of a common free-trading area within SEE would make the region more attractive for outside investors. Some countries benefit from low corporate taxation rates and labour costs that are well below those in EU countries, adding to the attractiveness for new investment.

International Trade

During the transition, enterprises in SEE have found it difficult to reach markets abroad. There are several reasons for this. In all transition countries it has taken time for businesses to make new contacts, acquire new marketing skills and convince clients abroad that they will be reliable partners. Other problems, however, are more specific to SEE, and especially those countries that were part of the former Socialist Federal Republic of Yugoslavia (SFRY). The break-up of the SFRY and the subsequent conflicts of the 1990s had a devastating effect on trade relations in the whole region.

The situation has improved in recent years. Expanding trade has become a priority of all governments in the region. The EU has helped significantly by lowering barriers and opening up markets to all countries in SEE, not just to those in the accession process. But trade flows, especially within the region, are still below their potential, suggesting that there is scope for direct action to promote trade even further.

The EU is generally the main destination for exports from the SEE region. Figure 4.5 shows the percentage of exports for each SEE country for both inter- and intra-regional trade. For most countries, at least half of exports go to the EU, although the figure is particularly large for Albania (almost 90 per cent), and Romania (two-thirds). Only Moldova has a relatively low share of exports to the EU, at just over a quarter. A breakdown of exports by country of destination shows that Italy is the main recipient of exports from six countries in the SEE region. Italy is also a major investor in SEE, highlighting the importance of distance and transportation costs as determinants of a country's trade orientation and investment flows.

Several initiatives are under way to enhance cross-border trading opportunities for enterprises in the region. A series of bilateral free trade agreements within the region have been signed, and many are under implementation. However, more work is needed in the coming years to ensure that both the spirit and the letter of each agreement are observed, and that the agreements become progressively more compatible with each other. Access to EU markets has been enhanced in recent years, but further measures are required to overcome technical barriers to trade.

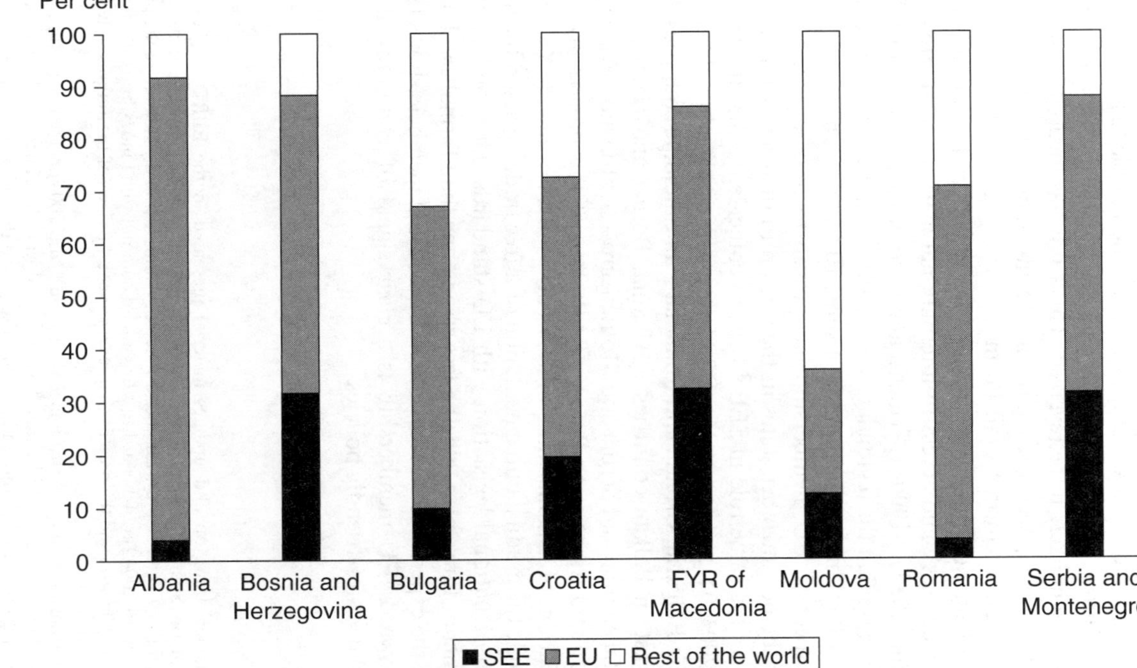

Source: IMF Direction of Trade Statistics, Vienna Institute for International Economic Studies and EBRD staff estimates.

Figure 4.5 Total exports of SEE countries, 2003

3. THE WAY AHEAD

In summary, there are strong grounds for optimism about SEE, tempered by caution. It is a region of opportunity and potential, but with considerable catching up to do. The citizens of SEE should be able to look forward to a bright future. Major challenges remain, but the positive trends of recent years are unlikely to be reversed. This study has focused on six prerequisites for private sector-led growth and investment: macroeconomic stability; structural reforms; a fair business environment; access to domestic sources of finance; inflows of foreign investment (with associated new skills and processes); and access to international markets. In all areas the progress since the late 1990s is evident, and in some cases remarkable. But it is also the case that the region lags behind the advanced transition countries of the EU. What can be done to ensure SEE catches up?

The prospect of EU membership has proven to be a key anchor for reform for the new member states in the run-up to their accession, and is likely to play the same role in SEE.[8] It is no coincidence that the reform leaders in 2003–04, as measured by EBRD transition indicators (described earlier) were Bulgaria, Croatia and Romania – all candidate countries. For the four western Balkan countries – Albania, Bosnia and Herzegovina, FYR of Macedonia, and Serbia and Montenegro – the EU has devised the Stabilisation and Association Process (SAP). Part of this process involves the negotiation of Stabilisation and Association Agreements (SAAs), which include the gradual implementation of a free trade area and the harmonization of national legislation with EU standards. This too has provided an anchor for reform, albeit a less strong one than formal candidate status. But the experience of accession in the new EU members shows that progress towards EU membership is a clear signal of commitment to reform and investor-friendly policies.

NOTES

1. This chapter draws on and updates material presented in the EBRD publication 'Spotlight on South-Eastern Europe: An Overview of Private Sector Activity and Investment', by Peter Sanfey, Elisabetta Falcetti, Anita Taci and Sladjana Tepic, published in April 2004 (available at http://www.ebrd.com/pubs/find/index.htm). Both the previous publication and the present chapter represent the views of the authors only and not necessarily of the EBRD.
2. The eight transition countries that joined the EU on 1 May 2004 are the Czech Republic, Estonia, Hungary, Latvia, Lithuania, Poland, the Slovak Republic and Slovenia. Two non-transition countries, Cyprus and Malta, also joined the EU on the same day.
3. In line with United Nations Security Council Resolution 1244, Kosovo remains a part of the territory of Serbia and Montenegro but is currently under interim UN administration, pending a resolution to its final status. This status is due for review in 2005.

4. Inflation in Serbia rose to double-digit levels again in 2004 partly because of the effects of higher oil prices and administered price increases.
5. See EBRD Transition Report (2004).
6. See EBRD Transition Report (2004).
7. The size of the increase in dollar value was partly due to the weaker dollar in 2003.
8. Moldova does not have any prospect at present of eventual membership, but it is part of the European Commission's 'Wider Europe' initiative. See Communication from the Commission to the Council and the European Parliament COM (2003) 104 Final: 'Wider Europe – Neighbourhood: A New Framework for our Relations with our Eastern and Southern Neighbours', available at http://europa.eu.int/comm/external_relations/we/intro/ip03_358.htm.

REFERENCES

EBRD (2004), 'Transition report 2004: infrastructure', London: European Bank for Reconstruction and Development.

Sanfey, P., E. Falcetti, A. Taci and S. Tepic (2004), 'Spotlight on South-Eastern Europe: an overview of private sector activity and investment', London: European Bank for Reconstruction and Development.

PART II

The Case of Dollarization and Euroization

5. The euro in Central and Eastern European countries: some introductory remarks

Josef Christl

The Eurosystem has, without doubt, established a truly credible and attractive European currency within a short period of time, and the euro has since come to play a significant role also outside the euro area – including the Central and Eastern European region. Before the cash changeover of national currencies to the euro there was an intense debate about whether the euro would be able to take over the role of the Deutsche mark in Central and Eastern Europe, and whether the euro would be able to attain the kind of reputation that the Deutsche mark – and the Austrian schilling – enjoyed.

Today, substantial amounts of currencies are circulating outside the countries in which they were originally issued. In most cases, however, little is known about their exact whereabouts, the extent of currency substitution and the motives behind the decision to hold foreign money rather than one's domestic currency. Yet it is important, for various reasons, to learn more about the extent a currency is used abroad. Among other things, large amounts of circulating foreign currency can add uncertainty to the results of monetary policy. Increases or decreases of domestic money demand might be wrongly appraised if foreign currency demand is incorrectly estimated. Furthermore, knowledge of the volume of currency circulating abroad can be revealing for domestic and foreign fiscal policy. In both cases, the size of unofficial dollarization or euroization might be related to the size of the foreign currency black market, reflecting a certain degree of tax evasion.

In 1997 the Oesterreichische Nationalbank started to commission representative semi-annual surveys in our neighbouring regions – specifically in Croatia, the Czech Republic, Hungary, Slovakia and Slovenia – to learn more about the amounts of foreign currency held by the population. Looking back, we are now able to analyse how the behaviour of Central and Eastern European countries has changed over time. For example the figures for the second half of 2003 show the percentage of private persons holding euros to have increased in all countries in the two preceding years. From 2001 to 2003, this share grew most strongly in the Czech Republic, from 13 per cent to 25 per cent; and in Slovakia, from 20 per cent to 27 per cent. Slovenia is the country with the highest share; in this country, 44 per cent of all respondents held euro assets.

Furthermore, the results illustrate that currency holdings are typically not motivated by domestic transactions – with one exception, namely Croatia, where 12 per cent of the respondents said that domestic transactions were their main motive for holding euros. Czechs, Slovaks and Hungarians tend to use euro holdings predominately for transaction purposes abroad – such as for holidays or for cross-border shopping. By contrast, in Croatia and Slovenia euro holdings are mainly motivated by the euro's store-of-value function. These differences are also reflected in the amounts of euros that people in Central and Eastern Europe hold. According to the survey for the second half of 2003, median euro holdings amounted to EUR 300 in Slovenia and EUR 130 in Croatia and ranged between EUR 80 and EUR 116 in the Czech Republic, Hungary and Slovakia.

The surveys also showed that in May 2001, that was before the cash changeover, the majority of people holding Deutsche marks or Austrian schillings were still unsure about their plans for conversion. Of those who had made up their minds, 58 per cent planned to exchange their mark or schilling holdings into euros, whereas 42 per cent wanted to convert them into 'other currencies'. The moderate perception of the euro before its cash debut can no doubt largely be attributed to uncertainties relating to the changeover. People were unsure about the exchange rate, they did not know who would be in charge of the exchange and they feared that they would have to pay considerable commissions. Many people were also uncertain whether the new single European currency would be as hard and stable as the Deutsche mark, or the Austrian schilling, had been. According to the 2002 survey, which reflects actual exchanges after the introduction of euro cash, 71 per cent of all respondents in the end exchanged their Deutsche mark holdings for euros and 21 per cent for local currencies. A much smaller fraction – just 4 per cent – was exchanged for US dollars.

What do people in Central and Eastern European countries think about the stability of the euro these days? The euro has excellent 'approval ratings' in this area. About 90 per cent of all respondents think that the euro is currently rather or very stable, and that it will remain stable or rather stable in the next two years. The results clearly show that the euro has successfully taken over the predominant role that the Deutsche mark and the Austrian schilling used to play in these countries. In other words, the euro has become a currency in which people in the region really have a lot of trust.

The survey conducted by the Oesterreichische Nationalbank only comprised one country located in South-East Europe, namely Croatia. However, the single European currency is important for the exchange rate regimes and for monetary policy in all South-East European countries. Most countries have geared their monetary policy to an external anchor, which is – without any exception – the euro. Bosnia and Herzegovina and Bulgaria have implemented currency boards, Macedonia has pegged its currency to the euro, Croatia and Serbia have practised a tightly managed float with the euro as the reference currency, and the two non-sovereign territories, namely Kosovo and Montenegro, have unilaterally adopted the euro. Two of the South-East European countries, Albania and Romania, have conducted a managed float, with the euro as the major reference currency, together with money growth targeting.

The euro plays a vital unofficial role in South-East Europe, with immense amounts of foreign currency held by inhabitants – the highest levels among the transition countries. The share of foreign currency holdings in broad money is very high, amounting, for example, to up to 75 per cent in Croatia and to 55 per cent in Bulgaria. In contrast to the case of unofficial euroization in South-East Europe, two parts of this region, namely the Republic of Montenegro and the Province of Kosovo, have officially euroized their economies. It is evident that in these two cases euroization took place in exceptional historical situations, which were the aftermath of the Kosovo war, as well as the conflict with the Milosevic regime and its inflationary policies.

Euroization can have some advantages but – as we know – it is also associated with high risks. A high degree of foreign currency held as a means of exchange is certainly an indicator that the domestic monetary system inspires little confidence. However, there has been considerable progress towards price stability: All countries of the region, with the exception of Romania, managed to archive single-digit inflation rates in 2003. Experience shows that price stability is positively influenced by the exchange rate as an external anchor. However, countries with a loosely managed float have also succeeded in bringing down inflation, such as in Albania. Overall, the experience in South-East Europe once more demonstrates that credibility of – and confidence in – monetary and economic policy is one of the most decisive factors for bringing down inflation. The improvement of price stability is also mirrored in an increasing monetization of most South-East European countries. Despite economic progress, euroization is likely to remain high in the future, which can to a large part be traced back to the growing trade and economic integration between South-East Europe and the EU countries.

While two countries, Romania and Bulgaria, are likely to join the EU in 2007, other countries or territories in the region still have a long way to go until they may enter the European Union. Eventually – once they have fulfilled all pre-conditions, especially the Maastricht Treaty – all new EU member states are also committed to adopt the euro. Yet it needs to be acknowledged that formal or de facto euroization is considered to be inconsistent with the Maastricht Treaty.

REFERENCES

Barisitz, S. (2004), 'Exchange rate arrangements and monetary policy in Southeastern Europe and Turkey: some stylized facts', in OeNB (ed.), *Focus on European Economic Integration*, No. 2/2004, pp. 95–118.

Stix, H. (2001), 'Survey results about foreign currency holdings in five Central and Eastern European Countries', in *CESifo Forum 3/2001*, pp. 41–8.

Stix, H. (2002), 'The euro in Central and Eastern Europe – survey evidence from five countries', in *CESifo Forum 3/2002*, pp. 33–8.

Stix, H. (2004), 'Foreign currency demand since 2002 – evidence from five Central and Eastern European countries', in *CESifo Forum 4/2004*, pp. 19–24.

6. *De jure* dollarization and euroization

Eduardo Levy Yeyati

A discussion of *de jure* dollarization *and* euroization presumes the presence of two different phenomena. Typically, *de jure* dollarization refers to the official adoption of a foreign currency – any foreign currency – in lieu of the national currency.[1] It follows that the standard definition of dollarization also comprises the unilateral adoption of the euro as exclusive – or parallel – legal tender. What do we talk about, then, when we talk about euroization?

Taking advantage of the absence of a standard definition of the term, I propose to understand euroization, more specifically, as monetary integration with the euro area. As I will argue below, this entails important differences with dollarization – as well as with monetary unions in general. But in order to frame the discussion, it is useful to revisit first the traditional dollarization debate.

This debate was reheated by the stream of emerging market crises in the late 1990s. The crises revealed the vulnerability of conventional pegs – which had regained popularity in the 1980s and early 1990s as a deflationary device – to self-fulfilling runs and speculative attacks, narrowing down the exchange rate regime debate to a credibility issue: unless a credible commitment device could not be engineered, governments would better avoid any commitment to a fixed exchange rate at all.

For a while, the so-called hard pegs were proposed as a partial solution to this dilemma. In a nutshell, this 'bipolar view' argued that the only alternative to floating was a pegged regime that was irreversible enough to eliminate the standard time inconsistency problem that plagued previous fixed arrangements.[2] If exit costs were enormously high – either due to legal constraints or to deleterious economic consequences – it would be ex-post optimal for a government to ensure the sustainability of the regime – and for market participants to believe in it.

Underlying this view was the belief that, in the absence of a strong national currency (as in most developing economies), the scope for an independent, counter-cyclical monetary policy – and, in general, the benefit of a floating exchange rate – was bound to be rather limited. While there were other aspects that matter in this discussion, the concept of a credible nominal anchor was certainly critical to the debate at the time.

If currency boards were the perfect example of a hard peg,[3] the Argentine crisis provided the perfect counter-example. Argentina not only showed how a long-standing currency board could be easily undone: it showed that this could be done endogenously while the currency board was still in place, through the printing of money by sub-national governments.[4] At any rate, as currency boards prove not to be hard enough, the bipolar view was left with unilateral *de jure* dollarization as the only possible (and more extreme) alternative to flexible exchange rates.

With the sole (debatable) exception of Liberia, there is no precedent of *de jure* de-dollarization: dollarization appears to be, indeed, more difficult to revert than any other fixed arrangement. The assessment of its pros and cons, however, suffers from a severe scarcity of relevant experiments. On the one hand, long-standing dollarized economies are largely due to historical and political reasons rather than economic motivations. More crucially, virtually all of them are very small sub-national economies that are hard to extrapolate in a meaningful way to the case of real countries. Panama, a small country by conventional standards, is a clear outlier within the group. On the other hand, potentially more revealing cases such as El Salvador or Ecuador are still too young to provide usable information.

THE DOLLARIZATION DEBATE

Keeping these caveats in mind, the dollarization debate can be broadly summarized by means of the following stylized trade-offs:

- Reduced transaction costs vs. exchange rate rigidity.
- Enhanced credibility vs. loss of counter-cyclical monetary policy.
- Reduced borrowing costs vs. financial fragility (loss of the lender of last resort).

The first trade-off is associated with the traditional Optimal Currency Area (OCA) theory. On one corner, there is the view that exchange rate volatility introduces transaction costs that reduce the efficiency and intensity of international trade. The popularity of this long-dated idea (of which McKinnon (1963) is an early reference) peaked with the work of Rose (1999), which estimated the impact of a common currency on trade flows to be up to 300 per cent (based, it has to be noted, on the sample of mostly sub-national entities mentioned above). These controversial results were toned down in subsequent work,[5] until a recent piece by Micco et al. (2003) shed new light on the discussion by working with the more relevant case of industrial economies at the time of the launch of the euro. Their preliminary evidence indicated that the effect of joining the European Economic and Monetary Union (EMU), while positive, was rather smaller than originally thought (about 15 per cent).

The flipside of these potential trade gains, still under the OCA view, lies in the loss of the exchange rate as an automatic absorber of real shocks. Given that the root of the problem lies in the asymmetries between the countries that share the currency, the cost would be smaller the greater the degree of factor mobility and the correlation of shocks within the region.[6] This concern is supported by the evidence that pegs tend to display greater output volatility (Levy Yeyati and Sturzenegger, 2003b) and greater output sensitivity to real shocks (Edwards and Levy Yeyati, forthcoming), particularly negative ones, which makes sense given the evidence that downward price rigidity tends to be greater than upward price rigidity.

The second trade-off is related with the 'modern' approach to the exchange rate debate, which, as noted, is centred on the concept of credibility. In particular, this approach views dollarization (as they viewed pegged regimes before) as a credible nominal anchor for non-credible monetary authorities. The evidence, which pertains almost exclusively to pegs, supports this claim: fixed regimes tend to be correlated with lower inflation – as long as they last.[7]

These inflation gains come at the expense of the loss of monetary policy.[8] In addition, one may argue that dollarization cripples any attempt at institutional building, which would require the successful implementation of a discretionary policy.

The existing evidence on this point is mixed. The fact that capital behaves pro-cyclically for most developing economies provides support for dollarization advocates, to the extent that it helps explain why flexible regimes do not appear to isolate domestic monetary variables from external shocks more effectively than rigid exchange rate arrangements.[9] However, as noted, monetary credibility cannot be achieved overnight, as witness some recent post-crisis success stories such as Chile, Mexico and even Brazil, which are gradually learning to disregard the exchange rate and to use monetary policy more actively.

Unlike the first two, the third trade-off, between reduced borrowing costs and lack of lender of last resort, is specific to *de jure* dollarization. On the one hand, dollarization eliminates currency risk by definition. If follows that, to the extent that currency risk has an adverse impact on sovereign risk, dollarization should lower the latter.[10] Conversely, inasmuch as the loss of the exchange rate as a shock absorber implies deeper recessions and greater default risk, dollarization may increase country risk premia. Moreover, dollarization makes the banking sector more fragile (or less efficient) due to the absence of a lender of last resort (or a presence of a costly substitute such as the holding of a substantial stock of liquid foreign assets).[11]

Short of testing the long-run effects on real-life dollarized economies, Powell and Sturzenegger (2003) examine the impact on sovereign risk of news that increases the probability of dollarization. Interestingly, they find that country risk in financially dollarized countries falls significantly on this news, while the opposite happens in non-financially dollarized ones.[12]

The incidence of financial dollarization leads directly into the crucial issue of the importance of initial conditions. On the one hand, de facto dollarization reduces the cost of *de jure* dollarization, since it already imposes many of the constraints associated with the latter. In particular, balance sheet effects reduce the tolerance for exchange rate fluctuations under a flexible regime, and the lender-of-last-resort function is limited to local currency intermediation.[13] Similarly, economic integration with the issuer of the foreign currency (or within the common currency region) increases trade gains, while credibility problems enhance the gains from importing monetary policy from more credible countries.

In short, we could then draw the following identikit of a prospective dollarizer:

- High financial dollarization.
- Important trade links with other users of the foreign currency to be adopted.
- Pervasive credibility problems that result in high country risk and persistent high inflation, or frequent currency collapses whenever they attempt to use an exchange rate anchor.

EUROIZATION

In this light, what can we say about euroization (in the particular definition used here)? The first thing to note is that, in general, there is mixed evidence on the relevance of OCA considerations in the political process that led to the launch of EMU. This is not specific to euroization: as noted, OCA was not relevant in any historical examples of unilateral dollarization – with the sole exception, perhaps, of El Salvador. At any rate, recent experiences show that substantial trade gains can be achieved without a common currency (as witnessed by NAFTA and the EU itself) and that additional gains induced by a common currency are likely to be moderate (as indicated by the preliminary evidence of the euro). More realistically, monetary integration is likely to be driven by credibility issues (for low credibility countries) and 'linkage' politics (for 'anchor' countries).[14]

But perhaps the main distinctive aspect between dollarization and euroization is the combination of a multilateral agreement and the presence of countries with policy credibility to export. Let me be more precise on this.

At the risk of oversimplifying a complex issue, one could summarize the euroization scheme from the perspective of a developing economy in this way: monetary and real integration plus a shared (implicit) lender of last resort that requires upward convergence to the anchor economies, a prerequisite that, in turn, works as a credible commitment mechanism to comply with the convergence criteria.

The exact nature of how this works is still an open question. In particular, European observers may dispute the idea of a regional lender of last resort within the euro area (let alone one that involves accession countries) and emphasize that it is the prize of integration that makes credible the commitment of governments to meet the accession criteria. However, besides trade gains (which in any case can be largely achieved through trade agreements), the other potential benefit from integration comes from nominal and financial stability, which hints at the presence of some implicit regional safety net.[15] At any rate, it is generally acknowledged that convergence to an anchor country (or countries) is crucial in this scheme.

Moreover, even in the absence of such a safety net, euroization (unlike dollarization) brings with it the additional benefit of a large degree of real integration, which reduces, through capital and labour mobility, the cost of losing the exchange rate as a mechanism to smooth out business cycle asymmetries between member countries. Indeed, with sufficient factor mobility, asymmetric business cycles may enhance the scope for regional risk-sharing.

From the perspective of a small developing country, then, euroization, by replacing the stick of exit costs by the carrot of integration, entails essentially a gentler and more effective version of dollarization which enhances substantially the associated credibility gains while it mitigates the cost of a rigid exchange rate.

In this light, we can address the question of whether euroization is a sensible prospect for a developing South-East European economy. Whereas the answer would still depend on the situation of individual countries, in this case we can afford to be more precise for at least two reasons.

First, a casual look at the identikit outlined above reveals that it matches relatively closely the situation of many of the countries involved. The example of Croatia is a case in point – it is safe to say that most other economies in the group largely fit the description. Second, as noted, euroization ensures a rapid convergence that goes beyond monetary policy.

Indeed, the existing evidence on the process of convergence has been striking by most standards. In particular, the narrowing of the spreads has often been accompanied by increased government efforts to comply with Maastricht conditionality, closing a virtuous circle. As a result, euroization (or, more precisely, its prospect) appears to bring the gains in terms of lower inflation and reduced borrowing costs often attributed (debatably) to unilateral dollarization.

Thus, euroization indeed appears to be a sensible prospect for South-East Europe – and, possibly, for developing economies in general. Ultimately, while unilateral dollarization is still under debate, one might argue that euroization may indeed be the peg pole that the bipolar view has been searching for.

NOTES

1. See Levy Yeyati and Sturzenegger (2003a), on which the present discussion is based. The definition excludes the use of foreign currency *alongside* the domestic currency, typically referred to as de facto or unofficial dollarization.
2. See for instance Fischer (2001).
3. Ghosh et al. (2000) is a good example of the case for currency boards, and the prominent role that Argentina played in this regard.
4. See De la Torre et al. (2003) for a detailed discussion of the collapse of the Argentine currency board.
5. See for instance Rose and Van Wincoop (2001).
6. Standard references on these issues are Mundell (1963) and Kenen (1969), respectively. One qualification may be in order. OCA theory assumes that common currency countries have no 'real risk-sharing' mechanism. If, by contrast, a regional transfer scheme is in place such that, whenever the macro context is better in one country than in the region as a whole, the country receives a subsidy for a given shock distribution, the more asymmetric the shocks, the larger the scope for regional risk-sharing.
7. See Ghosh et al. (1997) and Levy Yeyati and Sturzenegger (2001).
8. But, from the perspective of the modern view, this is exactly what dollarization is all about: if the policy maker is the source of the problem (due to lack of political will or mere ineptitude), losing him is more of an advantage than a disadvantage. In the end, dollarization advocates argue, the scope for a non-credible policy maker in a small open economy to run an autonomous monetary policy is bound to be limited anyway.
9. See for instance Frankel (1999), Hausmann et al. (1999) and Borensztein et al. (2001). Indeed, interest rates in Panama appear to be less significantly influenced by external rates than in countries with other, more flexible arrangements.
10. Currency risk may increase sovereign risk through balance sheet effects in de facto dollarized economies or, if a devaluation is successfully avoided, through the cost of the interest rate defence of the currency.
11. Other lender-of-last-resort substitutes are likely to be limited and unreliable (as the contingent credit lines subscribed in the 1990s by Argentina and Mexico with a consortium of international banks), or unpredictable (as the assistance from IMF-led rescue packages). See Broda and Levy Yeyati (2003) for a discussion.
12. Here, following Ize and Levy Yeyati (2003), financial dollarization denotes the holding by residents of foreign currency-denominated assets and liabilites in non-officially dollarized economies.

13. Hence, the different effect of dollarization on borrowing costs across financially dollarized and not financially dollarized economies.
14. Frieden (2002), for example, stresses the role of 'linkage' politics by which EMU may have helped Germany to gain European support for its foreign policy initiatives in Eastern Europe.
15. As stated in Levy Yeyati (2005), 'the perception that accession to EMU may enhance stability beyond what would be achieved by a set of good policies hints . . . at the presence of some implicit safety net that, at the very least, protects the country against exogenous shocks or liquidity runs, ensuring that these good policies are ultimately rewarded.'

REFERENCES

Borensztein, Eduardo, Jeromin Zettelmeyer and Thomas Philippon (2001), 'Monetary independence in emerging markets: does the exchange rate regime make a difference?' *International Monetary Fund Working Paper* No. 01/1.

Broda, Christian and Eduardo Levy Yeyati (2003), 'Dollarization and the lender of last resort', in E. Levy Yeyati and F. Sturzenegger (eds), *Dollarization*, MIT Press.

De la Torre, Augusto, Eduardo Levy Yeyati and Sergio Schmukler (2003), 'Living and dying with hard pegs: The rise and fall of Argentina's currency board', *Economía*, **5** (2), 43–99.

Edwards, Sebastián and Eduardo Levy Yeyati (forthcoming), 'Flexible exchange rates as shock absorbers', *European Economic Review*.

Fischer, Stanley (2001), 'Exchange rate regimes: Is the bipolar view correct?', *Journal of Economic Perspectives*, **15** (2), 3–24.

Frankel, Jeffrey (1999), 'No single currency regime is right for all countries or at all times', *National Bureau of Economic Research Working Paper* No. 7338.

Frieden, Jeffrey (2002), 'The political economy of dollarization: domestic and international factors', in E. Levy Yeyati and F. Sturzenegger (eds), *Dollarization: Debates and Policy Alternatives*, Cambridge: MIT Press.

Ghosh, Atish R., Anne-Marie Gulde and Holger C. Wolf (2000), 'Currency boards – more than a quick fix?', *Economic Policy*, **15** (31), 269–335.

Ghosh, Atish R., Anne-Marie Gulde, Jonathan Ostry and Holger Wolf (1997), 'Does the nominal exchange rate regime matter?', *National Bureau of Economic Research Working Paper* No. 5874.

Hausmann, Ricardo, Carmen Pagés-Serra, Michael Gavin, Michael Stein and H. Ernesto (1999), 'Financial turmoil and choice of exchange rate regime', *Inter-American Development Bank Research Department Working Paper* No. 400.

Ize, Alain and Eduardo Levy Yeyati (2003), 'Financial dollarization', *Journal of International Economics*, **59** (2), 323–47.

Kenen, Peter (1969), 'The theory of optimal currency areas: An eclectic view', in R. Mundell and A. Swoboda (eds), *Monetary Problems of the International Economy*, Chicago: University of Chicago Press.

Levy Yeyati, Eduardo (2005), 'Recurrent debt problems and international safety nets', in Miguel A. Centeno, Harold James and John Londregan (eds), *The Political Economy of Recurrent Debt*, Princeton Institute for International and Regional Studies Monograph Series, No. 3, Princeton, NJ: PIIRS, Princeton University.

Levy Yeyati, Eduardo and Federico Sturzenegger (2000), 'Is EMU a blueprint for Mercosur?', *Cuadernos de Economía*, **110**, 63–99.

Levy Yeyati, Eduardo and Federico Sturzenegger (2001), 'Exchange rate and economic performance', *IMF Staff Papers*, **47**, 62–98.

Levy Yeyati, Eduardo and Federico Sturzenegger (2003a), 'Dollarization: A primer', in E. Levy Yeyati and F. Sturzenegger (eds), *Dollarization*, MIT Press.

Levy Yeyati, Eduardo and Federico Sturzenegger (2003b), 'To float or to fix: Evidence on the impact of exchange rate regimes on growth', *American Economic Review*, **93** (4), 1173–93.

McKinnon, Ronald (1963), 'Optimum currency areas', *American Economic Review*, **LIII** (4), September, 717–25.

Micco, Alejandro, Ernesto Stein and Guillermo Ordoñez (2003), 'The currency union effect on trade: Early evidence from EMU', *Economic Policy*, **18** (37), 315–56, October.

Mundell, Robert (1963), 'Capital mobility and stabilisation policy under fixed and flexible exchange rates', *Canadian Journal of Economics and Political Science*, **29**, 475–85.

Powell, Andrew and Federico Sturzenegger (2003), 'Dollarization: The link between devaluation and default risk', in E. Levy Yeyati and F. Sturzenegger (eds), *Dollarization*, MIT Press.

Rose, Andrew (1999), 'One money, one market: Estimating the effect of common currencies on trade', *National Bureau of Economic Research Working Paper* No. 7432.

Rose, Andrew and Eric van Wincoop (2001), 'National money as a barrier to international trade: The real case for currency union', *American Economic Review*, **91** (2), 386–90.

7. Lessons from sustained cases of official dollarization/euroization*

Adalbert Winkler

1. INTRODUCTION

The official and unilateral adoption of a foreign currency, commonly known as dollarization or euroization,[1] has its place in the world economy's history, but was out of fashion for a long time – until Kosovo and Montenegro adopted the euro, and Ecuador, El Salvador and East Timor the US dollar as their currency. More important, international financial institutions and academic economists re-considered dollarization/euroization as a possible policy option when the crisis of many emerging market economies during the second half of the 1990s underlined the difficulties of managing exchange rates in a world of open capital accounts (Calvo, 1999 and 2001).[2] However, the costs and benefits of unilaterally adopting another country's currency have mainly been explored on theoretical grounds (Berg and Borensztein, 2000). Empirical analysis has been largely confined to the case of Panama (Edwards, 2001; Goldfajn and Olivares, 2002).

This chapter sheds light on the experience of countries and territories that have officially and unilaterally used a foreign currency for a long time.[3] In particular, it aims at answering the question concerning whether any lessons can be drawn from their experience for countries considering to unilaterally adopt another country's currency. The chapter is structured as follows. Section 2 discusses the pros and cons of such a move,[4] with a special focus on South-East European countries. Based on the criteria stressed by the bipolar view of sustainable exchange rate regimes and the optimum currency area (OCA) theory, sustained cases of dollarization/euroization are reviewed in section 3. The main results, summarized in section 4, are that dollarized/euroized countries have experienced a high degree of monetary stability and of integration with their anchor country. At the same time, sustained cases of dollarization/euroization have been characterized by substantial fiscal transfers from the anchor country, a high dependency on tourism, and financial integration via the establishment of offshore financial centres. These features, which have fostered integration with the anchor country, have been based on policies and attributes mainly exogenous to monetary policy, namely small country size as well as geographic and political proximity to the anchor country. By itself, the common currency has not served as a straightforward substitute for prior integration. Thus, despite the merits of (unilateral) dollarization/euroization as a device for achieving monetary stability, countries should carefully analyse integration prospects with the potential anchor country before opting for such a course, or consider other monetary policy options for achieving domestic monetary stability.

2. THE CURRENT DEBATE ON DOLLARIZATION/EUROIZATION

Theoretical Framework

The 'bipolar' or 'corner solution' view of sustainable exchange rate regimes (Fischer, 2001) and the theory of optimum currency areas, which exists in an 'old' and a 'new' version (Mongelli, 2002), form the theoretical framework of the debate on unilateral dollarization/euroization. The 'new' OCA theory and the bipolar view both emphasize the credibility of monetary commitments, whereas the 'old' OCA theory's assessment of benefits and costs of adopting a foreign country's currency is based on an analysis of the need for an independent monetary policy as an adjustment mechanism in case of asymmetric shocks and a low level of economic integration within the potential common currency area. In a nutshell, the theories identify the following main benefits and costs:

- Macroeconomic stability gains have been identified as the main benefit associated with dollarization/euroization.[5] By adopting the monetary policy of the anchor country, which enjoys a high degree of credibility, the dollarized/euroized country can achieve monetary stability by minimizing risks of output losses that arise when a domestic central bank aims at macro stabilization but is unable to pre-commit itself to a low rate of inflation (Barro and Gordon, 1983; Goldfajn and Olivares, 2000). Due to the credibility import, inflation and interest rates in the dollarized/euroized economy are assumed to converge rapidly towards the level of the issuing country.
- The loss of the monetary policy instrument as an adjustment instrument has been named as the most prominent cost of dollarization/euroization (Mundell, 1961).[6] Dollarized/euroized economies

have to rely on other adjustment mechanisms – like wage and price flexibility or fiscal transfers from the anchor country – to avoid substantial output swings in case of asymmetric shocks with the anchor country. Alternatively, they have to foster real and financial integration with the anchor country to ensure a high degree of business cycle correlation, thereby reducing the likelihood of asymmetric shocks.

Empirical evidence suggests that there are a number of countries that apparently suffer from a lack of monetary policy credibility owing to a history of monetary instability and a high degree of unofficial dollarization/euroization. These countries also seem to lack adjustment mechanisms beyond domestic monetary policy to counter asymmetric shocks. Moreover, the degree of integration with the potential anchor country is usually found to be underdeveloped. Thus, individual country analyses often lead to the conclusion that a possible move towards dollarization/euroization (both official and unilateral) could be highly beneficial with regard to monetary stability but come at a substantial cost, given the risk of asymmetric shocks and the lack of adjustment mechanisms.

The Case of South-East Europe

The South-East European region may serve as a prominent example for conflicting evidence on potential benefits and costs of unilaterally adopting a foreign currency.[7] Over the last decades the region has seen several periods of monetary and exchange rate instability,[8] accompanied by a high degree of unofficial euroization in the form of currency and asset substitution (see Table 7.1).[9] Yet countries in the area may, under some conditions, need an independent monetary policy to counter asymmetric shocks. While integration, in particular trade integration, with the euro area has quite advanced for some countries (Table 7.1), the degree of real and structural convergence is still limited. Per capita income levels, the most commonly used indicator of real convergence, albeit showing some signs of convergence in some countries, stand at less than 30 per cent of the euro area average in purchasing power standards, with the exceptions of Bulgaria and Croatia (Table 7.1). At the same time, despite remarkable progress in recent years, the process of institutional, legislative and infrastructure reforms related to the transition from a planned to a market economy is still ongoing, as shown by the EBRD transition indicators (Table 7.1). Thus, it is doubtful whether the economies of South-East European countries and the euro zone face symmetric shocks and whether they would react symmetrically to common shocks.[10]

Table 7.1 Selected indicators of South-East European economies

	Consumer prices (percentage change, period averages)		Foreign currency deposits (as a percentage of total deposits, 2003)	Trade in goods with the euro area (percentage of total trade in goods, 2003)	GDP per capita (PPP terms, USD, as a share of euro area GDP per capita)		EBRD Transition indicators***		
	1994–1998	1999–2004			1998	2004	Enterprises	Markets and trade	Financial institutions
Albania	19.2	2.4	30.8	75.4	12.3	15.9	2.8	3.6	2.2
Bosnia and Herzegovina	1.7	2.1	47.4	44.5	20.8	24.4	2.4	2.9	2.2
Bulgaria	272.2	5.8	48.0	51.9	24.1	30.6	3.4	3.7	3.0
Croatia	22.5	3.6	80.5	51.0	36.0	41.0	3.6	3.6	3.3
FYR of Macedonia	29.4	2.5	52.0	54.3	25.8	25.9	3.2	3.4	2.3
Romania	84.3	29.2	42.5	59.8	25.9	27.5	3.1	3.7	2.5
Serbia and Montenegro	n.a.	40.6	94.7*	≈80**	19.4	17.4	2.6	2.8	2.2

Notes:
* Serbia only.
** Share of the EU in total Serbian trade.
*** The transition indicators range from 1 to 4+, with 1 representing little or no change from a rigid centrally planned economy and 4+ representing the standards of an industrialized market economy.

Sources: IMF, EBRD, national sources, own calculations.

Moreover, the more recent South-East European experience also suggests that considerable progress in macroeconomic stabilization can be made with different exchange rate regimes. Disinflation and exchange rate stabilization have been achieved under euro-based currency boards (Bosnia and Herzegovina, Bulgaria), pegs and managed floats (Croatia, Serbia, FYR of Macedonia, Romania) and independent floating (Albania). Thus, the potential benefits of unilateral euroization in terms of domestic monetary stability seem to be limited, while the risks associated with prematurely forgoing the monetary policy instrument may be quite substantial. This is very much in line with the general economic reasoning of the ECOFIN Council's position on unilateral euroization in accession countries (see box 7.1): countries considering dollarization/euroization should follow a lengthy process of convergence or integration with the anchor country before adopting this country's currency.

BOX 7.1 THE ECOFIN COUNCIL POSITION ON UNILATERAL EUROIZATION IN ACCESSION COUNTRIES

The euro area represents a multilateral currency union formed by member states of the EU with common and shared responsibilities among its members. For the formation of Monetary Union, the EU Treaty specified certain economic and institutional criteria that have to be fulfilled by future member states of the common currency area in order to safeguard its sustainability. Moreover, the treaty provides that there has to be a Community assessment of the fulfilment of these criteria and mutual agreement on the appropriate exchange rates.

This is why with regard to current and future EU accession countries, the ECOFIN does not welcome unilateral euroization, as such an adoption of the euro outside the treaty process would run counter to the underlying economic reasoning of European Monetary Union. In particular, it would undermine the process of convergence prior to the adoption of the euro. Unilateral euroization would also imply circumventing the process of multilateral assessment of new members by current EU member states and as such would be difficult to reconcile with the cooperative spirit of a community of fellow members (ECOFIN, 2000; Duisenberg, 2001; European Commission, 2002).

The 'Endogeneity Hypothesis' of Optimum Currency Areas and the Rose Result

The view that an ex ante high degree of integration represents a precondition of a sustainable common currency area has recently been challenged by the 'endogeneity hypothesis' of optimum currency areas. According to this hypothesis, the criteria stressed by the old OCA theory will endogenously be fulfilled ex post once a common currency has been adopted (Frankel and Rose, 1998). For example, the adoption of another country's currency implies lower transaction costs in international trade between the two countries. This will lead to closer trade links (Dallas and Tavlas, 2001) and hence reduce the likelihood of asymmetric shocks between countries sharing a currency.

The empirical research originating from Rose (2000) supports this line of reasoning. Based on a sample including more than 180 countries and jurisdictions, it is shown that two countries sharing a common currency trade far more, perhaps over three times as much, than comparable countries with different currencies.[11] The result had a strong impact on the dollarization/euroization debate as it turned the old OCA view on its head: traditional OCA properties, like a high degree of integration or factor mobility, are not seen as a prerequisite, but as a consequence of a common currency.[12] A comprehensive analysis of sustained cases of dollarization/euroization,[13] considering a wide range of factors linked to costs and benefits of a common currency area, however indicates that integration efforts of dollarized/euroized countries have benefited not only from the common currency. Rather, they have relied to a significant extent on other policies and mechanisms facilitating integration with the anchor country.

3. CASES OF SUSTAINED OFFICIAL DOLLARIZATION/EUROIZATION

Overview

On the basis of the list of territories published by the United Nations[14] it is possible to identify 51 cases of sustained dollarization/euroization (Table 7.2).

Most of them are small, many even involving a population of less than 100 000. Moreover, almost two-thirds of the territories are politically dependent. Finally, with the exception of the island countries in the North Pacific, all independent countries use the currency of an anchor country that is either in their geographical vicinity or with whom they share a common border. Only dependent territories use the currencies of their home countries irrespective of how distant they are.[15]

Empirical research on the economic performance of sustained cases of

Table 7.2 Cases of sustained euroization/dollarization

Euroized countries (dependent territories)	Population	Dollarized countries (dependent territories)	Population	Other cases of official foreign currency adoption (dependent territories)	Population
Reunion	732 570	Puerto Rico	3 937 316	Jersey (GBP)	89 361
Guadeloupe	431 170	Guam	157 557	Isle of Man (GBP)	73 489
Martinique	418 454	Virgin Islands (US)	122 211	Guernsey (GBP)	64 342
French Polynesia	253 506	Northern Mariana Islands	74 612	Greenland (DKK)	56 352
New Caledonia	204 863	American Samoa	67 084	The Faeroes (DKK)	45 661
French Guiana	177 562	Bermuda	63 503	Gibraltar (GBP)	27 649
Mayotte	163 366	British Virgin Is.	20 812	Cook Islands (NZD)	20 611
Wallis and Futuna	15 435	Turks and Caicos Is.	18 122	St Helena (GBP)	7 266
St Pierre and Miquelon	6 928			Falkland Is. (GBP)	2 895
				Christmas Is. (AUD)	2 771
				Norfolk Is. (AUD)	1 879
				Tokelau (NZD)	1 445
				Cocos Is. (AUD)	633
				Pitcairn Is. (NZD)	47
Total	*2 403 854*	*Total*	*4 443 095*	*Total*	*394 401*

Table 7.2 (continued)

Independent euroized countries (date of independence)	Population	Independent dollarized countries (date of independence)	Population	Independent countries that have adopted another foreign currency (date of independence, currency adopted)	Population
Andorra (1278)	67 627	Panama (1903)	2 845 647	Lesotho (1966, ZAR)	2 177 062
Monaco (1419)	31 842	Bahamas (1973)	297 852	Bhutan (1949, INR)	2 049 412
San Marino (301)	27 336	Barbados (1966)	275 330	Namibia (1990, ZAR)	1 797 677
Vatican City (1929)	890	Belize (1981)	256 062	Swaziland (1968, ZAR)	1 104 343
		Micronesia, Fed. States (1986)	134 597	Kiribati (1979, AUD)	94 149
		Marshall Islands (1986)	70 882	Liechtenstein (1806, CHF)	32 528
		Palau (1994)	19 092	Nauru (1968, AUD)	12 088
				Tuvalu (1978, AUD)	10 991
				Niue (1974, NZD)	2 124
Total	*127 695*	*Total*	*3 899 462*	*Total*	*7 280 374*

Sources: CIA World Factbook, author's compilation.

dollarization/euroization has been rare. This reflects the difficulty of collecting relevant data as many countries are neither members of the IMF nor of the World Bank. Edwards (2001) and Edwards and Magendzo (2001, 2002) – analysing the macroeconomic performance of Panama and 13 other cases listed in Table 7.2[16] – found that dollarized/euroized countries have experienced significantly lower inflation, but have also grown at a significantly lower rate than countries with their own currencies. Moreover, fiscal records of the two groups of countries are rather similar. Overall, the available evidence seems to suggest that the adoption of a foreign currency does not automatically ensure a good, let alone superior, macroeconomic performance (Backé and Wójcik, 2003).

Optimum Currency Area Properties

Winkler et al. (2004) expand the analysis of sustained cases of dollarization/euroization. Keeping data limitations in mind, they focus on the criteria identified in the bipolar view as well as the new and old OCA theory to analyse how these countries have been able to sustain unilateral dollarization/euroization. Following the new OCA theory and the bipolar view on sustainable exchange rate arrangements, the alleged credibility gains of dollarization/euroization were assessed by looking at the inflation record, the level of interest rates and bond spreads, as well as fiscal and external imbalances of dollarized/euroized countries. Evidence on factor mobility, fiscal transfers from the anchor country as well as real and financial integration was collected in order to shed some light on the variables emphasized by the old OCA theory. Their results can be summarized as follows:

- Monetary stability has been a key feature of sustained cases of dollarization/euroization. Countries with a long history of dollarization/euroization seem to have inflation patterns similar to those of their respective anchor countries.[17] However, credibility issues did not play a role when countries opted for this monetary regime. In line with the findings of Edwards (2001) and Edwards and Magendzo (2001, 2002), there is also little evidence that dollarization/euroization has contributed to fiscal discipline. On the contrary, substantial fiscal deficits have been largely financed by transfers from the anchor countries. Financial sector development has advanced in many dollarized/euroized countries, but mainly in terms of offshore banking rather than in providing services to residents.
- Close integration with the anchor country has been a key feature of sustained cases of dollarization/euroization.[18] In addition to international trade and foreign direct investment, however, substantial fiscal transfers from the anchor country as well as integration via offshore finance and tourism have played a crucial role. Indeed, given the extent of use of these integration mechanisms – also compared to other countries – it can be argued that they have been decisive in supporting the exchange rate regime.[19]

Special Features: Fiscal Transfers, Offshore Activities and Tourism

The extraordinary degree of financial dependency on the anchor countries, the crucial importance of tourism as a means of real integration and the establishment of offshore centres as a means of financial integration are the main new findings of the empirical analysis of sustained cases of dollarization/euroization.[20]

- Fiscal transfers from the anchor countries have in some cases reached such dimensions that the relatively high per capita GDP of the respective dollarized/euroized countries largely depend on this support (Table 7.3). This is most pronounced for dollarized/euroized dependencies, as 17 out of 31 jurisdictions can be defined as financially dependent on the anchor country.[21]
- Ten dollarized/euroized economies are among the top 15 countries in terms of tourism activity (see Figure 7.1). About one-third of the 42 'highly tourist-oriented'[22] countries are dollarized/euroized, compared with only five of the 82 countries with a tourism inflow of less than 10 per cent of the domestic population.[23]
- 20 out of the 51 dollarized/euroized countries have established offshore financial centres. Given their small size and the substantial flows to offshore centres,[24] it can be assumed that in terms of GDP or expressed in per capita figures, financial integration with the anchor country is unusually large.[25]

Relevance for Other Countries Considering the Unilateral Adoption of a Foreign Currency

The empirical analysis of sustained cases of dollarization/euroization supports the reasoning in favour of a common currency stressed by the bipolar view as well as the new and old OCA theory. Dollarization/euroization has been associated with a high degree of monetary stability and a high degree of real and financial integration with the anchor country. In comparison to other countries, however, sustained cases of dollarization/euroization stand out with regard to the use of fiscal transfers, tourism and offshore finance as integration mechanisms with the respective anchor country. In doing so, they have benefited from three special characteristics:

- *Small size.* The small size of dollarized/euroized countries allows fiscal transfers from anchor countries to have comparatively large effects on income levels in the recipient countries. Only very small countries may benefit from taking a 'free-rider' position by offering non-residents a lenient fiscal and regulatory framework, for example by establishing offshore financial centres (Padoa-Schioppa, 2001; International Monetary Fund, 2000).

Table 7.3 Official development assistance/fiscal transfers and sustained cases of dollarization/euroization

Country	Political status	Qualitative evidence	ODA as % of GDP	Largest donor	Anchor country
American Samoa	dependent	'[I]mportant financial support from the US. [. . .] Transfers from the US Government add substantially to American Samoa's economic well-being.'	n/a	US	US
Cook Islands	dependent	'USD 13.1 million (1995); New Zealand continues to furnish the greater part.'	n/a	New Zealand	New Zealand
Faeroe Islands	dependent	'USD 135 million annual subsidy from Denmark (1999).'	n/a	Denmark	Denmark
French Guiana	dependent	'The economy is tied closely to that of France through subsidies and imports.'	n/a	France	France
French Polynesia	dependent	'The territory substantially benefits from development agreements with France aimed principally at creating new businesses and strengthening social services.'	9%	France	France
Greenland	dependent	The economy remains critically dependent on exports of fish and substantial support from the Danish Government, which supplies about half of government revenues. [. . .] USD 380 million subsidy from Denmark (1999)	n/a	Denmark	Denmark
Guadeloupe	dependent	'[The economy] depends on France for large subsidies and imports.'	n/a	France	France
Guam	dependent	'Guam receives large transfer payments from the US Federal Treasury (USD 143 million in 1997).'	n/a	US	US
Martinique	dependent	'[S]ubstantial annual aid from France.'	n/a	France	France
Mayotte	dependent	'USD 107.7 million (1995); note – extensive French financial assistance.'	n/a	France	France

Table 7.3 (continued)

Country	Political status	Qualitative evidence	ODA as % of GDP	Largest donor	Anchor country
New Caledonia	dependent	'In addition to nickel, the substantial financial support from France and tourism are key to the health of the economy.'	10%	France	France
N. Mariana Islands	dependent	'The economy benefits substantially from financial assistance from the US.'	n/a	US	US
Reunion	dependent	'The economic well-being of Reunion depends heavily on continued financial assistance from France.'	n/a	France	France
Saint Helena	dependent	'The economy depends largely on financial assistance from the UK, which amounted to about USD 5 million in 1997 or almost one-half of annual budgetary revenues.'	n/a	UK	UK
Saint Pierre et Miquelon	dependent	'The islands are heavily subsidized by France to the great betterment of living standards. [. . .] [A]pproximately USD 65 million in annual grants from France.'	n/a	France	France
Tokelau	dependent	'The people must rely on aid from New Zealand to maintain public services, annual aid being substantially greater than GDP.'	n/a	New Zealand	New Zealand
Wallis and Futuna	dependent	'Revenues come from French government subsidies, licensing of fishing rights to Japan and South Korea, import taxes, and remittances from expatriate workers in New Caledonia.'	n/a	France	France

Bhutan	independent	'The government of India finances nearly three-fifths of Bhutan's budget expenditures.'	12%	India	India
Kiribati	independent	'Foreign financial aid, from UK, Japan, Australia, New Zealand, and China, is a critical supplement to GDP, equal to 25%–50% of GDP in recent years.'	22%	Australia	Australia
Marshall Islands	independent	'US government assistance is the mainstay of this tiny island economy. . . . Under the terms of the Compact of Free Association, the US provides roughly USD 39 million in annual aid.'	57%	US	US
Micronesia, Fed. St.	independent	'[U]nder terms of the Compact of Free Association, the US will provide USD 1.3 billion in grant aid during the period 1986–2001'	40%	US	US
Niue	independent	'Government expenditures regularly exceed revenues, and the shortfall is made up by critically needed grants from New Zealand'	n/a	New Zealand	New Zealand
Palau	independent	'The government is the major employer of the work force, relying heavily on financial assistance from the US.'	21%	US	US
Tuvalu	independent	'Substantial income is received annually from an international trust fund established in 1987 by Australia, NZ, and the UK and supported also by Japan and South Korea.'	n/a	n/a	Australia

Sources: CIA World Factbook, OECD (2002).

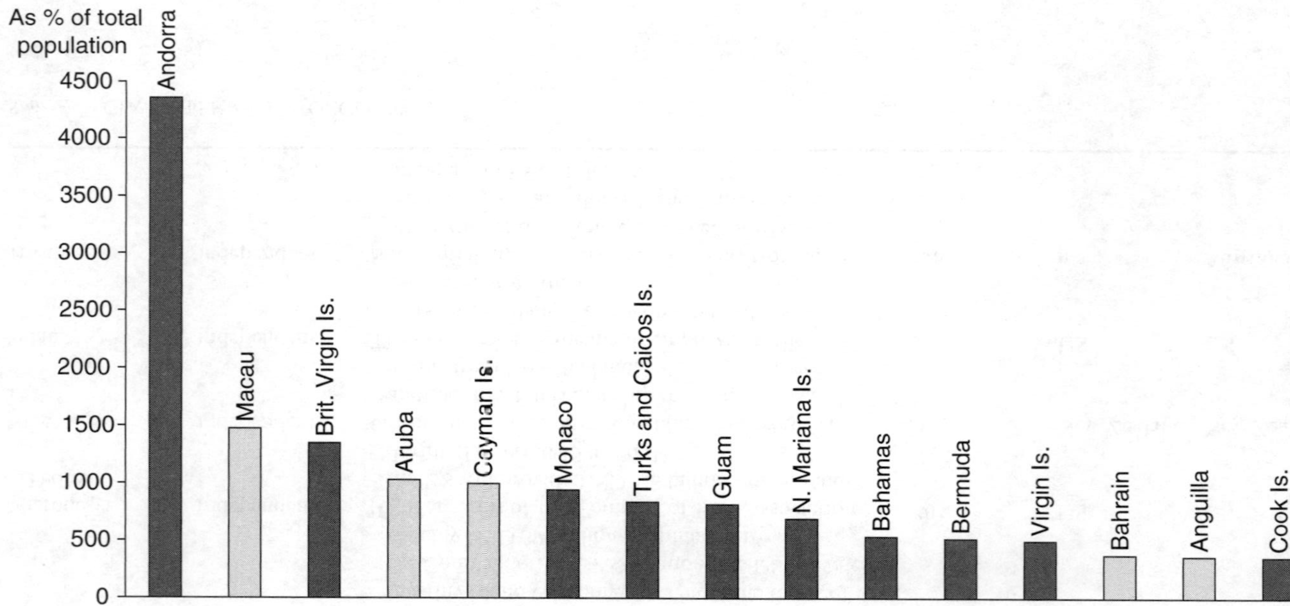

Note: Dark bars mark dollarized/euroized countries.

Sources: World Tourism Organization; authors' calculations.

Figure 7.1 Tourist-oriented countries: number of overnight visitors per year

- *Political status.* The fact that many dollarized/euroized economies are dependencies or have very close political relations with the anchor countries has a positive effect on all three integration mechanisms identified above. The willingness of a country to grant fiscal transfers to other countries is influenced by political considerations and affiliations. The success of offshore financial centres depends to a substantial degree on a stable political and regulatory environment which a dependency of a politically stable country can usually offer. Even with regard to tourism it can be argued that a beautiful landscape is of limited value if countries lack the political stability that is needed to attract tourists and investment into tourism infrastructure.
- *Location.* The potential for offshore finance and tourism seems to rely – at least to some extent – on the location of a country, namely geographical vicinity to the anchor country.

All these special characteristics are exogenous to the chosen monetary regime. Thus, the evidence on sustained cases of dollarization/euroization does not necessarily support the 'endogeneity hypothesis' of optimum currency areas. While a common currency may have been an important factor in strengthening trade links between dollarized/euroized countries and their anchor countries, it seems unlikely that the high degree of financial dependence and the importance of tourism and offshore centres for real and financial integration between dollarized/euroized and anchor countries have evolved endogenously through the sharing of a currency.

4. CONCLUSIONS

Recommendations in favour of unilateral official dollarization/euroization have become increasingly popular in recent years, as many countries have struggled with financial and exchange rate crises as well as domestic monetary instability. However, these recommendations have been largely based on theoretical arguments, as empirical research on countries that have opted for this exchange rate regime has been limited.

Against this background, this chapter summarized the findings on the actual experience of sustained cases of official dollarization/euroization, focusing on the criteria stressed by the bipolar view on sustainable exchange rate systems and the new OCA theory on the one hand and the old OCA theory on the other. Three conclusions seem to emerge:

1. In general, cases of sustained dollarization/euroization have experienced a high degree of monetary stability and integration with the

anchor country. Thus, they seem to have reaped the benefits and avoided the costs of dollarization/euroization stressed by the bipolar view on sustainable exchange rate systems and the new OCA theory on the one hand and the old OCA theory on the other.
2. There is evidence for a high degree of integration with the anchor country in terms of trade and foreign direct investment for many dollarized/euroized countries. However, substantial fiscal transfers from the anchor country, tourism and offshore finance have been identified as additional important and special features of the integration process.
3. Applying the experience of sustained cases to potential new cases is not straightforward. This is largely because special features, exogenous to the monetary regime, facilitated the integration of sustained cases of dollarization/euroization with the anchor country via fiscal transfers, tourism and offshore finance. These special features are the small country size, the political status as an anchor country dependency or as a country with close political ties to the anchor country, and geographical proximity to the anchor country.

In general, the analysis suggests that dollarization/euroization does not seem to be a straightforward substitute for prior integration. Countries that have sustained dollarization/euroization for a long time have relied to a significant extent on integration policies that took advantage of country characteristics exogenous to the exchange rate regime. Given the fact that most countries considering to adopt a foreign currency lack the special features of small country size, strong political affiliation and geographical proximity to the anchor country, they will not be able to draw on some key mechanisms these countries have employed to integrate with the anchor countries.[26] At the same time, the evidence for a broad 'endogenous' process of integration and convergence seems to be limited. Thus, it is difficult to derive strong and general lessons from the experience of sustained cases of dollarization/euroization.

Against this background, countries considering dollarization/euroization should either

- carefully consider the option of relying on a suitable domestic anchor for monetary policy before opting for unilateral dollarization/euroization, despite the latter's merits as a device for achieving macroeconomic stability, or
- ensure ex ante a high degree of integration with the potential anchor country to minimize the risks associated with the loss of the monetary policy instrument in case of asymmetric shocks.

NOTES

* This chapter is based on Winkler et al. (2004) and Mazzaferro et al. (2003) and has benefited from comments by Georges Pineau. The views expressed do not necessarily reflect those of the European Central Bank.

1. For simplicity and in line with standard practice, the term 'dollarization/euroization' is used throughout this chapter as a general term for the adoption of a foreign currency. Thus, it is not only used to characterize cases where the currency adopted is the US dollar or the euro, but also those cases where other foreign currencies are involved, for example the British pound or the Australian dollar.
2. Several papers have been produced by IMF or World Bank staff on this issue, and the World Bank also maintains a separate webpage on this topic. The *Journal of Policy Modelling* and the *Journal of Money, Credit and Banking* came out with special issues on this subject in 2001.
3. For simplicity, we refer to all cases of dollarization/euroization as 'countries'. This does not imply the expression of any opinion whatsoever on the part of the author or the European Central Bank concerning the legal status of any country, area or territory or of its authorities, or concerning the delimitation of its frontiers.
4. This chapter focuses only on the unilateral official adoption of a foreign currency and does not consider the unofficial or parallel use of a foreign currency (Baliño et al., 1999) or the multilaterally agreed adoption of a foreign currency (Angeloni, 2004).
5. Other benefits include (1) lower risk premia on financial assets and liabilities, (2) a more stable environment supporting domestic financial sector development, (3) the elimination of transaction costs when exchanging domestic into foreign currency and (4) stronger economic and financial integration with the anchor country.
6. Other costs include (1) the loss of the lender-of-last-resort function, and (2) the loss of seigniorage.
7. A similar analysis can be found in Berg, Borensztein and Mauro (2002) for Latin America and in Frankel (1999) for Argentina.
8. This has been most pronounced in the countries of the former Yugoslavia (Lahiri, 1991; Avramovic, 1995).
9. Indeed, focusing only on euro-denominated foreign exchange deposits, four South-Eastern European countries rank first on the list of EU neighbouring countries providing data on the share of foreign exchange deposits in total deposits.
10. With regard to the former acceding countries, this argument is developed in more detail in Backé et al. (2004).
11. This finding has proven to be statistically significant and robust with regard to other variables potentially affecting trade flows. By contrast, earlier research had largely failed to identify a significant and positive effect of exchange rate stability on trade. Thus, the Rose results triggered a debate on several aspects. Methodological issues and questions of data reliability were raised (see Nitsch, 2002; Persson, 2001; and Rose, 2002). Other observers wondered whether the results can be generalized (Quah, 2000; Obstfeld, 2000; Masson, 2000), given the special characteristics of many dollarized/euroized countries.
12. For example, Glick and Rose (2001), albeit pointing out that the trade effects of a common currency may take some time, claim that joining a currency union may cause bilateral trade between currency union members to almost double. Frankel and Rose (2002) suggest that dollarization/euroization might be associated with both enhanced economic integration and also higher economic growth.
13. The sample of currency unions in the Rose dataset includes countries and jurisdictions that form a regional currency union, in particular the CFA franc zone countries and the countries of the East Caribbean Currency Area, as well as the respective anchor countries. By contrast, the focus of this chapter is on the experience of countries that dollarized/euroized in a strict sense by unilaterally adopting the US dollar, the euro or any other third currency as legal tender. Thus, the total of 22 countries listed in Table 7.2 are part of the sample of currency unions in the Rose dataset.

14. See www.un.org/Depts/Cartographic/english/geoname.pdf.
15. The fact that many of the sustained cases of dollarization/euroization have been dependent territories indicates that political considerations seemed to have been highly relevant in the countries' 'choice' to adopt a foreign currency.
16. Andorra, Kiribati, Liechtenstein, the Marshall Islands, Micronesia, Monaco, Nauru, Panama, San Marino, Tuvalu, the Cook Islands, Greenland and Puerto Rico. In addition, Liberia and Palau were included.
17. Exceptions have been some island economies whose production structure is narrowly based on one or two key products. Here nominal convergence with the anchor country has been more limited.
18. A high degree of factor mobility has been an important characteristic of some dollarized/euroized countries.
19. In stating this, it is not intended to assert that the mechanisms have been deliberately employed to make the exchange rate regime sustainable. Rather, they were part of the general development strategy of the respective countries, as policies fostering real integration via tourism and financial integration have also been pursued by a number of other countries with similar characteristics, for example small size (Kose and Prasad, 2002), that are not dollarized/euroized.
20. Their relevance is also supported by evidence from a logit model on the role of financial transfers, tourism and offshore finance. Indeed, it can be shown that these characteristics have a statistically significant influence on the probability of two countries sharing a common currency, controlling for the influence of other variables. For details see Winkler et al. (2004, pp. 30ff.).
21. A country is defined as financially dependent when it either receives official development assistance (ODA) flows of more than 5 per cent of GNI, of which at least 20 per cent originates from one donor country. Data are taken from the OECD (2002) database. Given the limited country coverage of the OECD data, a country is also defined as financially dependent when it is referred to in the CIA World Factbook as receiving 'substantial transfers' or being 'highly dependent on subsidies'.
22. Countries are defined as 'highly tourist-oriented' if the number of annual overnight visitors exceeds the population.
23. Data are not available for 20 cases of dollarization/euroization.
24. For example, offshore centres account for roughly 8 per cent of total foreign claims by BIS reporting banks and for about 42 per cent of total foreign claims by BIS reporting banks that are held against non-developed countries.
25. The limited amount of information available suggests that funds from residents of the respective anchor countries account for a substantial share of assets managed in dollarized/euroized OFCs (see for example UK Home Office, 1998).
26. Winkler et al. (2004, pp. 40ff.) provide an analysis of the more recent cases of dollarization/euroization based on the criteria stressed by the bipolar view as well as the new and old OCA theory. While it is too early for a sustainability assessment, they stress that endogenous integration effects would be more than welcome to assure sustainability in the medium to long run. This is because, with the possible exception of El Salvador and the US, most traditional elements of integration between dollarized/euroized and anchor countries are still underdeveloped.

REFERENCES

Angeloni, I. (2004), 'Unilateral and multilateral currency unions: thoughts from an EMU perspective', in V. Alexander, G.M. von Furstenberg and J. Melitz (eds), *Monetary Unions and Hard Pegs: Effects on Trade, Financial Development and Stability*, Oxford and New York: Oxford University Press.

Avramovic, D. (1995), 'Reconstruction of the monetary system and economic recovery of Yugoslavia', *Forschungsberichte des Wiener Instituts für Internationale Wirtschaftsvergleiche*, No. 216, Vienna.

Backé, P. and C. Wójcik (2003), 'Unilateral euroization: a suitable road towards joining the euro area?', Paper presented at the conference on 'The Monetary Policy Role of Currency Boards: History and Practice', Central Bank of Bosnia and Herzegovina, Sarajevo, http://www.cbbh.gov.ba/april_konferencija/wojcik.pdf.

Backé, P., C. Thimann, O. Arratibel, O. Calvo-Gonzalez, A. Mehl and C. Nerlich (2004), 'The acceding countries' strategies towards ERM II and the adoption of the euro: an analytical review', *ECB Occasional Paper* No. 10, Frankfurt am Main.

Baliño, T., A. Bennett, E. Borensztein, A. Berg, Z. Chen, A. Ize, D.O. Robinson, A.E. Selassie and L. Zamalloa (1999), 'Monetary policy in dollarized economies', *IMF Occasional Paper* No. 171, Washington, DC.

Barro, R.J. and D. Gordon (1983), 'Rules, discretion and reputation in a model of monetary policy', *Journal of Monetary Economics*, **12**, 101–21.

Bayoumi, T. and P. Mauro (2001), 'The suitability of ASEAN for a regional currency arrangement', *The World Economy*, **24** (7), 933–54.

Berg, A. and E. Borensztein (2000), 'The pros and cons of full dollarization', *IMF Working Paper* WP/00/50, Washington, DC.

Berg, A., E. Borensztein and P. Mauro (2002), 'An evaluation of monetary regime options for Latin America', *IMF Working Paper* WP/02/211, Washington, DC.

Calvo, G.A. (1999), 'On dollarization', University of Maryland, mimeo.

Calvo, G.A. (2001), 'Capital markets and the exchange rate', *Journal of Money, Credit and Banking*, **33** (2), Part 2, 312–34.

Dallas, H. and G.S. Tavlas (2001), 'Lessons of the euro for dollarization: analytic and political economy perspectives', *Journal of Policy Modelling*, **23**, 333–45.

Duisenberg, W.F. (2001), 'The ECB and the accession process', Speech to the Frankfurt European Banking Congress at the Alte Oper in Frankfurt am Main, 23 November, http://www.ecb.int/key/01/sp011123.htm.

ECOFIN (2000), 'Report by the ECOFIN Council on the exchange-rate aspects of enlargement', submitted to the European Council of Nice.

Edwards, S. (2001), 'Dollarization and economic performance: an empirical investigation', *NBER Working Paper* No. 8274, Cambridge, MA, http://www.nber.org/papers/w8274.

Edwards, S. and I.I. Magendzo (2001), 'Dollarization, inflation and growth', *NBER Working Paper* No. 8671, Cambridge MA, http://www.nber.org/papers/w8671.

Edwards, S. and I.I. Magendzo (2002), 'A currency of one's own?', paper presented at a conference organized by the Sverige Riksbank and the IIES.

European Commission (2002), 'The euro area in the world economy – developments in the first three years, Communication from the Commission', *Euro Papers*, **46**, Brussels, http://europa.eu.int/comm/economy_finance.

Fischer, S. (2001), 'Exchange rate regimes: is the bipolar view correct?', Distinguished Lecture on Economics in Government, delivered at the meeting of the American Economic Association, New Orleans, 6 January.

Frankel, J.A. (1999), 'No single currency regime is right for all countries or at all times', *NBER Working Paper* No. 7338, Cambridge, MA.

Frankel, J.A. and A.K. Rose (1998), 'The endogeneity of the optimum currency area criteria', *The Economic Journal*, **108** (July), 1009–25.

Frankel, J.A. and A.K. Rose (2002), 'An estimate of the effects of common currencies on trade and income', *Quarterly Journal of Economics*, **67** (2), 437–66.

Glick, R. and A.K. Rose (2001), 'Does a currency union affect trade? The time series evidence', http://haas.berkely.edu/~arose.

Goldfajn, J. and G. Olivares (2000), 'Is adopting full dollarization the solution?', Pontífica Universidad Católica do Rio de Janeiro, Departamento de Economica, *Discussion Paper*, No. 416, Rio de Janeiro.

Goldfajn, I. and G. Olivares (2002), 'Full dollarization: the case of Panama', paper presented as part of the regional study on 'The choice of currency arrangements in Latin America and the Caribbean', LCSPR, Economic Management Group, http://wbln0018.worldbank.org/lac/lacinfoclient.nsf/0/188de6b8142bb478852569540076f3d1/$FILE/dollarpan.pdf.

International Monetary Fund (IMF) (2000), 'Offshore financial centers', *Background Paper*, Washington, DC.

Kose, M.A. and E.S. Prasad (2002), 'Thinking big', *Finance and Development*, **39** (4), 38–41.

Lahiri, A.K. (1991), 'Money and inflation in Yugoslavia', *IMF Working Paper* No. 91/50, Washington, DC.

Masson, P. (2000), 'One world, one currency: destination or delusion? Remarks', IMF Economic Forum, http://www.imf.org/external/np/tr/2000/tr 001108.htm.

Mazzaferro, F., C. Thimann and A. Winkler (2003), 'On the sustainability of euroization/dollarization regimes: how important are fiscal transfers, offshore finance and tourism receipts?', *Comparative Economic Studies*, **45** (3), pp. 421ff.

Mongelli, F.P. (2002), '"New" views on the optimum currency area theory: what is EMU telling us?', *ECB Working Paper* No. 138, Frankfurt am Main.

Mundell, R. (1961), 'A theory of optimum currency areas', *American Economic Review*, **51** (4), 509–17.

Nitsch, V. (2002), 'Honey, I shrunk the currency union effect on trade', *World Development*, **25** (4), 457–74.

Obstfeld, M. (2000), 'One world, one currency: destination or delusion? Remarks', IMF Economic Forum, http://www.imf.org/external/np/tr/2000/tr 001108.htm.

OECD (2000), 'Towards global tax co-operation', report to the 2000 Ministerial Council Meeting and Recommendations by the Committee on Fiscal Affairs, 'Progress in identifying and eliminating harmful tax practices', Paris.

OECD (2002), 'Geographical distribution of financial flows to aid recipients, 1960–2000', International Development Statistics, CD-ROM 2002 edition, Paris.

Padoa-Schioppa, T. (2001), 'Increased capital mobility: a challenge for the regulation of capital markets', in H. Siebert (ed.), *The World's New Financial Landscape: Challenges for Economic Policy*, Berlin; Heidelberg: Springer-Verlag.

Persson, T. (2001), 'Currency unions and trade: how large is the treatment effect?', *Economic Policy*, **16** (33), 435–48.

Quah, D. (2000), 'Discussion', *Economic Policy*, **15** (30), 35–8.

Rose, A.K. (2000), 'One money, one market: the effect of common currencies on trade', *Economic Policy*, **15** (30), 9–45.

Rose, A.K. (2002), 'Honey, the currency union effect on trade hasn't blown up', *World Development*, **25** (4), 475–79.

UK Home Office (1998), 'Review of financial regulation in the Crown Dependencies' (known as 'the Edwards Review'), www.official-documents.co.uk.

World Tourism Organization (2002), 'Compendium of tourism statistics', Madrid.

Winkler, A., F. Mazzaferro, C. Nerlich and C. Thimann (2004), 'Official dollarization/euroization: motives, features and policy implications', *ECB Occasional Paper* No. 11, Frankfurt am Main.

PART III

Monetary and Exchange Rate Policies: Circumstances and Choice in South-East Europe

8. Monetary policy in a euro-dominated environment: challenges for central banks in South-East Europe

Peter Mooslechner and Doris Ritzberger-Grünwald[1]

1. GENERAL INTRODUCTION

The political stabilization of South-East Europe (SEE), a region widely disadvantaged in the past, has paved the way for a new, much broader focus on Eastern Europe. In the 1990s the economic debate had concentrated on the countries coming within immediate reach as the Iron Curtain fell. These countries were not only the key agents of economic reform, but also the preferred destination of firms and banks trying to participate in the economic upswing. Going further south-east at the time would have meant leaving safe ground in a political and an economic sense. The attractiveness of, and the attention paid to, SEE has since increased significantly, however. The end of the wars that destabilized the region in the late 1990s led to an economic upswing, outperforming the upswing in the new EU member states – but also proceeding from a much lower base. With the prospect of EU accession in 2007 or 2008 at the latest for Bulgaria, Romania and – with some delay – for Croatia, growth rates are in fact likely to go up further. Unlike many other states located in the EU neighbourhood (Mediterranean countries or the CIS), all other SEE countries have in fact received clear signals from Brussels that in the long run they would also be welcomed as EU members. This makes the whole region interesting from a monetary policy point of view, as monetary policy becomes a matter of common interest upon EU accession (Fidrmuc and Korhonen, 2003). After all, these countries will also be obliged to adopt the euro.

2. SOME FUNDAMENTALS TO SHED LIGHT ON A WIDELY UNKNOWN REGION

An economic analysis of SEE is still an adventure, starting with the collection of data on the respective countries and territories, which is not an easy task. Yet as any economic judgment relies on data, this is where an assessment must start. In this context, this chapter is mainly aimed at providing a broad overview on monetary challenges and ongoing problems linked to the monetary integration process. After all, it would be much too early to try to give answers to more detailed, but frequently asked questions, such as how long the catching-up process is going to last or when the Maastricht criteria will probably be fulfilled.

2.1 Some Orders of Magnitude

Compared to the EU, SEE countries are economically small to miniscule players. South-East Europe – without Turkey – comprises a territory corresponding to about 15 per cent the size of the EU 25's area, its population comes to 12 per cent of that of the EU 25 and its GDP equals just 1.2 per cent of the GDP[2] of the EU 25 (see Table 8.1). The largest former socialist country of the region, Romania, commands an economic size of half a per cent of that of the EU 25. The smallest (non-sovereign) republic, Montenegro, accounts for 0.012 per cent of the EU 25's GDP. Average per capita GDP in SEE without Turkey comes to about a tenth of the average EU level.

In terms of size and population, a hypothetical new enlargement round comprising all South-East European countries would be only slightly smaller than the most recent enlargement in May 2004. But, not surprisingly, the SEE countries' total GDP and GDP per capita account for approximately only a third of the new member states' GDP and GDP per capita. These magnitudes reflect the high economic potential of the region, but also the large ground yet to be covered to reap it.

2.2 The Political Turmoil Hampered the Catching-up Process

SEE countries are typical transition countries on their way from a centrally planned economy or a system of workers' self management (market socialism) to a market economy. Yet the group of former Yugoslavian countries has to manage two more transition processes in parallel: the transition from being part of a larger state to a smaller independent democratic country, and the transition from war to peace. Even their neighbouring countries have been negatively affected in one way or the other, having lost potential

Table 8.1 South-East European countries' basic characteristics

Country	Territory (km²)	Population (2002 million)	GDP (2002, EUR billion)	GDP per capita (2002, EUR)
Albania	28 700	3.15	5.13	1630
Bosnia and Herzegovina	51 100	4.11	5.94	1445
Bulgaria	111 000	7.97	16.43	2060
Croatia	56 500	4.47	23.80	5325
Kosovo (Serbia)	10 900	1.96	1.40*	715*
FYR of Macedonia	25 700	2.02	4.02	2000
Montenegro	13 800	0.65	1.20*	1850*
Romania	238 400	21.75	48.52	2230
Serbia (without Kosovo)	77 500	7.52	14.00*	1860*
South-East Europe without Turkey	**613 600**	**53.60**	**120.44***	**2245***
EU 15	3 234 500	379.7	9234.3	24 320
New member countries	738 600	74.5	438.1	5880
EU 25**	3 973 100	454.2	9672.4	21 295

Notes:
* Estimate.
** EU 25 refers to all old and new EU member states after the enlargement round of 1 May 2004.

Source: Barisitz (2004).

export markets and being hampered by destroyed infrastructure, closed transport routes and migrating refugees.

Many of these countries are still in a post-war period, suffering from an unstable political situation, which has resulted in a very slow restructuring process, non-investment or even disinvestment behaviour, and a deep mistrust of national institutions and their often erratic policies. In their effort to stabilize the situation many successor countries to the former Socialist Federative Republic of Yugoslavia changed their currencies in the 1990s (see Table 8.3).[3] In view of still quite frequent devaluations, people preferred to hold their money in foreign currencies, but in cash rather than on foreign-denominated accounts, given widespread negative experience with foreign exchange deposit expropriations. Therefore the money did not find its way to potential investors, and the room for banking intermediation was limited.

2.3 Current Economic Environment

In 2004 the economies of the new EU members grew at a rather fast pace. On average their real GDP growth rate was 2 percentage points higher than output growth in the euro area. This makes the new EU member states one of the very few driving forces for the humbling euro area growth rate, and they are likely to maintain this margin in the years ahead, judging from IMF or European Commission forecasts for 2005 and 2006. SEE output growth has been even higher. As the region is very small in size, and as the starting level is more than low, this has only a minor positive effect on the euro area as a whole. But real GDP growth rates up to 8 per cent (Romania) or even 10 per cent (Montenegro) are impressive by themselves and a clear sign for the very fast catching-up process (see Table 8.2).

Inflation performance is extremely diverse across SEE countries. Whereas Romania and Serbia show relatively high inflation rates (between 11 and 12 per cent in 2004), other central banks have been quite successful in bringing inflation down to single-digit rates – or even below the rates of some euro area countries in some cases. This relatively fast disinflation process is somewhat surprising, especially when we look at the high growth rates of loans to the private sector and the rapid increase of domestic demand. At the same time, the labour market situation, which seems to be improving only very slowly, limits possible wage increases and reins in inflation expectations. Furthermore, re-monetization tendencies have evolved in a number of countries. In addition, the region is characterized by high unemployment rates, ranging roughly from 12 per cent in Bulgaria to 37 per cent in Macedonia. Only Romania has managed to bring the unemployment rate down significantly to 7 per cent in 2004. But with a huge shadow economy in place and vague labour market statistics, the economic message of these figures is questionable anyway.

Relatively low budget deficits reflect on the one hand the long history of state-owned firms taking care of the social welfare of their workers, and on the other hand the short history of central governments. Tax revenues are poor, but expenditures are low as well, resulting in a lack of social systems and infrastructure. Last but not least deficit ratios are arithmetically dampened by the sharp increase of GDP. Recently several countries (the Baltic states, Slovakia, Romania and Serbia) tried to limit tax evasion by introducing a flat tax. Still, this raises the questions of fairness and income distribution. Also the sustainability of the economic success is still not proven as these systems have only been in place for a short time. Given a downward spiral of competition, the economic success will moreover decrease with the number of countries introducing the flat tax.

Table 8.2 South-East European countries' economic fundamentals in 2003 and 2004

Country	GDP Annual real change in %		Unemployment rate based on LFS (annual average)		Consumer price index Period average, annual change in %		Current account balance % of annual GDP		General government balance % of GDP	
	2003	**2004**	**2003**	**2004**	**2003**	**2004**	**2003**	**2004**	**2003**	**2004**
Albania	6.0	6.0	15.0	14.4	2.3	2.9	−6.7	−4.3	−4.6	−5.2
Bosnia and Herzegovina	3.5	6.0	42.0	42.0	0.6	0.2	−30.2	−27.7	0.8	–
Bulgaria	4.3	5.7	13.6	12.0	2.3	6.2	−9.3	−7.4	0.6	1.4
Croatia	4.3	3.7	14.5	13.9	1.8	2.1	−7.0	−5.3	−6.3	−5.0
Kosovo (Serbia)[1]	3.1	3.2	30.0	30.0	1.0	1.5	−15.8	−17.1	2.5	−2.4
FYR of Macedonia[2]	3.4	2.0	36.7	37.0	2.4	0.9	−3.3	−7.1	−1.6	−1.9
Montenegro	2.4	10.0	20.0	20.0	6.7	2.4	−7.3	−5.7	–	–
Romania	5.2	8.3	6.8	7.1	15.3	11.9	−6.0	−7.5	−2.0	−1.4
Serbia (without Kosovo)	2.6	7.0	15.2	15.0	9.9	11.4	−10.2	−13.5	–	–

Notes:
1. 2004: projections; Unemployment rate: tentative estimate including informal employment.
2. Former Yugoslav Republic of Macedonia.

Source: WIIW; Bulgaria, Croatia, Romania: EC Economic Forecast Spring 2005; Kosovo: IMF.

Foreign direct investment (FDI) is relatively weak in SEE. The main reason for the hesitance of international investors is the often unclear legal and in some cases still unsettled political situation, whereas exchange rate instability is definitely no argument. But there are some promising exceptions. In 2004, the Austrian oil producing company OMV bought the Romanian Petrom (incidentally the single largest Austrian investment to date). Besides the banking sector, whose interests have also shifted to SEE, producers of construction material, hotels and real estate companies are also endeavouring to invest in the region.

Current account deficits are also diverse. Basically, countries fall into two different groups. In the EU- acceding countries and some others, deficits in 2004 were not higher than 7.5 per cent of GDP, whereas in Bosnia and Herzegovina, Kosovo and Serbia deficits reached up to 28 per cent of GDP. These data reflect small FDI inflows, a hindering bureaucracy, and a poor investment climate. Instead these economies are mainly driven by foreign financial aid and remittances from the diaspora. Therefore these figures do not necessarily call for a more restrictive monetary policy, but the timing of complete capital account liberalization is definitely important.

3. SOME IMPORTANT THEORETICAL CONSIDERATIONS SHAPING THE POLICY FRAMEWORK FOR SOUTH-EAST EUROPEAN COUNTRIES

To discuss the policy challenges facing central banks and, in general, the setting of macroeconomic policy in SEE, one has to rely on some fundamental guiding theoretical principles. Of course, the whole framework of macroeconomic policies is relevant for successful economic policies and smooth monetary integration in particular, but some elements have proven to be of specific importance by historical experience. Among these are some of the most basic challenges of the macroeconomic framework, like the question of fixed versus flexible exchange rates, the specific conditions relevant for small open economies (SMOPEC), the challenges created by the so-called policy trilemma and the overall determination of inflation dynamics. There seems to be a clear need to address all these fundamental questions at the very beginning of the expected convergence process, as they are relevant for the choice of macroeconomic policy strategies as well as for the choice of the institutional setup best suited to deliver an appropriate policy outcome.

From a historical perspective the breakdown of the Bretton Woods system in the early 1970s constitutes one of the key ingredients for this discussion (Eichengreen, 1998), as it was instrumental in favouring flexible exchange rates. In the end it took almost two decades until fixed exchange rate regimes regained importance as a reliable policy framework to stabilize the macroeconomic situation of a country.

The second important basic element to be considered in this respect is the SMOPEC characteristic or assumption that gained particular importance in the discussion following the Mundell-Fleming model of fundamental open-economy characteristics. Introduced at the time mainly to allow for differences concerning optimal currency area (OCA) preconditions between large and small countries, SMOPEC characteristics turned out to be instrumental in making open-economy analysis and results more realistic, given the differences in country size across the EU. Essential elements of this perspective are that small countries are usually price-takers on international markets, that they are characterized by a high share of constant return industries, a high concentration of product/industry specialization, a high geographic concentration of production as well as an overall high share of foreign trade in GDP. As a result small countries typically face a higher likelihood of asymmetric shocks, a fact that creates a challenge for all types of fixed exchange rate arrangements.

Based on these fundamental elements for smaller countries, a number of considerable challenges arise that have to be taken into account when going for real and nominal convergence and, eventually, joining Monetary Union.

3.1 The Policy Trilemma as a Guiding Principle

Obstfeld et al. (2004) forcefully restated the argument that policy makers in open economies face a macroeconomic trilemma of pursuing three typically desirable, yet contradictory objectives. The trilemma consists of stabilizing the exchange rate, enjoying free international capital mobility and employing monetary policy for domestic goals at the same time. With liberalized international capital flows generally considered a basic precondition for participating in international markets, to fix or not to fix the exchange rate, and at which level of development to decide on the issue, become fundamental questions for a small country's policy orientation. Moreover, Obstfeld et al. (2004) conclude that based on empirical evidence the trilemma still makes sense as a guiding policy framework and that the constraints implied by it are largely borne out by history.

Relating this to the situation of countries at an earlier stage of economic development or real convergence, it becomes immediately clear that one of their permanent and ultimate policy-making objectives is to balance the needs between domestic development goals and international monetary integration.

3.2 Balassa–Samuelson and the Scandinavian Model of Inflation

The goal and path of international monetary integration and of stabilizing the exchange rate is closely connected to the relative inflation dynamics of an economy, in particular if a country is expected to successfully tackle catching-up. While this fundamental issue is mainly discussed under the headline of the Balassa–Samuelson effect (Egert, 2002; Halpern and Wyplosz, 2002), its theoretical content and its policy consequences are covered best by the so-called Scandinavian model of inflation.

The once very popular Scandinavian model of inflation (Mooslechner, 2001) summarizes the basic issues to be addressed in a simple but structured way:

$$p_e = p_w$$
$$w_e = y_e + p_e$$
$$w_e = w_s$$
$$p_s = w_s - y_s$$
$$p = a_e p_e + a_s p_s \qquad a_e + a_s = 1$$
$$p = p_w + a_s (y_e - y_s)$$

Variables: p = inflation rate; y = productivity growth; w = wage growth; a = share of sector.
Subscripts: e = exposed sector; s = sheltered sector; w = world.

Starting from the SMOPEC characteristic that small countries are most likely price-takers in a world of fixed exchange rates, international inflation dominates domestic inflation via import prices on the one hand and the acceptance of (fixed) export prices on the other hand. At the same time, exposed and sheltered sectors of the (domestic) economy differ significantly in productivity growth but less in wage developments. Therefore, the overall domestic inflation rate will be determined by the international inflation rate plus the difference in productivity growth between the exposed and the sheltered sector of the economy (as well as the latter's share). Again, it becomes obvious that productivity growth in relation to wages, international competitiveness related to prices and the level of the exchange rate are the key to balancing domestic and international goals of a catching-up country.

3.3 Financial Market Development and Liberalization

Important framework conditions to be addressed include differences in starting points concerning the degree of financial market development and liberalization. Whereas the European economic integration process that took place in the 1970s and 1980s benefited from some degree of less than perfect financial market liberalization and therefore allowed for some room concerning the priority of domestic policy objectives, the current regime asks for almost perfect capital mobility and immediate financial market liberalization. For practical economic policy making, this results in a much stronger need to commit macroeconomic policies to integration objectives, while the potential risks coming from external shocks must be expected to be of a significantly higher likelihood. At the same time, it will take a while until financial deepening will have reached a level close to the EU average, dependent also on the dynamics of real convergence achieved.

In this respect, Braumann (2002) concludes from a detailed study of the Austrian case compared to international experience that (i) gradualism works well, (ii) the cyclical potential of financial market reforms should be handled with care and (iii) certain designs of financial systems seem to be more stable than others. As far as there is leeway to exploit these theoretical options, countries should make use of them in a careful way to minimize the risks and to maximize the benefits of the transformation process.

3.4 The Changing View and Role of Exchange Rate Developments

Finally, it has to be stressed that a considerable change in how the role of exchange rate developments is qualified has taken place, which broadly influences the hierarchy and sequence of economic policy strategies to be followed. After the breakdown of the Bretton Woods system and under the impression of the difficulties the system faced during its final decade, exchange rate movements and exchange rate flexibility were mainly seen as important economic policy tools to address important macroeconomic imbalances successfully. This perspective is also a dominant ingredient of the famous Mundell–Fleming (OCA) approach of open economy macroeconomics, which attributes a rather strong position to the exchange rate as a policy instrument (Frankel and Rose, 1998).

Compared to this – optimistic – view of the exchange rate as a macroeconomic policy tool, the experience of the 1980s and 1990s led to a completely different assessment of exchange rate developments. In the wake of the European exchange rate crises of the early 1990s, exchange rate developments were seen more and more as becoming a permanent source of international financial instability. To cope with this new understanding of exchange rates many initiatives were launched to create a new European framework of exchange rate stability. In the end this change in perspective led to the establishment of the euro area as an institutional framework making exchange rate volatility obsolete as a potential source of macroeconomic instability.

Of course, in this new world our overall understanding of the role of exchange rates in economic policy was not the only thing to change; the hierarchy of economic objectives and policies has also changed substantially. In particular, for countries intending to join the EU and – eventually – Monetary Union, stabilizing the exchange rate, via participation in ERM II first, has become an overriding goal in the integration and convergence process. This obviously gives the exchange rate a much greater weight in policy making even if countries are still at the beginning of the integration process.

4. IMPORTANT FRAMEWORK CONDITIONS

Theory but also practical experience paved the way for a renascence of fixed exchange rates in the 1990s. The increasing influence and the ongoing success of the hard currency block resulted in the decision to create the euro area, as a result of which the members' exchange rates were irrevocably fixed. EU-acceding countries also tied their hands. Initially they used several hard currencies as an anchor for their exchange rate. Since the introduction of the euro they have either pegged their currency to the euro directly, run a currency board, or increased the euro's share in the baskets. Only Poland has kept its pure float. In June 2004, shortly after EU enlargement, three countries (Estland, Lithuania and Slovenia) joined ERM II, and in April 2005 three others (Latvia, Cyprus and Malta) followed, committing themselves to keeping their exchange rates within a +/−15 per cent band or even closer to the central rate. In the meantime most of these countries have started to prepare the cash changeover (Gruber and Ritzberger-Grünwald, 2005). If everything goes smoothly the next Central and Eastern European countries will join the euro area in 2007. This will further push up the number of countries which have given up the exchange rate as a policy instrument. For obvious reasons this quick entry is a preferred solution for smaller countries, which increases the probability that SEE countries will adopt this strategy.

4.1 Official and Unofficial Euroization – A Unique Solution for a Special Environment?

The degree of euroization in Eastern European countries, measured by the share of foreign currency holdings in broad money, shows a wide range. It amounts to about 75 per cent in Croatia, 70 per cent in Latvia, 55 per cent in Bulgaria, 45 per cent in Slovenia, 38 per cent in Romania, 35 per cent in the Slovak Republic, 32 per cent in the Czech Republic, 30 per cent in Estonia,

25 per cent in Lithuania, 24 per cent in Hungary, 20 per cent in Poland and 18 per cent in Macedonia (Feige, 2002; see also Stix, 2004). This is broadly in line with the results of Reinhart and Rogoff (2004), indicating that in SEE Croatia, Romania and Bosnia and Herzegovina are the countries where unofficial euroization is the highest. In addition, there are some cases of official unilateral euroization in territories which started from scratch, namely Kosovo and Montenegro (see section 4.2).

Interestingly the list given by Feige (2002) is a mixture of new EU member states and SEE countries, reflecting that euroization is not necessarily an indicator for an early stage of transition. Instead it also reflects currency turmoils and periods of hyperinflation in the past, which eroded the trust of the population in the national currency (Levy Yeyati and Sturzenegger, 2003). Still, compared to the new EU member countries, SEE states have suffered more from political turmoil, corrupt governments, followed by several bank runs and the loss of personal savings deposits.

Finally, SEE countries used to complement their national currencies with a foreign one for decades. During the communist era the Deutsche mark and the Austrian schilling were used widely in the region, driven by tourism, remittances from guest workers and transfers from foreign pension systems. During the cash changeover in 2001/2002 holdings of the Deutsche mark and Austrian schilling circulating in these countries were converted into the euro. Many banks were able to convince their customers to open accounts in euros, as in the meantime the increased foreign ownership of many banks had led to more trust in the banking sector. In parallel, times had become politically more stable, and there was no longer any need for storing cash 'under the mattress'. As a result, at the end of 2003 euro-denominated deposits reached 83 per cent of total deposits in the banking system in Serbia, 76 per cent in Croatia, 41 per cent in Bosnia and Herzegovina, 19 per cent in Bulgaria, 13 per cent in Albania and 12 per cent in Romania (ECB, 2005). In contrast, the high rates in Kosovo (100 per cent) and Montenegro (88 per cent) reflect official euroization. Some of the new EU member countries (especially Slovenia, Latvia and Estonia as well as Slovakia) also show relatively high shares in this respect, ranging from 35 to 11 per cent. Interestingly, no clear trends can be detected in any of these groups of countries over the time horizon. On the lending side one can find a similar phenomenon, although most loans are indexed to foreign currency. For instance in Croatia in 2004 the structure of bank lending was as follows: 27 per cent in domestic currency, 12 per cent in foreign currency, and an overwhelming 61 per cent indexed to foreign currency.

Such a euro-dominated environment means a special challenge not only for commercial banks in hedging the currency mismatch of deposits and loans. It also creates an additional hurdle for central banks, apart from the challenges of being on the catching-up route and facing political instability. Overall, a high unofficial euroization restricts the independence and room for manoeuvre of monetary policy making. The exchange rate, for instance, cannot be geared properly, nor will it have a significant influence on the economy. The transmission mechanism will not work as usual either.

4.2 Monetary and Exchange Rate Regimes in Place

In an unstable environment and a situation in which it is difficult to establish internationally acknowledged institutions and to enforce sound decision-making, perhaps the biggest challenge for economic policy – and for monetary policy alike – is how to gain and preserve credibility. The preferred solution, anchoring the national currency somehow to a strong and stable neighbouring currency, is obvious. For SEE the euro is the obvious choice, given that trade figures indicate a close relationship between SEE and the euro area. Another advantage is that a stable exchange rate may enhance the already existing strong FDI between the two parties involved. Finally, this decision is based on the good experiences other small open economies have had with such a strategy. One can refer to the hard currency policy of Austria in the 1970s and 1980s in this respect (Handler, 1989); although the waters were much calmer then.

While it seems to be widely accepted that some orientation to the euro is helpful, a wide variety of different exchange rate regimes is in place in SEE countries (see Table 8.3). Two non-sovereign territories have adopted the euro as legal tender. A second group runs currency boards, another country has pegged its currency to the euro. A fourth group has established tightly managed, managed or loosely managed floats with the euro as a reference currency. In descending order of closeness to the euro, the following ranking applies:

- Montenegro and Kosovo, two non-sovereign territories, have adopted the euro as their legal tender. In general, euroization implies a trade-off between benefits associated with achieving monetary stability and costs related to the loss of independent monetary policy (Rose, 1999). Given the size of their territories, and given the urgent need for action because of the massive capital flight and the vanishing of the Yugoslav dinar as a means of transaction, installing their own currency may in fact not have been a choice for the monetary authorities of Kosovo (1.9 million people) and Montenegro (680 000 people) (Moalla-Fetini et al., 2004).
- Currency board arrangements have been in place in Bulgaria since 1997, and in Bosnia and Herzegovina since 1998. This transparent

solution provides a firm nominal anchor in the form of a fixed exchange rate vis-à-vis the euro. The central banks' monetary liabilities are fully backed by highly liquid foreign exchange reserves. As it introduces a simple and clear rule for money creation, a currency board is known as a stricter commitment than a conventional fixed exchange rate regime, thus enhancing credibility. Several new EU members have in fact been frontrunners in this respect and report quite good experiences with running euro-based currency boards.

- Macedonia has pegged its currency to the euro, Croatia runs a tightly managed float. Both use the euro as a nominal exchange rate anchor.
- Serbia and Romania conduct managed floats with the euro as the reference currency. In early 2003 Serbia, coming from a tightly managed float, somewhat loosened its stance and can now be characterized as pursuing a real exchange rate anchor. Romania couples a manged float with money growth targeting. Romania's exchange rate strategy, however, mirrors the increasing importance of the euro for the country. Since early 2002 Romania has run a managed float tied to a basket initially consisting of 40 per cent USD and 60 per cent EUR (75 per cent from 2004). Since early 2005, the euro has in fact been the sole reference currency. Moreover, Romania plans to switch to an inflation target of 7 per cent on 1 July 2005.
- Only one country runs a strategy that is more or less disentangled from the euro: Albania, a country that had to give up an exchange rate peg once before, as a result of which it suffered a sharp devaluation, is still running a loosely managed float. This is somewhat surprising as Albania is one of the smallest economies of the region and should be much more prone to a closer relationship to the euro. Albania, much like Romania, is aiming for inflation targeting in the near future.

Any such classification is of course somewhat arbitrary. We follow Barisitz (2004), which is slightly different from the IMF's concept, and the central banks involved tend to see things differently again. For instance Croatia, identified as having a tightly managed float with the euro as an exchange rate anchor by Barisitz (2004), might just as well claim to have a quasi-currency board in place. Without any doubt de facto euroization in Croatia is huge, and the room for manoeuvre for exchange rate policy is very limited. Another key criterion is convertibility, which determines the status of a currency in relation to other currencies. The currencies of Bosnia and Herzegovina, Bulgaria, Croatia, Kosovo and Montenegro are fully or almost fully convertible. Those of Macedonia, Romania and Serbia are convertible for current account transactions. The Albanian currency does not yet feature unrestricted current account convertibility. Obviously parts

Table 8.3 South-East European countries' monetary characteristics

Country	Currency (since); previous currency	Exchange rate regime (since); previous regime	Convertibility	Monetary policy framework (since); previous framework
Albania	Albanian lek (ALL)	Loosely managed float (early 1990s), major reference currencies: EUR (up to 1/1/1999: DEM), USD	Not yet unrestricted current account convertibility (IMF Art. XIV status)	Informal inflation targeting through money growth targeting (1998)
Bosnia and Herzegovina	Konvertibilna marka (BAM, June 1998); YUD and HRK (used regionally), DEM (country-wide) (until Dec. 1999); YUD (until early 1990s)	Currency board, peg to EUR (up to 1/1/1999: DEM) (formally introduced: August 1997, de facto since mid-1998); multiple currencies	Full (or almost full) convertibility	Nominal exchange rate anchor EUR (DEM) (August 1997)
Bulgaria	Bulgarian lev (BGN)	Currency board, peg to EUR (up to 1/1/1999: DEM) (since July 1997); managed float	Full (or almost full) convertibility (IMF Art. VIII acceptance Sept. 1998)	Nominal exchange rate anchor EUR (DEM) (July 1997); money growth targeting
Croatia	Croatian kuna (HRK) (May 1994); Croatian dinar (transitional); YUD	Tightly managed float, reference currency: EUR (up to 1/1/1999: DEM) (since Oct. 1993)	Almost full convertibility (IMF Art. VIII acceptance May 1995)	Nominal exchange rate anchor EUR (DEM) (Oct. 1993)
Kosovo/ Kosova (Serbia)	All foreign currencies legalized for transactions, EUR (DEM) predominant,		Full convertibility	EUR legal tender (September 1999)

	YUD used regionally (Sept. 1999); YUD			
FYR of Macedonia	Macedonian denar (MKD, April 1992); YUD	De facto peg to EUR (exchange rate target, up to 1/1/1999: DEM) (since early 1990s)	Current account convertibility (IMF Art. VIII acceptance: June 1998)	Nominal exchange rate anchor EUR (early 1990s)
Montenegro	Unilaterally euroized/ EUR (November 2000); November 1999–2000 EUR (DEM) parallel currency to YUD; before that YUD		Full convertibility	EUR legal tender (November 1999/2000)
Romania	Romanian leu (ROL)	Managed float (1991), reference currency: EUR (since early 2005); previously: reference basket: EUR (75%), USD (25%) (early 2004), EUR (60%), USD (40%) (early 2002); before that: reference currency: USD	Current account convertibility (IMF Art. VIII acceptance: March 1998)	Money growth targeting (early 1990s)
Serbia (without Kosovo/ Kosova)	(Yugoslav) dinar (YUD)	Managed float (January 2003), previously tightly managed float, reference currency: EUR (Dec. 2000); peg to EUR (DEM)	Current account convertibility (IMF Art. VIII acceptance: May 2002)	Real exchange rate anchor (January 2003), previously nominal anchor EUR (DEM) (1994)

Source: Barisitz (2004).

of the region are still in a process of early transition, as capital restrictions are necessary to prevent private capital flight.

4.3 National Financial Markets in Foreign Hands

Financial markets in SEE are characterized by high foreign ownership. In most of the countries foreign banks, mainly of Austrian or Italian origin, bought the overwhelming share of assets, then restructured, down-sized and modernized the local banks, and are running quite profitable entities by now. This process was a smooth one in some countries, while others (such as Albania, Bulgaria) underwent a major banking crisis. These banking crises were triggered by heavily distorted incentives, soft budget constraints, fraudulent behaviour, unsuccessful privatization efforts of state-owned banks, illegal gambling ('pyramids'), combined with macroeconomic and political instability and no or too little banking supervision. Bank runs and massive deposit withdrawals have been the result.

Although the SEE countries are still underbanked, financial intermediation is gaining momentum, reflecting the ongoing catching-up process. Banks are on their way to enlarging the range of products available. In parallel, credit growth to the private sector is increasing, leaving some countries with a sometimes worrying credit boom. This mirrors developments in the new EU member states. But as starting levels are lower, growth rates become double-digit numbers. For instance, in Bulgaria bank claims on enterprises and households accelerated by 31 per cent in 2002, 44 per cent in 2003 and around 47 per cent in the first half of 2004 (year on year) in real terms. Positively speaking, this is a clear sign that households trust banks again, and lending and deposits are on their way back to normal. The related (exchange rate) risks stem from the fact that most loans are in euros or indexed to the euro. On the macroeconomic side, up-side risks to inflation may exist.

5. WHAT ARE THE CHALLENGES?

Challenges are manifold, mainly because the countries of the region are at very different stages of political stabilization and integration. Monetary policy and exchange rate policy are instruments to enhance national price stability and international competitiveness, and are therefore important instruments in every catching-up process. But as some countries will become EU members soon, the fulfilment of the Maastricht Treaty, which was not necessarily designed for countries in transition in every respect, is also at the top of the agenda.

5.1 Monetary Policy Challenges in a Euro-dominated Environment

Monetary policy challenges reflect the early stage of the process of transition and/or catching up. Challenges include legal aspects, concerning the monetary institutions involved, but also economic challenges, resulting from the obvious contradiction between the urgent need for stability for this region, and the necessity of flexible policy instruments capable of absorbing shocks. Judging from the degree of central bank independence already achieved, using the Maastricht Treaty as a yardstick, a considerable number of weaknesses remain (Dvorsky, 2004). Although central bank laws already comply with Treaty requirements in some areas, a further strengthening of both legal and actual central bank independence will be necessary.

Another challenge for monetary policy results from low monetization which characterizes the region.[4] Low monetization is a clear sign of major inefficiencies still at work in the banking system, and the lack of experience of private agents to use money as a coordination device. This reduces the effectiveness of monetary policy by definition. In a nutshell, interest rates have less of an impact on economic activity. Quite often this problem is aggravated by FDI. Foreign owners tend not to use the local banking system. In general they prefer to involve the banks in their home country or they rely on their own conglomerate for financing.

A completely different challenge results from the close link to the euro. The peg to the euro – either in the form of a currency board or directly – is not only based on economic reasoning. It also reflects the political will to enter the EU and the euro area as quickly as possible. Sometimes the situation is topped by official or unofficial euroization. Empirical evidence suggests that euroization is no substitute for economic integration (Winkler et al., 2004). In addition, rules based on the 'principle of equal treatment' have to be followed. In November 2000 the ECOFIN adopted the position that countries aiming at EU accession cannot use unilateral euroization as a way of circumventing the stages foreseen by the Treaty establishing the European Community for the adoption of the euro.[5] It will be a major challenge to implement a currency or a national exchange rate policy on which the fulfilment of the Maastricht criteria can be checked properly.

5.2 Finding the 'Right' Exchange Rate – An Increasingly Difficult Task

Without doubt, changing framework conditions as well as the changing role of exchange rates in modern international financial markets create a number of new challenges for policy strategies in countries intending to strengthen monetary integration with the EU. To illustrate this, Bulir and

Smidkova (2005) assess these exchange rate challenges in comparison to the 'forerunners' joining EU, ERM II and Monetary Union up to now. The conclusion is rather straightforward. Based on their empirical estimates early adoption of the euro by latecomer countries is unlikely to be as smooth as that by the forerunner countries. The reasons for this are mainly that the real exchange rates of these countries are less in line with their fundamental-based values and that it would be rather costly to meet the convergence tests in the medium term.

Even if these estimates have to be interpreted with care and have to be taken as one particular estimate at a particular point in time, the basic problem faced becomes very clear: Finding the 'right' time and the 'right' exchange rate to cope with all the fundamental macroeconomic needs at the same time is likely to be much more difficult in the future than in the past (Backé and Wójcik, 2003).

6. CONCLUSIONS

In the case of South-East Europe, a widely unknown region is moving to the centre of economic interests. While parallels to the transition process of the now new EU member countries do exist, political changes were more violent in SEE, destabilizing the region for several years. Once the international community succeeded in stabilizing the region, the economic upswing was able to start. One of the major differences to the situation of the new EU member states is that the euro has now been established and as a result is more attractive to be used as a stable anchor for the region. This is in line with the fact that the SEE states have widely relinquished the exchange rate as a fine tuning policy instrument to influence their competitive situation.

The monetary policy solutions chosen are manifold, depending on the independence and the political will of the governments and central banks involved. From euroization to a loosely managed float one can find every sort of exchange rate regime, most of them are meant to import stability from the euro area. At the same time they reduce the flexibility which would be needed to improve the smooth running of a catching-up process. As a result, the necessary burden of economic adjustment has to happen on the real side.

Some SEE countries will become EU members relatively soon, others will have to wait a little longer. But all of them do see their future in the EU, which means that they will all have to introduce the euro in due time. The countries have to prove that they are able to cope with difficult situations: mainly that they are able to keep their currency stable vis-à-vis the euro. Some of the monetary and exchange rate regimes in place are compatible with the rules, others are not. Unilateral euroization is against the rules, but also countries with high unofficial euroization may face difficulties to gear the exchange rate accordingly. In any case new solutions have to be found.

NOTES

1. The authors wish to thank Stephan Barisitz for useful comments.
2. The GDP ratio is calculated on the basis of exchange rates. If purchasing power parities were used, the ratio might be about three times as large. See also Gligorov (2004, p. 52).
3. For more information on the – quite eventful – historical background of economic developments in the countries of the Western Balkans see Barisitz (1999).
4. For instance in Romania M2 accounted for only 24 per cent of GDP over the last decade, a ratio which is extremely low compared to developed economies, but also compared to other transition countries. In early 2003 the monetary base was covered almost four times by foreign exchange reserves (in 'normal' currency boards this ratio is one to one), rather pointing to the underdevelopment of the banking sector and low credit activity.
5. Report by the (ECOFIN) Council to the European Council in Nice on the exchange rate aspects of enlargement, Brussels, 8 November 2000, Council of the EU press release no. 13055/00. Also reiterated in 'Policy position of the Governing Council of the European Central Bank on exchange rate issues relating to the acceding countries', Frankfurt, 18 December 2003, www.ecb.int.

BIBLIOGRAPHY

Backé, P. and C. Wójcik (2003), 'The monetary integration of Central and Eastern European EU accession countries: the pros and cons of speedy versus more gradual strategies', in L. Vinhas de Souza and B. van Aarle (eds), *The Euro area and the New EU Member States*, Basingstoke: Palgrave Macmillan.

Barisitz, S. (1999), 'The South-East European nonassociated countries – economic developments, the impact of the Kosovo conflict and relations with the EU', in OeNB (ed.), *Focus on Transition*, **1**, 60–94.

Barisitz, S. (2004), 'Exchange rate arrangements and monetary policy in Southeastern Europe and Turkey: some stylized facts', in OeNB (ed.), *Focus on European Economic Integration*, **2**, 95–118.

Braumann, B. (2002), 'Financial liberalization in Austria: why so smooth?', in OeNB (ed.), *Financial Stability Report*, **4**.

Bulir, A. and K. Smidkova (2005), 'Exchange rates in the New EU accession countries: what have we learned from the forerunners?', IMF Working Paper 05/27, February.

Dvorsky, S. (2004), 'Central Bank independence in Southeastern Europe with a view to future EU accession', in OeNB (ed.), *Focus on European Economic Integration*, **2**.

ECB (2005), *Review of the International Role of the Euro*, January.

ECOFIN (2003), *Acceding Countries and ERM-II, EFC/ECFIN/109/03*, Athens, 5 April.

Egert, B. (2002), 'Investigating the Balassa-Samuelson hypothesis in the transition. Do we understand what we see?', *Economics of Transition*, **10**, 273–309.

Eichengreen, B. (1998), *Globalizing Capital: A History of the International Monetary System*, Princeton, NJ: Princeton University Press.

Feige, E. (2002), 'Empirical evidence on currency substitution, dollarization and euroization in transition countries', 8th Dubrovnik Economic Conference: Monetary Policy and Currency Substitution in the Emerging Markets.

Fidrmuc, J. and I. Korhonen (2003), 'The Euro goes East: implications of the 2000–2002 economic slowdown for synchronization of business cycles between the euro area and CEECs', *Comparative Economic Studies*, **46** (1), 45–62.

Frankel, J. and A. Rose (1998), 'The endogeneity of the Optimum Currency Area Criteria', *Economic Journal*, **108** (449), 1009–25.

Gligorov, V. (2004), 'South-East Europe (SEE) overview: diverse developments', in V. Gligorov, J. Poeschl, S. Richter et al. (2004), *As East You Go, the More They Grow: Transition Economies in a New Setting*, WIIW Research Report 308, July, 52–63.

Gruber, T. and D. Ritzberger-Grünwald (2005), 'The Euro changeover in the new member states – a preview', in OeNB (ed.), *Focus on European Economic Integration*, **1**, 52–75.

Halpern, L. and C. Wyplosz (2002), 'Economic transformation and real exchange rates in the 2000s: the Balassa-Samuelson connection', *UNO Economic Surveys of Europe*, **1**.

Handler, H. (1989), *Grundlagen der österreichischen Hartwährungspolitik*, Vienna: Manz.

Levy Yeyati, E. and F. Sturzenegger (2003), *Dollarization: Debates and Policy Alternatives*, Cambridge, MA and London, UK: MIT Press.

Moalla-Fetini, R., H. Hatanpää, S. Hussein and N. Koliadina (2004), 'Kosovo – gearing policies toward growth and development', IMF, 18 November.

Mooslechner, P. (2001), 'Vom skandinavischen Modell zur monetären Einheitserklärung der Inflation und zurück: ein unzeitgemäßes Plädoyer für die Rolle struktureller Erklärungsansätze zum Inflationsphänomen', in G. Chaloupek, A. Guger, E. Nowotny and G. Schwödiauer (eds), *Ökonomie in Theorie und Praxis* (Festschrift für Herrn Frisch), Berlin – Heidelberg: Springer-Verlag.

Obstfeld, M., Jay C. Shambaugh and Alan M. Taylor (2004), 'The trilemma in history: trade-offs among exchange rates', *Monetary Policies and Capital Mobility*, CEPR Discussion Paper 4352, April.

Reinhart, C.M. and K.S. Rogoff (2004), 'The modern history of exchange rate arrangements: a reinterpretation', *Quarterly Journal of Economics*, **CXIX** (1), 1–48.

Rose, A.K. (1999), 'One money, one market: the effect of common currencies on trade', CEPR Discussion Paper 2329, Center for Economic Policy Research, London.

Stix, H. (2004), 'Foreign currency demand since 2002 – evidence from five Central and Eastern European Countries', *CESifo Forum*, **5** (4), 9–24, Winter.

Winkler, A., F. Mazzaferro, C. Nerlich and C. Thimann (2004), 'Official dollarization/euroization: motives, features and policy implications of current cases', European Central Bank, Occasional Paper Series 11.

9. Disinflation and monetary policy arrangements in Romania

Daniel Daianu and Ella Kallai

1. INTRODUCTION[1]

Disinflation has been pursued successfully in Romania in recent years. Inflation came down from over 40 per cent in 2001 to 14 per cent in 2003 and 9.3 per cent in 2004. By 2007 it should come down to around 3 per cent.

The benefits of a low-inflation environment are unquestionable, as price stability is the ultimate objective of monetary policy. In addition, low inflation is a pre-condition for EU accession. There only remains the other critical question, namely, what is the proper strategy to achieve the ultimate objective? Different central banks have adopted different strategies, placing a different emphasis on the various pieces of information, elements of their decision-making process or different aspects of their communication policies. Inflation targeting (IT) is one of those strategies.

The National Bank of Romania (NBR) plans to introduce IT in 2005. This regime brings a series of benefits for a central bank, including a clear policy focus on inflation. At the same time the Romanian central bank needs to unburden its monetary policy to achieve further disinflation. But three main contradictory pressures are likely to arise: first, the requirements imposed by the need to achieve nominal and real convergence with a view to joining the EU in 2007 and European Monetary Union (EMU) at a later stage push the central bank toward a policy mix that is able to ensure growth and further disinflation simultaneously. Second, under inflation targeting the 'divine coincidence' of inflation stabilization and real stabilization objectives can be achieved only in specific economic circumstances. Third, the operational requirements of a 'hard' inflation targeting regime are unlikely to exist under the current monetary transmission conditions.

The central question of this chapter is under what circumstances can inflation targeting be implemented in Romania? Section 2 summarizes the recent history of inflation in Romania. Section 3 presents the context of disinflation and dilemmas of monetary policy. Section 4 reviews distinguishing features of the IT monetary policy framework and experience with IT in various countries. Section 5 examines challenges posed by IT implementation in Romania. Section 6 discusses policy choices.

2. WHERE DOES ROMANIA'S MONETARY ECONOMY COME FROM?

From the beginning of transition monetary policy had to carry the burden of too slow a restructuring of the economy. Price stability, which should have been the prime aim of monetary policy, was frequently sacrificed, causing Romania to build up an image as a high-inflation country (Figure 9.1). The dramatically high inflation rates at the beginning of the 1990s were not the result of central bankers' disinterest in pursuing price stability; in the absence of a functioning tax system, seigniorage was simply the only way to finance government expenditures aside from borrowing. The multiple and varying objectives to be met by monetary policy in the 1990s were rarely consistent with the achievement of inflation reduction. Therefore the policy choices may appear unsystematic, myopic and even inconsistent with basic principles of what macroeconomic models suggest is good policy practice. Arguably, structural features of the economy (including *structural strain*, which is illustrated by arrears[2]) undermined the conduct of monetary policy.

Disinflation (Figure 9.2) coincides with the institutional context created by a more independent NBR.[3] In 1998 inflation was 40.6 per cent. At the time, monetary aggregates were used as a monetary policy anchor – neither the exchange rate nor interest rates were an option, given the small amount of foreign reserves and the unpredictable relationship of interest rates with inflation. The NBR's monetary policy framework was based on minimum reserves and frequent 'deposit-taking' operations for liquidity control. When foreign debt service payments peaked and the danger of insolvency loomed large in 1999, adjusting the current account became the first aim of monetary policy; consequently, inflation climbed to 54.8 per cent. In 2000 inflation came down to 40.7 per cent. By then the exchange rate had replaced monetary aggregates as the anchor of monetary policy, but the need to finance the budget deficit and to keep the current account deficit within reasonable limits prevailed over disinflation considerations.

In 2001, while exceeding the target of 25 per cent, inflation declined to 30.4 per cent. Helped by declining interest rates on T-bills, the NBR also succeeded in imposing its interest rate policy for the first time. The NBR avoided a large real appreciation of the domestic currency, but again failed to sterilize the mounting liquidity following the purchases of foreign exchange. In 2002 inflation went down to 17.8 per cent, below the target of

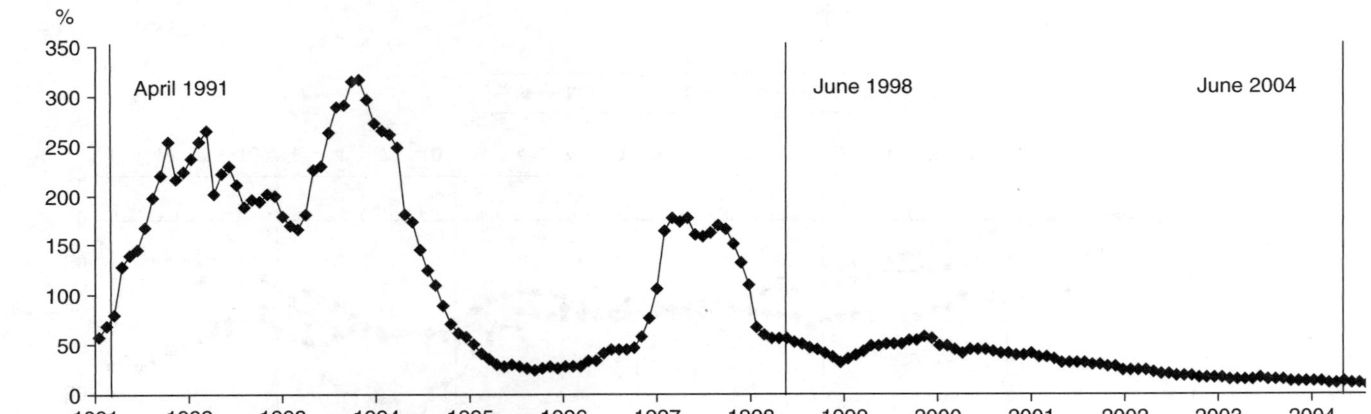

Source: INSSE.

Figure 9.1 *CPI (monthly change in per cent, year-on-year) and the institutional changes*

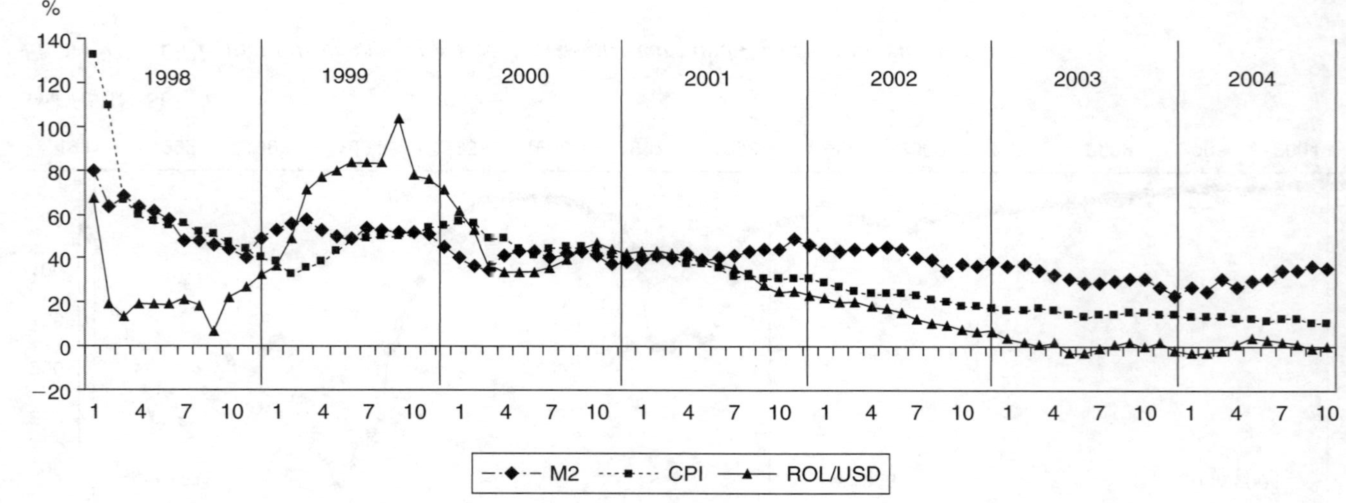

Source: INSSE.

Figure 9.2 M2, CPI and ROL/USD exchange rate (monthly change in per cent, year-on-year)

22 per cent. While pushing disinflation, the NBR also kept an eye on economic growth and external equilibrium. The control of monetary aggregates (via base money) continued to shape monetary policy. Liquidity was controlled through reverse repos and deposit-taking.

In 2003 the inflation target – 14 per cent – was attained. The traditional conflict between disinflation and mitigation of the external disequilibrium tendency eased, while the euro was adopted as a reference exchange rate. Disinflation progressed further in 2004 and inflation has fallen to 9.3 per cent. The NBR relied on the stability of the exchange rate as an anchor and the control of liquidity through heavy sterilization operations.[4] Keeping the budget deficit low has helped disinflation.

3. THE CONTEXT OF DISINFLATION

In mid-1999 Romania went through a short but serious financial crisis, and avoided default on the external debt by drastically adjusting the balance of payments, among other things, by halving the budget deficit. Prior to the crisis, an overvalued Romanian leu (ROL) gradually eroded export competitiveness and depleted the NBR's foreign exchange reserves. Since 2000 the NBR has directly pursued the policy goals of

1. rebuilding and consolidating the stock of foreign exchange reserves and of preventing an excessive ROL appreciation (consistent goals);
2. achieving gradual disinflation.

Since goals (1) and (2) are not mutually consistent, the NBR has had to rely on two instruments. To achieve the goals of recovering reserves and limiting real ROL appreciation so as to support export competitiveness, the NBR has bought large amounts of foreign currency since 1999, increasing its current foreign exchange reserves cover to more than four months of imports. This substantial accumulation of reserves contributes to reducing the country-specific risk and to improving Romania's credit rating and implicitly its terms of borrowing. In turn, the cheaper access to international capital comes with additional pressure on the NBR to buy foreign currency if it keeps fighting ROL appreciation. When, at the end of the period (2002–2003), the NBR slowed down the pace of buying foreign currency, the ROL appreciated slightly against the reference currency basket.[5]

When buying foreign currency, the NBR also injected liquidity into the economy, and these interventions were never fully sterilized. The monetary base (M0) and the money stock (M2) increased throughout this period and the consequences on inflation were almost immediate.[6] Up to 2003 disinflation occurred while the NBR tried to prevent the ROL from appreciating against the euro and the US dollar. Since then the ROL has undergone steady real appreciation against the reference currency basket.[7]

Unlike in industrial countries, where the central bank is a net creditor of the banking sector,[8] in Romania – as in the transition countries that joined the EU in 2004 – the central bank is a net debtor. In Poland, Hungary and the Czech Republic, the central bank's monetary management consists in adjusting the monetary base by modifying the volume of resources borrowed from commercial banks (for one-week or two-week periods) through regular tender operations. The target instrument is the interest rate that the central bank pays for these credits. Of course, the interest rate the central bank must pay depends on interest rates reported on commercial bank deposits, reserves and loans to households. This is an equilibrium price and is driven by market forces.

Since 2001 the NBR has 'attracted deposits', that is, borrowed resources for one-month periods from commercial banks. Unlike in the case of the above-mentioned monetary policy regimes, the underlying target seems to be rather quantitative. It appears that the NBR first defines the volume of resources it wants to borrow (as a means of controlling liquidity), and then sets the interest rate at a level at which commercial banks will want to lend.

The NBR's method of attracting deposits may have been quite effective in dragging liquidity,[9] but is atypical since most other countries follow the opposite strategy, that is, first choose and announce the interest rate, then see how many resources are attracted; in a third step, adjust the instrument if the target is missed. In the NBR procedure, the interest rate does not seem to be the key variable; thus it may not convey high-quality information about the monetary policy stance, in particular when some form of rationing occurs in the demand for borrowed resources.

Arguably, the recent years' successful disinflation has brought the interest rate pass-through in Romania closer to the pass-through levels prevailing in other Central European economies (Tieman, 2004). But the central bank's heavy net debtor position and commercial banks' oligopoly status, as well as still immature financial markets, stand in the way of an effective interest rate policy.

Unsurprisingly, the rapid accumulation of foreign exchange reserves after 1999 and a contained expansion of the monetary base, given these sterilization operations, led to quite a bizarre monetary structure where, since 2003, the monetary base has been covered almost four times by foreign exchange reserves. In other words, the relationship between the monetary base and hard currency reserves has been tighter than in standard currency board agreements, where this ratio is one-to-one. This does not necessarily imply that Romania has abnormally high reserves, but rather points to the underdevelopment of the banking sector and credit activity (low monetization).

4. INFLATION TARGETING (IT)

The NBR has announced its intention to introduce inflation targeting as a new monetary policy regime during 2005 in order to help continue disinflation (bring it to around 3 per cent by 2007) and bolster the central bank's credibility.

4.1 IT as a Monetary Policy Regime

The broadest definition of inflation targeting is a monetary policy framework that accords overriding importance to the maintenance of price stability. The narrower definition says that inflation targeting is a monetary policy framework based on the adoption of a monetary policy rule in which forecasts of future inflation play a central role, either in the form of instrument rules or of target rules. An instrument rule expresses the monetary policy instrument as a simple and usually linear function of deviation of a few key macroeconomic variables from their target level. A target rule expresses the monetary policy instrument as the solution to an optimization problem defined by a loss function describing the costs associated with deviations of specific goal variables from their target levels subject to the constraints imposed by the model of the economy's structure.

Since monetary policy works its effect on inflation with a significant delay (at least nine months and up to two years) inflation targeting is in fact inflation forecast targeting (Svensson, 1997). Inflation forecasts are contingent upon the central bank's view of the transmission mechanism, the current state of the economy and a planned path for the instrument. Complex econometric modelling and statistical inference building on high-quality data and economic information are needed in order to produce reliable forecasts (a subjective assessment of the inflation path may be included too). All this highlights the logistical challenge linked with IT implementation.

The inflation targeters are explicit about the long-run inflation rate that constitutes price stability. The inflation target announcement aims at increasing credibility and anchoring inflation expectations. It is useful in establishing the political legitimacy for an independent central bank, especially when taking unpopular decisions.

4.2 The Economics of Inflation Targeting

The strongest rationale of the inflation targeting regime is that under some reasonable conditions stabilization of prices is equivalent to the stabilization of output around its natural level – that is, the level of output that would prevail if there were no nominal rigidities (Blanchard, 2003). The equivalence holds in models with staggered price setting and rational expectations. Achieving the natural level of output, though, may not maximize welfare if it comes at the cost of large distortions in the composition of output. The class of models for which full price stability is optimal from the point of view of welfare maximization requires a sum of restrictive assumptions (Woodford, 2004).

One restrictive assumption is that there are assumed to be no shocks that would require the relative price of any good to vary over time in an efficient equilibrium. If an efficient allocation of resources requires relative price changes, due to asymmetries in the way different prices are affected by shocks, maintaining the stability of a symmetric index of prices is not generally optimal (Aoki, 2001).

The second restrictive assumption is the flexibility of wages. Although this assumption is one common in the sticky price models (Christiano et al., 2001), it might not be validated in practice. If both wages and prices are sticky with price stabilization, the real wage will be frequently misaligned, as will the relative wages of different types of labour if these are not set in perfect synchronization.

The third restrictive assumption is the lack of market power and distorting taxes. In the case when these are present, the equilibrium level of economic activity is likely to be too low on average. When this is true, not only is the flexible price equilibrium level of output different from the optimal level, but real disturbances will not shift these two quantities to quite the same extent. This means that the gap between the level of output associated with a policy that maintains stable prices and the optimum level of output will be varying in time. As a consequence, it will not be possible to simultaneously stabilize inflation and the welfare relevant output gap.

4.3 Experience with Inflation Targeting Worldwide, in Transition (Emerging) Economies

Whether the macroeconomic effects of inflation targeting are better than the effects of any other monetary policy pursuing price stability is controversial. Levin et al. (2004) investigate the experience of inflation targeters and non-targeters since 1994 in a number of OECD countries and emerging countries. They find that inflation is more persistent for non-targeters especially when the focus is on core inflation and not consumer price index (CPI). They also find that GDP growth volatility is the same for targeters and non-targeters, but inflation volatility is higher for inflation targeters. However, they recognize that the extent to which the reduction of inflation can be credited to IT is not obvious. As for emerging markets (including the Czech Republic, Hungary and Poland), the results document that the introduction of the inflation target moves inflation expectations down gradually, the transition is a smooth one and not characterized by a break at the introduction of IT. Again, the question is the extent to which the reduction of inflationary expectations can be due to the introduction of inflation targeting and not due to a whole range of other institutional changes (fiscal consolidation, a greater degree of central bank independence) which are introduced alongside inflation targeting.

Bernanke et al. (2001) analyse the macroeconomic effect of inflation targeting using three different tests. First, they use the so-called sacrifice ratio and Phillips curve equation in order to decide whether disinflation has been achieved at a lower cost than otherwise expected. The results suggest that the adoption of inflation targeting in New Zealand, Canada, the United Kingdom and Sweden did not alter significantly the real economic costs of achieving disinflation. Second, they test whether the private sector inflation expectations inferred from surveys or forecasters and from interest rate differentials have declined after targeting beyond the degree associated with a drop in inflation. The evidence from both the survey data and interest rate differentials suggests that the adoption of inflation targeting does not establish immediate credibility for monetary policy. However, inflation targeting does help to pin down inflation expectations as the new regime becomes established. The third test tries to determine whether the interaction between inflation, monetary policy and real GDP has changed following the adoption of inflation targeting. The results show that the economic performance of non-targeters over the period considered is not appreciably different from that of inflation targeters.

Inflation targeting has been a more challenging task in transition economies than in developed countries. As experience with IT in transition economies shows, the central banks in these countries often missed inflation targets by a significant amount. Jonas and Mishkin (2003) look at the potential difficulties and evaluate the outcome in the three East European countries – the Czech Republic, Hungary and Poland – that claim to use the IT system. They conclude that although the progress with disinflation has been good, the comparatively high level of uncertainty in these countries makes it relatively difficult to predict inflation over the medium term as required by the inflation targeting framework. These difficulties result in frequent undershooting and overshooting of the inflation target. Undershoots of the inflation targets have resulted in serious economic downturns that have eroded support for the central bank in both Poland and the Czech Republic.

The same conclusion arises from the Daianu and Lungu (2004) study of the performance in the three East European inflation targeters. The central banks in all three countries have had limited success in hitting inflation targets. Moreover the inflation volatility has become larger. The authors point out several possible explanations. First, it is difficult in these countries to disentangle the source of the shock, which stems from the fact that the effects of structural changes these economies undergo overlap with those brought about by external causes. Second, there is the possibility for monetary policy to pursue multiple objectives. Fearing political tension, these countries might assign higher weights to economic growth than the central banks would acknowledge and thus deviate in fact from the inflation targeting framework. Third, fiscal policy, on an unsustainable path, might play a damaging role in influencing inflation expectations.

5. IMPLEMENTING INFLATION TARGETING IN ROMANIA

The European Commission's Regular Report on Romania's progress towards accession from October 2004 acknowledges that 'Romania complies with the criterion of being a functional market economy. Vigorous implementation of its structural reform programme should enable Romania to cope with competitive pressure and market forces within Union.' Moreover, 2007 is confirmed as the year of EU accession.

The objectives of monetary and fiscal policy for the coming years are indirectly set by the requirements of nominal and real convergence criteria.

In the years ahead, monetary and fiscal policies should give priority to preserving the momentum in disinflation and growth (see Table 9.1). The question is how fast Romania should bring down inflation to the EU rate without incurring an excessive output loss. The recent experience shows that an annual 3–4 per cent of real appreciation of the domestic currency is manageable against the backdrop of increasing remittances from abroad. But how would steady appreciation of the domestic currency impact on competitiveness over the longer run? Is inflation targeting an appropriate monetary policy regime?

5.1 Rationale for Adopting IT in Romania

The adoption of IT could bring major benefits for Romanian monetary policy. First of all, by enlarging the projection period in which an inflation

Table 9.1 The constraints of nominal criteria for euro adoption (data for 2003)

	Budget deficit (% of GDP)	Public debt (% of GDP)	Inflation (%)	Interest rate on 10 years EUR bond (%)	Exchange rate stability
Target	**−3**	**60**	**<2.8**	**<6.8**	**Yes**
Czech Republic	−7.8	34.5	0.4	4.63 (23/6/2014)	No
Hungary	−5.5	56.8	4.7	5.5 (6/5/2014)	No
Poland	−4.6	44.8	0.8	4.5 (5/2/2013)	No
Slovakia	−5.2	43.8	8.1	4.5 (20/5/2014)	No
Romania	−2.7	27	14.1	–	No

Source: National central banks.

target is pursued, the central bank would escape from the trap of time inconsistency. Second, by adopting a single publicly acknowledged goal, such as an inflation target pursued over the medium term, the central bank could manage inflation expectations so that the required short-run deviation from the target does not jeopardize the final goal. Third, the central bank might benefit from a kind of 'demonstration effect' by using a method adopted in some of the EU's newest members.

In order to benefit from these advantages the NBR needs to choose an appropriate time for introducing inflation targeting. Most inflation targeting countries have chosen to adopt the new regime only after having some initial success in lowering inflation from previously high levels; this happened in Romania during 2001–2004. In order to gain credibility for the new regime it is important to be able to meet the target with a high probability. This means benefiting from proper logistics and a thorough understanding of the monetary transmission mechanism. A clear signal that both government and central bank support and share responsibility for the new approach enhances the success.

The choice of the target is critical. The right target should mitigate the adverse effect of economic conditions, which could move away the inflation targeting from an optimum monetary policy. Although there is an agreement that inflation and not the price level be targeted and that the optimal target is not zero but a small positive rate of inflation, there is no consensus on what measure of inflation should be targeted. The choice of the latter depends on which characteristics of the economy divert inflation targeting from an optimal monetary policy: wage stickiness, market power and distortionary taxes, relative price adjustments (a series of nominal rigidities).

5.2 Features of the Monetary Economy in Romania

Understanding the monetary transmission process is vital to the appropriate design and implementation of monetary policy (of IT). This proves to be a fairly challenging task even for developed economies when there is uncertainty about the way monetary impulses propagate into the real sector. In Romania the task is harder since the undergoing structural changes add more uncertainty regarding the economic effects of a given monetary policy measure. Uncertainties revolve around the 'fiscal dominance' issue as well. It is essential to identify factors that influence the effectiveness of the monetary transmission mechanism significantly.[10]

5.2.1 The structure of the banking sector

As in other accession countries, banks hold by far the bulk of financial intermediation in the Romanian economy. The banking sector is largely dominated by a few private banks and a very large majority state-owned bank (BCR, which is basically a market maker[11]) and is characterized by a low ratio of assets to GDP. At the end of 2003 the share of banks' total assets in GDP was 33 per cent (this ratio is one of the lowest compared to other Eastern European economies). Moreover, the banking sector has all the characteristics of an oligopoly (Antohi et al., 2003). In the first semester of 2004 the five largest banks representing 13 per cent of total banks held around 62 per cent of assets and deposits, and 58 per cent of loans. This degree of market power diminishes the effectiveness of monetary policy, given that under such a market structure, the control of the central bank over liquidity in the banking system is weakened (commercial banks may use their abnormal oligopoly profits to counter an NBR impulse).[12]

5.2.2 Low monetization

The share of M2 in GDP has been fluctuating around 24 per cent over the last decade, which is extremely low compared with developed economies and even with other transition economies. The low level of monetization is indicative of major inefficiencies still at work in the banking system and the lack of experience of private agents in using money as a coordination device. The low monetization bears on the effectiveness of monetary policy. For instance, if private agents do not finance investment projects through bank credits or bonds, interest rates have less of an impact on economic activity.

5.2.3 Euroization/dollarization (on both asset and liability sides)

In a partially dollarized (euroized) economy, the dollar (euro) is used in any of the three classical roles of money: unit of account, instrument of exchange and store of value, the more relevant being the first two (Calvo, 1999).

Given Romania's inflation history over the last 14 years it is therefore not very surprising that the dollarization/euroization phenomenon should be so entrenched. After reaching a peak of 46 per cent at the beginning of 2002 the proportion of the hard currency component in M2 has steadily fallen to around 40 per cent at the end of 2003 and 35 per cent at the end of 2004 against the backdrop of the ROL's sharp appreciation.[13,14] Compared to other Eastern Europe economies, Romania is one of the most highly dollarized/euroized countries.[15] Asset substitution leads, inevitably, to an increased volatility of demand for domestic money, which makes the management of monetary policy by the NBR more difficult. The success of disinflation and the ROL's appreciation are likely to reverse currency substitution.

Recent literature on financial crises focuses on the other side of private agents' balance sheets and puts forward financial risks associated with liability dollarization, for example a situation where private and public debts are denominated in a foreign currency. As compared to currency substitution (asset dollarization), this is quite a different perspective on dollarization (euroization) and must be explicitly dealt with (Reinhart et al., 2003). Various risks indeed may be connected to a significant dollar debt, in particular if the international value of the local currency can slide down.[16]

5.2.4 The informal sector and the demand for cash

A factor that generates additional complications when attempting to forecast the effects of monetary policy on aggregate demand is the existence of a large informal sector, which, to some extent, explains why the demand for cash is so important in the Romanian economy. In general, the size of the informal sector has followed an upward trend,[17] growing from a low of 9 per cent in 1993 to a (possible) high of 42 per cent in 2000.[18] Since then it has been on a decline.

From a monetary point of view, the existence of a large informal sector increases the demand for cash (both ROL and hard currency). Since factors that affect the informal sector change, so does the demand for money.

5.2.5 Size and openness

As Romania is a small open economy, the exchange rate is by far the most important channel of the monetary transmission mechanism because, in contrast to other channels, it affects not only aggregate demand but also aggregate supply. A depreciation of the exchange rate, caused by a loosening of monetary policy, for example, could induce firms to raise their domestic prices even in the absence of any increase in aggregate demand. Moreover, as exchange rate information is available instantaneously on financial markets, wages and prices tend to adjust before movements in import costs have worked their way to the cost structure. This is a particular feature of the economies with a high inflation track record, such as Romania.

One indicator of a country's degree of trade openness is the average share of foreign trade with respect to GDP.[19] In Romania, this share has been growing constantly since 1998 – from 23 per cent in that year to over 40 per cent in 2004, which shows increasing integration within the world economy. Although the Romanian economy is one of the least open economies among the newest EU members, its trade shares are still higher than the average for the euro area.[20]

The NBR's policy of a real appreciation of the ROL together with an impressive increase in the domestic credit have led to an increase of the current account deficit up to 5.8 per cent of GDP in 2003 and, probably, beyond 6 per cent in 2004. This forced the NBR to postpone its plans for further capital account liberalization. Among the transactions that were scheduled to be liberalized at the end of 2003 were trading by residents in foreign securities, short-term financial loans and credits (obtained by residents from non-residents) as well as allowing non-residents to open ROL-denominated bank accounts and trade in domestic securities.[21]

The timing of the complete capital account liberalization is important. A premature opening of the capital account could translate into financial turmoil if other macroeconomic criteria are not met first (Daianu and Vranceanu, 2003). In a small open economy like Romania the world interest rate is given. Large speculative foreign inflows tend to exploit the interest rate differentials and thereby take advantage of the existing arbitrage opportunities. This would make the Romanian economy a potential target, as real interest rates here are high and would thus ensure that a capital gain is realized.

The low diversification of trading instruments in Romanian financial markets could limit speculative inflows to some extent. The Bucharest Stock Exchange Market (BSE) had a small capitalization-to-GDP ratio of 9 per cent at the end of September 2004. The bond market is also underdeveloped with issuance of corporate bonds being virtually absent. Arguably, government T-bills are among the most traded instruments but a tight fiscal stance imposes a ceiling on the quantity that is currently issued.[22] Nonetheless, the range of financial instruments has only one direction to go and, thereby, it does not eliminate the threat posed by speculative flows.

5.3 Structural Constraints of IT Implementation

The 'divine coincidence', which is associated with inflation targeting, is not easy to achieve. Arguably, Romania's economy does not fit into the class of models which ensures the simultaneity of inflation stability and output stability around its natural or optimal level. At the same time, the dampening effects on economic activity of nominal rigidities could be counteracted by significant efficiency reserves which exist in the Romanian economy; these reserves could fuel growth in the years to come. But the issue posed by nominal rigidities is significant.

Thus, relative prices need further adjustment. Administered prices represent still 21 per cent of total prices (which are included in the consumer price index). The productivity growth differential between traded and non-traded goods is larger than in developed countries, and the relative price of non-traded goods to traded goods would tend to increase. Under a flexible exchange rate regime, as it will be under IT, the Balassa–Samuelson effect will result in some combination of inflation and nominal appreciation. If the Balassa–Samuelson effect is large, the authorities in countries with flexible exchange rate regimes might feel compelled to allow the exchange rate to appreciate rapidly, which may attract more volatile capital inflows and hurt competitiveness.

Second, wages might not be flexible enough in Romania. Iara and Traistaru (2004) found no evidence for the adjustment of regional average pay to local unemployment in Romania – unlike in Poland, Bulgaria or Hungary, where the unemployment elasticity of pay hovers around −0.1 found in advanced economies. The new Labour Code does not help flexibility either. Employment declined by 2.3 million between 1990 and 2003, with 10 per cent of the decline occurring during the last expansion cycle: between 2000 and 2003.[23] In addition, most wages are pegged to the minimum wage. The frequency of the change in minimum wage and the magnitude of change have a considerable effect on wage dynamics.

Third, concentration is high in many industrial sectors and gives considerable market power to economic agents. This can easily be seen in the case of basic products (steel, cement, and so on) and utilities.

5.4 Policy Implications of IT

Inflation targeting in Romania would have to cope with a series of challenges, which bear on the concrete form of its implementation.

5.4.1 The credibility challenge

If targets are missed by large margins this would undermine the credibility of the new policy regime. In order to avoid this situation the models used need to be thoroughly worked out and tested. As mentioned already the construction and use of proper models is a formidable logistical problem in an economy that is still undergoing structural change.

5.4.2 Overburdening of budget policy

The coordination between monetary and fiscal policies is crucial in achieving macroeconomic stability (Mishkin, 2000). Given the choice of monetary targets to set prices, fiscal policy is significantly constrained because it has to achieve optimality in tax patterns, solvency, and ensure long-run consistency between debt and money holdings. In Romania fiscal policy has been rather restrictive over the last years.[24] However, the budget deficit picture is more complicated because of, primarily, two phenomena. The first is the social security system crisis. Here, the pension system is probably in the most precarious state. In 2004, Romania had three officially registered workers for every four retired persons. However, the picture is distorted by the fact that, out of the country's working population of around 9.5 million, only 4.5 million appear to be employed. With around 0.6 million being unemployed the remainder of the labour force work either abroad or in the informal economy under the status of unpaid family worker or self-employed. One should also consider the large part of the population in the rural area.[25]

Since 1996, the share of pension expenditure in total government expenditure has grown from 5.2 per cent to 14.2 per cent in August 2004. The pension costs will, undoubtedly, continue to pile up the pressure on government expenditure. This phenomenon is likely to be further exacerbated by a declining birth rate and increased emigration with expected EU entry. Addressing the pension system issue means reforming the existing pay-as-you-go (PAYG) system, where pension expenditure in any given year is financed by that year's contributions in the form of payroll taxes.

The second issue is the poor financial discipline that has been persisting within the economic system. The establishment of such a culture in which the non-payment of utility bills and other budgetary debts has been tolerated has meant, in effect, that large implicit subsidies have been draining the budget. A large part of these arrears can be found in the energy sector. Low collection rates and a long-lasting policy of keeping prices below current costs have pushed up the quasi-fiscal deficits in this sector to several percentages of GDP in recent years. Only in the last couple of years have energy prices approached market clearing levels.

It is difficult to predict a time horizon under which the volume of arrears could be brought steadily under control. Therefore, the indirect potential future threat to the government budget is going to persist, endangering the course of macroeconomic stabilization. One should also factor in the expenses related to the implementation of the *acquis communautaire*.

It is arguable that IT would strain the budget through its deflationary bias. And there could be a reverse of the fiscal dominance issue in this regard. This is why there is need for multi-annual budget programming and further fiscal consolidation. What brings some light, however, is that revenue collection seems to have improved lately.

5.4.3 Excessive appreciation of the ROL

Due to massive capital inflows and 'free floating' and since full capital account opening is to happen by 2007, a substantial real appreciation of the domestic currency is to be expected.[26] Unless productivity gains are adequate (substantial) a sort of a 'Dutch disease' could be in the making. This issue poses a challenge to exchange rate policy in the framework of IT. As Chang and Velasco (2000) said, 'how to float is the problem'.

5.4.4 Possible large variability of output dynamics

There is an agreement in the literature that a central bank should care about asset prices, including exchange rates, at least to the extent they influence inflation and output. Within an inflation targeting framework a forward-looking central bank would bear in mind how asset price movements affect output and inflation forecasts. These policy implications outline a policy challenge for NBR: what form of IT to adopt?

6. POLICY CHOICES (MP AND ERP)

The Romanian economy has some distinct characteristics that ask for a careful consideration of the appropriate monetary (MP) and exchange rate policies (ERP). The large stock of arrears and potential future pressures on the government budget, such as the high cost of pensions expenditure or fiscal costs in the run up to EU entry, require a close coordination of monetary and exchange rate policies with budget policy.

The NBR has announced publicly the introduction of inflation targeting in 2005. Arguably, a 'soft' form of IT (a gradual introduction) is appropriate. This 'soft' monetary framework would focus on inflation but would consider shorter horizons (two to four quarters) than the medium term, would not neglect exchange rate completely, would work closely with the government on budget policy and would further delay the full opening of capital account.

The ECB's monetary policy regime is also an option to consider. Another option would be to keep the current policy and wait for better conditions in order to introduce IT. As some say, 'if it ain't broke why fix it'. Trying to adopt a 'hard' form of IT would be highly risky.

6.1 Inflation Targeting: Why a 'Hard' Version is not Recommended[27]

The benefits derived from an IT regime, in terms of accountability and credibility, stem from using reliable conditional forecasts and using effective policy instruments. Obtaining a reliable conditional forecast is a difficult task. The relationship between the instruments is in general assumed to be known. In practice, inflation targeting central banks need one (several) stable macro-econometric model(s) to get the inflation forecast and simulate the impact of a change in the set of instruments over the inflation path. Arguably, the interest rate on resources borrowed by the NBR from commercial banks (so-called 'attracted deposits') might be this instrument. Yet, the interest rate pass-through remains a policy challenge in view of the NBR's massive sterilization operations, the market power of some commercial banks and still immature domestic financial markets.[28]

Furthermore, it is the challenge of econometric modelling. It may be argued that for no country can correct econometric models be built. True, all models are subject to estimation biases; furthermore, model parameters change when policy changes. But estimating a model for a relatively stable economy with relatively stable policies (for example the UK or Sweden) is not the same thing as estimating a model for an economy whose structure and policies are changing. Econometric modelling is almost an impossible task when the structure of an economy is changing, which is obviously the case for a transition country; that difficulty prompted ECB officials not to seriously consider a euro area macro-econometric model (in particular, given that the adoption of the euro is altering the inner structure of EMU). And the IT attempts in Central European countries are very 'loose' in reality.[29]

The NBR needs to improve its basic forecasting tools; without an appropriate bond yield curve, tracking inflation expectations is quite hard. As a substitute, before a wide range of bonds with various maturities become available, NBR could implement some form of survey on inflation forecast of market analysts. Notice that it is difficult to forecast the money demand given the weight of the informal sector and because shifts in expectations make private agents arbitrate between local and foreign currencies, which may all legally be used as a store of value (and even as a transaction instrument).[30] Supply in the broad money stock is also hard to monitor since a substantial portion of the money stock is in hard currency and cash in circulation holds a large portion of base money.

Given these uncertainties, the risks of taking decisions on the basis of a wrong two-year forecast are quite high. Today the NBR's credibility is quite high, in view of the disinflation achieved until now. This capital of credibility can only be adversely affected if the NBR forecasts come out to be wrong systematically.

What about the timing of IT implementation? If Romania has to follow (with a lag) the same path as the most advanced transition economies (Poland, Hungary, the Czech Republic) it may face massive capital inflows in the near future, which would push towards a sharp real appreciation of the domestic currency. To put some breaks on the decline in export competitiveness, from a social welfare point of view it may be useful to push down the interest rate. But independent employment and competitiveness goals may clash with the low inflation goal, as required by the IT regime.

Romania is set to join the EU by 2007; it must then set its monetary institutions and policy in line with the euro area, so as to join, at a later date, EMU. But the European Central Bank (ECB) itself is not a genuine IT central banker. Like the Fed, the ECB made the choice of flexibility, although it has precise quantitative targets in terms of inflation. Probably this would be an option for the NBR, as a pretty loose form of IT.

The ECB experience is enlightening on several other issues; many empirical studies have shown that the ECB is not indifferent either to fluctuations in economic activity or the exchange rate. It seems that for a central bank, 'flexibility' is an asset at least as important as 'credibility'. Early studies in the credibility of monetary policy argued that discretion is at the origin of all the evils in monetary management. In more recent analyses, it came out that if the lack of flexibility (discretion) casts serious doubts on the sustainability of the banking system itself, then the credibility risk may occur at a deeper layer.

6.2 Exchange Rate Policy

Romania's foreign financial position is sound, with a satisfactory (and improving) country risk rating,[31] a relatively low external debt, and no difficulties in financing the debt service. The NBR stock of foreign exchange reserve is quite normal according to international standards.

Lately the NBR allowed for more flexibility in the determination of the exchange rate. This trend should continue. Direct interventions might still be conducted in an exceptional way, to fend off speculative attacks or terminate a bubbly behaviour of the domestic currency.

This does not imply a fully hands-off attitude over the international value of the ROL, but a managed, market-based influence of the NBR over the exchange rate, consistent with its price stability goal via its (direct or indirect) influence over short-term interest rates. Flexibility in the realm of exchange rates will enhance the capacity of the NBR to pursue the goal of internal price stability by increasing the effectiveness of monetary policy; the latter's effectiveness would be helped by controls on speculative capital flows.

After Romania joins the EU, it should also join the ERM II (by 2009 or later) with a view of becoming an EMU member. This will shift the NBR's focus back from price stability to exchange rate stability. But the two goals are not inconsistent, since in the medium run the international value of the currency can be stable only if its internal value is stable.

7. CONCLUSION

All in all, Romania is on a favourable economic track: growth is back and inflation declines at a steady pace (Table 9.2). Further progress hinges on deepening structural reforms, with reducing overall economic inefficiency and quasi-fiscal deficits. The country seems poised to attract more foreign investment.

In this context, in order to support effective monetary policy management, the exchange rate flexibility should be enhanced. In turn, this might call for more gradualism than currently agreed in the process of capital account opening.

The characteristics of the Romanian economy do not favour the 'divine coincidence' if hard inflation targeting is implemented in the near future. The economy still needs substantial relative price adjustments, wages have to be more flexible, the economic structure shows too much market power, and the tax system is still pretty distorting. In addition, the NBR needs to develop its own capacity to implement inflation targeting.

Since the NBR has announced its intention to introduce IT in 2005 a 'soft' form (a gradual introduction of this regime) is, arguably, a better choice than a hard version. A 'soft' IT framework would focus on inflation but would consider shorter horizons (two to four quarters) than the medium term, would not neglect the exchange rate completely, would work closely with the government on budget policy and would further delay the full opening of the capital account.

An ECB-like system, as a very loose form of IT, is also an option (Issing, 2004). Under such an arrangement, the policy maker focuses on price stability too, but monetary policy management builds on the 'just-do-it' principle. In the case of a small and still fragile economy, flexibility does not clash with credibility; to the contrary, both back each other. Sophistication required by a genuine (hard) IT regime would introduce unnecessary risks, and additional noise in the economy, deemed to accentuate, not to dampen fluctuations.[32]

Table 9.2 Macroeconomic indicators, 1998–2004

	1998	1999	2000	2001	2002	2003	2004.Q3
GDP, ROL billion	373 798.2	545 730.2	803 773.1	1 167 687	1 512 616.8	1 890 778.3	2 254 600[1]
GDP, annual growth, % change	−4.8	−1.2	2.1	5.7	5	4.9	7.2[1]
CPI, % change	40.6	54.8	40.7	30.3	17.8	14.1	9.6[1]
Net foreign assets, ROL billion	16 162.1	41 380.7	92 911.7	168 511.7	236 923.5	252 094.3	337 000.8
Net domestic assets, ROL billion	76 367.7	92 741.7	92 148.2	102 000.3	136 789	208 929.4	230 403.3
Domestic credit, ROL billion	79 919.3	101 340.4	112 885.5	143 244.7	200 221.1	301 225.5	354 638.4
Non-government credit, ROL billion	59 086.5	57 719.4	75 007.1	118 254.4	178 727.9	302 879.3	393 446.3
Non-government credit, annual growth, % change	64.5	−2.3	30	57.6	51.1	69.5	29.9
Foreign currency loans, ROL billion	34 813.9	33 274.5	44 596.2	70 721.1	111 999.1	167 838.9	239 496.8
Foreign currency loans, annual growth, % change	77	−4.4	34	58.6	58.4	49.8	42.7
Broad money, M2, ROL billion	92 529.9	134 114.3	185 060	270 512	373 712.5	460 741.3	567 404.1
Broad money, M2, annual growth, % change	48.9	44.9	38	46.2	38.1	23.3	23.1
T-bills with discount, average yield, %	72.7	76	49.7	35.7	17.3	18	16.4
Attracted deposits, stock, daily average, ROL billion	699.8	3 653.3	3 817.2	24 835.1	63 602.2	65 219.6	92 159

Table 9.2 (continued)

	1998	1999	2000	2001	2002	2003	2004.Q3
Attracted deposits, interest rate, %	106.3	66.2	49.2	34.9	20.8	20.95	18.75
Share of foreign currency deposits in M2, %	32.6	37.6	40.4	42.8	39.3	37.1	35
M1, ROL billion	22 109.7	29 668.9	46 331.1	64 308.8	88 304.6	113 259.8	142 811.3
M1, % growth	18	34.2	56.2	38.8	37.3	28.3	26
Current account deficit, EUR million	−2 575	−1 355	−1 494	−2 488	−1 623	−2 877	−2 098[2]
Current account deficit, % in GDP	−8	−3.5	−3.6	−6	−3.4	−5.8	−6.2
Budget deficit, % of GDP	−2.8	−2.5	−3.6	−3.1	−3.1	−2.6	−1.6
Exchange rates, ROL/EUR (average)	9 989.25	16 295.57	19 955.75	26 026.89	31 255.25	37 555.87	40 745.9
Exchange rates, ROL/USD (average)	8 875.55	15 332.93	21 692.74	29 060.86	33 055.46	33 200.07	33 242.2
Real appreciation (−)/depreciation (+), against the basket[3]	–	–	−5.7	−5.64	−2.37	−3.22	−4.9

Notes:
1 Estimated for 2004.
2 January–August, 2004.
3 The basket was 0.6 EUR–0.4 USD up to 2003 and 0.75 EUR–0.25 USD since 2003.

Source: NBR.

NOTES

1. Daniel Daianu is Professor of Economics at the School of Political and Administrative Studies (SNSPA) in Bucharest; Dr Ella Kallai is Senior Economist at Alpha Bank Romania. The authors thank Laurian Lungu and Thomas Reininger for their comments on the chapter. It goes without saying that the authors bear sole responsibility for its content.
2. Daianu (1994).
3. According to Law 101/1998, which has replaced Law 34/1991, the fundamental objective of the NBR was to ensure the stability of domestic currency with a view to maintaining price stability. Only the latest Law 312/2004 stipulates the fundamental objective as being the maintenance of price stability.
4. The exchange rate pass-through between 1997 and 2003 was found large and fast (Gueorguiev, 2003) justifying the choice of exchange rate as a basic anchor for disinflation.
5. During 2002–2003 the currency basket was made up of 60 per cent euro and 40 per cent US dollar. In January 2004 the currency basket composition changed to 75 per cent euro and 25 per cent US dollar. In November 2004 the NBR announced that the basket was to become 100 per cent euro-based.
6. As put forward by Daianu and Vranceanu (2001), a shock to the money stock reached its maximum impact on inflation three months later.
7. The currency basket was dropped (in favour of the euro) in November 2004.
8. For instance, the ECB will lend money for a one-week period, in a reverse-repo operation. It alters the amount of borrowed reserves by tuning the marginal interest rate required on these resources.
9. A Granger causality test over the inflation rate (INF) and the NBR liabilities towards commercial banks (LLNBR) (in logarithms) over the period 1998.01–2003.09 shows that the latter has a strong impact on inflation rates (in a six lag model). A simple regression model (Daianu et al., 2004), reveals that: $INF_t = 5.33 + 0.26INF_{t-1} - 0.41LLNBR_{t-2}$. The negative and statistically significant sign of the LLNBR coefficient suggests that the deposit attracting operations had a stabilizing impact on prices (R2A=0.50).
10. Traditionally, four channels of transmission of monetary policy have been identified in modern financial systems. The first channel is the direct interest rate effect, with the central bank's key rates affecting market interest rates. This in turn will affect the spending, saving and investment behaviour of individuals and firms. The second channel is credit availability. The third channel is asset prices such as bonds, equities, and physical assets (for example housing). The fourth channel is the exchange rate. In all transmission channels, expectations intervene significantly.
11. Not infrequently the NBR has relied on BCR in order to relay its interest rate policy signals.
12. There is a vast theoretical and empirical literature which shows that the impact of a given monetary policy on banks depends on the industrial organization of the sector. One implication of this is that larger banks are able, in principle, to shelter their profits from fluctuations in monetary policy.
13. Arguably, the indicator used to measure the degree of currency substitution could somehow underscore the extent of the phenomenon since it does not include foreign currency in circulation due to the inherent difficulties in measuring the latter.
14. As a comparison, Reinhart et al. (2003) has shown that between 1996 and 2001, the average ratio of foreign currency-denominated deposits in broad money for a sample of selected emerging market economies was 18.4 per cent. In their sample Argentina had the highest ratio, 52.5 per cent, followed by Turkey with 45.9 per cent.
15. In 2001, for example, the ratio of foreign exchange deposits in M2 was 9.9 per cent for the Czech Republic, 13.3 per cent for Poland, and 30.1 per cent for Slovenia.
16. For an explanation of this balance sheet effect see Aghion et al. (2001); Jeanne and Zettelmeyer (2002).

17. The reasons why it has been so are multiple. First, the choice of economic agents to operate in the informal sector is a natural response to avoid an excessive tax burden (social security contributions are, probably, the highest in Europe). Second, because of a complicated mechanism of regulation an increasing number of companies have switched parts of their activities to the informal sector. Third, a still underdeveloped financial system has increased the probability of economic agents to engage in informal cash transactions.
18. Ciupagea (2001); Albu et al. (2001); French et al. (1999).
19. Exports plus imports divided by two as a share of GDP.
20. According to the 1999 EBRD Transition Report the average share of trade in GDP for the EU candidate countries was 45 per cent.
21. Some of the capital control regulations have been changed, however. For example, from 2004 residents are allowed to take abroad any amount of foreign currency with the requirement to declare sums that exceed EUR 10 000.
22. In September 2004 almost 50 per cent of the total internal public debt of EUR 3.3 billion represented T-bills, and 12 per cent represented T-bills issued in foreign currency (down from 14.4 per cent registered in December 2002).
23. It seems that the recent growth cycle is jobless-driven and productivity-driven.
24. The general government deficit has been cut from 5.4 per cent (without privatization revenues) of GDP in 1998 to an estimated 2.4 per cent of GDP in 2003. For 2004 the deficit is forecast at 1.6 per cent.
25. In comparison, the ratio of workers to pensioners in Europe, already considered to be in the crisis zone, currently stands at four to one and is forecast to decline to two to one by the year 2040.
26. See also Isarescu et al. (2003).
27. See also Daianu et al. (2004).
28. Tieman (2004) is more optimistic in this regard.
29. Levin et al. (2004) show that in emerging economies the weight of food in the price index is much higher than in developed economies. This increases inflation volatility, and makes more difficult for the policy makers the task of reaching their targets, with adverse consequences on central bank credibility; they also argue that most developing countries cannot afford to neglect the exchange rate, which is often a focal point for inflation expectations. But a dual objective is contradicting the IT principle. Levin et al. (2004) also show that in the emerging economies that adopted IT (including the Czech Republic, Hungary and Poland) there was no significant reduction in long-term expected inflation after the introduction of IT. Neither was there any significant reduction in short-term expected inflation after the introduction of IT; the downward trend in inflation expectations could be put forward well before adoption of IT. Another observation is that in emerging economies the adoption of IT has been frequently associated with overshooting or undershooting; possible explanations for missing the targets are: difficulties of controlling and forecasting inflations, larger shocks, the lower credibility of the central bank.
30. Antohi et al. (2003) document well the difficulties the NBR staff faced to forecast the demand for money.
31. Fitch-IBCA raised Romania's sovereign rating to investment grade (BBB–) in November 2004.
32. As Greenspan (2004) put it when referring to easing monetary policy in 1998 'the product of a low probability event and a potentially severe outcome can be judged as a more serious threat to economic performance than the higher inflation that might ensue in the more probable scenario'. The uncertainties clouding the way the monetary transmission works render the eventual inflation forecasts too approximate and make it advisable to embody a risk management policy in the monetary policy. Central banks need to consider not only the most likely future path, but also the distribution of possible outcomes about the path.

REFERENCES

Aghion, Philippe, Philippe Bachetta and Abhijit Benerjee (2001), 'Currency crises and monetary policy in an economy with credit constraints', *European Economic Review*, **45**, 1121–50.

Albu, Lucian, Lucian Croitoru, Daniel Daianu, Cornel Tarhoaca and Clementina Ivan-Ungureanu (2001), 'The underground economy in Romania', mimeo, Bucharest: CEROPE.

Antohi, Dorina, Ion Udrea and H. Braun (2003), 'The transmission mechanism of monetary policy in Romania', *NBR Working Paper* No. 13.

Aoki, Kosuke (2001), 'Optimal monetary policy responses to relative price changes', *Journal of Monetary Economics*, **48** (1), August, 55–80.

Bernanke, Ben S., Thomas Launbach, Frederic S. Mishkin and Adam S. Posen (2001), *Inflation Targeting: Lessons from the International Experience*, Princeton: Princeton University Press.

Blanchard, Olivier (2003), 'Comments on *Inflation Targeting in Transition Economies; Experience and Prospects* by J. Jonas and F. Mishkin', NBER Conference on Inflation Targeting.

Calvo, Guillermo (1999), 'On dollarization', mimeo, University of Maryland.

Chang, Roberto and Andrés Velasco (2000), 'Exchange-rate policy for developing countries', *The American Economic Review*, **90** (2), 71–5.

Christiano, Lawrence J., Martin Eichenbaum and Charles L. Evans (2001), 'Nominal rigidities and the dynamic effects of a shock to monetary policy', *NBER Working Paper* No. 8403.

Ciupagea, Constantin (2001), 'The size and determinant of the informal economy in Romania', mimeo, Institute of World Economy, Bucharest.

Daianu, Daniel (1994), 'Arrears in a post-command economy', *IMF Working Paper*, No. 54.

Daianu, Daniel and Radu Vranceanu (2001), 'Subduing high inflation in Romania. How to better monetary and exchange-rate mechanism?', *WDI Working Paper* 402, William Davidson Institute.

Daianu, Daniel and Laurian Lungu (2004), 'Inflation targeting, between rhetoric and reality. The case of transition economies', Paper prepared for the 8th EACES Conference, Belgrade, September.

Daianu, Daniel and Radu Vranceanu (2003), 'Opening the capital account of developing countries: some policy issues', *Acta Oeconomica*, **53**, 245–70.

Daianu, Daniel, Laurian Lungu and Radu Vranceanu (2004), 'Romania's monetary institutions and policy: meeting the EU challenge', Bucharest: Romanian European Institute.

De Menil, Georges, Nina Budina, Wojtek Maliszewski and Geomina Turlea (2004), 'Monetary policy in Romania: 1992–2002', forthcoming in *Journal of International Money and Finance*.

EBRD Transition Report (1999).

European Commission (2004), 'Regular report on Romania's progress towards accession', October.

French, R., Matei Balaita and M. Ticsa (1999), 'Estimating the size and policy implications of the underground economy in Romania', Study by the Ministry of Finance, Bucharest.

Greenspan, Alan (2004), 'Risk and uncertainty in monetary policy', *American Economic Review*, May, **94** (2), 33–40.

Gueorguiev, Nikolay (2003), 'Exchange rate pass-through in Romania', *IMF Working Paper* 130.

Iara, Anna and Iulia Traistaru (2004), 'How flexible are wages in EU accession countries?', *Labour Economics*, **11** (4), 431–50.

Isarescu, Mugur, Lucian Croitoru and Cornel Tarhoaca (2003), 'Politica monetara, inflatia si sectorul real', in Lucian Croitoru, Daniel Daianu, George de Menil, Cornel Tarhoaca (eds), *Cadrul Macroeconomic si Ajustarea Structurala*, Bucharest, CEROPE, pp. 47–71.

Issing, Otmar (2004), 'Inflation targeting: A view from the ECB', *Federal Reserve Bank of St. Louis Review*, July–August, **86** (4), 169–79.

Jeanne, Olivier and Jeromin Zettelmeyer (2002), '"Original sin", balance sheet crises and the role of international lending', *IMF Working Paper* WP/02/234.

Jonas, Jiri and Frederic S. Mishkin (2003), 'Inflation targeting in transition countries: Experience and prospects', *NBER Working Paper* No. 9667.

Levin, Andrew T., Fabio M. Natalucci and Jeremy M. Piger (2004), 'The macroeconomic effects of inflation targeting', *Federal Reserve Bank of St. Louis Review*, July–August, **86** (4), 51–80.

Mishkin, Frederic S. (2000), 'What should central banks do?', *Federal Bank of St. Louis Review*, **82**, 1–13.

NBR, Annual Reports, 1998–2003.

Reinhart, Carmen, Kenneth Rogoff and Miguel Savastano (2003), 'Addicted to dollars', *NBER Working Paper* No.10015.

Svensson, Lars E.O. (1997), 'Inflation forecasts targeting: Implementing and monitoring inflation targets', *European Economic Review*, **41**, 1111–46.

Tieman, Alexander (2004), 'Interest rate pass-through in Romania and other central European economies', *IMF Working Paper*, November, No. 211.

Woodford, Michael (2004), 'Inflation targeting and optimal monetary policy', *Federal Reserve Bank of St. Louis Review*, July–August, **86** (4), 15–41.

10. Choice of exchange rate regime: implications for South-East Europe

Julius Horvath

1. INTRODUCTION

This contribution discusses the choice of exchange rate regimes by the countries of Southern and Eastern Europe, that is Albania, Bosnia and Herzegovina, Bulgaria, Croatia, Macedonia, Romania, and Serbia and Montenegro. The chapter is structured as follows. Section 2 sketches – in a historical perspective – specific factors of development in South-East Europe. Section 3 evaluates recent positive developments. Section 4 reviews the literature on the exchange rate regime choice, while Section 5 connects exchange rate regimes with growth performance. Section 6 discusses the experience of Central European countries. Finally, Section 7 derives some tentative suggestions for South-East Europe.

2. SOME SPECIFICS OF SOUTH-EAST EUROPE

First, from a historical perspective, the area of South-East Europe has quite often been a source of political tensions. These tensions, together with other factors, typically had a negative impact on growth and development, and on different occasions led to currency and price vulnerability and to periods of high inflation and currency depreciation. It is an open question to what extent this political economy argument has implications for current policies concerning the exchange rate regime choice.

Second, South-East Europe has long been one of the most underdeveloped areas in Europe. In the last 200 years or so, the countries of South-East Europe stayed on the periphery of European growth and off the convergence paths that would have brought them closer to the more developed areas of Europe. Bairoch (1976) and Berend and Ranki (1982) document that the gap between South-East Europe and other parts of Europe was widening already between 1800 and 1860. At the time, Great Britain and other early industrializing countries took a significant lead, and the Mediterranean and Scandinavian countries assumed a convergence path to the core, while countries of South-East Europe were lagging behind. Half a century later, in the period 1920–1938, the gap between Romania, Bulgaria or Yugoslavia on the one hand and Germany on the other hand was still widening or stagnating.[1]

The gap did not narrow during the period of socialism, either. As Estrin and Urga (1997) show, the countries in South-East Europe were not on a convergence path towards Western economies in the period 1970–1990, and the situation even worsened in the early years of transition, especially in the period 1990–1995, when convergence-supporting policies were all but absent.[2] By 2003, average GDP in the South-East European countries had in fact dropped to approximately 86 per cent of the GDP level prevailing in 1989.[3]

Furthermore a process of de-industrialization swept the region. By 2003, real gross industrial output, for example, had dropped to 28.0 per cent (Albania), 13.5 per cent (Bosnia and Herzegovina), 51.7 per cent (Bulgaria), 66.2 per cent (Croatia), 52.6 per cent (Romania), 38.8 per cent (Serbia and Montenegro) and 45.5 per cent (Macedonia) of the 1989 level (1989 = 100).[4]

These are important observations. The development gap facing these countries is immense. In a more traditional approach – such as in Gerschenkron (1962) – laggards are considered to have an advantage since the gap between what is and what can be is an investment opportunity. More recent literature, however – for instance Landes (1990), is rather sceptical about the real convergence perspectives of laggards.[5]

To sum it up, growth is of primal importance for this geographical area, a factor that should be duly considered when discussing monetary and exchange rate issues.

3. RECENT POSITIVE DEVELOPMENTS

More recent developments make for a more positive vision. First, the macroeconomic environment is relatively stable in all countries. Central bank policies have been successful in curbing inflation from high levels in the early 1990s to one-digit levels at present; disinflation prevails and currencies are stable.

In 1993 no country in this sample had inflation rates below 70 per cent per annum. By 1998 only Serbia and Romania still had inflation rates over 30 per cent. In 2003 Romania was the only country to post more than 10 per cent inflation; yet inflation continued to decrease in the first two quarters of 2004. Recent monetary stability in Croatia, Macedonia, Bosnia and Herzegovina, and Bulgaria is impressive.

Second, increased deregulation decreases the importance of political economy aspects in the macroeconomic operation of these countries. Today most countries in South-East Europe have opened up and seek to incorporate their economies into European structures. Those countries in the area that are expected to accede to the EU have enhanced incentives to create patterns of behaviour which may be favourable for breaking up the vicious circles for lagging regions.[6]

Third, in 2002 and 2003 we observe fairly strong growth in the region. There has also been a significant increase in the size of foreign direct investment flowing to the region. The reform efforts in Bulgaria, Croatia and Romania related to their goal of joining the EU seem to be paying off.

Fourth, some governments in the region are now increasingly responsive to the concerns of foreign and domestic businesses. Despite some negative experience during the privatization process it seems that governments are supporting undertakings that will foster economic growth, whereas in the past they used to act more like redistributive-oriented protection organizations with very short time horizons.[7]

Despite these positive results one cannot see a clear concept of development for this region. Stabilization by itself is not enough to trigger a virtuous circle of growth.[8] The question is whether there are policies that could help stabilize growth without endangering macroeconomic stability. It seems that to boost development some trigger mechanism is needed. Traditionally, large-scale development plans, like the Dawes Loan or the League of Nations loans in the pre-war period, served as triggers. Today, joining the Western European structures may have the same positive trigger effect.

As Dornbusch (1990) suggested, after successful stabilization, countries with low historical growth patterns need the leverage of foreign capital combined with local belief – which is still lacking in South-East Europe – that a sustainable and stable growth pattern is possible. These are the preconditions for a virtuous circle of investment, savings and sustainable growth to begin. The beginning of the 21st century would appear to provide a historic opportunity for the region in this respect.

In the following sections we try to apply these observations to the more specific issues of currency and exchange rate.

4. EXCHANGE RATE REGIME CHOICE

The choice of an exchange rate regime is one of the most intricate topics of international macroeconomics. This issue can be approached from various directions.

First, one possibility is to evaluate which exchange rate regime could ease the response of the economy to given kinds of disturbance.[9] In summary, a country exposed to external nominal shocks should use flexible rates to insulate the domestic economy. A fixed regime can be useful when dealing with domestic nominal shocks, while domestic real shocks are best handled under a flexible regime. This approach has relatively little practical application – even if the results have serious conceptual validity – since most of the economies face various combinations of real, nominal, domestic and external shocks.

A second approach deals with the problem of the exchange rate regime in the context of stabilization plans.[10] It considers a country with high inflation that wishes to stabilize while minimizing the costs of adjustment. The stabilizing country first needs to correct the source of its imbalances. However, Bruno (1991) shows that the corrected system can be consistent with different inflation rates. For this reason a clear signal of a shift in policy is needed, which is usually provided by a nominal anchor in the form of a fixed exchange rate regime.

A third approach stems from the time inconsistency literature. This literature puts forward the idea that an exchange rate peg can help the domestic economy by importing credibility. In other words a country with (relatively) high inflation and thus lower credibility of its monetary authorities could import credibility from a country with a proven commitment to low inflation and a stable currency.[11]

A fourth approach is rooted in the theory of optimal currency areas. This approach investigates structural characteristics of a given country that determine whether maintaining internal and external balance is better achieved with fixed or floating rates.[12]

A fifth approach tries empirically to evaluate the weight of different variables appearing in other approaches.[13] For example von Hagen and Zhou (2002) distinguish three groups of factors affecting a country's exchange rate regime choice: economic fundamentals, variables relating to macroeconomic stabilization and variables relating to the risk of currency crisis.

When it comes to selecting *the* optimal exchange rate regime combination from among these approaches, a country's characteristics, the nature of shocks, stabilization goals and credibility issues will matter most.

5. EXCHANGE RATE REGIME AND GROWTH PERFORMANCE

Levy Yeyati and Sturzenegger (2001) point out that the impact of exchange rate regimes on economic growth is under-investigated, 'probably due to the fact that nominal variables are typically considered to be unrelated to longer-term growth performance' (p. 2). Proponents of both neo-classical and endogenous growth theory do not see the exchange rate as one of the factors potentially affecting long-run growth rates. Conversely, Dooley et al. (2003) argue that Asian economies moving from the periphery to the core benefited significantly from maintaining relatively fixed but undervalued currencies stimulating export-led growth.[14] This discussion would exceed the scope of this chapter; the following is limited to presenting the results of some interesting empirical investigations into this issue.

Ghosh et al. (1997) using a comprehensive dataset for more than 100 countries show that across different exchange rate regimes there are only slight differences in the rate of growth. In their sample – on average – the highest growth (2.1 per cent) is associated with intermediate exchange rate regimes, while 1.7 per cent growth is with floating regimes and 1.4 per cent growth with fixed exchange rate regimes. In their sample, inflation is both lower and more stable, and output more volatile under fixed exchange rate regimes.

The fact that one needs to distinguish between the de facto and *de jure* exchange rate regime makes the problem more complicated. Reinhart and Rogoff (2004, p. 38) document how different exchange rate classification matters. However, the growth performance of different exchange rate regimes is quite similar; only the growth results under a freely falling regime are clearly discouraging.

These results were obtained in a set consisting of a large number of countries for a relatively long period of time, and they do not provide us with clear operational advice. Having in mind the specificities of South-East Europe we look at the issue whether historically lower growth rates or more unstable domestic politics could have implications for the exchange rate policy choice.

Edwards (1996, p. 14) writes, 'countries with a historically low rate of growth will be more tempted to "overinflate" as a way to accelerate growth, even in the short run. If this is the case, then low-growth countries will have an incentive to "tie their own hands" as a way to avoid falling into this temptation.' In a similar spirit one could also argue that countries with a history of unstable domestic political relations may also opt to 'tie their own hands' to prevent these tensions from being transmitted into their monetary and currency relations. However, results of Edwards (1996) for the set of 63 countries and for the period 1980–1992 suggest that the more unstable a country with other things given, the lower is the probability of choosing a pegged exchange rate system (p. 15). An intuitive explanation may lie in the fact that more stable governments are better able to withstand the political costs of a currency crisis and, thus, these governments will be more willing to adopt fixed exchange rate regimes.

6. EXPERIENCE OF CENTRAL EUROPEAN COUNTRIES

Central European countries began transition with exchange rate-based stabilization programmes. A fixed exchange rate regime was crucial in preventing run-away inflation, delivering macroeconomic stability and facilitating the liberalization of foreign trade and the introduction of current account convertibility. In order to ensure the credibility and sustainability of the peg, the currency had to undergo a substantial initial devaluation at the outset of transition. This reflected commitment to price stability and also the fact that they had already accumulated sizable international reserves or received support from international financial organizations. With time, all four Central European countries relaxed and eventually abandoned fixed exchange rates in favour of more flexible regimes.

Exchange rate arrangements in these countries in the period 1990–2004 document the tendency to move from fixed towards more flexible arrangements. This is especially obvious in case of the Czech and Slovak koruna, and also the Polish zloty, but even the Hungarian forint has quite a degree of *de jure* flexibility in a wide symmetric band of 15 per cent.

The first steps towards more flexible exchange rate regimes had occurred in the second half of the 1990s when the Czech Republic, Poland and Slovakia extended their fluctuation bands; this step was precipitated by pressures for appreciation. The Czech Republic moved towards a more flexible regime in reaction to a currency crisis in May 1997.[15] Similar developments unfolded in Slovakia, where a more flexible exchange rate was adopted in October 1998. In January 1999, Poland extended the fluctuation bands for the Polish zloty; simultaneously, the National Bank of Poland announced plans to float the zloty, a step eventually implemented in April 2000. Hungary sustained a crawling peg with narrow fluctuation bands until spring 2001. In May 2001 Hungary introduced a regime shadowing ERM II with its central parity towards the euro and a ± 15 per cent band.

Despite the adoption of more flexible exchange rate regimes monetary authorities in these countries continue to view exchange rate stability as one of their major policy objectives. Therefore, they frequently engage in interventions against fluctuations of the exchange rate, though not against the trend development of the exchange rate.

In these countries movement toward more flexible regimes was substantiated by the fact that rigidly fixed rates could lead to an untenable appreciation of the real exchange rates, and that they provide worse protection against potential speculative attacks. Another reason for this move was that the fixed exchange rate regimes made it difficult to advance the disinflation process further, mainly due to the fact that large capital inflows contributed to higher growth of monetary aggregates, creating inflationary pressures.

It is a sign of maturity in the conduct of monetary policy that no major exchange rate regime changes were undertaken in recent years. Quite the contrary, the stability of these currencies is magnified by the fact that some of these currencies significantly appreciated. Significant inflows of capital also act towards pushing up currency values. In addition there is an upward pressure due to the Harrod–Balassa–Samuelson effect. Exchange rate risks remain still high especially in countries with high fiscal deficits and rising debt. The volatility of short-term capital flows and possible currency crises before joining the EMU structure is still a possibility. Nerlich (2002, p. 3) raises a point that while there were shifts in the exchange rate regimes, these shifts were the result of proactive policy management, which was largely facilitated by the institutional framework for EU integration; that is, these shifts did not represent a passive response to actual or potential currency crisis perspectives.

Building credible monetary institutions was a difficult task that all new member countries accomplished, though.

7. IMPLICATIONS FOR SOUTH-EAST EUROPE

- Optimum currency area considerations would suggest that small and open economies in South-East Europe trading mostly with euro area countries should opt for exchange rate regimes pegged to the euro.
- A long-standing experience of low growth rates together with a recent history of domestic political tensions suggests that building monetary credibility is a top priority for countries in the area.
- Building stable monetary institutions is crucial also because empirical findings do not clearly connect a particular exchange rate regime with better growth results.
- The experience of other countries suggests that there is no exchange rate regime that would fit all countries.[16] The final decision is in some sense an 'art'. As Calvo and Mishkin (2003, p. 28) put it, 'an informed choice of exchange rate regime requires a deep understanding of a country's economy, institutions, and political culture.'
- Decision on a proper exchange rate regime also requires an ability to create a consensus across different political strata to avoid creating new tensions through monetary and exchange rate policy.

- After successful and credible stabilization of currency and inflation – in the medium term – central banks in the region should get more involved in helping to create the long-run growth potential. This involves, among others, a policy avoiding non-competitive exchange rates.

NOTES

1. For example, in 1938 the net national income per head as compared to Germany was approximately 20 per cent in Bulgaria; 24 per cent in Yugoslavia, and 21 per cent in Romania. See Kaiser and Radice (1985, p. 532).
2. Fischer et al. (1998) data show that in 1995 Romania accounted for 18.6 per cent, Bulgaria 27 per cent, Macedonia 8.8 per cent, and Croatia 21.8 per cent of Germany's per capita income adjusted for purchasing power parity.
3. In comparison, the ratio between 2003 and 1989 levels is approximately 1.22 for the Central European countries. See United Nations Economic Commission for Europe, Economic Survey of Europe, 2004, No. 2.
4. See United Nations, Economic Commission for Europe, Economic Survey of Europe, 2004, No. 2, p. 82.
5. Landes (1990) argues that to be late leads to unnecessary high pressures on policy makers, which increases the probability of bad government and bad policy decisions, which again worsens the perspective of real convergence.
6. However, in some countries in South-East Europe – where prospects of accession to the EU are very low – no such incentives exist.
7. Historically, as Landes (1998, p. 252) mentions, government policies would not always be favourable for those involved in trade and money affairs. For example, when independence and modern politics came to the Balkans, the representatives of the new countries paradoxically drove out from these countries the most active elements in terms of trade and money – the foreigners.
8. The widespread belief that 'growth is natural' prevails. One can say that Central European countries have followed similar patterns. However, geo-political factors work in favour of the Central European countries, since in these countries the transition process was not only a movement towards markets and democracy but also a geo-political shift towards Western Europe and the United States. This is what gives credibility to policies in these countries. These geo-political factors play – at least till today – a much lower role in South-East Europe than in Central Europe.
9. Following Poole (1970), this literature includes, among others, Frenkel and Aizenman (1982). For a survey see Argy (1990).
10. See, for example Dornbusch (1986) and Bruno (1991).
11. Among others see Giavazzi and Giovannini (1989), Giavazzi and Pagano (1988), and Fratianni and von Hagen (1992).
12. For a recent survey see Lafrance and St-Amant (1999) and Horvath (2003).
13. Heller (1978) and Melvin (1985) are early attempts in this approach while Edwards (1996), Berger et al. (2000) and von Hagen and Zhou (2002) are more recent contributions.
14. In this respect see also Williamson (2004).
15. For a more detailed description see Horvath (1999).
16. Currently, one finds different exchange rate regimes in the area. These include unilateral dollarization in Kosovo and in Montenegro; currency boards in Bosnia and Herzegovina and in Bulgaria; euro-based exchange rate regimes in Croatia, Macedonia, Romania and Serbia; and float in Albania.

REFERENCES

Argy, Victor (1990), 'Choice of exchange rate regime for a smaller economy: A survey of some key issues', in Victor Argy and Paul de Grauwe (eds), *Choosing an Exchange Rate Regime: The Challenge for Smaller Industrial Countries*, International Monetary Fund, Katholieke Universiteit Leuven, Macquarie University, pp. 6–81.

Bairoch, Paul (1976), 'Europe's gross national product: 1800–1975', *The Journal of European Economic History*, **5** (2), 273–340.

Berend, Ivan T. and Gyorgy Ranki (1982), *The European Periphery and Industrialization 1780–1914*, Cambridge; New York: Cambridge University Press.

Berger, Helge, Jan-Egbert Sturm and Jakob de Haan (2000), 'An empirical investigation into exchange rate regime choice and exchange rate volatility', *CESifo Working Paper* No. 263.

Bruno, Michael (1991), 'High inflation and the nominal anchors of an open economy', *Essays in International Finance*, No. 183, Department of Economics, Princeton University, June.

Calvo, Guillermo A. and Frederic S. Mishkin (2003), 'The mirage of exchange rate regimes for emerging market countries', *NBER Working Paper* No. 9808, National Bureau of Economic Research, June.

Dooley, Michael P., David Folkerts-Landau and Peter Garber (2003), 'An essay on the revived Bretton Woods system', *NBER Working Paper* No. 9971, National Bureau of Economic Research.

Dornbusch, Rudiger (1986), 'Inflation, exchange rates and stabilization', *Essays in International Finance*, No. 165, Princeton University, International Finance Section, October.

Dornbusch, Rudiger (1990), 'From stabilization to growth', *NBER Working Paper* No. 3302, National Bureau of Economic Research, March.

Edwards, Sebastian (1996), 'The determinants of the choice between fixed and flexible exchange-rate regimes', *NBER Working Paper* No. 5756, National Bureau of Economic Research, September.

Estrin, Saul and Giovanni Urga (1997), 'Convergence in output in transition economies: Central and Eastern Europe, 1970–1995', *CEPR Discussion Paper* No. 1616, London: Centre for Economic Policy Research, April.

Fischer, Stanley, Ratna Sahay and Carlos Végh (1998), 'How far is Eastern Europe from Brussels?', *IMF Working Paper* No. 98/53, International Monetary Fund.

Fratianni, Michele and Jürgen von Hagen (1992), *The European Monetary System and European Monetary Union*, Boulder: Westview Press.

Frenkel, Jacob A. and Joshua Aizenman (1982), 'Aspects of the optimal management of exchange rates', *Journal of International Economics*, **13**, 231–56.

Gerschenkron, Alexander (1962), *Economic Backwardness in Historical Perspective*, Boston: Harvard University Press.

Ghosh, Atish, Anne-Marie Gulde, Jonathan Ostry and Holger Wolf (1997), 'Does the nominal exchange rate regime matter?', *NBER Working Paper* No. 5874, National Bureau of Economic Research, January.

Giavazzi, Francesco and Alberto Giovannini (1989), *Limiting Exchange Rate Flexibility, The European Monetary System*, Cambridge, Mass.: MIT Press.

Giavazzi, F. and M. Pagano (1988), 'The advantage of tying one's hands: EMS discipline and the central bank credibility', *European Economic Review*, **32** (5), 1055–82.

von Hagen, Jürgen and Jizhong Zhou (2002), 'The choice of exchange rate regimes: An empirical analysis for transition economies', International Macroeconomics, *CEPR Working Paper* No. 3289, Centre for Economic Policy Research.

Heller, Robert (1978), 'Determinants of exchange rate practices', *Journal of Money, Credit and Banking*, August, 308–21.

Horvath, Julius (1999), 'Currency crisis in the Czech Republic in May 1997', *Post-Communist Economies*, **11** (3), 277–98.

Horvath, Julius (2003), 'The optimal currency area: A selective review', *BOFIT Discussion Papers*, No. 2003/15, Bank of Finland.

Kaiser, M.C. and E.A. Radice (ed.) (1985), *The Economic History of Eastern Europe 1919–1975*, Oxford and New York: Clarendon Press.

Lafrance, Robert and Pierre St-Amant (1999), 'Optimum currency areas: A review of the recent literature', *Bank of Canada Working Paper* No. 99–16.

Landes, David S. (1998), *The Wealth and Poverty of Nations*, New York; London: W. W. Norton Company.

Landes, David S. (1990), 'Why are we so rich and they so poor?', Richard T. Ely Lecture, *American Economic Review*, May, pp. 1–13.

Levy Yeyati, Eduardo and Federico Sturzenegger (2001), 'To float or to trail: Evidence on the impact of exchange rate regimes', mimeo, January.

Melvin, Michael (1985), 'The choice of and exchange rate system and macro-economic stability', *Journal of Money, Credit and Banking*, **17** (4), November, 467–78.

Nerlich, Carolin (2002), 'Exchange rate strategies of EU accession countries: Does exchange rate policy matter?', prepared for the KOBE Research Seminar, European Central Bank.

Poole, William (1970), 'Optimal choice of monetary policy instruments in a simple stochastic macro model', *Quarterly Journal of Economics*, **84** (2), May, 197–216.

Reinhart, Carmen M. and Kenneth S. Rogoff (2004), 'The modern history of exchange rate arrangements: A reinterpretation', *The Quarterly Journal of Economics*, **119** (1), February, 1–48.

Williamson, John (2004), 'The choice of exchange rate regime: The relevance of international experience to China's decision', lecture at a conference on exchange rates organized by the Central University of Finance and Economics in Beijing on 7 September. http://www.iie.com/publications/papers/williamson0904.pdf.

11. Euroization in Montenegro: benefits, weaknesses and economic implications

Ljubiša Krgović

1. INTRODUCTION

The last decade was characterized by an accelerated development of monetary theories, as well as the implementation of new ideas and financial innovations. These developments have confirmed yet again that there is no generally accepted monetary theory, that is, no common pattern of monetary policy to be followed by central banks.

Although this decade was also characterized by a more intensified implementation of inflation targeting, we can still conclude that, in practice, central banks are dominantly focused on exchange rates. This hypothesis has been confirmed by research conducted by Fry (2000) on a sample of 94 countries. Figure 11.1 shows the most important results of this research.

The figure clearly shows that of the 94 central banks analysed, for 33 the exchange rate represents the main objective, and for 34 an important objective. In other words, 67 central banks recognize the exchange rate as an important objective, while inflation represents an important objective for 61 central banks.

There are a great number of different currency regimes in the world today. The following 11 regimes have been distinguished both in theory and practice:

1. Currency union
2. Currency board
3. Fixed peg to one currency
4. Fixed peg to a group of currencies
5. Horizontal band
6. Crawling peg
7. Crawling band
8. Tightly managed float

9. Other managed float
10. Free floating
11. Dollarization

Various exchange rate regimes have different implications for economic policy. Figure 11.2 illustrates the existing flexibility in accordance with the selected exchange rate regime.

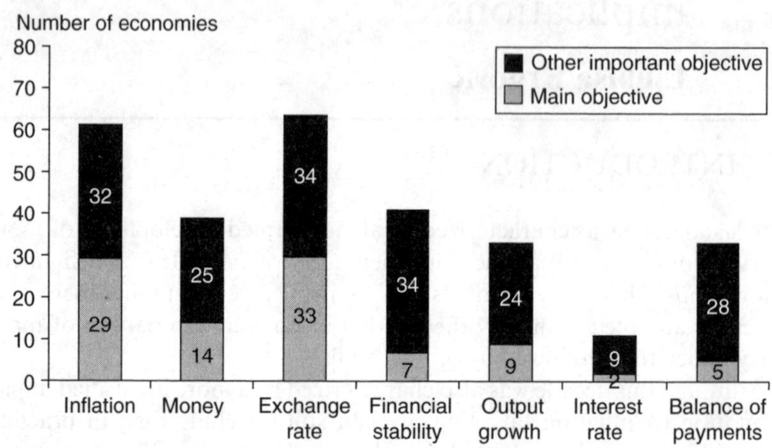

Source: Fry (2000).

Figure 11.1 The most important objectives of central banks

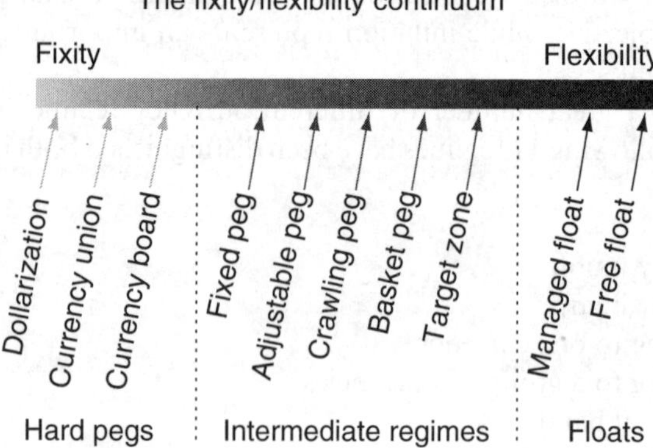

Source: Author's compilation.

Figure 11.2 Types of exchange rate regimes

From the aspect of the country that uses it, dollarization represents the strictest variant of exchange rate regimes, as such a regime does not offer any possibility of influencing the exchange rate. Currency, that is, monetary union, is a more flexible type because a currency/monetary union member country may have an influence on the exchange rate policy through common bodies.

With the increase in the number of independent countries after World War II, the number of currencies has grown dramatically. Following inadequate economic policies, the existence of a great number of currencies proved to be misguided. In the last decade, a reverse trend has emerged – the number of world currencies has been reducing.

2. THE TERM 'DOLLARIZATION'

Dollarization is not a new term, but comes from a phenomenon that was 'out-of-date'[1] but re-emerged as an economic policy instrument recommended by economists in the last decade.

The term 'dollarization' – and 'euroization'[2] – implies several different monetary systems sharing one common characteristic: the broad use of a foreign currency as the means of exchange for formal or informal transactions. The two most widespread currencies are, undeniably, the US dollar and the euro. The degree of dollarization can be best verified by the fact that some two-thirds of the USD issue are held outside the USA.[3] In the mid-1990s, the Bundesbank estimated that some 40 per cent of the issued value of the German mark was used by foreigners.[4]

Official dollarization occurs when a foreign currency has the exclusive status as legal tender[5] in the absence of a national currency. Another option is that several foreign currencies are used as legal tenders, but this is rather rare.[6] The group of officially dollarized economies includes only 16 independent countries at present, Montenegro being one of them.

Official semi-dollarization implies the situation where a foreign currency is used alongside a national currency as legal tender. Montenegro was a case in point at the beginning of its monetary reform when the German mark was first introduced as a means of payment. This system is used today in Haiti, the Bahamas, Liberia, Cambodia, and some other countries.

Unofficial dollarization is the situation where, due to the lack of confidence in the national currency, a foreign currency is used as a means of payment, a unit of account, and a store of value,[7] but not as the official legal tender. It is not possible to provide accurate statistics on the number of countries with unofficial dollarization, but this type of dollarization is more widespread than official adoption. Another way to measure unofficial dollarization is by the proportion of the national currency deposits and foreign currency deposits in the domestic banking system. A recent survey carried out by the IMF in the mid-1990s showed that, according to this methodology, 52 countries could be categorized as unofficially dollarized.[8] Montenegro before monetary reform was a case in point, as are most economies in transition and most developing countries.

Monetary union can be considered as the fourth variant of dollarization, namely a common currency shared by several countries. At the moment, the European Monetary Union is the only true example[9] of this variant, although there are some indications that monetary union could be established on the American Continent in the future or in the south of Africa.

Almost all countries that have accepted either full or partial dollarization went through a stage of unofficial dollarization first. As a rule, unofficial dollarization comes after or during periods of hyperinflation and/or devaluations (depreciations), that is, anticipating their occurrence. First, a foreign currency becomes the means of saving to avoid potential losses due to macroeconomic instability. Then, the foreign currency becomes the unit of account, first in property and higher-value products transactions, then gradually including more products; and finally, it becomes a means of payment. In fact, dollarization is the result of rational behaviour by individuals, undertakings, and others who strive to protect their property from losing its value, as the result of disastrous economic policy.

Dollarization makes sense if the following requirements are met:

- A country is rather small[10] and dependent upon foreign trade,
- a country had a recent history of hyperinflation,
- revenues from seigniorage are relatively small due to widespread unofficial dollarization, and
- there are foreign currency reserves which would enable the exchange of the national currency with another foreign currency.[11]

The additional criterion that has been emphasized lately relates to close economic relations with the USA (that is, with the EU in the case of euroization).

Earlier economic analyses suggested that the cost of official dollarization is too high. However, unofficial dollarization was widespread in the last decade, and the financial innovation that reduced the share of currency in GDP, together with the reduction in inflation in most countries has diminished the potential costs of dollarization.[12] It is obvious that full dollarization has numerous advantages, but also a number of weaknesses. Table 11.1 shows the benefits and weaknesses of aspects of the policy of full dollarization.

Table 11.1 Benefits and weaknesses of full dollarization

Benefits	Weaknesses
Provides low inflation rate (similar to that in the country of 'reserve currency')	Loss of foreign currency reserves
Limits the possibility of misuse of monetary policy	There is no opportunity to adjust the level of foreign exchange
Lower interest rates as the result of low inflation and lack of devaluation risk	Limited possibility of conducting an independent monetary policy
Accelerates development of domestic capital market	There is no issue premium
Transaction costs in international economic relations reduce	There is no possibility of using inflation tax in extraordinary situations
Alleviates integration of domestic companies in international economy, and induces an increase of direct foreign investments	Limits possibilities of using the lender-of-last-resort policy
Induces an increase in foreign trade	One-off shocks: currency translation, new software, changes in accountancy, and similar
Greater budgetary discipline	Increased value drain in balance of payments problems
Eliminates currency risk	
Countries might also strengthen their financial institutions and create positive sentiment toward investment, both domestic and international	

Source: Author's compilation.

The effects of dollarization on the economic performance of a country are difficult to determine since, on one hand, a very small number of countries have a statistically important dollarization history,[13] and on the other hand, most of the dollarized countries are very small and specific in terms of their geographical position and the structure of their economic activities. Table 11.2 shows the performance of some independent dollarized countries.

The experiences of many countries have shown that drastic monetary reform (dollarization is just one of the options) is fruitful, as a rule, at least in its initial stages. This was undoubtedly confirmed by currency boards in

Table 11.2 Characteristics of independent dollarized countries

Country	Population	GDP (USD billion)	Currency	Year of dollarization
Andorra	73 000	1.2	EUR banknotes but own coins	1978
Northern Cyprus	180 000	1.4	Turkish lira	1974
East Timor	857 000	0.2	USD	2000
El Salvador	6 100 000	12.2	USD, Colon	2001
Ecuador	12 400 000	18.7	USD	2000
Kiribati	82 000	0.1	Australian dollar banknotes but own coins	1943
Liechtenstein	31 000	0.7	Swiss franc	1921
Marshall Islands	61 000	0.1	USD	1944
Micronesia	120 000	0.2	USD	1944
Monaco	32 000	0.8	EUR	1865
Nauru	10 000	0.1	Australian dollar	1914
Palau	17 000	0.2	USD	1944
Panama	2 700 000	8.7	USD banknotes but own coins	1904
San Marino	26 000	0.1	EUR banknotes but own coins	1897
Tuvalu	11 000	n.a.	Australian dollar banknotes but own coins	1892
Vatican	1 000	n.a.	EUR banknotes but own coins	1929

Source: Author's compilation.

Bulgaria and Bosnia and Herzegovina, monetary reform in Argentina (initial stages), the introduction of a new currency in Brazil, the stabilization programme in Israel, the dollarization in Panama, and many others.

Dollarized countries have higher GDP per capita, on average, than countries with their own currency. Twelve dollarized countries belong to the group of the 40 richest countries in the world, and only five dollarized countries have GDP per capita lower than USD 1500. Table 11.3 confirms the aforementioned.

Edwards (2001) has come to a somewhat different conclusion. He points out that dollarized economies have much lower inflation rates, lower GDP rates, and similar fiscal performances than the countries with their own

Table 11.3 GDP per capita in dollarized economies and countries with their own currency

	Average value	Median
World (all countries and jurisdictions – total of 228)	8800	4780
Countries with their own currency (all countries and jurisdictions – total of 228)	8200	4200
Dollarized countries (all countries and jurisdictions – total of 46)*	11 120	8850
Independent	*9400*	*4500*
Dependencies	*12 340*	*11 150*

Note: *Excluding Pitcairn Islands, Cocos Islands, Vatican, Easter Island, and Norfolk Island.

Source: Winkler et al. (2004).

currency. He does not give any definite conclusions regarding dollarization, but suggests that dollarization would generate more costs than profit to large countries with volatile terms of trade, and which are not integrated in the international economy to a great extent, and in which financial transactions are mostly in domestic currencies. However, bearing in mind a relatively small sample, its specificity, and the lack of sufficient reliable data (which Edwards also points out), it is difficult to accept these conclusions as generally acceptable theoretical postulates. One definitely valid conclusion that can be drawn from this research is that dollarization itself is not an arrangement which guarantees economic prosperity.

Some dollarized economies have relatively bad economic performances. This can be explained primarily by the fact that this group of countries opted for dollarization after deep recessions, hyperinflation episodes, macroeconomic instability, and so on. Therefore, it is unreasonable to expect that dollarization itself can lead to an accelerated economic growth. It can create only one of the necessary prerequisites – stable economic conditions.

3. THE HISTORY OF THE MONETARY SYSTEM IN MONTENEGRO

The SFRY (Socialist Federal Republic of Yugoslavia) used to have a two-tier banking system consisting of the central monetary institution – the National Bank of Yugoslavia (NBY), which was the core of the system – as well as six national banks of the member republics and two national banks in autonomous provinces. Commercial banks existed in the form of primary banks, specialized financial institutions, post office savings banks, saving and credit cooperatives, and the so-called internal banks that were financial services to large enterprises with limited financial autonomy. The Social Bookkeeping Department (SDK), as an 'independent' state agency, provided financial control of all enterprises, and simultaneously functioned as the state treasury and auditor.

The main characteristics of the financial system in the 1970s and the 1980s were high inflation, growing quasi-fiscal deficit financed by the NBY, a soft currency, and a growing problem of illiquidity and insolvency of banks. Besides inflation, this system generated periodical devaluations, which led to the redistribution of wealth and income from dinar asset owners to the owners of net dinar debts and foreign currencies (privileged socially owned enterprises and individuals). So, the average annual inflation in the twenty-year period from 1971–91 amounted to 76 per cent, which put the SFRY third from last in a group of 108 countries (only Zaire and Brazil were behind it). High inflation, which induced the fall in effective interest rates (which were usually negative), and frequent devaluations led to a decline in citizens' confidence in the national currency. Consequently, this resulted in the fall in dinar deposits as citizens switched the latter for hard currency deposits, usually in German marks and rarely in US dollars. That way the former SFRY also became an unofficially dollarized country.

The aforementioned situation eventually led to hyperinflation of 2040 per cent in 1989. In response to this worrying situation, the Federal Government of that time, supported by the IMF, introduced a detailed stabilization programme aimed at reducing the inflation. Thus, on 18 December 1989 the dinar was pegged to the (West German) mark in a ratio of 7:1, which enabled the partial convertibility of the dinar as of 1 January 1990. However, the maintenance of a fixed exchange rate, even temporarily, and the conduct of an autonomous monetary policy was practically possible only in the short term. So, while the reduction in inflation was successful until June 1990, the annual inflation rate that year still amounted to 300 per cent, which was 100 times more than in Germany. As a result, the real effective exchange rate of the dinar grew by 85 per cent, which caused exports and real GDP to fall by 7.6 per cent.

The increase in subsidized loans, which the NBY had to grant to certain enterprises and banks, significantly contributed to the failure of this stabilization programme. At the same time, the necessary institutional changes were not conducted, the NBY continued to take over foreign exchange losses from commercial banks, and it was simultaneously exposed to the pressures and unsynchronized behaviour of the republic's national banks.

After the disintegration of SFRY, two former member republics – Montenegro and Serbia – formed the Federal Republic of Yugoslavia (FRY) on 28 April 1992. In the new country the monetary system was re-centralized, with the National Bank of Montenegro (NBM) losing its autonomy and becoming a regional office of the National Bank of Yugoslavia (NBY) whose main office was in Belgrade. Thus, the National Bank of Montenegro was no longer governed by a Governor, who had been previously appointed by the Parliament or the Government of the Republic of Montenegro, but by a Director General, who was appointed by the Governor of the NBY in Belgrade.

The payment system, as the 'nervous system' of the financial system in FRY, consisted of several entities: NBY/ZOP (Institute for Payment Operations), banks, the Post Office, and so on. At the same time, the NBY managed the giro accounts of these entities, that is, the bearers of payment operations, and giro accounts of economic and other legal entities. The NBY performed the daily and periodical clearing of liabilities by accounts, managed accounts for money issue, deposits and loans. The roles of banks and the Post Office were far less important (receiving payments and payments for private citizens' accounts, and similar operations for private citizens). A participant in payment operations (an enterprise, institutions and other legal entities, a private citizen) could have only one commercial account.

A high level of monetary and financial centralization was established, which was easy to be manipulated and which enabled unbelievable misuse due to the absence of the rule of law and financial discipline, and this resulted in hyperinflation in the period 1992–94. Full responsibility for this fell on the NBY (as the centre of monetary and financial discipline), Central ZOP (there were also republic Institutes for Payment Operations), and interest groups which were able to control them. Due to its position in the hierarchy and its economic (lack of) power, Montenegro was not able to match the NBY in the misuse of this centralized system.

In February 1992, after the crash of the Common Market and simultaneous outbreaks of war in two former Yugoslav republics, the monthly inflation rate in Serbia and Montenegro was 50 per cent, reaching 100 per cent in June the same year. The latter figure represents the general threshold that defines hyperinflation. At the end of 1993, inflation amounted to 3 508 091 786 746 per cent, which represents the longest in duration, and the second highest hyperinflation rate in the world.

The embargo that the United Nations imposed against SRY in May 1992 on almost all commercial transactions and later expanded to all commercial transactions (except for humanitarian aid) in April 1993, additionally caused the overall economic situation to deteriorate. At the same time, all

SRY state subjects' foreign currencies and physical assets held abroad were frozen. This drastic limitation was effective until January 1994.

Burdened with a harder and more chaotic situation in the economy and unsatisfied citizens who, besides the poverty, were affected by the war conditions and sanctions, the government conducted a monetary reform in January 1994. This programme introduced a 'super dinar' pegged to the German mark in a ratio of 1:1, which means that 15 zeros were taken off the old dinar. Although the programme was promoted as reflecting a modified variant of a currency board, this was only declarative. The de facto non-convertibility, the existence of foreign exchange controls, and a non-market use limitations of foreign currencies and foreign trade flows (only for the import of 'essentially important goods') represented the key features of the 'super dinar' system, inherited from the former system in essence. Additionally, the programme did not impose institutional limits for issuing the new dinar, which are the main request and the rule of the currency board.

The programme itself failed because instead of reducing fiscal expenditure, which was estimated as impossible in those conditions, including salaries and social security expenditure from the budget, the programme introduced a tax reform which was characterized by some unpopular measures, such as lump sum, fixed corporation taxes differentiated by sectors and enterprises. Moreover, a tax on trips abroad, payable in German marks, was introduced.

At the same time, although they were finally relieved of the destructive hyperinflation as prices fell, and although they accepted the dinar for some small payments, the citizens never trusted the programme entirely. Therefore, all larger transactions remained in foreign currency, usually the German mark, which continued to be the citizens' savings currency. Thus, after a short increase in dinar deposits lasting a few months only, they fell again.

As the implementation of the programme continued, the NBY lowered interest rates to 9 per cent and maintained them at that level until July 1994, using them as previous monetary authorities had done – as a support for agriculture. However, banks soon started to compensate for the lost interest earnings by introducing special fees on financial services, demanding high collateral for loans and, finally, by setting higher interest rates than those previously agreed with the NBY. In spite of large fines, the banks soon started paying unofficial premiums of 15–20 per cent on the dinar exchange rate to the German mark, thus indicating a devaluation of the dinar in the near future. Such devaluation happened on 26 November 1994 – the dinar depreciated by 62.6 per cent in comparison with the US dollar, and then again by 57.9 per cent on 1 April 1998. In October 1999, the dinar was two-and-a-half times weaker in the black market than its official value of 6 dinars for 1 German mark (DEM 1 = DIN 15).

4. EUROIZATION IN MONTENEGRO AND ITS EFFECTS

At the beginning of 1999 the Montenegrin government started looking for a way to establish monetary independence for Montenegro. Given that both citizens and the business sector had been used to performing transactions and to saving in German marks for years, the Montenegrin government chose a dollarization model with the German mark as the local national currency.[14] Instead of the dinar, the world's worst-performing currency at the time, as estimated by Hanke (2000b), Montenegro introduced a parallel currency system – one in which the German mark was made legal tender and allowed to freely float alongside Montenegro's other legal money, the dinar (2 November 1999). The entire process was conducted swiftly and without IMF support or guidance. At the time when the German mark was introduced as the means of payment, the government was operating with a fiscal deficit of about 20 per cent of GDP.[15] In January 2001 the German mark (DEM) became the only legal tender, until the euro became the official means of payment in June 2002.

The Monetary Council[16] ran the National Bank of Montenegro of that time, from the moment the German mark was adopted until the establishment of the Central Bank of Montenegro. Until the establishment of the central bank, during 2000 and 2001, this body enacted numerous regulations and acts which enabled the German mark to be fully accepted as the means of payment, accounting and hoarding.

Montenegro also met all theoretical requirements for a successful implementation of dollarization. It was a small, highly open country with experience of hyperinflation in the past, with almost no seigniorage income, with a great contribution of foreign trade with the EU, and substantial flexibility in the labour force (a great number of people were employed outside Montenegro).

The Central Bank of Montenegro has no primary issue or the possibility to issue its own securities, which practically disables the rediscounted rate management policy. The only real instrument is the reserve requirement policy, and an indirect possibility to influence interest rates is through the issue of treasury bills. Through this policy Montenegro has lost some important monetary policy instruments, primarily instruments to conduct monetary and foreign exchange, but at the same time, it has gained credibility and economic stability.

These specific circumstances beg questions regarding the efficiency of monetary policy. Both the central banks of the EMU member states and the Central Bank of Montenegro use the same currency, the euro, which is issued by the European Central Bank. However, the Central Bank of

Montenegro has somewhat greater freedom to influence the secondary issue since it can autonomously establish the reserve requirement rate, which is a right that central banks of member states of the EMU do not have. The existing system is very similar to a currency board because money in circulation depends on money inflows from abroad. The difference is that the money that enters Montenegro represents actual money, whereas in the currency board system the incoming foreign currencies are exchanged for a domestic currency.

Euroization has proved to be very successful in reducing inflation. After its introduction, inflation in Montenegro did not automatically balance with that in Germany, that is, the EU. This had been anticipated since dollarization leads to price equalizations only in the long term. The first years bring normal price growth since some prices tend to equalize with those of the country of primary issue.

A trend of a gradual convergence of the inflation rates in Montenegro to those in the EMU was present in the last two years and has continued in 2004, so the anticipated inflation rate in 2004 was 4.3 per cent (see Figure 11.3).

If we compare the minimum and the maximum interest rates, we can conclude that interest rates are falling. This is not only the result of dollarization but also that of a successfully implemented banking system reform. However, interest rates are still high because euroization has eliminated only one of the risks, the currency risk, while from the banks' perspective, other risks are still present – namely country and client risk. The possibilities to influence interest rates are very limited, and they are reduced to T-bills management and decision-making regarding the amount of T-bills that should be held as a part of reserve requirements.

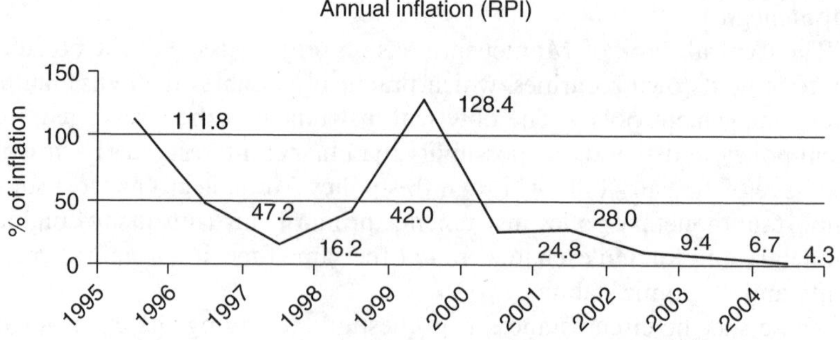

Source: Monstat (The Republic of Montenegro Statistics Office).

Figure 11.3 Inflation rates in Montenegro

Following the introduction of dollarization, the situation in the monetary, financial and banking sectors of Montenegro began slowly but surely to show signs that citizens' confidence in the new monetary regime was increasing. Modest at first, the increase in deposits soon became notable (see Figure 11.4).

Fiscal deficits have been reduced to a reasonable level; following 20 per cent of GDP in 1999, the deficit ranged from 8.6 per cent to 6.9 per cent in the period 2000–03 and is anticipated to have dropped below 3 per cent of GDP for the whole of 2004.

Euroization and stable business conditions encouraged an intensive inflow of foreign investments. Table 11.4 shows these inflows by years.

Foreign trade deficit is still very high due to several important reasons. For small dollarized/euroized countries a high liberalization level of foreign

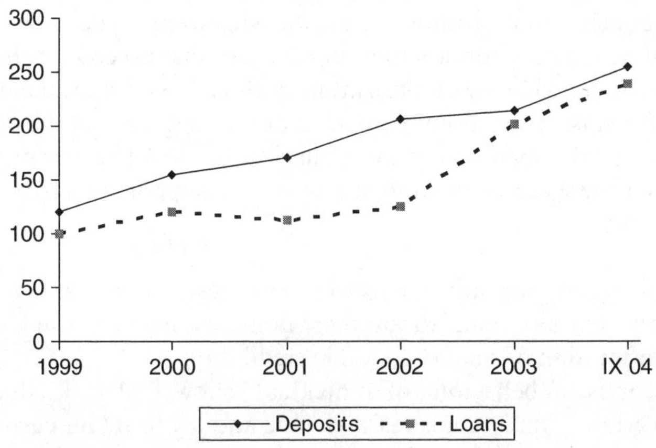

Source: Banks from Montenegro.

Figure 11.4 *Change in deposits and loans with banks in Montenegro (in EUR million)*

Table 11.4 *Foreign direct investments (in USD million)*

Year	2001	2002	2003	2004*
	4.3	77	52.2	46.4

Note: *Data for the first nine months of 2004.

trade regime is important. However, if domestic manufacturers are not sufficiently competitive, a deficit is an inevitable consequence. Additionally, Montenegro is very dependent on the import of oil and oil derivatives, and the explosion in the prices of these products in the world market induced the increase in deficit. The unfavourable EUR/USD exchange rate encourages the import of consumer goods. In the end, it should be noted that there are substantial inflows to tourism and transfers from abroad, which have not been registered in the balance of payments.

Ultimately, the challenges for the future consist primarily in maintaining macroeconomic stability and in controlling the budget deficit.

It may appear at first sight that there is a dilemma regarding whether Montenegro should retain the euro or introduce its own currency. There is no empirical evidence on the abandonment of dollarization in modern history, so there are no examples of other countries whose experiences could be used to draw some conclusions. The only example is Liberia, but Liberia abolished dollarization during the whirlwind of a civil war and an extremely difficult economic situation. The fact that no country has opted for the abandonment of dollarization, although some of them have a dollarization history of more than one century, suggests that the prevailing opinion is that the abandonment of dollarization would be detrimental. We believe that there are many more arguments to support this hypothesis at this moment:

- Macroeconomic stability has just been established, and it is most likely that switching to another monetary regime would induce a deterioration of macroeconomic credibility;
- Theories of behaviour of individuals show that in a situation of uncertainty individuals resist change and try to retain current positions;
- The hyperinflation experience is still 'vivid' and it is likely that in a situation of uncertainty, economic entities would try to protect their property by increasing prices;
- The experience of unofficially dollarized countries has shown that the strong hysteresis effect would still be present once macroeconomic stability has been established, which would probably happen in Montenegro. This means that a part of transactions would be in euros, which would contribute to an increase in the grey economy and a reduction in fiscal income;
- The introduction of a domestic currency would be a bad signal for investors who prefer doing business in a hard currency;
- Except for the state, which would restore its foreign exchange reserves, the currency conversion would generate expenses for

the currency conversion commissions for both citizens and the economy, and increase costs in software conversions, accountancy, and so on;
- In a situation of macroeconomic stability there are almost no examples of radical monetary reforms.

It is obvious that economic policy should be in line with all the Maastricht criteria, and the only criterion with significant discrepancies is the movement of interest rates. That is why the maintenance of a sound banking sector is of extreme importance wherein bank supervision process will continue to have an important role. This role is stressed by the fact that in the circumstances of unilateral euroization the Central Bank of Montenegro has a limited possibility to act as the lender of last resort.

Of critical importance is the maintenance of a sound fiscal policy because the euroization system does not allow high fiscal deficits. Such a policy will mean a reduction in interest rates on T-bills, which will cause the reduction in other interest rates as an end result, as well as the elimination of any suspicious capital that could seriously jeopardize monetary reform.

An open issue in the future may be the high foreign trade deficit that could lead to an outflow of euros. Currently, this gap is to a great extent covered by donations, foreign credits, and the inflow of foreign investments. Bearing in mind that donations and credits are only temporary instruments, it will be vital to balance the balance of payments.

Foreign debt repayments will also represent money outflow. It accentuates the importance of the balance of payments balancing, that is, inflows of foreign investments. Another option may be the issue of state bonds in the domestic market, which would be successful if it were covered by idle money (money hoarded in mattresses).

The achievement of a social consensus about the salaries is crucial because of the pressure to increase salaries (which is higher than productivity), primarily in state-owned enterprises may represent an important element in the deterioration of macroeconomic stability.

Finally, we may conclude that the euroization in Montenegro has had an effect on the increase in stability and business predictability. However, euroization itself cannot start economic growth, and it should not be a substitute for economic reforms. Therefore, the continuation and the acceleration of economic reforms is, in fact, the only possible solution.

APPENDIX 11A DOLLARIZED ECONOMIES

Officially Dollarized: Dollar as a Legal Tender

1. Independent states: East Timor, Marshall Islands, Micronesia, Palau, Panama, Ecuador, El Salvador;
2. Dependencies: the Pitcairn Islands (New Zealand), Cocos Islands (Great Britain), British Virgin Islands (Great Britain);
3. The USA territories: Guam, American Virgin Islands, Puerto Rico, American Samoa, North Mariana Islands.

Officially Dollarized: Other Currencies

1. Independent states: Andorra (euro), Liechtenstein (Swiss franc), Monaco (euro), Nauru (Australian dollar), San Marino (euro), Tuvalu (Australian dollar), Vatican (euro);
2. Dependencies: Cocos Islands (Australian dollar), Cook Islands (New Zealand dollar), Greenland (Danish krone), Niue (New Zealand dollar), Norfolk Island (Australian dollar), St. Helena (British pound), Tokelau (New Zealand dollar);
3. Other regions: Montenegro (euro), Kosovo (euro).

Officially Semi-dollarized: Dollar as a Legal Tender

The Bahamas, Cambodia, Laos, Haiti, and Liberia.

Officially Semi-dollarized: Other Currencies

Bhutan (Indian rupee), Brunei (Singapore dollar), Canary Islands (British pound), the Isle of Man (British pound), Lesotho (South African rand), Namibia (South African rand), Tajikistan (use of other currencies permitted).

Table 11.1A Review of macroeconomic indicators in Montenegro

Basic components and data	1999	2000	2001	2002	2003	Jan.–Sep. 2004
REAL SECTOR DEVELOPMENTS						
GDP (in current prices in EUR million)			**1049**	**1221**	**1.375**	**1010.8**
Industrial output index (compared to the same period the year before)	−8%	4%	−0.70%	0.60%	2.4%	11.9%
Forestry (compared to the same period the year before)			−14%	−9.90%	0.60%	0.114
Construction (compared to the same period the year before)			5.0%	0.0%	−9.0%	−7.9%
Revenues from tourism (EUR million)			128.2	144	151.2	171.7
Employment						
Number of employed people (average)	115 349	113 818	114 100	113 775	111 856	110 049
Number of unemployed people (average)	75 303	84 092	81 612	80 582	71 678	60 447
Inflation rate						
CPI (compared to December the year before)	145.3%	21.9%	26.50%	9.2%	6.2%	−0.5%
RPI (compared to December the year before)	128.4%	24.8%	28%	9.4%	6.7%	1.9%
Average salaries (EUR)						200.6
MONETARY DEVELOPMENTS						
M1 (EUR million)					**402**	**425**
Total deposits (EUR million)	**121**	**155**	**171**	**206**	**211**	**255**
Deposits by corporate sector				76	91	77
State deposits				61	45	51
Central government				39	14	11
Funds and municipalities				7	21	25
Deposits by financial institutions				8	6	23
Deposits by citizens (savings)		3	6	24	45	64

Table 11.1A (continued)

Basic components and data	1999	2000	2001	2002	2003	Jan.–Sep. 2004
Total credits (EUR million)	**100**	**120**	**124**	**125**	**201**	**240**
Credits to corporate sector			49	79	127	152
Credits to state			15	21	20	11
Central government				16	16	6
Funds and municipalities				4	4	5
Credits to banks and financial institutions			3	0.7	1.6	0
Credits to citizens			6	22	49	64
Turnover in stock exchanges (EUR thousand)						
NEX Montenegro stock exchange				6.153	17.115	10.114
Montenegroberza stock exchange				8.719	26.429	8.788
Stock exchange indices (change at end-August 2004 compared to December previous year)						
NEX 20 index					1219.38	1736.62
NEX PIF index					1122.46	1394.15
MOSTE index					131.31	102.07
Average interest rate on 28-day T-bills				8.14%	10.08%	9.75%
Average interest rate on 56-day T-bills				8.13%	10.13%	9.78%
Average interest rate on 91-day T-bills					–	0.098
Average interest rate on 182-day T-bills					–	0.108
FISCAL DEVELOPMENTS (EUR million)						
Original revenues				229.8	337.5	273.4
Total expenditure and net borrowings				250.7	371.4	270.8
Surplus/deficit of the state				**−20.9**	**−33.9**	**2.6**
Financing				60.8	22	1.4
Grants				26.9	12.6	5.9

Revenues from privatization		37.7	12.6	3.2
Net indebtedness		−3.8	−3.2	−7.8
EXTERNAL DEVELOPMENTS				
Current account balance (USD million)	**−61**	**−154**	**−114**	**−62**
Trade balance	−375	−402	−409	−311
Balance of services (tourism +transport + financial services + other services)	106	94	127	146
% coverage of trade deficit with other balances	84		72	80
Current account balance, in % of GDP (in USD)		**−14.3**	**−7.3**	
Frozen foreign currency deposits (EUR million)			127	
External debt (EUR million)			438.8	

Source: Author's compilation.

NOTES

1. The greatest number of countries used foreign currencies as legal tenders in the 19th and at the beginning of the 20th century.
2. The term dollarization is accepted for all countries that use foreign currencies as their legal tenders, no matter which currency it is.
3. Aguado (2000).
4. Schuler (2000).
5. In some dollarized economies, the US dollar circulates along with the national currency, but solely as small-value coins. This is primarily due to the relatively high transport cost of coins.
6. An interesting fact is that the USA belonged to the category of 'dollarized economies' at one point, because a foreign currency was used until 1857.
7. Foreign bonds, foreign currency deposits abroad, foreign currency deposits in the domestic banking system, and foreign notes in wallets and mattresses may be used as a store of value (Savić, 1999).
8. Schuler (2000).
9. Some types of monetary union exist in Africa in the rand zone.
10. If the last two dollarized countries, Ecuador and El Salvador, are excluded, the populations in other officially dollarized economies are around 20 million.
11. The optimal currency area theory is not given special attention in the chapter as the authors accept the position of economists who believe that the older variant of this theory is not applicable since with accepted dollarization the requests set out in this theory become endogenous variables.
12. Bogetić (2000).
13. Currently, only 16 independent countries are dollarized.
14. Regulation of the Use of the German Mark as the Means of Payment With a View to Protecting the Economic Interests of Montenegro (Official Gazette of the RM, No. 41/99 and 22/00).
15. Hanke (2000a).
16. The Regulation on the Appointment of the Members of the Monetary Council (Official Gazette of RM, No. 41/99, 45/99 and 39/00).

REFERENCES

Aguado, S. (2000), *Transatlantic Perspectives on the Euro and the Dollar: Dollarization and Other Issues*, Spain: University of Alcalá.

Bogetić, Ž. (2000), 'Official dollarization: Current experiences and issues', *Cato Journal*, **20** (2), 179–213.

Edwards, S. (2001), 'Dollarization and economic performance: An empirical investigation', *NBER Working Paper* No. 8274, Cambridge.

Fry, M. (2000), 'Key issues in the choice of monetary framework', in *Monetary Policy, Frameworks in a Global Context*, London: Routledge.

Hanke, S. (2000a), 'Some reflections on monetary institutions and exchange-rate regimes', Testimony before the International Financial Institutions Advisory Commission United States Congress.

Hanke, S. (2000b), 'The beauty of a parallel currency', CATO Institute, www.cato.org/cgi/bin/scripts/printtech.cgi./dailys/01-14-00.html.

Meyer, S. (2000), 'Dollarization: an introduction', presentation for the Friends of Global Interdependence Centre.

Monstat (Montenegro Office for Statistics), *Saopštenja o kretanju stope inflacije (Announcement about Inflation)*, različiti brojevi (different numbers), Podgorica.
Ponsot, J. (2002), 'Dollarization and currency boards as instruments of monetary integration', Conference on 'Exchange rates, economic integration and the international economy', Toronto, Canada: Ryerson University.
Savić, N. (1999), 'Valutni odbor, dolarizacija i eurizacija', *Ekonomist*, No. 14, Beograd.
Schuler, K. (2000), *Basics of Dollarization*, Joint Economic Committee Staff Report, USA.
Schuler, K. (2002), 'Dollarization at the intersection of economics and politics', luncheon speech at the conference 'Euro and dollarization', New York: Fordham University Graduate School of Business.
Winkler, A., F. Mazzafero, H. Nerkich and C. Thimann (2004), 'Official dollarization/euroization: motives, features and policy implications of current cases', *Occasional Paper Series*, No. 11, European Central Bank.

12. Exchange rate and monetary policies in Bulgaria since 1990

Mariella Nenova

In its recent economic history Bulgaria has applied two approaches to macroeconomic stabilization that involved completely different exchange rate and monetary policies: first a floating exchange rate (from 1991 to July 1997) and then a fixed exchange rate under a currency board arrangement (CBA), (since July 1997). Correspondingly, the period up to 1997 was characterized by a quite active monetary policy and the use of a wide range of monetary policy instruments: a basic interest rate, minimum reserve requirements, refinancing facilities, open market operations and last resort lending. Since July 1997 money supply has reflected the strict rule that the national currency can be issued only in exchange for foreign currency at the given statutory exchange rate.

Both approaches were introduced via macroeconomic stabilization programmes, supported by the IMF. The design of both programmes took into account the stance of the economy and existing constraints. The economic conditions amid which each stabilization package was launched were in fact pretty similar – a huge drop in output, depletion of foreign reserves, accumulation of inflationary pressures and demands for exchange rate depreciation, and heating up social unrest (see Appendix Table 12.1A). Initially, the two programmes also shared common constraints – a high government debt burden, significant share of non-performing loans in banks' portfolios, predominance of the state sector operating under soft budget constraints, an unsustainable fiscal position, and no access to international financial markets.

However similar the starting conditions for the two programmes had been, the factors causing the destabilization in each period were quite different. The macroeconomic turmoil and the output decline in 1990–1991 originated from the collapse of the socialist countries' Common Market and the denied access to international financial markets due to the moratorium on debt payments.[1] The stabilization effort of 1997 was necessitated by the inconsistent and incoherent macroeconomic policy implemented in the previous years. To a great extent the problems were due to the deliberate delay in structural reforms. As of the beginning of 1997 Bulgaria was rightly considered a laggard in transition.

After the severe crisis in 1996 and a run on banks, which led to the collapse of the banking system, Bulgaria introduced a currency board arrangement in July 1997 and fixed the exchange rate to the Deutsche mark, later to the euro. Almost instant macroeconomic stabilization followed, creating a favourable environment for economic growth. The currency board arrangement was fortified by prudent fiscal policy, fast privatization of state enterprises and banks, and liquidation of loss makers. Nowadays the deepening of the structural reforms continues and increases substantially the efficiency of the economy – a key factor for enhancing its competitiveness. Today the country is successfully completing its preparation for EU accession in 2007.

The chapter describes briefly the main components of the two stabilization programmes of 1991 and of 1997 as well as the exchange rate and monetary policy incoherence in 1992–1996. Against this backdrop, it analyses the causes for the failure of 1991–1996 economic policies and for the success of the currency board arrangement since 1997.

THE 1991 HETERODOX STABILIZATION PROGRAMME WITH A FLOATING EXCHANGE RATE: WAS THERE AN ALTERNATIVE?

Two blueprints for macroeconomic stabilization were proposed to decision makers in 1991: one perceived a standard IMF-supported heterodox stabilization programme based on restrictive monetary, fiscal and income policies and a freely floating exchange rate, while the other one, not discussed in public, reflected on the pros and cons of introducing a currency board (Hanke and Schuler, 1991).

The choice fell on the first option and reform started in February 1991. The aim of the stabilization programme was to eliminate the monetary overhang and stabilize the economy, and to take steps towards establishing market institutions and mechanisms (see Appendix Table 12.2A). The main components of the stabilization programme were as follows: price liberalization, introduction of a free exchange market for the commercial banks and a freely floating exchange rate. The basic interest rate of the central bank was the prime tool of monetary policy, providing the major nominal anchor. Complementary instruments, supportive to the restrictive monetary policy, were also included: limits to nominal wage growth rate, ceilings on bank lending to the non-government sector, fiscal policy with a target deficit of 3.5 per cent to GDP and a constraint on the net domestic credit to government. Monetary policy had to solve the problem of the monetary overhang, inherited from the socialist economic system, while the tight fiscal and incomes policies had to suppress aggregate demand.[2] Ultimately, the implemented programme had to result in an improvement of the current account balance by limiting its deficit.

The programme also enumerated, but did not accentuate, structural reforms, in particular the privatization of state-owned enterprises, agricultural reform, the establishment of an independent central bank and financial sector reform. The operational targets of the 1991 programme envisaged growth to recover and the monthly inflation rate to subside to 2 per cent in the second half of 1991.

The effective implementation of the programme was launched in February 1991 and economic developments during the first three months were according to expectations. Following an initial price rise in February–March of about 280 per cent, inflation subsided below 2 per cent per month in the next few months.

However, the trade unions gathered strength as the social tension continued rising, and in the second half of the year the initial tightening was gradually relaxed (Agency for Economic Coordination and Development, 1991). On an annual basis some of the targets had been met; the fiscal balance, for instance, and other targets were even exceeded (the current account deficit improved more than projected). Yet, from a social point of view, the two most important targets for the second half of the year – the recovery of growth and the persistent reduction of monthly inflation rate to 2 per cent – were missed. Data for 1992 provide evidence that growth did not resume even in 1992, and the inflation rate remained quite high (see Table 12.1).

Table 12.1 Bulgaria: main macroeconomic indicators in 1991–1992

	1991 programme	1991 actual	1992 actual
Real GDP growth rate (%)	−11.3	−8.4	−7.3
Inflation – average (%)	287.5	338.5	91.3
Inflation – end of year (%)	234	473.7	79.5
Annual nominal average wage growth rate (%)	151.5	168.0	102.2
General government deficit (in % of GDP)	−3.5	−3.3	−5.2
Current account balance (in USD million)	−2016.0	−77.0	−360.5
Gross official reserves with monetary gold (in USD million)	625	516	1207

Sources: National Statistical Institute; Bulgarian National Bank; Ministry of Finance.

The softening of the programme implementation was followed by a withdrawal of the IMF for a couple of years. In the period up to 1997, macroeconomic policy applied the instruments of the 1991 stabilization programme but in a rather controversial and inconsistent manner, and the economy fluctuated accordingly in a stop and go fashion.

With the benefit of hindsight, what might have happened if the second option – the introduction of a currency board – had been selected in 1991? Strictly speaking, the necessary minimum set of pre-conditions, justifying the introduction and guaranteeing the successful operation of a currency board, did not exist in 1991. The next section will try to explain why.

PREREQUISITES FOR A CURRENCY BOARD

In practice, the introduction of a currency board as a macroeconomic stabilization tool is not widely accepted and even less widely applied. This type of monetary arrangement is considered as a last resort for countries with high inflation and fast progressing currency substitution. Even in those cases it is recommended specifically for small open economies.

Concisely, the benefits from a currency board encompass: the preservation of the national currency and hence, of seigniorage; a higher confidence in the national currency via the credibility of the reserve currency; a clear and transparent rule of money supply, which anchors expectations. In the short run, the fixed exchange rate is more or less bound to bring down domestic inflation and interest rates and stimulate growth.

The major flaw of the currency board is the straightjacket it imposes on the economy by requiring a very high level of fiscal and financial discipline. It prohibits central bank financing of government in any form, restricts or eliminates last resort lending and severely limits the number of instruments with which the government may respond to shocks.

Apart from the benefits and flaws of a currency board arrangement a number of prerequisites need to be considered. The first set of criteria, as with all fixed exchange rate regimes, concerns the choice of the reserve currency and the level of pegging. The second set of criteria should reflect a probabilistic approach and assess at least quantitatively the likelihood of success of the arrangement in the longer run.

The choice of the reserve currency might seem pre-determined by the currency substitution process. Yet, it is very important to take into account the regional perspectives of foreign trade re-orientation and expected foreign direct investment (FDI) host countries. While the US dollar dominated the national currency substitution process in Bulgaria in 1997, the impending changeover to the euro within the EU and the prospect of

EU membership for Bulgaria tipped the scales in favour of the Deutsche mark as the reserve currency. However, the US dollar was the dominant foreign currency already in 1991 and at the time there was not even a hint of the possible accession to the EU of any of the ex-socialist countries. With the benefit of hindsight, in view of Bulgaria's pending EU accession, a peg to the US dollar would have been a wrong policy choice.

The level of pegging should not be of much concern because it highly depends on the ratio of the monetary base to the available foreign reserves. The best case for an introduction of a currency board is when the ratio of the monetary base to international reserves equals the market exchange rate. When the liberalization of the markets was implemented in Bulgaria, the exchange rate rose from 2.88 in January up to 20.7 BGN/1000 USD in February 1991. If the exchange rate level had to match the currency board requirement it had to be further devalued to reach the ratio of 94.2 BGN/1000 USD. Higher exchange rate devaluation was surely going to pass through to inflation and maintain inflation at high levels in the next months. Since economic agents' behaviour was completely unpredictable under the new environment, developments in the real exchange rate could not be foreseen. Of course, it is always possible to borrow funds if the discrepancy between the actual and the implicit exchange rate is very large and the pegging would lead to a much stronger depreciation (Hanke and Schuler, 1991), but at least the country should have access to the international financial markets. In 1991 Bulgaria depended entirely on IMF and World Bank financing.

The second set of criteria should help evaluate the future sustainability of the currency board arrangement. In very few cases the exit from a currency board may be clearly outlined at the very beginning. In this respect Bulgaria in 1997 had an advantage – the adoption of the euro in a foreseeable future represented an acceptable exit strategy. But even if there is no clear-cut exit strategy, it is still possible to maintain the credibility of the currency board arrangement by a supportive mix of fiscal policies and structural reforms. As it has already been pointed out in the short run the fixed exchange rate is doomed to insert confidence in the system. The government receives a time out to fortify the initial confidence and to strengthen it further. During the honeymoon (which may last for one or two years after the introduction of the currency board) the government has to lay the foundations for the sustainability of the regime. Then it should continuously provide evidence of its firm commitment to the currency board arrangement. The longer-run sustainability may be assessed within the framework of a repetitive game during which the arrangement is stable only if in each round of the game the government sticks firmly to its pre-commitments.

In this respect the government should answer the expectations of the economic agents for restructuring the fiscal sector and maintaining a balanced budget, for consolidating the banking system as a guarantee for its health and ability to withstand shocks, for imposing financial discipline on all economic agents and not allowing leakages by bailing out state-owned enterprises and banks.

As Calvo accentuates (Liviatan, 1992, p. 23) the potential of growth and capital inflow are important for going ahead with the decision to implement a currency board. I would make this statement more precise: it is the potential for efficiency improvement that supports expectations of smooth operation of a currency board. The growth of efficiency of the economy provides the guarantee for a stable operation of a currency board arrangement. So, all efforts should be focused on restructuring and enhancing competitiveness, which may compensate for the volatility of capital flows. In the medium term an improved current account balance should strengthen the external position of the country.

In 1991 Bulgaria faced rather obscure economic perspectives. With scarce financial resources, relying entirely on IMF and World Bank financing, and against the backdrop of political instability, the transition path was extremely dubious. Severe political discussions about the pattern of privatization hampered the process. The banking system had to be restructured while most banks were burdened with non-performing loans and were technically bankrupted. Even the IMF programme of 1991 proposed no solution to the bad debt problem. Moreover, the government had lost a substantial amount of revenue because of output drops, tax reform and massive tax avoidance, while an abrupt reduction of expenditures was unacceptable in the short run. It was obvious that the central bank was going to finance the budget deficit and refinance the commercial banks.

Since neither of the elaborated requirements was achievable in 1991, it was a better choice to go for a standard stabilization programme with the opportunity to conduct a more relaxed economic policy than a currency board arrangement required. If a currency board had been introduced in 1991 it was surely going to be a failure.

EXCHANGE RATE AND MONETARY POLICIES IN 1992–1996

In the second half of 1991 the first effort to stabilize the economy and launch the necessary structural reforms lost momentum. All consecutive negotiations with the IMF to conclude another stand-by agreement failed, too. The economic policy mix implemented in the following years reflected the basic principles of the 1991 stabilization programme. Monetary policy had to supply the major nominal anchor. However, the process of implementation had been contaminated by controversial measures, making the overall policy mix inconsistent and incoherent.

One of the objectives of the 1991 stabilization programme was the establishment of an independent central bank capable of conducting a monetary policy in support of the external and internal stability of the national currency. Although the Law on the Bulgarian National Bank (BNB), adopted in June 1991, stated the required independence, and even forbade central bank lending to government unless repayable in the course of the calendar year, the central bank was not able to execute its independence effectively. In contradiction of the BNB law, the annual government budget Act provided for longer-term central bank financing of government expenses. As the country remained cut off from international financial markets, the issue policy of the central bank became subordinated to fiscal policy.

The severe government debt burden exacerbated by the lack of structural reforms and the high share of non-performing loans in the banking system kept driving up liquidity requirements. The debt burden of the state-owned enterprises, accumulated in the years up to 1990, continued to grow. Instead of privatizing or liquidating loss-making enterprises right away, the governments got involved in a sequence of debt relief operations (Nenova et al., 1997) in the period 1992–1996. This approach allowed loss makers to survive; the state-owned enterprises enjoyed an easy money environment to prolong the period of inefficient functioning. The tolerance of state enterprises' loose finances encouraged private firms to follow suit and soften their budget constraints by taking advantage of loopholes in legislation and weak law enforcement.

The commercial banks, stuck with the non-performing loans of the state enterprises, asked for liquidity injections (see Appendix 12.2A). The loose stance of monetary policy in 1992–1993 led to a new rise in the domestic credit-to-GDP ratio (Table 12.2). It also generated an exchange rate crisis in March 1994. An attempt was made in 1994–1995 to tighten monetary policy, followed by another loosening in the second half of 1995.

Under the pressure of liquidity claims the central bank developed the range of liquidity instruments trying to eliminate unsecured lending to commercial banks. Government securities became more important as collateral for central bank refinancing. Figure 12.1 shows that financing the government by selling government securities to the commercial banks replaced direct central bank loans in 1994–1995, but the central bank continued indirectly to finance the deficit by refinancing the commercial banks via repurchase agreements or outright purchases of government securities from the commercial banks.

Table 12.2 Bulgaria: monetary and credit aggregates, 1990–1996 (in per cent of GDP)

	1990	1991	1992	1993	1994	1995	1996
Broad money	110.6	76.1	76.8	78.5	79.5	66.3	74.8
Domestic credit	148.6	118.5	120.7	132.7	103.4	68.8	108.7
Government domestic credit	30.1	34.0	44.7	64.9	52.6	28.9	45.7
Non-government domestic credit	118.5	84.5	76.0	67.8	50.7	39.9	63.0

Source: Bulgarian National Bank.

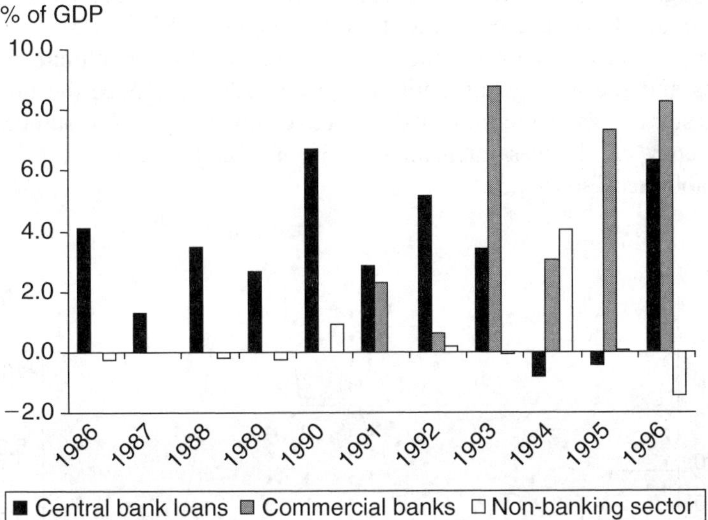

Source: Ministry of Finance.

Figure 12.1 Bulgaria: domestic financing of the budget

In late 1995 growing liquidity constraints at a growing number of commercial banks caused the volume of unsecured lending to rise anew. By the end of 1995, unsecured lending to the commercial banks was the major source of liquidity provision, and in 1996 it reached 92 per cent of all refinancing provided by the central bank.

The crisis of 1996/early 1997 was caused by the incongruity of economic policies. The central bank did try to fulfil the objective of maintaining the stability of the national currency. Credit ceilings, which had been in effective use from 1991 to June 1994, were abolished with the development of open market operations. Basically, the central bank applied two instruments: it set a key interest rate and manipulated banks' minimum reserve requirements. From 1993 the interest rate policy was openly targeted at maintaining the stability of the national currency.

However, taking into account the external financial constraints, the central bank's interest rate policy was under very strong pressure from powerful debtors – the government, state-owned enterprises, and commercial banks. Counteracting the central bank's efforts to defend the stability of the national currency, the debtors opted for a lower interest rate and higher liquidity. A decline in the interest rate against the backdrop of the accommodative money supply policy created inflationary pressure and caused the exchange rate to depreciate, forcing a round of interest rate increases. Time deposit and lending rates followed suit (see Figures 12.2 to 12.5).

From 1994 the central bank frequently changed the minimum reserve ratios and the underlying methodology in order to reduce the nominal interest rate while retaining its restrictive monetary policy stance. The frequency of changes intensified as the financial system became more unstable (see Table 12.3).

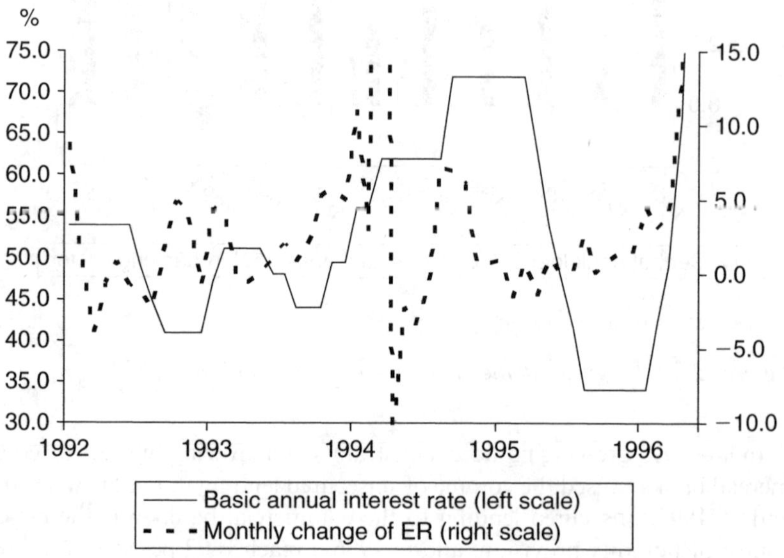

Source: Bulgarian National Bank.

Figure 12.2 Bulgaria: exchange rate fluctuations and the basic interest rate (January 1992–May 1996)

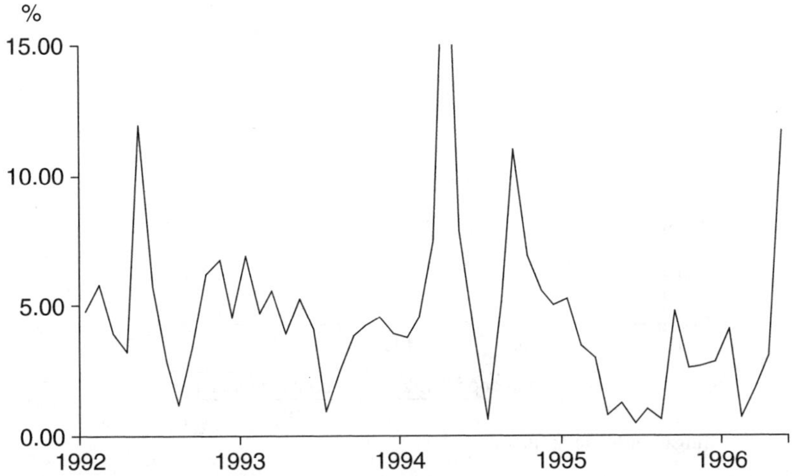

Source: National Statistical Institute.

Figure 12.3 Bulgaria: monthly inflation rates (January 1992–May 1996)

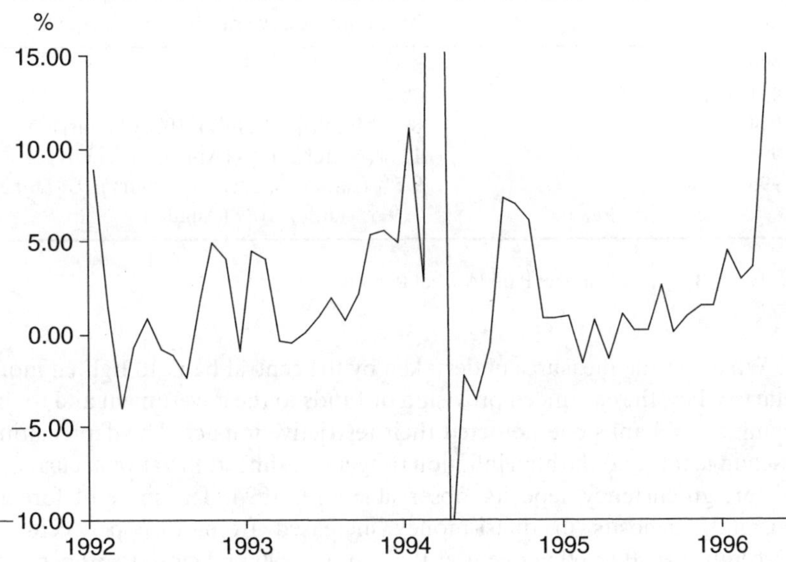

Source: Bulgarian National Bank.

Figure 12.4 Bulgaria: monthly exchange rate changes (January 1992–May 1996)

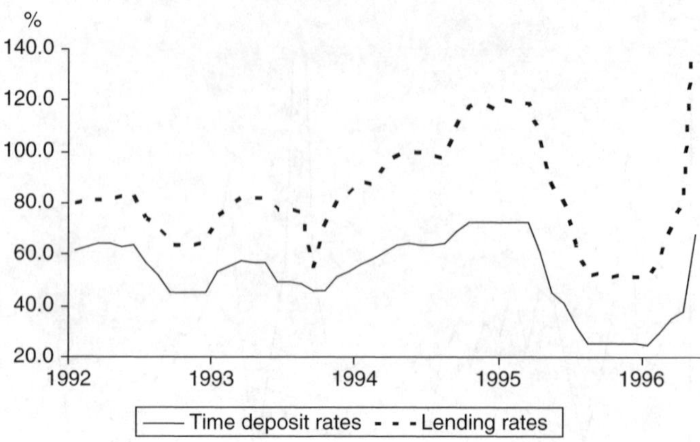

Source: Bulgarian National Bank.

Figure 12.5 Bulgaria: annual time deposits and short-term interest rates (January 1992–May 1996)

Table 12.3 Bulgaria: minimum reserve requirements (1990–1996)

	Minimum reserve ratios
1990	5%
1991–1993	7%
1994	8% (March), 9% (July), 10% (August)
1995	11% (March), 12% (April), 11% (July)
1996	9.5% (January), 8.5% (February), 9% (June), 9.5% (July), 10% (August)

Source: Bulgarian National Bank Annual Reports.

Whatever the measures undertaken by the central bank to tighten monetary policy, the continued provision of funds to the government and to the commercial banks counteracted their restrictive impact. The depreciating exchange rate and the high inflation triggered a shift from national currency to foreign currency deposits, observable after 1994. The share of foreign currency deposits in quasi-money increased from 20.7 per cent in December 1990 to 60 per cent at the end of 1996 and close to 80 per cent at the end of 1997 (see Figure 12.6). In the turbulent environment of 1996 (a run on banks) and the hyperinflationary first two months of 1997 dollarization spread to most retail trade operations, too. By then economic agents, having become highly sensitive to the exchange rate fluctuations,

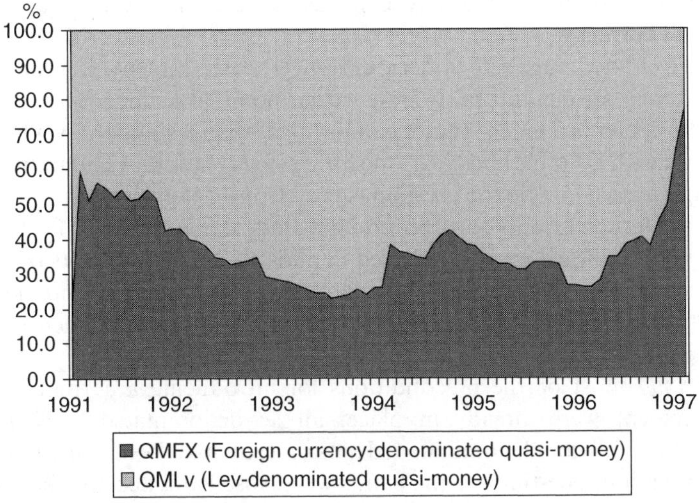

Source: Bulgarian National Bank.

Figure 12.6 Bulgaria: currency structure of quasi-money (1991–1997)

were immediately converting their wages into foreign currency (predominantly US dollars). Demand for foreign currency spiked and the depreciation of the exchange rate quickly spilled over to prices. The annual nominal interest rate reached three-digit levels.

The welfare and output loss caused by the crisis were much higher than the initial costs of transition (see Appendix Table 12.1A). At the beginning of 1997 the Bulgarian economy was characterized by: total loss of confidence; a significant loss of income and wealth; preserved dominance of the inefficient economic structure created under the socialist regime; a high sensitivity of prices to exchange rate dynamics and a high degree of dollarization. It seemed at that time that only a crucial change in economic policy might bring back confidence, establish macroeconomic stability and restore growth prospects.

EXCHANGE RATE AND MONETARY POLICIES SINCE 1997: THE CURRENCY BOARD ARRANGEMENT

In the first two months of 1997 the country was in chaos, with unwinding hyperinflation, and on the verge of complete dollarization. The currency board seemed the best policy capable of restoring confidence in the national currency.

The fixed exchange rate under a currency board framework usually provides a very strong and fairly transparent nominal anchor. The currency board represents a much stricter commitment than a standard peg because it comes with a simple and clear rule for money creation. A commitment to manage a currency board presupposes a strong determination to impose hard budget constraints on all economic agents, as announced in Parliament by the new political majority elected in mid-1997. The prospects of future EU membership for Bulgaria, though quite vague at that time, provided an exit strategy, very important for building up the implied confidence in the arrangement.

By 1997 most of the preconditions for introducing a currency board arrangement were already in place: all lev-denominated debt in real terms (and all lev-denominated deposits too) had been wiped out by hyperinflation; one-third of the banks were closed and declared bankrupt, only the strongest survived; the reserve money level in USD was twice below the level of the international reserves at the prevailing exchange rate (see Figure 12.7).

The loss of output was so deep in 1997 that the potential growth rate was quite high. The obsolescent fixed assets coupled with skilled-but-low-paid

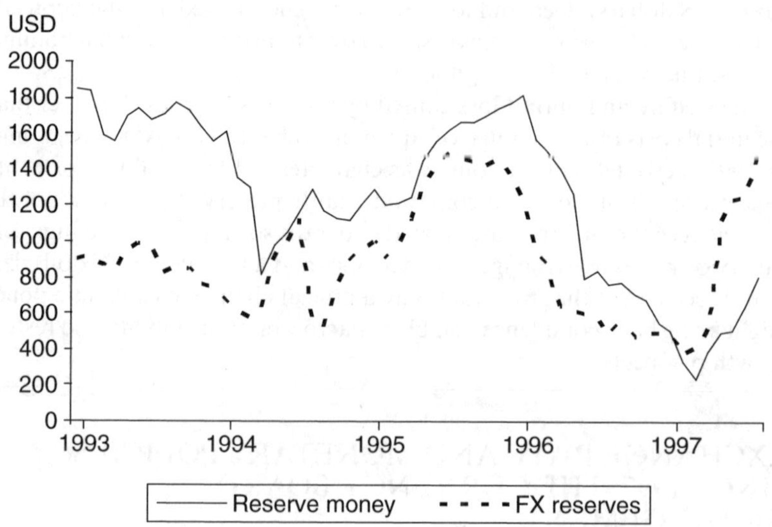

Source: Bulgarian National Bank.

Figure 12.7 Bulgaria: reserve money and international reserves (in USD)

Table 12.4 Bulgaria: monetary and credit aggregates, 1997–2003 (in per cent of GDP)

	1997	1998	1999	2000	2001	2002	2003
Broad money	34.1	29.6	31.7	36.8	41.7	42.9	46.3
Domestic credit	20.8	15.6	15.3	17.8	20.2	23.7	28.7
Lev-denominated domestic credit	6.3	7.3	5.6	8.1	10.1	13.1	15.8
Government domestic credit	11.48	5.07	3.22	5.26	5.27	3.90	2.14
Non-government domestic credit	9.33	10.56	12.08	12.57	14.95	19.79	26.53

Source: Bulgarian National Bank.

labour had to attract foreign investment. Moreover, while the EU rejected Bulgaria's request for opening accession negotiations in 1997, there was still hope that the EU might one day arrive at a different opinion if the necessary reforms took place.

At that time the government was running huge primary surpluses and the expected decline in domestic interest rates after the introduction of the currency board had to reduce the cash deficit and hence government debt to a sustainable level (see Table 12.4).

The stabilization programme of 1997 was supported by the IMF and its goals were: to restore the confidence in the national currency and the banking system and to lay the foundations for sustained economic growth. The main components of the economic policy mix of the programme were the establishment of the currency board arrangement and the prohibition of central bank financing of the budget. Price liberalization was again on the agenda since in the efforts to contain inflation the governments in 1992–1996 had increased the number of goods and services with administered prices, pushing their weight in the consumption basket beyond 50 per cent. Furthermore, the agricultural reform was in the middle of nowhere. The privatization of state-owned enterprises and the liquidation of the loss makers was of the highest priority.

In general, under a fixed exchange rate regime the structural changes may be as likely to happen as they may not happen. The government still has some freedom to continue with a policy of interventions and protection of loss makers, deliberately building shelters against competition. In such a case the peg will soon be undermined. The collapse of a fixed exchange rate regime, especially under a currency board regime, would bring much higher

Table 12.5 Bulgaria: main macroeconomic indicators in 1997–1998

	1997 programme	1997 actual	1998 actual
Real GDP growth rate (%)	−4.8	−5.6	4.0
Inflation – average (%)	–	1058.4	18.7
Inflation – end of year (%)	768.8	547.7	1.6
Annual nominal average wage growth rate (%)	–	884.2	146.9
General government deficit (in % of GDP)	−4.1	−2.0	+0.9
Current account balance (in USD million)	7.0	1046.3	−61.4
Gross official reserves with monetary gold (in USD million)	1621	2474	3056

Source: National Statistical Institute; Bulgarian National Bank; Ministry of Finance.

losses than a floating exchange rate (the regrettable example of Argentina). For this reason the introduction of the currency board arrangement in Bulgaria was tightly packed with an ambitious programme to implement the long-postponed structural reforms and to insert financial discipline into the system – the core difference between the economic policies of the period before 1997. It should be reported that the objectives of the 1997 stabilization programme have been met well (see Table 12.5).[3] Since 1997 Bulgaria has maintained the selected macroeconomic policy mix, sponsored by a sequence of IMF stand-by agreements, the last – a precautionary one – having been approved in August 2004.

In July 1997, when the new BNB Law entered into force, the exchange rate was fixed at DEM 1 to BGL 1000, and later to the euro, under the currency board arrangement.[4] The BNB's monetary liabilities are fully covered by foreign reserves. The monetary base consists, roughly in equal halves, of the monetary liabilities and the government's accounts with the central bank. The excess of foreign reserves over the monetary liabilities accumulates in a special account that can be used when a lender of last resort is needed.

According to the money supply rule the central bank exchanges unlimited amounts of national currency against reserve currency at the fixed exchange rate. The BNB Law forbids any central bank financing of budgetary expenses either directly or by purchases of government securities or in any other form. So, unlike under the failed currency board of Argentina, in Bulgaria national government securities are not included in the foreign reserves and no distortions in the balancing level of the exchange rate might happen.[5] The BNB Law also prohibits commercial banks refinancing except in the case of systemic crisis and against collateral of highest quality, when the lender-of-last-resort facility might be activated.[6]

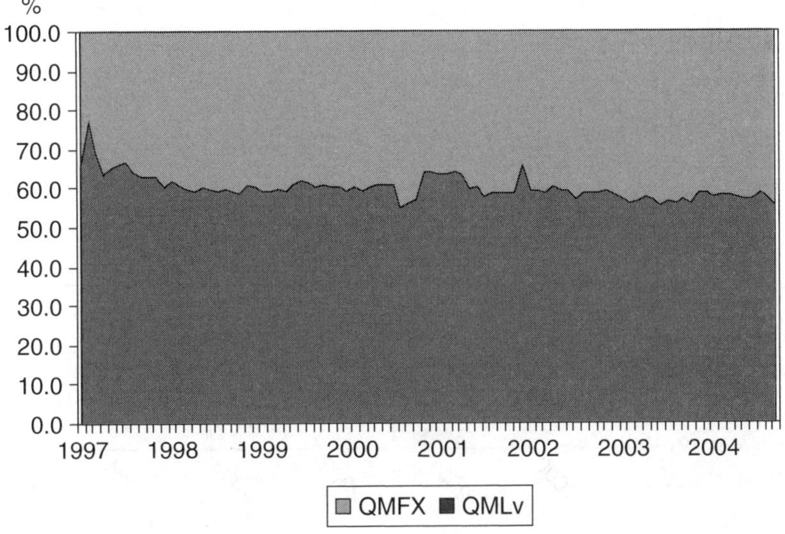

Source: Bulgarian National Bank.

Figure 12.8 Bulgaria: currency structure of quasi-money (1997–2004)

The economic policy implemented was capable of blocking the process of dollarization and of inspiring confidence in the national currency.

Recent research based on data covering the period after the introduction of the currency board arrangement did not detect a permanent effect of the USD/BGL dynamics on consumer prices and wages, which represents statistical evidence that the period of dollarization in Bulgaria is over.[7] The most important change occurred in the currency structure of exports and imports due to the fixed exchange rate of the national currency, and motivated by the substantial reduction in custom tariffs between Bulgaria and the EU. The share of European currencies in exports increased from 36.7 per cent in 1999 to 60.7 per cent in 2003 and in imports respectively from 46.8 per cent to 62.7 per cent. The level of dollarization, measured by the share of foreign currency deposits in quasi-money remains relatively high with a subtle tendency of a decline (see Figure 12.8).[8]

The most important outcomes of the currency board arrangement are the stability of nominal variables, the continuously improving economic performance and the acceleration of economic growth (see Figures 12.9 and 12.10).[9]

Macroeconomic stability based on the currency board arrangement reduced the overall level of interest rates. The deposit rate remains quite

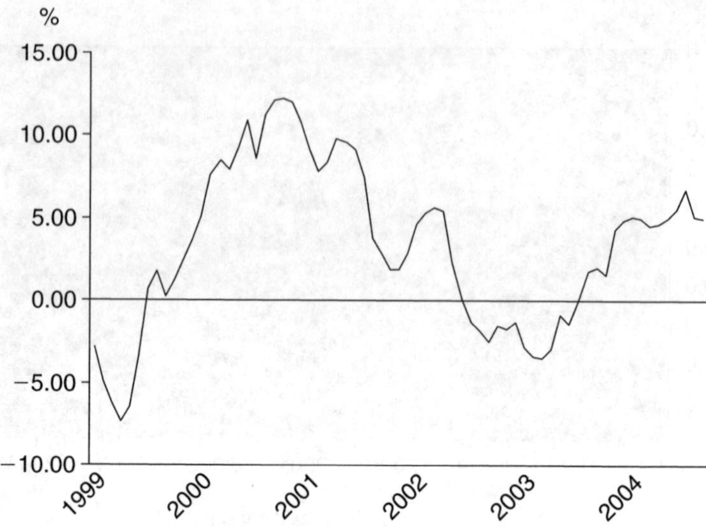

Source: National Statistical Institute.

Figure 12.9 Bulgaria: core inflation annual rates (1999–August 2004)

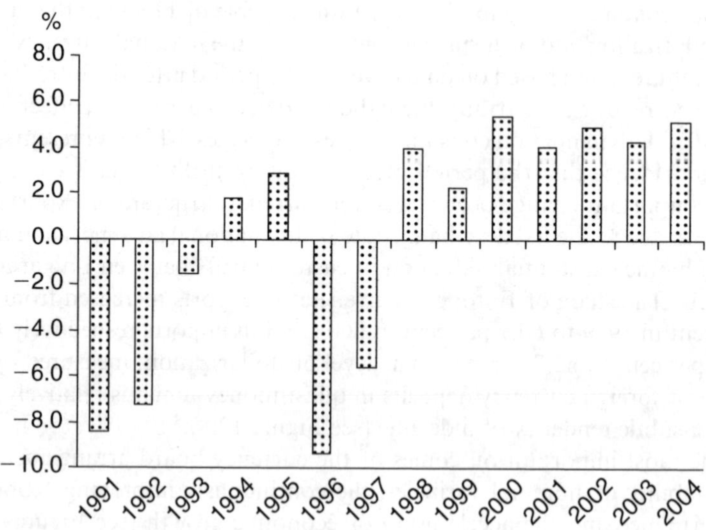

Source: National Statistical Institute.

Figure 12.10 Bulgaria: economic growth

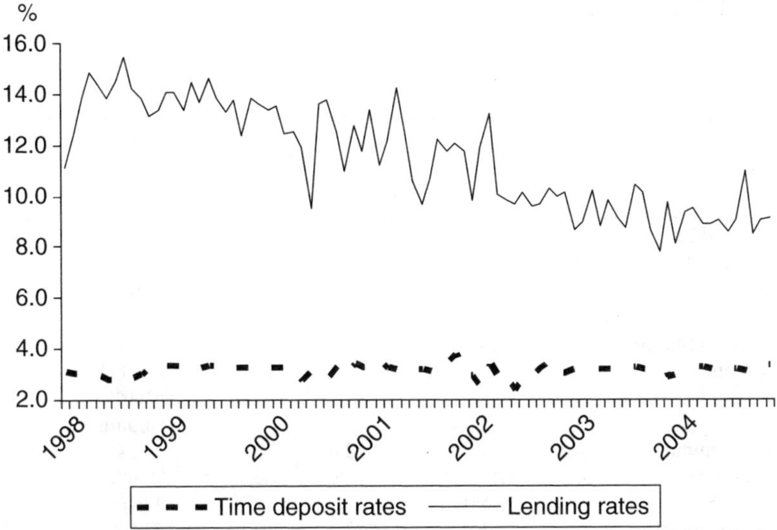

Source: Bulgarian National Bank.

Figure 12.11 Bulgaria: time deposits and lending rates (October 1997–August 2004)

stable while lending rates are gradually declining and may converge to the average euro area level in the near future (see Figure 12.11).

THE PERSPECTIVES

Bulgaria is expected to join the EU in January 2007. A national consensus has been achieved that the currency board arrangement will be operated until Bulgaria's entry in the EU and in the euro area.[10] All components of the macroeconomic policy mix will be subordinated to achieving the Maastricht criteria in the interim period of the exchange rate mechanism (ERM) II. Bulgaria has made the commitment to maintain the currency board arrangement unilaterally until euro area entry, perceived to happen in 2009–2010.

The potential for relatively high growth rates is far from exhausted and Bulgaria has become an attractive FDI destination in the last couple of years. The continuing deepening of structural reforms, initiated by the comprehensive privatization, enhances the efficiency of production and persistently reduces unit labour costs – a measure of improving competitiveness.

APPENDIX 12A.1

Table 12.1A Bulgaria: main economic indicators (per cent)

	1990	1991	1992–1995 (average)	1996	1997	1998–2003 (average)
GDP growth rates	−9.1	−8.4	−1.7	−9.4	−5.6	4.2
Average inflation rate	26.3	338.5 (Feb–122.9)	80.0	122.0	1058.38 (Jan–242.3)	8.0
Average exchange rate (annual change)	–	5-fold (Feb–6-fold)	68.0	165	9-fold (Jan and Feb – by 100% per month	2.1
Average annual interest rate	4.5	45.8 (August 54)	52.6	127 (Sept 300)	72.4 (March 136.6)	4.2
Average annual short-term lending interest rate	–	65.6	83.2	291.06	213.0	11.7
Broad money to GDP ratio	110.6	76.3	75.3	74.8	34.1	38.2
Net domestic credit to GDP	148.6	118.5	106.4	108.7	20.8	20.2
Level of foreign reserves (USD million, monetary gold excluded)	125 (end of year)	516 (end of year)	1236.5 (end of 1995)	483 (end of year)	2111.6 (end of year)	6291.0 (end of 2003)

Table 12.2A Bulgaria: the stabilization programmes of 1991 and 1997

	1991 (February 14 letter of Intent and Memorandum of Economic Policy)	1997 (March 24 1997 Memorandum of Economic Policy)
The programme aims at:	1. To end the chronic excess demand and stabilize the economy in new macro-framework 2. To take essential steps towards adopting market mechanisms in the economic system	1. Stabilizing the economy 2. Restoring the confidence in the national currency – the lev and the banking system 3. Alleviating the very high costs stemming from the recent crisis, addressing long-standing structural problems in the real sector

Table 12.2A (continued)

	1991 (February 14 letter of Intent and Memorandum of Economic Policy)	1997 (March 24 1997 Memorandum of Economic Policy)
		4. Laying the foundations for sustained economic growth and external vulnerability
Specific targets	1. To contain the further decline of the economy by striving for a recovery in the second half of the year 2. To rapidly reduce the rate of inflation to a monthly rate of 1–2 per cent in the second half of the year 3. To limit the external current account deficit	1. The economy is expected to begin recovering during the second quarter of the year 2. Inflation is expected to decline to 2 per cent monthly by year end 3. A small current account surplus
Main stabilization components	1. A comprehensive price reform (liberalization of prices) 2. A reform of the exchange rate system – the introduction of a free exchange market for commercial banks and a free floating exchange rate 3. The basic interest rate of the central bank is the main instrument to implement a tight monetary policy 4. Nominal anchors: • Limits on the growth of nominal wages • Nominal consolidated budget deficit target and a target for 3.5 per cent deficit to GDP in 1991 • Ceilings on the net credit to government • Credit ceilings for non-government sector • *Tax reform and budgetary expenditures restructuring (reduction in subsidies, reducing the number of government employees,*	1. Establishment of a currency board arrangement in order to anchor the exchange rate expectations 2. Prohibition of central bank financing of the budget 3. Financial and banking sector reform that restores confidence in and the soundness of the banking system and prepares it for operation under the CBA 4. Enterprise reform to substantially reduce quasi-fiscal deficits and to liquidate unviable enterprises 5. Other structural reforms including land reform and price and trade liberalization, especially in the agricultural sector, and removal of impediments to the development of markets and foreign investment.

Table 12.2A (continued)

	1991 (February 14 letter of Intent and Memorandum of Economic Policy)	1997 (March 24 1997 Memorandum of Economic Policy)
	reducing expenditures on defence and security, improving the efficiency of budgetary expenses allocation)	
Structural reforms	1. Transformation of the state enterprise sector 2. Agricultural reform 3. Financial sector reform – establishing an independent central bank	

APPENDIX 12A.2

Central Bank: Commercial Banks Relationship in 1991–1996

The interrelations between the central bank and commercial banks developed in the period 1991–1996 against the backdrop of the ongoing banking system reform based on the introduction of market mechanisms. During the socialist rule the central bank centralized all financial resources of the few existing banks and also provided them with liquidity according to the approved national development plans. In 1990 the central bank stopped collecting commercial banks' resources and imposed minimum reserve requirements (5 per cent of the deposit base). In 1991 the establishment of the interbank money market allowed the commercial banks to trade their excess reserves. Since the process of transformation needed time, at the beginning the central bank deposited resources in the commercial banks on bilateral terms in order to provide them with liquid funds. Later this facility was transformed and the central bank offered deposits at regular auctions. In late 1991 the central bank started discount operations, granting loans to the commercial banks against collateral, promissory notes in particular. In 1992 as the government securities market developed and deepened the Lombard loans were introduced. In June 1994 open market operations were launched and they initially squeezed out the other standing facilities of the central bank.

NOTES

1. The moratorium was announced in March 1990.
2. It is important to note that wages in 1990 had been raised considerably and coupled with the uncertainty about the exact moment of price liberalization caused an excess stockpiling of households and firms, initiating huge shortages of food.
3. See the IMF reports on the progress of Bulgaria under the EFF (Extended Fund Facility (IMF)) programme.
4. Under the currency board arrangement the national currency, the lev, was fixed to the Deutschmark by law, which also provided for an automatic re-pegging to the euro, once it should come into existence. Due to this provision the switch from the Deutsche mark as an anchor currency to the euro took place without a concomitant amendment of the BNB Law and without speculations about the exchange rate. In July 1999 due to the overall macroeconomic stabilization and restoration in confidence, the national currency was redenominated at the rate of DEM 1 = BGN 1.
5. The design of the Bulgarian currency board contains two safeguards – a fiscal reserve account and a banking department account. The foreign reserves cover more than twice the monetary base.
6. Since the introduction of the currency board, until now no commercial bank has resorted to central bank refinancing.
7. I am indebted to Ilijan Georgiev (European University Institute, Florence) for this co-integration analysis.
8. In Liviatan (1992, p. 2) Sebastian Edwards notes: 'It now appears that when currency substitution comes, it's there to stay'.
9. For information of recent economic developments in Bulgaria and the short-term projections see the quarterly publication of the Bulgarian National Bank 'Economic Review'.
10. On 25 November 2004 the Council of Ministers of the Republic of Bulgaria and the Bulgarian National Bank signed an Agreement on the policy and commitments to be followed in the process of introducing the euro in the Republic of Bulgaria in the period until 2009/10. The Agreement was signed in keeping with the announced Negotiation Position under Chapter 11 'Economic and Monetary Union' and in line with the Pre-accession Economic Programme of the Republic of Bulgaria (PEP) 2002–2005, and PEP 2004–2007. As from the date of its membership of the European Union (EU) the Republic of Bulgaria will also join the Economic and Monetary Union (EMU) taking the irrevocable commitment to become a member of the euro area and to introduce the single European currency, the euro, in compliance with the procedures provided for in the Treaty on the European Community, in the Report of the Council of Economics and Finance Ministers (Ecofin Council) of 7 November 2000 regarding the aspects of the exchange rate policy during the enlargement process, and in accordance with the position of the Governing Council of the European Central Bank (ECB) of 18 December 2003.

REFERENCES

Agency for Economic Coordination and Development (1991), *The Year of the Iron Sheep*, Sofia: Agency for Economic Coordination and Development.

Camilleri Gilson, Marie-Thérèse (2004), 'An institutional framework for comparing emerging market currency boards', *IMF Working Paper* No. 04/180, International Monetary Fund.

Gulde, Anne-Marie, J.S. Kahkonen and P.M. Keller (2000), 'Pros and cons of currency board arrangements in the lead-up to EU accession and participation in the euro zone', *IMF Policy Discussion Paper* No. 00/1, International Monetary Fund.

Hanke, S. and K. Schuler (1991), 'Teeth for the Bulgarian Lev: A currency board solution', Washington, DC: International Freedom Foundation.

Liviatan, Nissan (ed.) (1992), 'Proceedings of a conference on currency substitution and currency boards', *World Bank Discussion Papers*, 207, The World Bank.

Nenova, M. (2004), 'The relationship between real convergence and the real exchange rate: The case of Bulgaria', *BNB Discussion Papers DP/41/2004*, Bulgarian National Bank.

Nenova, M., N. Micheva, Tz. Manchev and A. Mihailov (1997), *Financial Policy in Bulgaria in the Period of Transition to a Market Economy*, Sofia: Bulgarian National Bank.

Perry, Guillermo E. (ed.), G. Calvo, M. Corden, S. Fischer, Sir A. Walters and John Wiliamson (1997), *Currency Boards and External Shocks. How Much Pain, How Much Gain?*, Washington: The World Bank.

PART IV

FDI and Trade as Pivotal Elements for Catching up and Competitiveness

13. FDI and trade as pivotal elements for catching up and competitiveness

Ewald Nowotny

1. SOUTH-EAST EUROPEAN COUNTRIES AND A STRATEGY OF EXPORT-LED GROWTH

The countries of South-East Europe (SEE) are a very inhomogeneous group, both with regard to their economic and political structures and with regard to their relationship with the EU. But for all of these countries a strategy of export-led growth appears to be the most promising way for economically sustainable development. This is immediately obvious for the many small countries of this region, but is relevant also for Romania, the biggest country.

A policy of export-led growth is directly relevant for tackling the problems of high current account deficits. This problem is relevant for most of the countries of the region and has to been seen as one of the major policy restrictions for more expansionist government policies – policy restrictions in many cases institutionalized by IMF agreements (see Table 13.1). One also has to be aware that for the countries of the Western Balkans the external balances shown in this table are the current account deficits after grants. Current account deficits before grants are substantially higher in some countries; in Bosnia and Herzegovina for instance they account for 21.3 per cent of GDP – which is clearly an unsustainable situation.

From a longer-term perspective a policy of export-led growth has the even more important effect of enforcing international standards of quality and reliability and thus advancing long-term structural change with regard to institutions, educational and training systems. First of all to be able to qualify as a reliable supplier, economic and political stability is an important condition, as is an adequate supply of infrastructure services with regard to transportation, telecommunication and energy. In South-East Europe (but also in other regions), there is a short-term and medium-term problem of power shortages in many cases, which may become one of

Table 13.1 Foreign trade and FDI

	Current account in % of GDP	FDI (inflow, net) in EUR billion
Romania		
2000	−3.7	1.2
2003	−5.8	1.4
2004	−6.2	3.0
2005	−5.8	2.2
Bulgaria		
2000	−5.6	1.0
2003	−8.4	1.2
2004	−8.2	1.8
2005	−8.0	1.7
Croatia		
2000	−2.5	1.2
2003	−7.3	1.7
2004	−6.4	1.1
2005	−5.5	1.1
Macedonia		
2000	−2.0	0.2
2003	−6.0	0.08
2004	−6.1	0.1
2005	−5.7	0.1
Serbia and Montenegro		
2000	−3.9	0.03
2003	−8.8	1.1
2004	11.7	n.a.
2005	−11.7	n.a.
Albania		
2000	−7.4	0.2
2003	−8.5	0.1
Bosnia and Herzegovina		
2000	−12.5	0.2
2003	−17.5	0.3

Sources: European Commission, DG for Economic and Financial Affairs, Occasional Papers No. 5, 'The Western Balkans in transition', Brussels, January 2004; L. Podkaminer et al. (2004), 'Transition countries on the eve of EU enlargement', The Vienna Institute for International Economic Studies, wiiw Research Reports 303, Vienna; Bank Austria, CEE Report, 3/2004. 2004, 2005: forecasts.

the major obstacles for foreign direct investment (FDI) in the industrial sectors.

A further important macroeconomic condition is a monetary policy that avoids an overvaluation of the national currency. Here a conflict of goals with policies of strict stability orientation may arise. Experience shows that it might be better to follow a 'middle way' – after all a policy of following unrealistic fixed exchange rate regimes has often been a sure recipe for disaster.

Another important prerequisite for a strategy of export-led growth is, of course, adequate access to export markets. There are encouraging developments concerning overcoming the fragmentation of the regional SEE market. To a large extent thanks to the efforts of the Stability Pact for South Eastern Europe, 28 bilateral free trade agreements between the countries of SEE have been signed up to now and it can be expected that this will boost intra-regional trade. To a large extent this will also depend on technical–institutional improvements, for instance with regard to border procedures.

The main issue for the region is, however, full access to EU markets. This will be the case for new EU members. For all other countries in the region Association Agreements are in different stages of existence or preparation. With regard to trade policy this means the creation of free trade arrangements, which, however, do not fully apply to agricultural products – an area where the region has special comparative advantages.

There is a certain fear that EU membership of Romania and Bulgaria (and hopefully also Croatia) in 2007/09 could create new trade barriers in the region. To a certain extent this is an unavoidable side effect of a step-by-step admission procedure. But the examples of Slovenia and Hungary seem to demonstrate that closer proximity to EU members has overall positive effects for the countries of the SEE region and also offers learning experiences.

2. THE FDI EXPERIENCE

Whereas current account developments are still unsatisfactory in most countries of SEE, recent developments with regard to FDI show a mixed picture. (For detailed country reviews and an institutional and legal overview see: OECD, Stability Pact, 2003).

2003 and especially 2004 have brought about a substantial increase of FDI in the EU accession countries Romania and Bulgaria, which is in remarkable contrast to developments in the new EU member countries, where in 2003 a rapid decline of FDI from EUR 21 billion to EUR 9.3 billion was observed. Obviously after a first round of FDI very much connected with privatizations in the new EU members, interest – and chances – for FDI is now moving to the next round of accession countries. In the past, new EU members have often enjoyed above-average FDI inflows after entry, a process that now seems to be accelerating in the cases of Romania and Bulgaria.

For the other countries of the region FDI inflows still show an unsatisfactory performance with little prospect of improvement (see Table 13.1). Yet it has to be recognized that even this slow process has led to massive structural changes. As in other countries, in the countries of SEE, inward FDI stock as a percentage of GDP also increased substantially in the relatively short period from 1995 to 2001 (Table 13.2). This has a substantial impact not only on economic, but also on institutional developments in the respective countries, an impact that is bound to increase in the near future. So for instance in Romania inward FDI stock as a percentage of GDP, which had been only 2.3 per cent in 1995, increased to 20.5 per cent in 2001

Table 13.2 Catching up: inward FDI stock as a percentage of GDP in CEE, 1995 and 2001 (per cent)

Country/Region	1995	2001
Estonia	14.4	65.9
Czech Republic	14.1	64.3
Moldova, Republic of	6.5	45.0
Slovakia	4.4	43.2
Hungary	26.7	38.2
Latvia	12.5	32.4
Lithuania	5.8	28.9
Croatia	2.5	28.4
Bulgaria	3.4	25.0
Poland	6.2	24.0
FYR of Macedonia	0.8	23.9
Slovenia	9.4	23.1
Albania	8.3	21.0
Romania	2.3	20.5
Serbia and Montenegro	2.7	20.1
Bosnia and Herzegovina	1.1	15.8
Memorandum:		
Central and Eastern Europe	5.3	20.9
World	10.3	22.5

Source: UNCTAD, FDI/NC database.

and will have increased substantially in 2004/05 due to the recent massive inflow of privatization-connected FDI.

The notion of FDI is however a very inhomogeneous one. On the one hand there are greenfield investments, typically in the automobile industry. These investments are mostly export-oriented, which is of special relevance for a strategy of export-led growth. The main challenge for the host countries in these cases is to provide adequate infrastructure for the greenfield investment sites. This relates especially to transport and power supply and may involve substantial public investments to be undertaken within a tight time schedule. Apart from technical and financial challenges this may also involve the need to deal with private land owners hoping to exploit their specific strategic position. Strange as it may sound, therefore fair but effective expropriation laws for the benefit of public infrastructure are an important element of efficient investment promotion policies – and also an important element in the fight against some form of corruption and 'Mafia'-related activities. 'Greenfield' FDI is also of special relevance for investment activities by foreign small and medium-sized companies (SMEs). These companies shy away from the risks of privatizing big, usually overstaffed existing companies, but look for ways of outsourcing labour-intensive parts of their production. A successful example is for instance the cluster of investments by North Italian SMEs in Croatia.

3. FDI AND PRIVATIZATIONS

Up to now most FDI in SEE (and also in Central Europe) has been related with privatization activities. This process is almost finished in Central Europe but will continue to be a main driving force for FDI in SEE. SEE thus has the chance to learn some lessons from privatization-related FDI from Central Europe, but also from other EU countries, such as Spain. There are a number of cases where nationally or otherwise collectively owned enterprises have suffered an economic breakdown or have no chance to become internationally competitive. The (near) collapse of some major banks of the region or the fate of some basic industry state conglomerates are cases in point. Here selling these companies to foreign investors is usually the only alternative to a total breakdown with – as in the case of financial institutions – far-reaching damaging effects for the whole economy.

A more difficult question arises with regard to public-owned companies that are, at least in the medium term, economically viable and are thus, of course, of special interest for foreign investors. As the strategy of these potential investors may also influence the positions of the EU side in negotiations, this is a field where conflicts between the EU and national governments may come up – as became evident for instance during Slovenia's accession negotiations. First of all it has to be recognized that the EU treaty in the context of the Single European Market has a number of provisions against distorting state interventions but is neutral with regard to the question of public or private ownership – a distinction which is not always fully observed in actual EU policy. The volume and structure of privatizations thus remains the responsibility of national governments and should be discussed with pragmatic, rather than ideological perspectives.

A particularly sensitive point is whether in connection with privatization-related FDI it is possible or advisable to refer to a notion of 'public' or 'national interest'. This, by the way, is a discussion not restricted to SEE but one of high importance in many EU countries such as France, Germany and Austria. Following a pragmatic approach there are no general recipes, but one important aspect will be to what extent foreign ownership can influence the medium- to long-term development perspectives of the company involved. In some cases for companies in SEE the long-term chance for survival may be to become beneficiaries of outsourcing activities of big international companies, exploiting the advantages of low labour costs. Yet this also implies that these investments will move on to still cheaper sites as soon as this becomes politically and economically feasible. Some of the more advanced Central European countries are already experiencing this problem, but it also affects countries like Spain, where most of the export-related industries are in foreign ownership.

Under a longer-term perspective a more promising – but difficult to achieve – approach may be to try a policy that in addition to offering low-cost production sites also creates chances for entrepreneurial activities especially with regard to 'own' R&D activities or 'own' international marketing strategies by the companies involved. Such a policy of keeping a certain element of strategic decision making and thus to keep some 'headquarter-functions' in the countries involved, will usually also involve the need to exert some influence on the ownership side, at least by retaining the position of a 'core shareholder'. Such a strategy may be relevant especially with regard to export-oriented industries with a certain potential for 'own' technological and marketing know-how. This is the case for instance with regard to certain export-oriented industries in Slovenia and Croatia, whereas unfortunately in most countries of SEE chances for such a long-term strategy seem to be rather limited. This strategy of securing 'endogenous development perspectives' is also less relevant with regard to ownership in the fields of financial services, where the need to get rid of distorting political influences and the need to 'import' reputation and efficiency may be of higher importance. Nevertheless it may also be advisable for SEE countries to have, in addition to a strong private, foreign-owned banking sector, some public, 'KfW type'[1] financial instruction that may serve as a public development bank, for instance for aspects of regional development or for supporting SMEs. In some countries financing institutions of this kind do exist; for instance KfW has a substantial presence in Croatia.

4. FDI IN INFRASTRUCTURE

A differentiated approach is also necessary with regard to FDI in infrastructure. In fields like energy and telecom investments, FDI – connected with privatizations – may give access to new technological and managerial know-how. Moreover, besides financing new investments, foreign ownership may be seen as a guarantee for providing adequate maintenance; neglect of maintenance being one of the main problems of 'traditional' infrastructure management in SEE. Obviously the privatization of infrastructure will be connected with the need to install efficient and fair national regulating agencies. Efficient regulation of what had been natural monopolies has proved to be an extremely difficult task all over the world – it is all the more so in SEE. This holds especially for small countries, where per capita costs of efficient regulation will be very high. In the medium and long run regulation problems, connected with questions of pricing policy, may create serious tensions between foreign investors and national governments and are thus one of the main risks for infrastructure-related FDI. There exist valid economic and governance arguments to install something like regional regulating agencies, instead of many national institutions, for major fields of infrastructure; the political chances to put such a proposal into practice are however very small at the moment.

With regard to transport infrastructure, especially roads and motorways, there exist many proposals to involve foreign private investors, sometimes advocating very sophisticated financing schemes. Experience in Central Europe and also in SEE has shown that in many cases 'simple is better'. That means that direct public financing, supported for instance by long-term EIB loans, or in the case of EU member countries structural funds or a 'simple' concession model for financing a new motorway may be preferable to a sophisticated private/public partnership structure. It is also important to have a realistic forecast with regard to the level of fees, tolls, and so on that are needed for private financing of infrastructure projects. The low per capita income in most SEE countries means that for instance with regard to toll roads the level of tolls that is 'acceptable' for the public may be too low for a realistic financing plan.

5. SUMMING UP

There is no doubt that FDI and trade are pivotal elements for catching up and competitiveness for the countries of SEE. Both trade and FDI are central elements for a strategy of export-led growth, which is the most promising development strategy especially for the smaller countries of the region. Up to now, however, most countries have shown substantial external imbalances, which underlines the need for an export-oriented economic policy on the one hand and better access to EU markets on the other hand.

FDI has shown a very volatile development in the past years. But for those countries close to EU accession it can already be observed that interest for FDI has grown substantially. This holds both for privatization-related FDI and for greenfield FDI. A major challenge for the region will be to be able to participate in the car assembly bonanza currently observed in Central and Eastern Europe. According to UNCTAD Investment Report (2003) as many as 13 car industry projects are under way or in concrete preparation in the CEE countries, compared with only one project (Renault in Pitesti, Romania) listed for SEE. As the car industry is a leading industry for a great number of suppliers, some of them also SMEs, it will be of strategic importance for SEE to profit from this big eastward shift of one of Europe's major industries. Given the huge amounts of capital involved and the special infrastructure needs of this industry, political and economic stability are necessary conditions to be successful in the challenging competition for this kind of FDI. But, of course, not only for this kind. . .

NOTE

1. KfW: Kreditanstalt für Wiederaufbau, the big development bank owned by the German government.

REFERENCES

OECD Stability Pact (2003), 'South-East Europe Compact for Reform, Investment, Integrity and Growth. National Treatment of International Investment in South-East European Countries: Measures Providing Exceptions', Paris, October.

UNCTAD (2003), *World Investment Report 2003. FDI Policies for Development: National and International Perspectives*, New York; Geneva: UN.

14. Foreign direct investment in South-East Europe: what do the data tell us?

Dimitri G. Demekas, Balázs Horváth, Elina Ribakova and Yi Wu[1]

INTRODUCTION: WHY ANOTHER PIECE ON FOREIGN DIRECT INVESTMENT?

Foreign direct investment (FDI), its determinants and its effects, has been extensively studied. It has long been recognized that the benefits for the host country can be significant, including knowledge and technology transfer to domestic firms and the labour force, productivity spillovers, enhanced competition, and improved access for exports abroad, notably to the source country. Moreover, since FDI flows are non-debt creating, they are a preferred method of financing external current account deficits, especially in developing countries, where these deficits can be large and sustained. At the same time, FDI can be a mixed blessing. In small economies, large foreign companies can – and often do – abuse their dominant market position. Large investors are sometimes able to coax concessions in return for locating investment there, and aggressively use transfer pricing to minimize their tax obligations. Multinational corporations attempt to influence the domestic political process, especially in developing countries. And FDI can give rise to potentially volatile balance of payment flows.[2] Graham (1995), Borensztein et al. (1995) and Lim (2001), to name but a few, provide useful overall surveys of the literature on the impact of FDI on the host country. Holland and Pain (1998) present the evidence on diffusion of innovation, and Javorcik (2004), Javorcik et al. (2004) and Alfaro et al. (2003) discuss productivity spillovers. Finally, Lipschitz et al. (2002) present a good theoretical overview of the policy implications of large capital flows, including FDI.

The case for FDI is particularly compelling in transition economies. The need for extensive enterprise restructuring and modernization against the background of limited domestic resources creates an environment where the potential benefits of FDI are especially valuable. Also, transition economies are well placed to benefit from the technology transfer associated with FDI: they are relatively developed and possess a highly educated labour force (the aforementioned study by Borensztein et al., 1995, finds that the impact of FDI on growth is larger when the host country labour force is highly educated). Finally, the balance of payments crises of the 1980s and 1990s have highlighted the importance of non-debt creating capital flows for external sustainability during the transition process (underscored by the evidence presented in Frankel and Rose, 1996). As a result, attracting FDI has become a prominent item on the policy agenda, especially in transition economies, and research on the determinants of FDI has been expanding rapidly.

SO WHY ANOTHER PIECE ON FDI?

- First, because the proliferating 'initiatives' to attract or promote FDI, often enthusiastically supported by donors and international organizations, though well-intentioned, overestimate the impact of policies and sometimes rest on false premises: the extensive literature reviewed in the following section, as well as our own findings, suggest that factors outside the reach of policy makers are at least as important as policies in influencing FDI; and that the impact of some policies widely seen as good for the economy as a whole may actually have ambiguous effects on FDI. Re-assessing the received wisdom can thus contribute to more realistic and better-targeted policies.
- Second, because the existing empirical literature focuses on the analysis of total FDI flows, including for privatization. In transition economies, however, privatization-related FDI flows can be sizeable, lumpy, and time-bound, and their inclusion in the analysis may distort the results. We correct for privatization-related foreign inflows and examine the determinants of 'underlying' FDI.
- Third, because the prevailing empirical approach implicitly assumes that policies to attract FDI operate in a vacuum: in reality, however, there are limits to how much the host country's policies can be adjusted, and these limits are often given by what neighbours and competitors are doing. We develop techniques that can gauge what policies can realistically be expected to achieve in terms of additional FDI in this environment.
- And fourth, because South-East (SE) Europe is largely absent from the existing literature:[3] of over 40 original empirical studies

we reviewed, only four cover some of the SE European countries, and the coverage is patchy and inconsistent. Our chapter covers all seven SE European countries and compares their experience with that of their neighbours in Central Europe, the Baltics, and the CIS.

THE RECEIVED WISDOM: THE FINDINGS OF PREVIOUS EMPIRICAL RESEARCH INTO THE DETERMINANTS OF FOREIGN DIRECT INVESTMENT

The existing empirical literature on the determinants of FDI can be categorized into two groups: studies focusing on aggregate, economy-wide FDI flows, and microeconomic (firm- or sector-level) studies, building on the work of R. Vernon (Vernon, 1966). In this section, we concentrate on the former, with emphasis on research covering transition economies.

To interpret the findings of the literature on the determinants of FDI, it is useful to keep in mind the distinction between two types of FDI identified in theory – although in real life this distinction is often blurred. Horizontal FDI (HFDI) is market-seeking investment, aimed primarily at the domestic market in the host country, when local production is seen as a more efficient way to penetrate this market than exports from the source country. Vertical FDI (VFDI) is cost-minimizing investment, when a multinational corporation chooses the location of each link of its production chain to minimize global costs. As a result of these differences in motivation, a number of host country factors, such as market size, trade restrictions, and transport costs, can be expected to have different effects on HFDI and VFDI. There is broad agreement that HFDI is more prevalent (Navaretti and Venables, 2004), but also some evidence that the recent surge in FDI flows to developing countries, in particular, was mainly VFDI (Hanson et al., 2001; Markusen and Maskus, 1999). Both types of FDI are in principle subject to 'agglomeration', that is clustering in certain locations where the existing business infrastructure is set up to serve a particular industry, and 'herding', where investors tend to follow a leader that establishes operations in a particular country.

Virtually all empirical studies find that gravity factors (market size and proximity of host to source country) are the most important determinants of FDI. Just as with trade flows (Breuss and Egger, 1999; Di Mauro, 2000; Feenstra et al., 2001), the gravity model consistently explains about 60 per cent of aggregate FDI flows to individual host countries, regardless of the region. Lankes and Venables (1996) and Lim (2001) provide useful literature surveys; Singh and Jun (1996) report the evidence on a large sample of developing countries; and Estrin et al. (1997); Claessens et al. (1998); Brenton et al. (1999); Bevan and Estrin (2000); Resmini (2000); Carstensen and Toubal (2004), and Janicki and Wunnava (2004) are among the most important studies focusing on transition economies. Since gravity factors are exogenous to policies, this finding puts into perspective the efforts of policy makers in host countries to attract FDI.

The policy environment, of course, does matter for FDI. At a very general level, a policy environment that promotes macroeconomic stability, ensures the rule of law and the enforcement of contracts, minimizes distortions, supports competitiveness, and encourages private sector development can be expected to stimulate all private investment, including foreign investment. But when empirical studies attempt to estimate the impact of individual policies on FDI, the results are often ambiguous.

Trade policies and, more broadly, trade costs (tariffs, non-tariff barriers, and transportation costs) are generally found to have a significant impact on FDI flows, but in aggregate regressions their sign is ambiguous. This is probably due to the different effect barriers to trade can be expected to have on horizontal and vertical FDI: they tend to attract HFDI, which aims at penetrating the domestic market, but repel VFDI. At the aggregate level, the sign would thus depend on which kind of FDI is prevalent in the particular host country. Empirical studies that decompose FDI into horizontal and vertical tend to support this hypothesis: Brainard (1997) finds that freight costs and tariffs have a positive effect on HFDI; Barrel and Pain (1999) report a similar result for protectionist measures; and Markusen and Maskus (1999), decomposing the sales of foreign-owned firms in the host country, find that higher trade costs stimulate HFDI and repel VFDI.

The evidence on the impact of tax policies on FDI is evolving. Earlier studies found only a negligible effect (and, at times, with the 'wrong' sign – Brainard, 1997). But more recent work shows increasing evidence that a low tax burden attracts FDI (for instance, Hines, 1999). The apparent increase in the responsiveness to tax policies in recent years could be explained by VFDI, which is mainly driven by the relative cost of production, becoming more prominent. The sensitivity of VFDI rather than HFDI to taxation seems also more pronounced in developing countries (Mutti and Grubert, 2004). The evidence on tax incentives is not conclusive, but there are some indications that transparent and simple tax systems tend to be most attractive for FDI (Hassett and Hubbard, 1997). This is also supported by an OECD study on the use of tax incentives for investment (Box 14.1).

BOX 14.1 OECD STUDY ON THE USE OF TAX INCENTIVES FOR INVESTMENT

This study (OECD, 2003) found tax incentives generally inefficient in promoting investment. It argued that multinational companies have significant scope in effectively setting their tax burden through aggressive and sophisticated tax planning. As a result, specific tax incentives, such as tax holidays or exemptions, ran the risk of being abused, ignored, or even proving counter-productive (when they are non-transparent, are changed often, or if they involve large administrative discretion). The study recommended lowering labour taxes and allowing general accelerated depreciation combined with five-year loss carry-forward rules for both domestic and foreign investors. It also suggested strengthening thin-capitalization rules (to avoid showing capital investment as debt to reap tax advantages) and regulations on transfer pricing (to counter the most egregious examples of tax planning). Finally, it advised against (i) multiple tax incentives to avoid the possibility of their 'stacking'; (ii) special economic zones, which often result in distorting the location decisions of foreign investors; and (iii) 'non-automatic' criteria involving administrative decisions for triggering tax relief eligibility, to minimize the scope for rent-seeking and corruption.

There is evidence that regional integration reduces HFDI and stimulates VFDI. In the context of transition economies, studies generally find that steps toward integration with the EU have a positive effect on FDI flows (Braconier and Ekholm, 2001, Bevan et al., 2001). These results, however, need to be interpreted with caution: it is not clear that they capture the effect on FDI of increasing regional integration rather than the prospect of greater political and institutional stability expected to accompany EU accession.

Low institutional development, structural rigidities, and poor governance could be thought of as a tax on investment, as shown by Wei (2000). A wide variety of indicators have been used in empirical studies as proxies for these underlying factors, such as the Index of Economic Freedom of the Heritage foundation, the EBRD indices on progress with transition or the quality of the institutions, dummies for the method of privatization, and various country risk indicators. While most studies on the determinants of FDI find some of them to be significant, these proxies are particularly susceptible to being correlated with other underlying explanatory factors and their estimated coefficients can thus be hard to interpret.

The evidence on production costs and factor endowments is mixed. Labour costs are often not found to be significant, due perhaps to the difficulties in measuring accurately productivity differentials. Labour skills, on the other hand, have generally positive effects on FDI. Skill-rich countries also tend to attract high-skill industries. Marin (2004) finds that Austrian and German companies are outsourcing the most skill-intensive activities into Central and South-East European countries to take advantage of relatively inexpensive skilled labour.

Some studies find agglomeration and herding to be important (Barrel and Pain, 1999; Campos and Kinoshita, 2003) but further research is needed to separate spurious and real agglomeration. Agglomeration effects are most commonly proxied by the quality of infrastructure, degree of development, and lagged stock of FDI, but these variables may influence FDI through other channels as well. Finally, Bevan and Estrin (2000) report some evidence of feedback effects (FDI contributing to changes in the host environment that in turn stimulate more FDI) that might explain the emergence of leaders and laggards among host countries.

The coverage of South-East European countries in the empirical literature is scant, mainly due to lack of data. A number of papers provide stylized facts on FDI to SE Europe (Lankes and Venables, 1996; Hunya, 2004; European Commission, 2004). A handful of econometric studies focusing mainly on Central Europe include one or two countries from SE Europe in the sample, typically Bulgaria and Romania, the two SE European EU candidates. Only four studies (Christie, 2003, Garibaldi et al., 2002, Deichmann, 2001; Holland and Pain, 1998) cover more than these two SE European countries, and the coverage is not uniform. None of them covers all seven SE European countries.

The findings of this relatively small body of research are generally in line with those of the broader literature reviewed above. Gravity factors are important determinants of FDI. Labour costs and institutional variables (various indicators of progress in transition, the method of privatization, index of economic freedom, political stability, progress in EU accession) also play a significant role. However, openness to trade, the tax regime, and infrastructure are statistically significant only in some of the studies. Christie (2003) examines whether horizontal or vertical FDI is predominant in the region and reports that in Central European economies HFDI is prevalent, but the evidence for SE European countries is inconclusive.

FOREIGN DIRECT INVESTMENT IN SOUTH-EAST EUROPE: THE EVIDENCE

Size and Distribution of FDI

SE European countries as a group generally lag behind Central European countries in attracting FDI (Figure 14.1). There is significant differentiation within the group, with Romania and Croatia having attracted more than their peers. Additional insight is provided by Figure 14.2, which pairs the rank resulting from Figure 14.1 with the stock of FDI. Four separate clusters emerge: the big three Central European countries (Czech Republic, Hungary, and Poland on the lower right-hand side); then Croatia, Slovakia, Romania and the Baltics; followed by an 'intermediate' cluster with Slovenia, Bulgaria, and Serbia and Montenegro; and finally the 'laggards' (Albania, Bosnia and Herzegovina, FYR of Macedonia, and Moldova).

FDI flows into all these economies since the beginning of transition were closely associated with the privatization process. Privatization-related FDI is arguably a special case, not determined (or not influenced to the same extent) by the same variables as 'underlying' FDI. Because consistent data on privatization-related FDI are not available for all these countries, Figure 14.3 uses data on cross-border mergers and acquisitions as a proxy.[4] While looking only at non-privatization-related FDI changes the ranking of some individual countries, the broad picture remains the same.

The country ranking is also influenced by the size of these economies. Figure 14.4 adjusts for scale by showing the stock of aggregate FDI at end-2003 in per capita terms. While the ranking of some countries has again changed (Croatia moves up the rank; Poland is ranked between Slovakia and the Baltics; Romania has moved several notches down), the SE European countries – except for Croatia – still lag well behind their Central European neighbours. A per capita FDI stock of about USD 1000 provides a clear demarcation line between the two groups.

Turning finally to the sources of FDI flows to the region, Figure 14.5 provides two interesting insights. First, the sources of FDI are highly concentrated: Germany, Austria, Italy and Greece are among the top five sources for almost all SE European countries. This, as well as the case of Moldova, where FDI originates mostly in Russia, provides strong prima facie support to the hypothesis that gravity variables – in particular, proximity – play a major role in determining FDI flows. Second, some of the more advanced countries in the region, themselves important hosts of FDI flows from Western Europe, are gradually emerging as sources of FDI in the less advanced SE European countries (Bosnia and Herzegovina, FYR of Macedonia).[5]

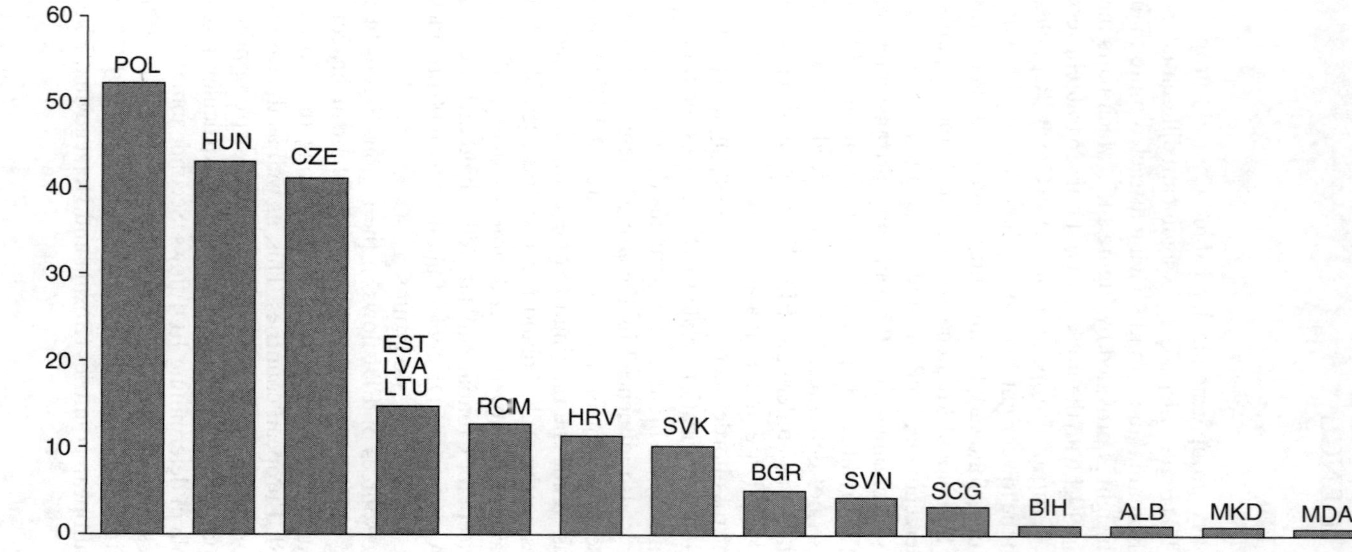

Note: Key to country labels used in Figures 14.1–14.7: ALB: Albania; AUS: Austria; BEL: Belgium; BGR: Bulgaria; BIH: Bosnia and Herzegovina; CHN: China; CZE: Czech Republic; CYP: Cyprus; DEU: Germany; ESP: Spain; EST: Estonia; FRA: France; GBR: Great Britain; GRC: Greece; HRV: Croatia; HUN: Hungary; ITA: Italy; KWT: Kuwait; LVA: Latvia; LTU: Lithuania; MDA: Moldova; MKD: FYR of Macedonia; NLD: Netherlands; POL: Poland; ROM: Romania; RUS: Russian Federation; SCG: Serbia and Montenegro; SVN: Slovenia; SVK: Slovakia; TUR: Turkey; USA: USA.

Source: UNCTAD database.

Figure 14.1 Total FDI stock, 2003 (USD billion)

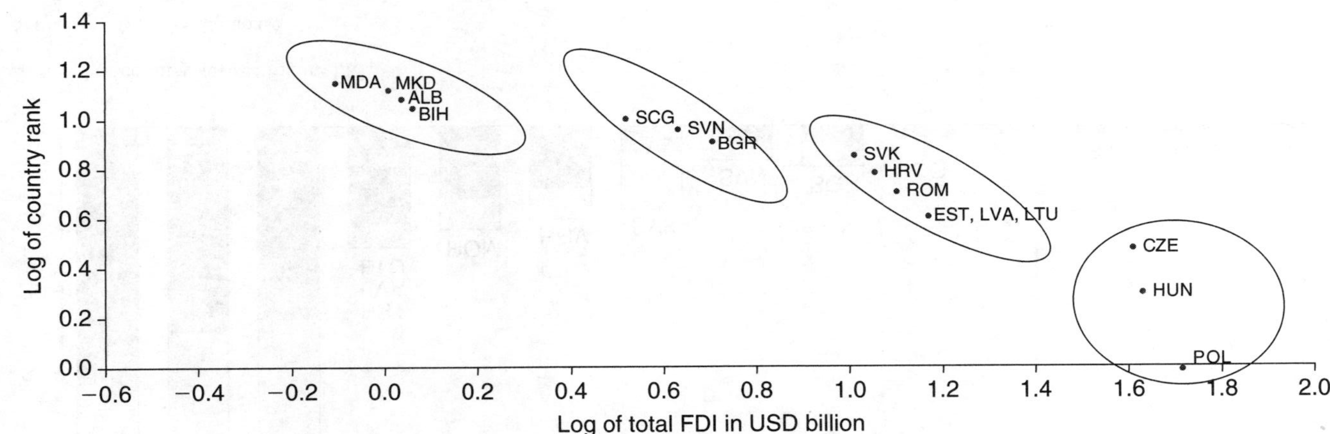

Note: For country key see Figure 14.1.

Figure 14.2 FDI clusters in Central and South-East Europe (logs of rank and total FDI in USD billion)

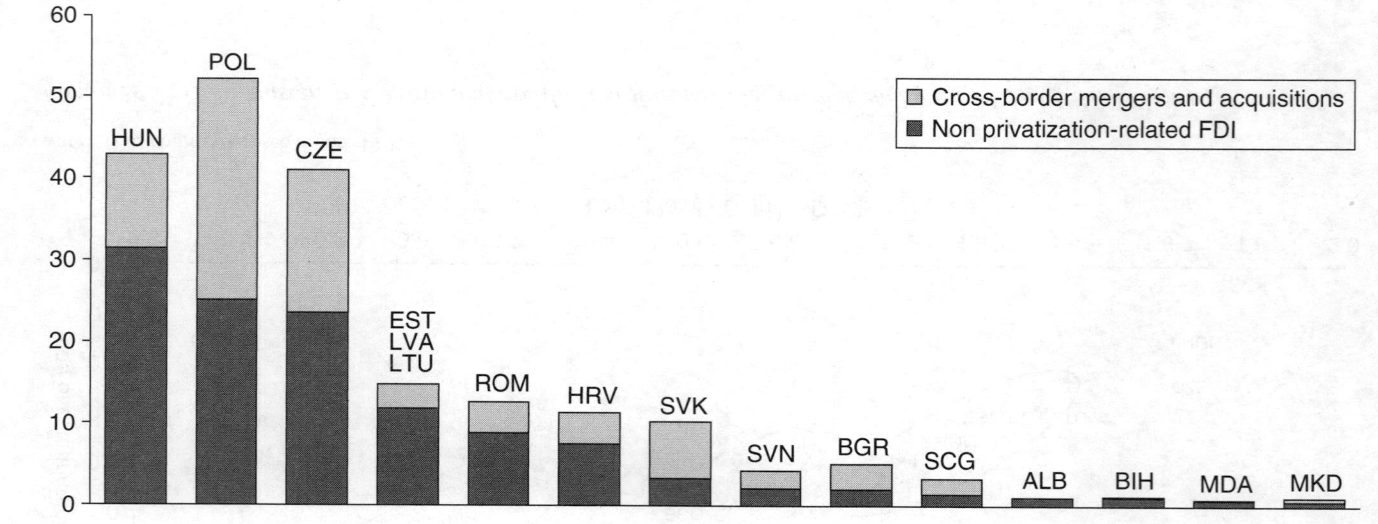

Note: For country key see Figure 14.1.

Source: UNCTAD database.

Figure 14.3 Privatization and non-privatization-related FDI stock, 2003 (USD billion)

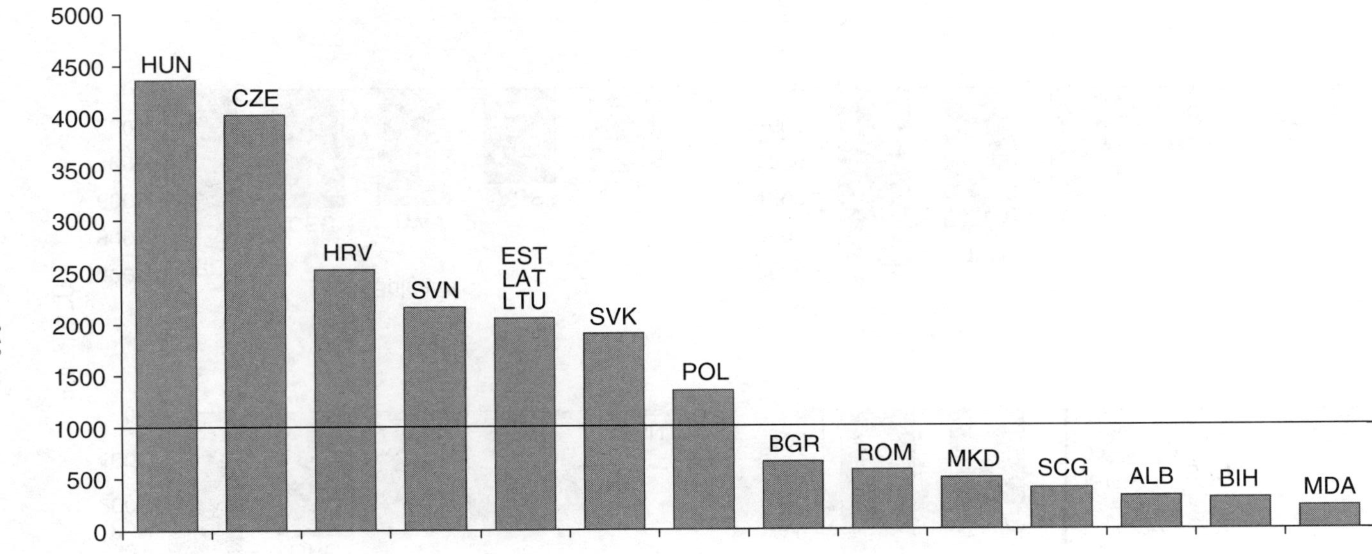

Note: For country key see Figure 14.1.

Source: UNCTAD database.

Figure 14.4 FDI stock per capita, 2003 (in USD)

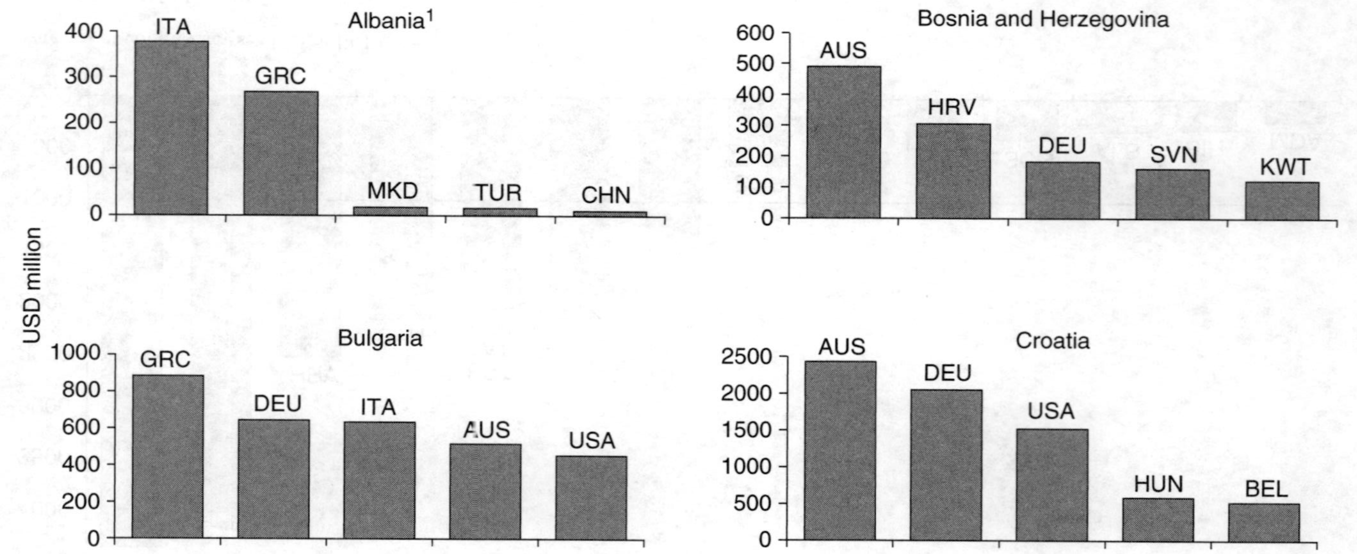
USD million
Albania[1]
400
300
200
100
0
ITA
GRC
MKD
TUR
CHN
Bosnia and Herzegovina
600
500
400
300
200
100
0
AUS
HRV
DEU
SVN
KWT
Bulgaria
1000
800
600
400
200
0
GRC
DEU
ITA
AUS
USA
Croatia
2500
2000
1500
1000
500
0
AUS
DEU
USA
HUN
BEL

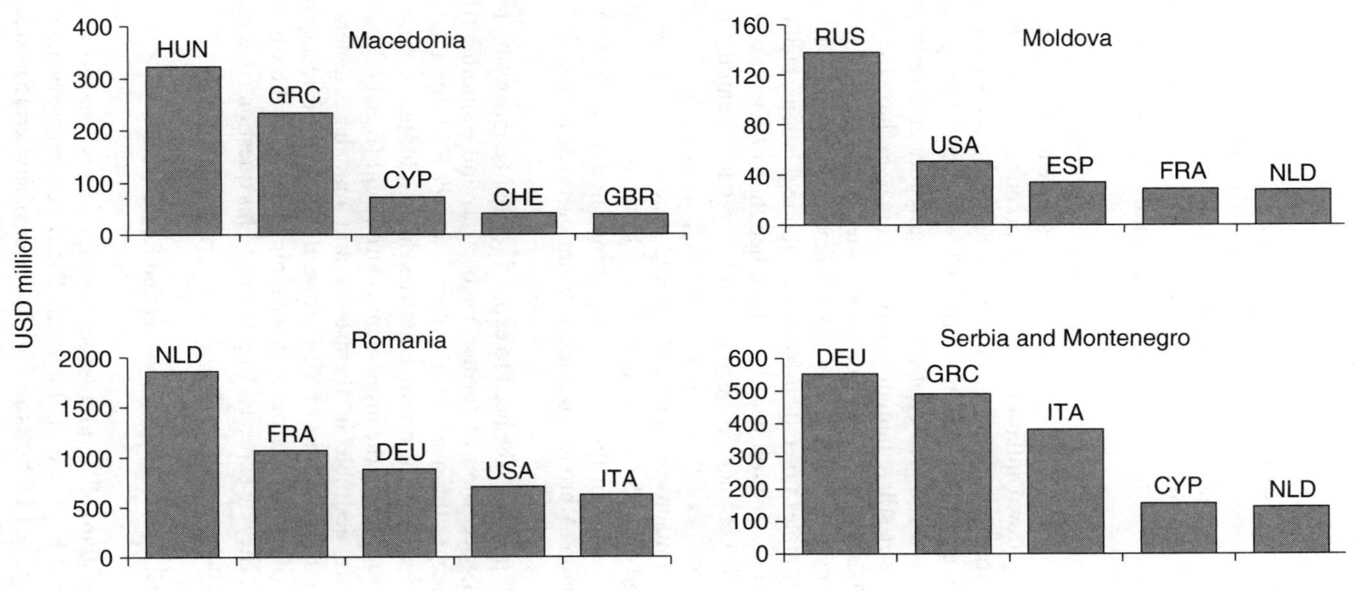

Notes:
1. End-2001 Stock.
* For country key see Figure 14.1.

Source: OECD.

Figure 14.5 Top five source countries (2003 FDI stock)*

The Policy Environment

The successful transition experience of Central European countries and the Baltics, attributed to some extent to their ability to attract large amounts of foreign investment at an early stage, and the sizeable gap between these countries and the SE European group in terms of FDI, has drawn attention to the importance of the policy environment and catalysed efforts to encourage FDI flows.

The policy environment in SE European countries has been steadily – if unequally – improving in recent years. All countries have made significant progress in bringing down inflation; promoting private sector development through privatization, deregulation, and a better business environment; and improving public administration. These policies, though not specifically targeted to FDI, are doubtless encouraging foreign investment.

Weaknesses, however, still remain in a number of areas. Perhaps the most fundamental weakness relates to governance and the business environment. All SE European countries, each to a different degree, need to make further efforts to simplify complex tax and customs laws and regulations, facilitate access to land and construction permits, strengthen the judiciary, accelerate the resolution of commercial disputes, and eliminate remaining discriminatory provisions against foreign investors. A joint IMF–World Bank paper taking stock of macroeconomic policies and structural reforms in SE Europe since the end of the Kosovo conflict (Demekas et al., 2002) provides a more detailed discussion of the outstanding agenda in these areas for the countries in the region. A broader but more recent overview is provided in World Bank (2005).

For reasons both political (the need to expand regional cooperation following the wars of succession of former Yugoslavia) and economic (the desire to avoid a 'beggar-thy-neighbour' policy to attract FDI through tax and other incentives), SE European countries have adopted a unique regional approach to shaping the investment environment (Box 14.2).

These policies are desirable in themselves and may have generally beneficial effects on the economies of SE Europe. But given the evidence on the preponderance of gravity factors in determining FDI flows, how much additional FDI can they be expected to generate? This question is tackled in the following sections.

Econometric Results: Bilateral FDI Cross-section Regressions

We start with the standard bilateral cross-section regressions – the tool often used in the empirical literature of this kind. The dependent variable is a cross-section of bilateral FDI flows and stocks (in logs) between 15 host and

BOX 14.2 THE SOUTH-EAST EUROPE COMPACT FOR REFORM, INVESTMENT, INTEGRITY AND GROWTH

The Investment Compact, a component of the Stability Pact for South-Eastern Europe, is an example of a group of countries – Albania, Bosnia and Herzegovina, Bulgaria, Croatia, FYR of Macedonia, Moldova, Romania, and Serbia and Montenegro – joining forces to encourage high quality FDI. It aims to unify the approach toward foreign investors across countries on the principle of equal treatment with domestic investors. While this principle is embodied in an (incomplete) web of bilateral investment treaties and OECD Investment Instruments (legal instruments that establish rules of conduct for capital movements, which are binding commitments for member governments but recommendations for multinational enterprises), a uniform region-wide approach was seen as preferable, owing to its transparency and universal coverage. It also sends a clear signal of the cooperative approach taken by this group of host countries. The Investment Compact clearly lays out existing exceptions from national treatment for foreign investors (that is, when treatment is not as favourable as that of domestic investors) by country, with the objective that these exceptions be eliminated over time. In the context of the Investment Compact, SE European countries have agreed to work toward

- unifying FDI registration and approval procedures with those for domestic firms;
- allowing acquisition of real estate by foreign investors for FDI purposes;
- minimizing FDI-related requirements on statistical reporting, work and residence permits;
- eliminating discrimination in access to government procurement contracts; and
- removing obstacles to FDI in financial and professional services.

24 source countries averaged for 2000–2002, from OECD's International Direct Investment Statistics, updated and supplemented by data provided by country authorities and Hunya (2004).[6] On the right-hand side, we use population (a proxy for market potential), distance between source and host

capitals (also in logs), and a dummy capturing cultural or historical ties between source and host country as the gravity variables. Additional regressors (their sources in parentheses) include the ratio of tariff revenues to the value of imports (EBRD Transition Reports); the statutory corporate income tax rate (IMF); the EBRD index of foreign exchange and trade liberalization (EBRD Transition Reports);[7] the EBRD index of infrastructure reform, a composite index measuring the degree of reforms and decentralization in electricity generation and distribution, roads, railways, and telecommunications (EBRD Transition Reports); a dummy capturing tax holidays (compiled from PricewaterhouseCoopers' Worldwide Tax Summaries); unit labour costs in manufacturing, calculated as the ratio of manufacturing wages to GDP per capita (IMF); and an estimate of the 'bribe tax' as a share of annual firm revenues (from the business environment surveys by the EBRD and World Bank).

The results are shown in Table 14.1. They are broadly consistent regardless of whether bilateral FDI flows or stocks are used as the left-hand side variable. As in all other studies, gravity variables are very significant: the larger the size of the host economy and the closer the geographical and cultural proximity to the main FDI source countries, the greater the cumulative FDI attracted.

Several policy variables also have a statistically significant effect on FDI flows and stocks. The EBRD index of foreign exchange and trade liberalization has a significant positive effect on FDI in all specifications, while unit labour cost – a variable representing productivity-adjusted wage rates – has a negative effect in some. The tax burden on business, captured by the statutory tax rate, also has a significant negative impact. But not all policy variables work equally well. The index of infrastructure reform is significant in only one specification. Tax incentives appear to be insignificant (consistent with the findings of the OECD survey in Box 14.1), as does the 'bribery tax', an estimate of the burden of corruption on business.

The Determinants of Non-privatization FDI: Aggregate FDI Panel Regressions

As shown in Figure 14.3, FDI flows related to privatization can be very sizeable in some of the countries in our sample. Because the pace of privatization differs from country to country, privatization deals can be large and lumpy, and the process itself is time-bound, the associated FDI flows may distort the results of the bilateral panel regressions. In addition, it is possible that the determinants of privatization-related FDI are different from those of all other FDI.

Table 14.1 Bilateral FDI cross-section regressions[1, 2, 3]

Dependent variable	FDI flows	FDI flows	FDI flows	FDI stock	FDI stock
Size (population)	1.260***	1.080***	1.050***	1.507***	1.220***
	(0.158)	(0.153)	(0.219)	(0.135)	(0.185)
Distance between host and source	−3.037***	−2.666***	−2.607***	−2.970***	−2.623***
	(0.358)	(0.366)	(0.378)	(0.344)	(0.391)
Cultural ties	0.760**	1.036***	1.068***	0.982**	1.321***
	(0.365)	(0.397)	(0.410)	(0.405)	(0.468)
Foreign exchange and trade liberalization (EBRD index)		1.556***	1.370***		0.503*
		(0.307)	(0.349)		(0.304)
Tariff revenue/ imports		0.004	−0.004		0.016
		(0.047)	(0.046)		(0.037)
Statutory corporate income tax rate		−0.115***	−0.080*		0.020
		(0.040)	(0.043)		(0.028)
Unit labour cost[4]		−0.846*	−0.578		0.222
		(0.432)	(0.533)		(0.404)
Infrastructure reform (EBRD index)			0.128		0.768*
			(0.443)		(0.410)
Tax holidays			0.370		0.408
			(0.361)		(0.311)
Corruption (bribery tax)[5]			−0.115		−0.101
			(0.287)		(0.255)
R-squared	0.62	0.68	0.68	0.69	0.72
Number of observations	179	179	179	202	202

Notes:

1. All variables except dummies in logs. Source countries: EU-15 plus the US, Switzerland, Russia, Poland, Hungary, Cyprus, Croatia, Slovenia, and Czech Republic. Host countries: Albania (for stock regressions only), Baltic countries (as a group), Czech Republic, Hungary, Poland, Slovak Republic, Slovenia, Bulgaria, Croatia, Moldova, FYR of Macedonia, Romania, Serbia and Montenegro, and Bosnia and Herzegovina (for stock regressions only).
2. *, **, and *** represent significance at 10%, 5%, and 1% respectively. A source country dummy is included in all regressions.
3. All variables are averaged over 2000–2002 when data are available. The end-2001 stock is used for Albania and the end-2004 stock for Bosnia and Herzegovina.
4. Unit labour costs are calculated as the ratio of wage rate manufacturing to GDP per capita.
5. Average bribe tax as a percentage of annual firm revenues.

Unfortunately, there are no consistent data on privatization-related FDI on a bilateral basis. As discussed earlier, a good proxy for privatization-related FDI is cross-border mergers and acquisitions (M&A) for which, however, data are only available on an aggregate basis for each host country. Therefore, we conduct a panel analysis using aggregate FDI data excluding cross-border M&A for each host country for the period 1995–2003.[8]

The use of panel regressions with both a time and a cross-country dimension, as opposed to a simple cross-section regression, allows a more sophisticated examination of country-specific effects. We use the following specification

$$\ln \mathrm{FDI}_{it} = \theta X_{it} + u_i + v_{it},$$

where X_{it} is a vector of explanatory variables in host country i that affect its attractiveness as a destination of non-privatization-related FDI (including two time-invariant variables: weighted distance from and cultural ties to source countries), u_i captures any country-specific effects, and v_{it} is the disturbance term.

The country-specific term u_i may be either fixed parameters that can be estimated ('fixed effects') or random disturbances characterizing the ith country ('random effects'). In the first case, since the fixed country effects are time-invariant, they would be perfectly correlated with the other two time-invariant explanatory variables. As a result, we would not be able to estimate accurately the impact of location and cultural ties on FDI. The random effects specification, on the other hand, would allow us to estimate the impact of these variables and actually provide more efficient estimates if the country-specific term u_i is not correlated with the other explanatory variables.[9] To distinguish between the two hypotheses regarding the country-specific term, we can test for the orthogonality of u_i to the other regressors with a Hausman test. The results, reported in Table 14.2, suggest that the random effects specification is indeed appropriate for our benchmark regressions.

The results for the random effects regressions, presented in Table 14.2 (for FDI stocks) and Table 14.3 (for FDI flows), are consistent with those from the bilateral regressions, although regressions using the FDI stocks as the dependent variable perform generally better than those with FDI flows. Gravity variables are still strongly significant, as is the degree of liberalization of the trade and foreign exchange regime. The tariff revenue as a share of imports and the unit labour cost have a significant negative impact in most regressions. The EBRD infrastructure reform index also appears to have a major positive effect on FDI in most regressions. The corporate tax burden, however, is significant only in some regressions. This may be

Table 14.2 Aggregate non-privatization FDI stock panel regressions, 1995–2003[1]

	(1)	(2)	(3)	(4)	(5)	(6)	(7)
Specification	Random effects						Fixed effects
Sample	SEE + CEE[2]					SEE + CEE + CIS[3]	SEE + CEE[2]
Year dummies?	No	No	Yes	No	Yes	No	No
Size (population)	0.976***	0.641***	0.721***	0.522***	0.593***	0.912***	2.105
	(0.297)	(0.193)	(0.212)	(0.140)	(0.126)	(0.167)	(3.468)
Weighted distance[4]	−15.381***	−8.417***	−12.353***	−8.288***	−10.280***	−2.806***	
	(3.904)	(2.402)	(2.764)	(1.720)	(1.605)	(0.887)	
Weighted cultural ties[4]	0.071	6.368**	4.949	3.769	4.894**	1.799	
	(5.191)	(3.229)	(3.634)	(2.344)	(2.104)	(3.267)	
Foreign exchange and trade liberalization (EBRD index)		0.776***	0.401***	0.362***	0.407***	0.238**	0.318*
		(0.149)	(0.122)	(0.130)	(0.116)	(0.112)	(0.181)
Tariff revenue /imports		−0.094***	0.004	−0.038**	−0.012	−0.041**	−0.044**
		(0.019)	(0.018)	(0.017)	(0.016)	(0.018)	(0.020)
Corporate income tax/GDP		−0.146**	0.036	−0.025	0.019	−0.125***	−0.030
		(0.071)	(0.054)	(0.060)	(0.053)	(0.047)	(0.068)
Unit labour cost[5]		−0.856**	−0.680**	−0.363	−0.639**	0.123	0.077
		(0.372)	(0.330)	(0.287)	(0.257)	(0.256)	(0.606)
Infrastructure reform (EBRD index)				0.884***	0.409***	1.008***	0.897***
				(0.120)	(0.150)	(0.121)	(0.139)

Table 14.2 *(continued)*

	(1)	(2)	(3)	(4)	(5)	(6)	(7)
Specification	Random effects						Fixed effects
R-squared	0.62	0.84	0.88	0.90	0.74	0.81	0.93
Number of observations	124	115	115	115	115	172	115
p-value for Hausman test[6]	0.15	0.67	0.95	0.87	0.22	0.48	0.87

Notes:

1. All variables except dummies in logs. *, **, and *** represent significance at 10%, 5%, and 1% respectively.
2. Albania, Bosnia and Herzegovina, Baltic countries (as a group), Czech Republic, Hungary, Poland, Slovak Republic, Slovenia. Bulgaria, Croatia, Moldova, FYR of Macedonia, Romania, Serbia and Montenegro.
3. Countries in note 2 plus non-oil exporting CIS countries (Armenia, Belarus, Georgia, Kyrgyz Republic, Tajikistan, Ukraine, and Uzbekistan).
4. Sum of bilateral distance (or culture tie dummies) to source countries as specified in the bilateral regressions in Table 14.1 weighted by source countries' GDP.
5. Unit labour costs are calculated as the ratio of wage rate manufacturing to GDP per capita.
6. The null hypothesis for the Hausman test is that the difference in coefficients between fixed effects and random effects specifications is not systematic. Thus a small p-value suggests the rejection of random effects specification.

Table 14.3 Aggregate non-privatization FDI flow panel regressions, 1995–2003[1]

	(1)	(2)	(3)	(4)
Specification		Random effects		Fixed effects
Year dummies?	No	No	Yes	Yes
Size (population)	0.745***	0.562***	0.597***	4.205
	(0.201)	(0.165)	(0.162)	(6.608)
Weighted distance	−6.545***	−5.793***	−6.892***	
	(2.414)	(1.854)	(1.874)	
Weighted cultural ties	6.145*	5.743**	6.518***	
	(3.320)	(2.584)	(2.533)	
Foreign exchange and trade liberalization (EBRD index)	0.862***	0.471**	0.541***	1.117***
	(0.210)	(0.210)	(0.209)	(0.351)
Tariff revenue /imports	−0.012	0.009	0.022	0.098**
	(0.027)	(0.024)	(0.025)	(0.046)
Corporate income tax/GDP	−0.136	0.028	0.057	−0.007
	(0.109)	(0.107)	(0.105)	(0.135)
Unit labour cost	−0.890**	−0.525	−0.650*	−2.599**
	(0.421)	(0.346)	(0.341)	(1.165)
Infrastructure reform (EBRD index)		0.626***	0.379	−0.354
		(0.204)	(0.244)	(0.414)
R-squared	0.63	0.66	0.70	0.76
Number of observations	113	113	113	113
p-value for Hausman test	0.13	0.03	0.06	

Note: 1. See notes in Table 14.2.

attributed to the use of the corporate income tax-to-GDP ratio as a proxy, instead of the statutory tax rate. The corporate tax ratio is also influenced by factors unrelated to the corporate tax burden faced by foreign investors, such as the efficiency of tax collection, and may indeed be correlated with other institutional factors that could be expected to have a positive impact on FDI.

We also replicate the key regressions including year dummies, which yield broadly similar results. As a further robustness check, we have expanded the sample of host countries to include the non-oil exporting CIS countries (Armenia, Belarus, Georgia, Kyrgyz Republic, Tajikistan, Ukraine, and Uzbekistan).[10] The result is again broadly consistent with that of the original sample. Results from fixed effects regressions are reported in the last column of Tables 14.2 and 14.3. The population variable becomes insignificant, while many of the policy variables remain significant with the expected sign. Finally, we tried using per capita FDI stock and flows as the dependent variable, and again the results (not reported) are broadly similar.

Who Stands to Gain the Most from Good Policies? Potential FDI Estimation

The preponderance of gravity variables among the determinants of FDI, underscored both by the existing empirical literature and our own findings, suggests that policies can have a relatively limited, albeit still significant, impact. It is the size of this impact that is of interest to the policy makers, since they cannot affect the size, location, or history of their country. Moreover, even if certain policy variables are unambiguously identified as significant determinants for FDI, there is a limit to the discretion policy makers have.

To capture the impact that policies could have on FDI in this environment, we distinguish between exogenous determinants – the gravity variables – that are taken as given by policy makers, and endogenous or policy-related variables that are under their control. We can then estimate a 'potential' level of FDI for each host country using the actual values of exogenous variables for each host country and the 'best' values of the policy variables. The gap between actual FDI and this 'potential' would measure how much each host country stands to gain from getting its policies right.[11]

What is the 'best' value of the policy variables? Clearly, the corporate tax rate, for instance, cannot be driven to zero – even if this were beneficial for FDI. In reality, policy makers in host countries use the level of policy variables in their neighbours and competitors as a benchmark. To estimate a realistic level of 'potential' FDI in these conditions, we use the 'best' level of the policy variables across the sample, that is the highest degree of foreign exchange and trade liberalization and the lowest unit labour cost, tariff level, and corporate tax burden across the countries in Central and SE Europe in 2003. While 'better' values for these variables are of course possible, this approach gives an idea of the level of non-privatization-related FDI that could realistically be expected if policy makers in each host country emulated their best-performing neighbours.

To estimate the 'potential' FDI stock, we use equation (2) from Table 14.2, in which all explanatory variables are highly significant. Table 14.4 presents the results and Figure 14.6 shows the ratio between actual and 'potential' non-privatization FDI stock at end-2003. Hungary, the Czech Republic and Romania appear to be already above their 'potential'. For all other Central and SE European countries, on the other hand, greater effort on the policy front would have a substantial payoff in terms of additional FDI.

Table 14.4 Estimated potential and actual non-privatization FDI stock, 2003 (USD million)

Country	Potential FDI[1]	Actual FDI	Gap[2]
Hungary	16600	31488	−90%
Czech Republic	15999	23550	−47%
Romania	7886	8848	−12%
Croatia	10389	7547	27%
Bulgaria	3053	2063	32%
Slovak Republic	5810	3316	43%
Slovenia	3810	2170	43%
Poland	45233	25080	45%
Macedonia, FYR	1418	611	57%
Moldova	1821	742	59%
Albania	2870	1067	63%
Serbia and Montenegro	5774	1441	75%
Bosnia and Herzegovina	6151	1064	83%

Notes:
1. Potential FDI is estimated on the basis of the regression reported in column 2 of Table 14.2. For foreign exchange/trade liberalization index the maximum value from the 2003 sample is used, and for tariff revenue/imports, corporate income tax/GDP, and unit labour costs the lowest values from the 2003 sample are used.
2. Gap = (potential FDI–actual FDI)/potential FDI.

Not surprisingly, this payoff appears to be relatively smaller in the case of Croatia, which has already attracted significant FDI, but larger in the case of the other SE European countries. The ones with the most to gain from getting their policies right are Bosnia and Herzegovina, Serbia and Montenegro, and Albania, whose FDI levels are estimated at 60 to 80 per cent below 'potential'.

These results should be treated with caution. First, as mentioned above, using the 'best' values of the policy variables from the sample does not mean that these policies cannot be improved further. In that case, the calculated 'potential' may underestimate what countries can achieve through better policies. And second, the estimated coefficients of the time-invariant variables, in particular that for distance, are consistently significant but not stable, suggesting the need to expand the sample.

Does Size Matter? Threshold Effects Estimation

Although the empirical results presented in the previous sections appear to be relatively robust, the relationship between FDI and the various

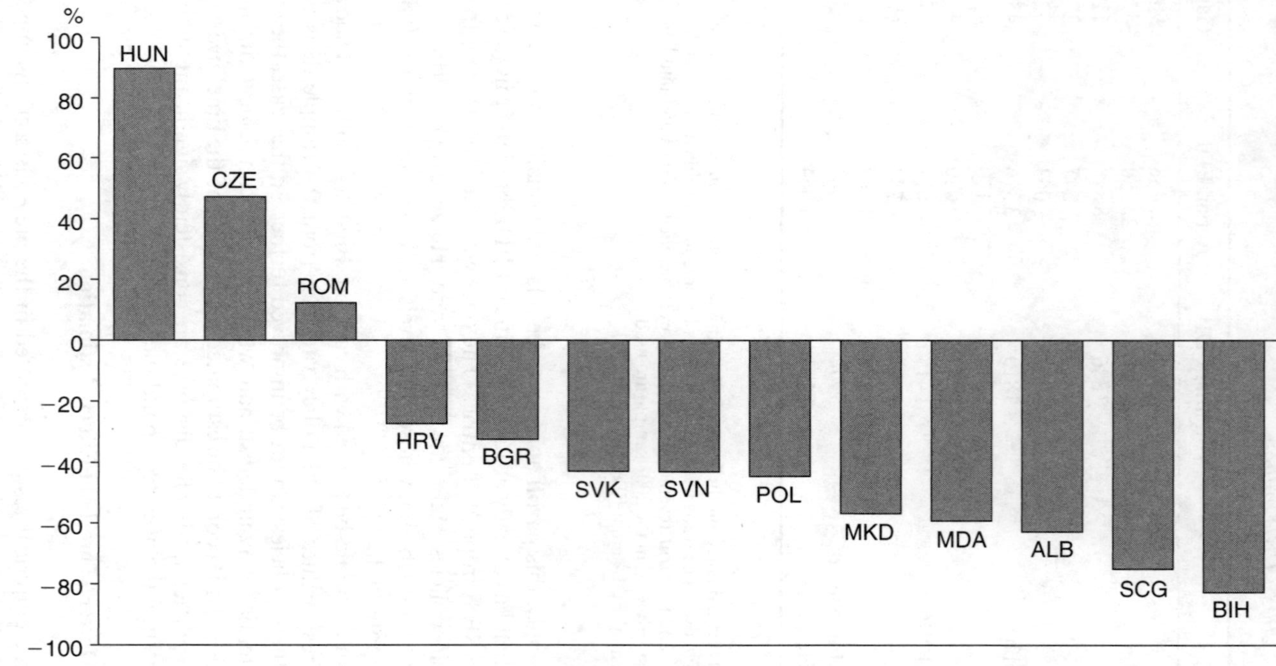

Note: For country key see Figure 14.1.

Figure 14.6 Non-privatization-related FDI stock at end-2003 compared to estimated potential (in per cent)

explanatory variables may not be constant across our sample. Indeed, the emergence of distinct clusters of 'leaders' and 'laggards' suggests that the nature of this relationship may be changing as the level of FDI increases. Threshold effects estimation, along the lines of Hansen (1996), provides the tool to test this hypothesis.

This technique essentially tests the hypothesis that the sample can be split into two sub-samples depending on the value of a threshold variable q_{it}:

$$\ln \mathrm{FDI}_{it} = \theta_1 X_{it} + u_i + v_{it,} \quad q_{it} \leq \gamma,$$
$$\ln \mathrm{FDI}_{it} = \theta_2 X_{it} + u_i + v_{it,} \quad q_{it} > \gamma,$$

The advantage of this technique is that it allows the threshold value to be endogenously estimated, as well as the calculation of an asymptotic p-value for the null hypothesis of no threshold effect using simple simulation techniques.

To test this hypothesis, we use equation (4) in Table 14.2, setting the number of bootstrap replications to 1000. The results are presented in Table 14.5 and Figure 14.7. There is strong evidence of a threshold at a level of non-privatization FDI of 11 per cent of GDP (roughly the level in Bulgaria, Poland, Slovakia, and FYR of Macedonia): the null hypothesis (no threshold) can be rejected at the 1 per cent confidence level. Indeed the hypothesis that the difference between the estimated coefficients in the two sub-samples is not statistically significant is rejected for all but two explanatory variables (column 3 of Table 14.5).

When moving from below to above the threshold, the relationship changes dramatically: size and distance, while still significant, become less important as determinants of FDI. The unit labour cost, which has a major negative impact on FDI below the threshold, becomes insignificant. In contrast, cultural proximity, the degree of foreign exchange and trade liberalization, and the extent of reform in the infrastructure sector become (more) important above the threshold.

The estimated coefficient of the corporate tax burden is a minor puzzle: while significant in both sub-samples, it appears with a negative sign in the sample below and with a positive sign in the sample above the threshold. One possible explanation is that the corporate tax-to-GDP ratio used as the proxy is also capturing the effect of other underlying variables – such as the quality of public administration – which may have a positive impact on FDI, and that these variables become more important than the tax burden as FDI moves above the threshold.

An intuitive interpretation of these findings is that in the early stages, when a host country first opens its door to foreign investors, the size of the domestic market, distance, and cheap labour are the most important

Table 14.5 Threshold effects estimation aggregate non-privatization FDI stock regressions, 1995–2003[1]

	(1)	(2)	(3)
Specification	Random effects	Random effects	p-value for H_0:
Estimated threshold[2]	FDI/GDP≤11%	FDI/GDP>11%	Difference between coefficients in (1) and (2) is not significant
Size (population)	0.676***	0.434***	0.01
	(0.148)	(0.124)	
Weighted distance[3]	−9.441***	−5.566***	0.01
	(1.631)	(1.630)	
Weighted cultural ties[3]	2.483	5.647***	0.11
	(3.175)	(2.048)	
Foreign exchange and trade liberalization (EBRD index)	0.433***	0.522**	0.69
	(0.129)	(0.258)	
Tariff revenue/ imports	−0.021	−0.023	0.89
	(0.019)	(0.017)	
Corporate income tax/GDP	−0.139**	0.304***	0.00
	(0.066)	(0.086)	
Unit labour cost	−0.911***	−0.194	0.01
	(0.355)	(0.268)	
Infrastructure reform (EBRD index)	0.531***	0.816***	0.03
	(0.150)	(0.146)	
Year dummies?	No	No	
R-squared	0.90	0.97	
Number of observations	64	51	

Notes:
1. See note 1 to Table 14.2 for country coverage.
2. The null hypothesis of no threshold can be rejected at 1% level. The estimated threshold is FDI/GDP = 10.98%.
3. See notes in Table 14.2.

determinants of FDI. As the country succeeds in attracting more foreign investment, the importance of these factors declines and other factors come increasingly into play: the degree of openness and institutional development, the business environment, and possibly a sense of shared values and attitudes. This interpretation is also consistent with the hypothesis that successful host countries are able to attract increasingly high

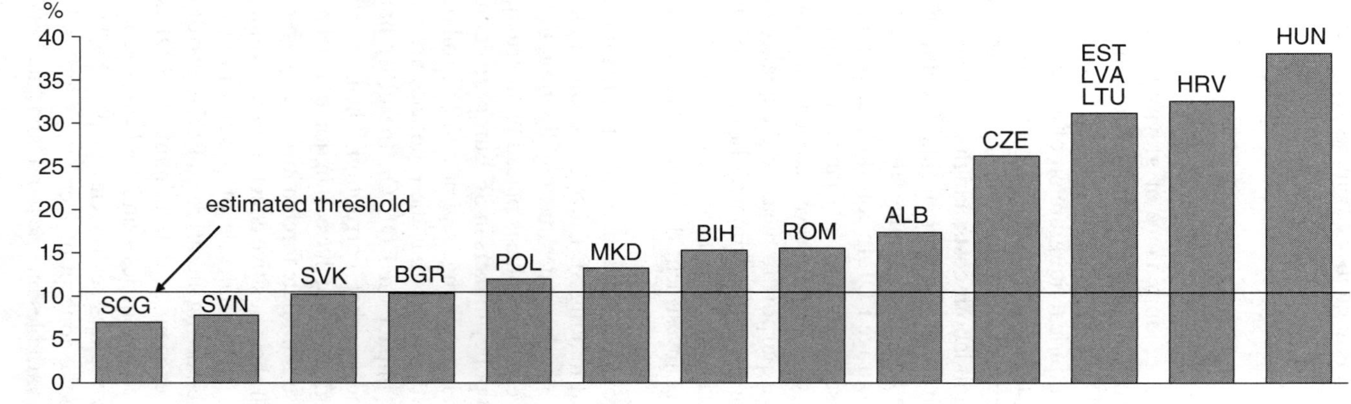

Note: For country key see Figure 14.1.

Figure 14.7 Estimated threshold for non-privatization FDI (in per cent of GDP, end-2003)

value-added, sophisticated foreign investment, as suggested by the 'Flying Geese Model' (WIIW, 2004).

CONCLUSIONS

Our analysis confirms the predominance of gravity factors (host market size and geographical and cultural proximity between source and host country) in explaining FDI flows to Central and SE Europe, in line with the findings of the existing empirical literature on other regions. This conclusion holds even after adjusting for privatization-related FDI flows.

Nevertheless, the policy environment in the host country still matters for FDI. We find that high unit labour costs, a high corporate tax burden and, to a lesser extent, a high level of import tariffs discourage FDI, while a liberal foreign exchange and trade regime and advanced reforms in the infrastructure sector encourage FDI. In contrast, tax holidays and domestic corruption do not seem to have a significant impact. The results concerning institutional variables, however, come with a health warning: explanatory variables that purport to measure the quality of institutions, such as the index of reforms or the estimated 'bribery tax', may be imperfect proxies. Since they may also be correlated with each other or with other factors that also influence investment decisions, their coefficients may be hard to interpret.

These findings can provide a solid analytical foundation for the evaluation of policies aimed at making SE European countries more attractive to foreign investors while, at the same time, highlighting the limits of what these policies can achieve. The emphasis placed by international financial institutions, donors, and policy makers in SE European countries on liberalizing the trade and foreign exchange regime and controlling labour costs is appropriate: our results suggest that these policies are indeed likely to have a beneficial direct impact on FDI. On the other hand, efforts to improve governance and combat corruption, their broader economic benefits notwithstanding, may not have a major *direct* impact on FDI. They could still, of course, stimulate foreign investment – indeed all investment – *indirectly* through their positive effects on the economy.

To explore further the potential role of policies in attracting foreign investment, we extend the existing literature on FDI in two directions. First, we distinguish between exogenous determinants of FDI (size, location, cultural links to source countries) and policy-driven determinants. Recognizing that policy makers set policies in part by looking at their competitors, we develop the concept of a country's 'potential' FDI determined by the exogenous variables on one hand, and the 'best' values of the endogenous variables in our sample on the other. This concept should be seen as a benchmark, not a ceiling: countries can (and do) attract FDI beyond their 'potential' by adopting more FDI-friendly policies than their competitors. But it gives an idea of the level of non-privatization-related FDI that could realistically be expected if policy makers in each host country emulated their best-performing neighbours. The comparison between 'potential' and actual non-privatization FDI at end-2003 shows that SE European countries, especially Albania, Bosnia and Herzegovina, FYR of Macedonia, and Serbia and Montenegro stand to gain the most in terms of additional FDI by getting their policies right. That margin is smaller in Croatia and Bulgaria, which have already attracted considerable FDI given their size, location, and cultural ties with source countries, while Romania seems to have reached its 'potential' FDI level. To continue attracting sizeable FDI inflows, countries that are already close to or above 'potential' should strive to go beyond the policy norms prevailing in the region.

The second direction in which we extend the existing literature is to test for threshold effects, that is the hypothesis that the impact of the various determinants on FDI changes once FDI increases beyond a certain level. We find strong evidence of a threshold at a level of non-privatization-related FDI of 11 per cent of GDP, roughly that in Bulgaria, Poland, Slovakia, and FYR of Macedonia. Below that level, gravity variables and labour costs are the predominant determinants of FDI. As FDI rises above the threshold, however, the importance of these factors declines (although gravity variables continue to be significant), and that of trade and foreign exchange liberalization, cultural proximity, and other institutional factors increases. While not conclusive, this evidence suggests that the nature of FDI changes as the host country attracts more foreign investment. The initial wave of foreign investors is attracted primarily by market size, ease of access, and low labour costs but, once a 'critical mass' of foreign investment is reached, a new kind of investor appears, drawn more by the degree of openness and institutional development, the business environment, and possibly a sense of shared values and attitudes.

NOTES

1. International Monetary Fund (IMF), Washington, DC. This is an interim summary of results of an ongoing project at the IMF. An initial version of this chapter was presented at the conference on 'Southeastern European Challenges and Prospects' during 28–30 November, 2004 in Vienna. The authors are grateful without implication to Hans-Peter Lankes for encouragement, support, and many helpful comments; to the Oesterreichische Nationalbank and the participants to the aforementioned conference; to Harald Hirschhofer, Jan-Peter Olters, Kevin Ross, Edgardo Ruggiero, Graham Slack, Thanasis Vamvakidis (IMF Resident Representatives in various SE European countries)

and Gábor Hunya (Wiener Institut für Internationale Wirtschaftsvergleiche) for help in compiling the database for this project; and to Madhuri Edwards for excellent research assistance. The views expressed in this chapter are the authors' and do not necessarily represent those of the IMF.

2. In addition to the large, lump-sum inflows, FDI can also cause outflows related to profit or capital repatriation. Paradoxically, the most investor-friendly host countries may be at a higher risk of such outflows when parent firms are in distress or regional contagion raises perceived risk because they have more liquid capital markets and minimal obstacles to capital and current transactions (see Lehman, 2002; Lehman and Mody, 2004).
3. We include in SE Europe Albania, Bosnia and Herzegovina, Croatia, FYR of Macedonia, Serbia and Montenegro (sometimes collectively referred to as the 'Western Balkans'), as well as Bulgaria and Romania.
4. Mergers and acquisitions data are from UNCTAD (www.unctad.org) and include purchases via domestic and international capital markets. Some of these transactions, depending on the share acquired in the domestic company, may not be included in national FDI statistics.
5. Notably Hungary (telecommunications, banking) and Slovenia (retail trade, banking). This phenomenon is in line with the pattern described as the 'Flying Geese Model' (WIIW, 2004). According to this model, transnational companies locate low- and medium-technology export-oriented subsidiaries in leading transition economies first. As wages in those countries rise, these subsidiaries move on to countries with lower wage costs, replaced by medium-tech and (increasingly) high-tech subsidiaries. Thus, the manufacturing base in more advanced transition economies is increasingly concentrated in medium- and high-tech areas.
6. Source countries are the EU-15 plus Croatia, Cyprus, the Czech Republic, Hungary, Poland, Russia, Slovenia, Switzerland, and the US. Host countries are Albania, Bosnia and Herzegovina, Bulgaria, Croatia, the Czech Republic, FYR of Macedonia, Hungary, Moldova, Poland, the Slovak Republic, Slovenia, Serbia and Montenegro, as well as Estonia, Latvia, and Lithuania treated as one host destination, as in the OECD database. Due to lack of data, the 2001 FDI stock for Albania and the 2004 FDI stock for Bosnia and Herzegovina are used.
7. This index measures the degree of liberalization of the trade and foreign exchange system. A '1' rating means widespread import and/or export controls or very limited legitimate access to foreign exchange. A '2' rating signifies some liberalization of import and/or export controls, almost full current account convertibility, but a foreign exchange regime that is not fully transparent (possibly multiple exchange rates). A '3' rating means that almost all quantitative and administrative import and export restrictions have been removed. A '4' rating is given when all quantitative and administrative import and export restrictions and all major export tariffs have been removed (except for agriculture) and the tariff scale for non-agricultural imports is fairly uniform. A '4+' rating means that the country has adopted standards and norms of advanced industrial economies and has become a WTO member.
8. Distance and cultural proximity variables for each host country are now weighted by source countries' GDP. Since only one or two observations of the variable on tax holidays are available for each host country during the observation period, this variable is omitted. Also, because statutory tax rates are not available for every year in every host country in our sample, we use the corporate tax as a share to GDP to proxy the corporate tax burden.
9. Conceptually, the random effects approach is more appropriate if the sample is a random drawing of individual observations from the population of all FDI host countries.
10. FDI in oil-producing Russia, Azerbaijan, and Turkmenistan is driven by additional explanatory factors that are not relevant for the rest of our sample.
11. Christie (2003) also presents a 'potential' FDI and reports that SE European countries as a group were 47 per cent below that level. His estimate, however, is the predicted value of FDI on the basis of the gravity factors plus an institutional variable (index of economic freedom by the Heritage Foundation – which confusingly includes the size of total capital inflows as an indicator) and ignores the impact of policy variables.

REFERENCES

Alfaro, L., A. Chanda, S. Kalemli-Özcan and S. Sayek (2003), 'FDI spillovers, financial markets, and economic development', *IMF Working Paper* WP/03/186, Washington, DC: International Monetary Fund.

Barrel, R. and N. Pain (1999), 'Domestic institutions, agglomeration and foreign direct investment in Europe', *European Economic Review*, **43**, 925–34.

Bevan, A. and S. Estrin (2000), 'The determinants of foreign direct investment in transition economies', *CEPR Discussion Paper* No. 2638.

Bevan, A., S. Estrin and H. Grabbe (2001), 'The impact of EU accession prospects on FDI inflows to Central and Eastern Europe', *Sussex European Institute Policy Paper* 06/01, Sussex, UK: University of Sussex.

Borensztein, E., J. De Gregorio and J.W. Lee (1995), 'How does foreign direct investment affect economic growth?', *NBER Working Paper* No. 5057.

Bos, J.W.B. and M. van de Laar (2004), 'Explaining Foreign Direct Investment in Central and Eastern Europe: an extended gravity approach', Utrecht, the Netherlands: Utrecht School of Economics.

Braconier, B.H. and K. Ekholm (2001), 'Foreign direct investment in Central and Eastern Europe: employment effects in the EU', *CEPR Discussion Paper* No. 3052.

Brainard, L.S. (1997), 'An empirical assessment of the proximity-concentration trade-off between multinational sales and trade', *American Economic Review* **87**(4), 520–44.

Brenton, P., F. Di Mauro and M. Luecke (1999), 'Economic integration and FDI: an empirical analysis of foreign investment in the EU and in Central and Eastern Europe', *Empirica*, **26**, 95–121.

Breuss, F. and P. Egger (1999), 'How reliable are estimations of East–West trade potentials based on cross section gravity analysis?, *Empirica*, **26**, 81–94.

Campos, N.F. and Y. Kinoshita (2003), 'Why does FDI go where it goes? New evidence from the transition economies', *IMF Working Paper* WP/03/228, Washington, DC: International Monetary Fund.

Carstensen, K. and F. Toubal (2004), 'Foreign direct investment in Central and Eastern European Countries: a dynamic panel analysis', *Journal of Comparative Economics*, **32**(1), 3–22.

Christie, E. (2003), 'Foreign direct investment in South-East Europe', The Vienna Institute for International Economic Studies, *Working Paper* No. 24.

Claessens, S., D. Oks and R. Polastri (1998), 'Capital flows to Central and Eastern Europe and the former Soviet Union', *World Bank Policy Research Working Paper* No. 1976, World Bank, Washington, DC.

Deichmann, J.I. (2001), 'Distribution of foreign direct investment among transition economies in Central and Eastern Europe', *Post-Soviet Geography and Economics*, **42**, 142–52.

Demekas, D., J. Herderschee, J. McHugh and S. Mitra (2002), 'Building peace in South-East Europe', A Joint World Bank–International Monetary Fund paper, Washington, DC.

Di Mauro, F. (2000), 'The impact of economic integration on FDI and exports: a gravity approach', *CEPS Working Document* 156.

Estrin, S., K. Hughes and S. Todd (1997), *Foreign Direct Investment in Central and Eastern Europe*, UK: Cassel.

European Bank for Reconstruction and Development, *EBRD Transition Report*, various issues, London: EBRD.
European Bank for Reconstruction and Development and World Bank, *Business Environment and Enterprise Performance Survey*, various issues, World Bank.
European Commission (2004), 'The Western Balkans in transition', *Occasional Paper* No. 5, European Commission, Brussels.
Feenstra, R.C., J.R. Markusen and A.K. Rose (2001), 'Using the gravity equation to differentiate among alternative theories of trade', *Canadian Journal of Economics*, **34** (2), 430–47.
Frankel, J. and A.K. Rose (1996), 'Currency crashes in emerging markets: an empirical treatment,' *Journal of International Economics*, **41**, 351–66.
Garibaldi, P., N. Mora, R. Sahay and J. Zettelmeyer (2002), 'What moves capital to transition economies', *IMF Working Paper* WP/02/64, Washington, DC: International Monetary Fund.
Graham, E. (1995), 'Foreign Direct Investment in the World Economy', *IMF Working Paper* WP/95/59, Washington, DC: International Monetary Fund.
Hansen, B.E. (1996), 'Inference when a nuisance parameter is not identified under the null hypothesis', *Econometrica*, **64** (2), 413–30.
Hanson, G., R. Mataloni and M. Slaughter (2001), 'Expansion strategies of the U.S. multinational firms', *NBER Working Paper* No. 8433.
Hassett, K.A. and R.G. Hubbard (1997), 'Tax policy and investment' in A. Shah (ed.), *Fiscal Policy: Lessons from Economic Research*, Cambridge: MIT Press.
Hines, J.R. Jr. (1999), 'Lessons from behavioral responses to international taxation', *National Tax Journal,* **52**, 305–22.
Holland, D. and N. Pain (1998), 'The diffusion of innovations in Central and Eastern Europe: a study of the determinants and impact of foreign direct investment', *NIESR Discussion Paper* No. 137.
Hunya, G. (2004), *Foreign Direct Investment in South-East Europe 2003–2004*, The Vienna Institute for International Economic Studies.
Janicki, P.H. and P.V. Wunnava (2004), 'Determinants of foreign direct investment: empirical evidence from EU accession candidates', *Applied Economics*, **36**, 505–9.
Javorcik, B.S. (2004), 'Does foreign direct investment increase the productivity of domestic firms? In search of spillovers through backward linkages,' *American Economic Review*, **94** (3), 605–27.
Javorcik, B.S., K. Saggi and M. Spatareanu (2004), 'Does it matter where you come from? Vertical spillovers from foreign direct investment and the nationality of investors', *World Bank Policy Research Working Paper* 3449, Washington, DC: The World Bank.
Lankes, H.-P. and A.J. Venables (1996), 'Foreign direct investment in economic transition: the changing pattern of investments', *Economics of Transition* **4** (2), 331–47.
Lansbury, M., N. Pain and K. Smidkova (1996), 'Foreign Direct Investment in Central Europe since 1990: an econometric study', *National Institute Economic Review*, **156**, 104–13.
Lehman, A. (2002), 'Foreign direct investment in emerging markets: income, repatriations and financial vulnerabilities', *IMF Working Paper* WP/02/47, Washington, DC: International Monetary Fund.
Lehman, A. and A. Mody (2004), 'International dividend repatriations', *IMF Working Paper* WP/04/5, Washington, DC: International Monetary Fund.

Lim, E.-G. (2001), 'Determinants of, and the relation between, foreign direct investment and growth: a summary of the recent literature', *IMF Working Paper* WP/01/175, Washington, DC: International Monetary Fund.

Lipschitz, L., T.D. Lane and A.T. Mourmouras (2002), 'Capital flows to transition economies: master or servant', *IMF Working Paper* WP/02/11, Washington, DC: International Monetary Fund.

Marin, D. (2004), 'A nation of poets and thinkers – less so with Eastern Enlargement? Austria and Germany', *CEPR Discussion Paper Series* No. 4358, Centre for Economic Policy Research.

Markusen, R.M. and K.E. Maskus (1999), 'Discriminating among alternative theories of the multinational enterprise', *NBRM Working Paper* No. 7164.

Mutti, J. and H. Grubert (2004), 'Empirical asymmetries in foreign direct investment taxation', *Journal of International Economics* **62**, 337–58.

Navaretti, G.B. and A.J. Venables (2004), *Multinational Firms in the World Economy*, UK: Princeton University Press.

OECD (2003), *Tax Policy Assessment and Design in Support of Direct Investment*, OECD.

PricewaterhouseCoopers (PWC), *Corporate Taxes: Worldwide Summaries*, various issues, John Wiley & Sons.

Resmini, L. (2000), 'The determinants of foreign direct investment in the CEECs: new evidence from sectoral patterns', *Economics of Transition*, **8** (3), 665–89.

Singh, H. and K. Jun (1996), 'The determinants of foreign direct investment in developing countries', *Transnational Corporations*, **5** (2), 67–105.

Vernon, R. (1966), 'International investment and international trade in the product cycle', *Quarterly Journal of Economics*, May, 190–207.

Wei, S. (2000), 'How taxing is corruption on international investors?', *Review of Economics and Statistics*, February, **82** (1), 1–11.

WIIW (2004), 'Are the geese flying? Comparing the industrial restructuring role of FDI in South-East Asian and Central European countries', Jubiläumsfonds Project No. 9958, The Vienna Institute for International Economic Studies.

World Bank (2005), *World Development Report*, Washington, DC: World Bank.

15. Trade integration of the new EU member states and selected South-East European countries: lessons from a gravity model

Matthieu Bussière, Jarko Fidrmuc and Bernd Schnatz[1]

1. INTRODUCTION

Over the past ten years, Central and South-East European countries (CEECs and SEECs) experienced rapid trade integration with the euro area, which had two major implications. From a euro area perspective, the share of these countries in extra-euro area trade[2] almost doubled between 1993 and 2003, from 7 per cent to 13 per cent.[3] Taken as an aggregate, the whole region now represents the euro area's third largest trading partner behind the United Kingdom (15.8 per cent) and the USA (13.6 per cent). For the CEECs and SEECs, in turn, the euro area represents the most important trading partner. The share of the euro area in the Czech Republic, Hungary, Poland, Slovenia and Romania (measured as percentage of imports and exports of these countries), is close to 60 per cent; for Albania it reaches almost 80 per cent, while for Bosnia and Herzegovina, FYR of Macedonia, Bulgaria and the Slovak Republic it is closer to 50 per cent but quickly rising.

The natural question that arises from these stylized facts is whether the increasing integration of the CEECs and SEECs with the euro area is likely to continue in the years to come, or rather to slow down. The answer to this question depends to a large extent on the interpretation of past developments. Clearly, the fact that integration between Eastern European transition countries and the more mature economies of the euro area increased in the 1990s should not, by itself, come as a surprise. The sheer geographical proximity of these countries, the large economic weight of the euro area and the rapid economic catching up of the transition economies are three likely factors accounting for this development. In addition, the transition process itself – combined with the removal of trade hurdles through accession to the EU – most certainly further enhanced trade between these two groups of countries. An open question, though, remains: is the rise in market shares observed so far largely coming to an end or is it still likely to continue? This requires having a view on what would constitute 'normal' trade relationships for these countries with the euro area.

The aim of this chapter is to set up a methodological framework to tackle this question empirically. For that purpose, the chapter uses a standard gravity model, where trade between country pairs is modelled as a function of their economic size and of the geographical distance between them. While this standard and relatively simple model constitutes a useful starting point, the chapter enriches this model by adding other variables to account for a common language or common border between two countries, free trade agreements, valuation effects and foreign direct investment (FDI) flows. These additional variables extend the scope of the standard model and allow a wide range of issues related to the transition process to be discussed. As recent research on the subject recommends the application of the fixed effects model (to account for unobservable factors), the chapter discusses the implication of using fixed effects in the particular case of transition economies.

To estimate the model, we use a database of bilateral trade flows across 61 countries, observed at annual frequency over the period 1980–2003. Estimations are therefore performed with roughly 50 000 observations, which is more than in most studies on the subject. Pooling so many observations has two main advantages: first it yields tightly estimated coefficients. Second, it allows us to draw from the experience of other dynamically developing countries at a similar stage of economic development. The model's performance in terms of goodness of fit is found to be highly satisfactory as the right-hand side variables explain a significant share of the variance of the dependent variable.

The model also successfully passes several robustness tests. A detailed analysis of the predicted values for the three largest euro area countries yields two key results. First, the values of trade flows between France, Germany and Italy with other large industrialized economies are close to the model's predictions. This result is intuitive as one would expect that trade flows between mature economies should be close to their 'normal' level in the long term, and are therefore more amenable to estimation with a gravity model. Second, the ratio of predicted to actual trade flows between the euro area's three largest economies on the one hand and the CEECs on the other hand was falling sharply throughout the 1990s. As argued in the chapter, the level of this ratio is difficult to interpret due to specific econometric problems. Yet, the evolution of this ratio through time can give an indication that the CEECs were trading below potential in the early 1990s, and that the gap has been narrowing since then.

The rest of the chapter is organized as follows. The next section presents some stylized facts on the issue. Section 3 reviews the existing literature on gravity models – focusing predominantly on Central and Eastern European countries – and introduces the gravity model. Section 4 reports the estimation results and the last section concludes.

2. STYLIZED FACTS: TRADE BETWEEN THE EURO AREA, NEW EU MEMBER STATES AND THE SEECS

For the CEECs, the euro area represents the most important trading partner. In the case of the Czech Republic, Hungary, Poland, Romania, Slovakia and Slovenia, for instance, trade with the euro area now amounts to nearly 60 per cent of their total trade (see Figure 15.1). In the case of the Slovak Republic, trade with the euro area started from a relatively low level in 1993 (less than 30 per cent) and quickly increased in the following ten years. The magnitude of the increase was also high for Romania, whose trade share with the euro area rose from 40 per cent to 60 per cent over the same period. For the countries that were already trading a lot with the euro area in 1993 (such as Slovenia, Hungary and Poland), the share of the euro area seems to have remained roughly constant over the past ten years. In the particular case of Hungary, the share of the euro area in foreign trade rose above 60 per cent in the late 1990s but abated somewhat since then. The pattern observed in Figure 15.1 would therefore suggest that the share of the euro area external trade in the above-mentioned countries tends to converge towards a common level. However, there are some exceptions to this general pattern. In the Baltic countries, for example, the share of the euro area in foreign trade is significantly lower (around 40 per cent) and seems to remain stable at that level. Similarly, the market share of the euro area in Turkey has remained stable in the past ten years at around 40 per cent. To anticipate the analysis of the gravity model that will be developed in the following sections, one could partly attribute the lower share of the euro area in the Baltic countries and in Turkey to their higher distance from the euro area.

The large share of euro area trade in the new EU member states reflects predominantly the high weight of Germany. A geographical decomposition of trade by partner country[4] reveals for instance that the share of Germany in these countries is higher than the share of Italy (Romania being a noticeable exception). Furthermore, trade with other new EU member states is still large for many of them. Trade between the Czech Republic and Slovakia especially is comparably high due to their common history (see Fidrmuc and Fidrmuc, 2003). Also, the share of Russia in the CEECs remains high (5 per cent on average, which is more than the shares of the UK and the USA), especially for the Baltic countries (where Russia's share is above 10 per cent), reflecting the importance of distance and traditionally strong supplies of raw materials and fuels.

Turning to the SEECs, the share of the euro area is quickly rising in Bosnia and Herzegovina and in FYR of Macedonia (from 30 per cent in 1993 to roughly 50 per cent in 2003), while for Croatia it has remained roughly stable at 50 per cent in the past ten years. Albania has the highest share of trade with the euro area at nearly 80 per cent. Yet, by contrast with the other countries, this reflects mostly trade with Italy (more than 50 per cent) and Greece (at around 20 per cent in the late 1990s and slightly less in 2002 and 2003), rather than trade with Germany.

From a euro area perspective, the most noticeable changes that occurred in the past ten years have been an increase in the market shares[5] of the new EU member states and of China – providing an unprecedented example of integration dynamics (see Djankov and Hoekman, 1997) – and a continuous decrease in the share of Japan (see Figure 15.2). Between 1993 and 2003, the share of the new EU member states in extra-euro area trade almost doubled, from 5.7 per cent to 10.6 per cent. Overall, the new EU member states increased their market shares in the euro area countries almost continuously, with the exception of 1999 and 2000 when it temporarily levelled off. More recently the prospect of EU membership might have given a new impetus to these dynamics.

Trade between the euro area and other candidate and accession countries (Bulgaria, Croatia and Romania) has also increased substantially since 2000, similarly to the experience of the new EU member states during the 1990s (see Figure 15.3). Finally, bilateral trade with other countries in South-East Europe (Albania, Bosnia and Herzegovina, and FYR of Macedonia) has started to pick up since 2000, raising the question whether these countries may experience a similar dynamic development of their trade with the euro area as the new EU member states did in the past decade.

Taken together, the CEECs and the SEECs are a fairly important trading partner of the euro area. In 2003, the region as a whole traded roughly as much with the euro area as the USA (13.6 per cent) and significantly more than Japan (4.3 per cent), China (5.4 per cent) or Russia (1.5 per cent), but it is still less important than the UK (15.9 per cent). Among the CEECs, the market shares of the Czech Republic, Hungary and Poland in the euro area are between 2–3 per cent, while the other shares of the other CEECs are commonly at or below 1 per cent (Figure 15.3).

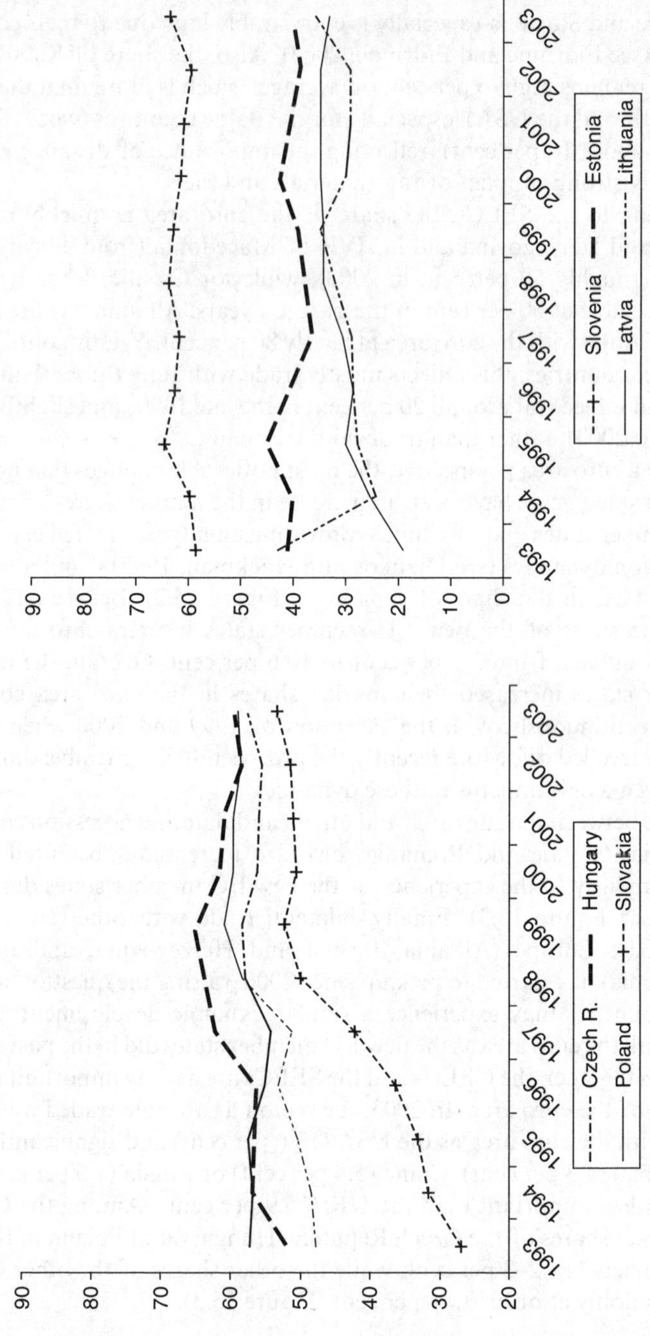

90
80
70
60
50
40
30
20
1993
1994
1995
1996
1997
1998
1999
2000
2001
2002
2003
Czech R.
Hungary
Poland
Slovakia
90
80
70
60
50
40
30
20
10
0
1993
1994
1995
1996
1997
1998
1999
2000
2001
2002
2003
Slovenia
Estonia
Latvia
Lithuania

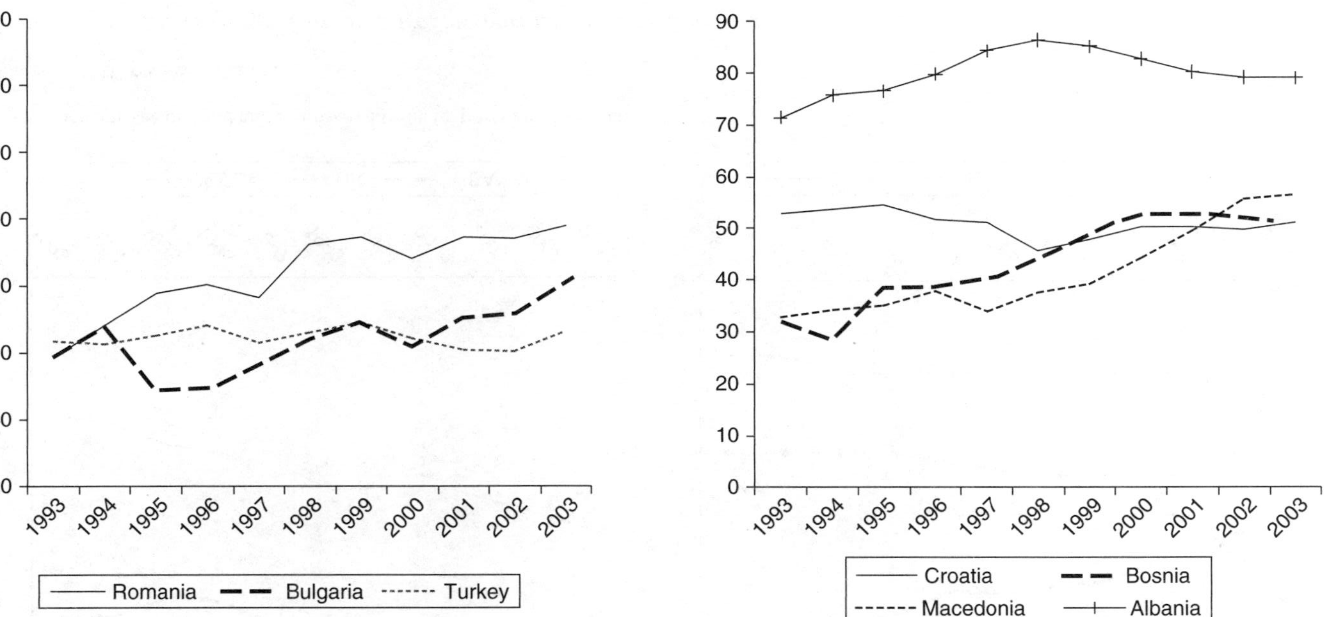

Note: Share of trade flows with the euro area as a percentage of total trade flows (exports and imports).

Source: IMF, own calculations.

Figure 15.1 The importance of the euro area for the CEECs and the SEECs

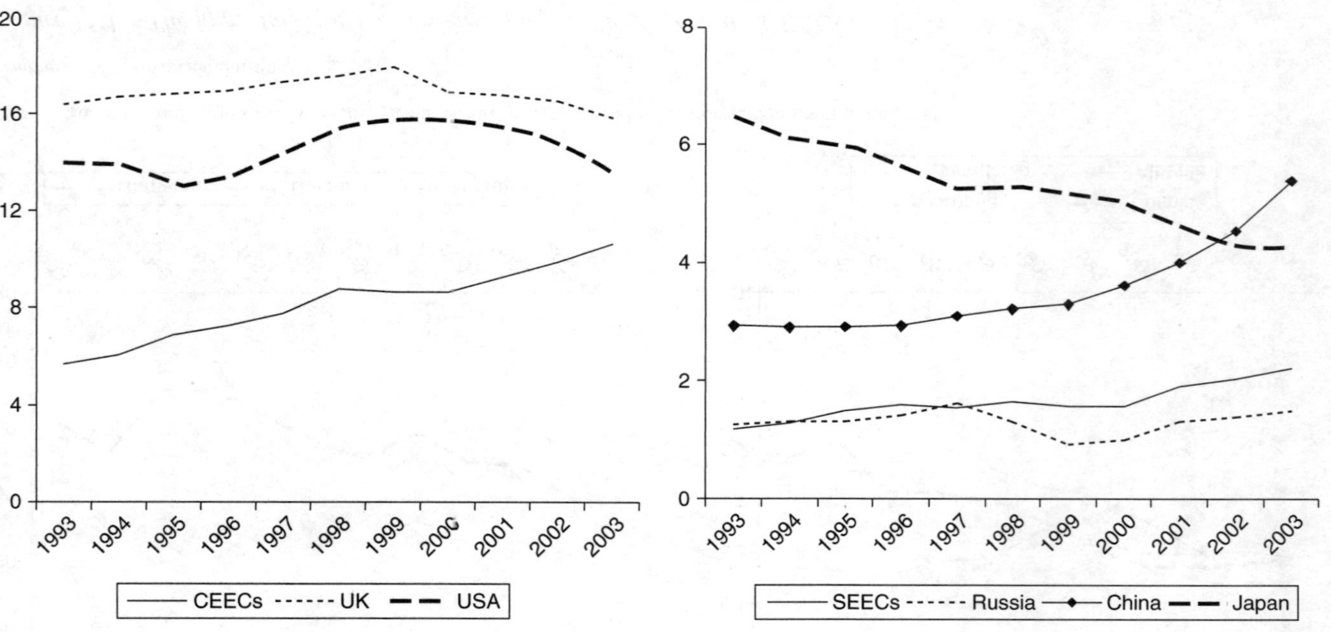

Note: Percentage of total extra-euro area trade (exports and imports).

Source: IMF, own calculations.

Figure 15.2 Share of key euro area trading partners in euro area trade

Finally, it is worth mentioning the role of FDI for the CEECs. Table 15.1 reports FDI outflows of the six largest world economies by destination. Between 1995 and 2001, Germany invested much more than any other country in CEECs, both in absolute value and in percentage of total FDI outflows. However, there are a few exceptions: France invested nearly as much as Germany in Poland. Italy was the largest investor in Bulgaria. Finally, France invested more than Italy and Germany together in Romania. By contrast, investment from the other large industrialized countries (UK, USA and Japan) in CEECs and SEECs was rather low. Both the UK and Japan invested a sizeable fraction of their total FDI in the USA (around 40 per cent), while 50 per cent of US investment went to the EU. These developments are consistent with the trade patterns observed above, in particular with the predominant weight of Germany in CEECs trade.

In sum, the stylized facts on trade between the euro area and the CEECs and the SEECs show significant adjustments over the past decade. The new member states made dynamic gains in market shares in the euro area and vice versa. This raises the question whether the integration of these economies with the euro area and, more generally, into the world economy is already at an advanced stage, or whether more integration can be expected. In the following, this is assessed quantitatively on the basis of a gravity model which explains trade between countries or regions as a function of other economic fundamentals.

3. EMPIRICAL METHODOLOGY: THE GRAVITY MODEL

Gravity models, which were originally proposed by Linder (1961) and Linnemann (1966), have become one of the most commonly used workhorse models to analyse geographical patterns in trade flows. By analogy with Newton's theory of gravitation, gravity models express bilateral trade as a function of two key variables: the economic size of two given countries engaged in trade and the distance between them. Gravity models, which in their most general form suggest that the magnitude of trade between countries depends on supply in the source country, demand in the host country, and other factors which may stimulate or hinder bilateral trade, are consistent with standard models of international trade (see Deardorff, 1995; Anderson, 1979; Anderson and van Wincoop, 2003). Gravity models can be directly related to the above-mentioned stylized facts on trade of the CEECs and SEECs. The relevance of economic size is apparent from the fact that the shares of the larger CEECs (Poland, Hungary, the Czech Republic) in euro area trade are higher than those of smaller CEECs. At the

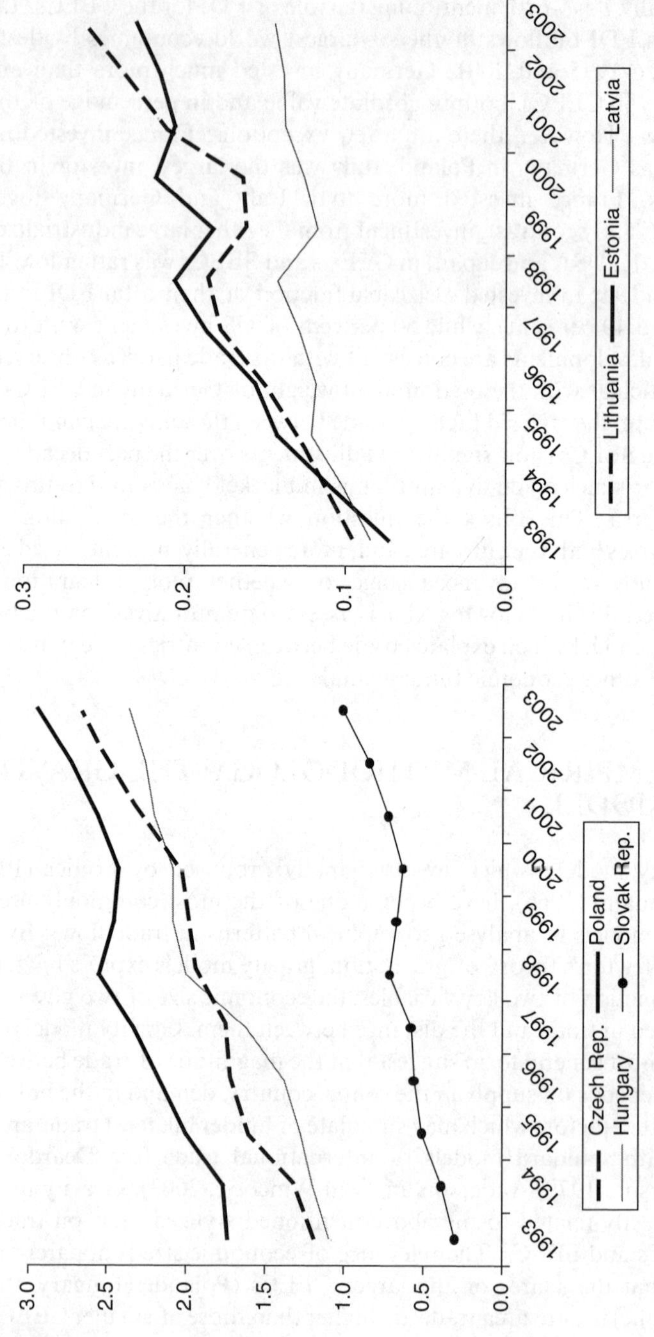

Czech Rep.
Poland
Hungary
Slovak Rep.
3.0
2.5
2.0
1.5
1.0
0.5
0.0
1993
1994
1995
1996
1997
1998
1999
2000
2001
2002
2003
Lithuania
Estonia
Latvia
0.3
0.2
0.1
0.0
1993
1994
1995
1996
1997
1998
1999
2000
2001
2002
2003

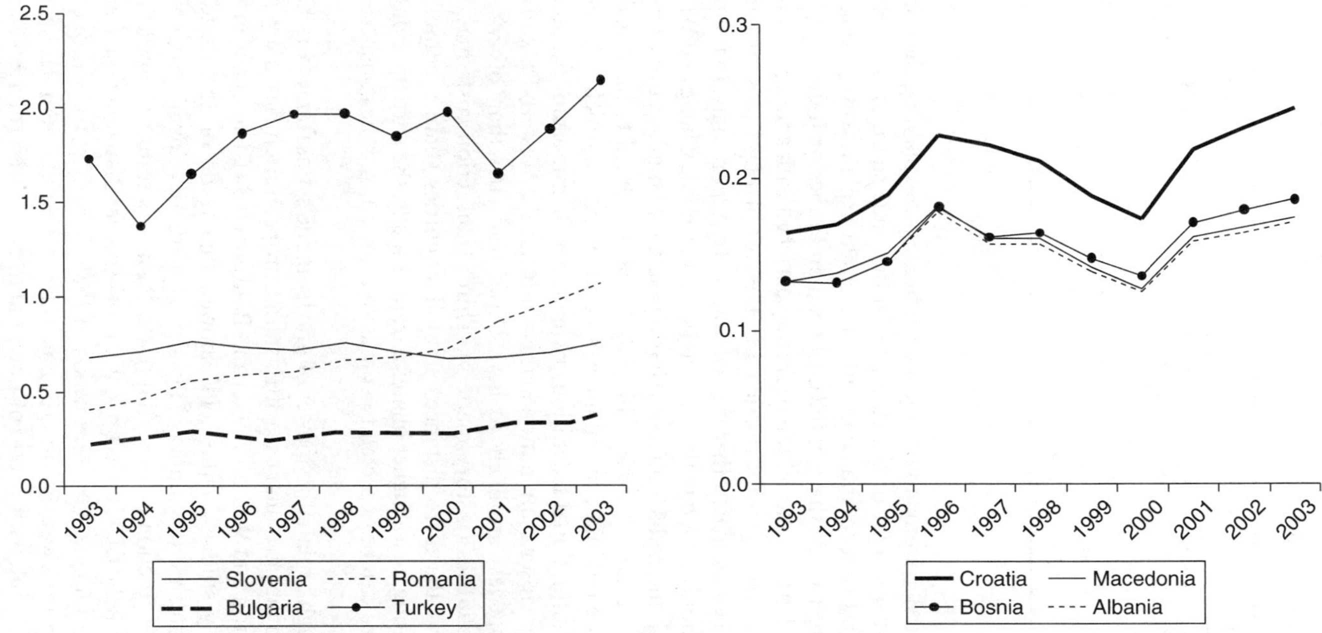

Note: Percentage of total extra-euro area trade (exports and imports).

Source: IMF, own calculations.

Figure 15.3 Shares of CEECs in euro area trade

Table 15.1 Cumulated FDI in CEECs and SEECs, 1995–2001 (USD billion)

	Poland	Hungary	Czech R.	Slovakia	Slovenia	Bulgaria	Romania	World
France	9631	1483	2060	168	317	181	1038	493 674
Germany	10 000	5973	5207	1748	179	252	575	406 249
Italy	1469	258	107	72	74	355	219	67 706
UK	1151	412	603	26	21	47	49	660 510
USA	1051	1116	146	36	30	18	80	462 161
Japan	266	500	244	0	0	0	40	303 541

Source: OECD.

same time, distance seems to be a good candidate for explaining the comparatively smaller weight of the euro area in the trade share of the Baltic countries. Both distance and economic size could explain why Germany has a much larger trade share in the CEECs than France or Italy.

The standard gravity model can be further enriched with additional variables, as trading costs are not restricted to the cost of physically shipping goods, but also encompass other transaction costs. Accordingly, four variables are commonly added to the analysis (see for example Cheng and Wall, 2004). First, it is likely that countries sharing the same language trade more with each other than otherwise. This may be partly related to historically established trade ties and cultural links. Second, countries which belonged to the same multinational federations (which may be important for some countries under closer examination in this study like the Western Balkan or the Baltic countries) are likely to have closer trade ties than otherwise comparable countries (history matters). Third, transaction costs may be reduced beyond the mere distance factor if countries share a common border, translating into a higher bilateral trade. Finally, the participation in a free trade area can be expected to stimulate trade among the constituent countries.

In view of high explanatory power of gravity models, this framework has been applied to the particular case of Eastern European countries in several studies. Hamilton and Winters (1992) and Baldwin (1994), two of the most influential early studies in the field, showed that trade of the Eastern European countries (excluding Yugoslavia) with developed countries has been only a fraction of potential trade. Baldwin's results showed that actual trade with the EU-12 was up to five times smaller than potential trade for Bulgaria and former Czechoslovakia in 1989. Some Central European transition economies were found to be much closer to equilibrium (Hungary being a case in point, with a ratio of potential to actual trade of 1.8), while countries like Romania and Albania, which did not participate in the Council of the Mutual Economic Assistance, started trade liberalization with regional trade structures closer to the gravity predictions estimated by Baldwin. Havrylyshyn and Al-Atrash (1998) found that Romania achieved a significantly higher actual share of trade with the EU than predicted by the model in 1996. Kaminski et al. (1996) and Jakab et al. (2001) suggest a rapid convergence towards trade potential levels by the CEECs. Egger (2003) and Fidrmuc and Fidrmuc (2003) found trade between the EU-15 and the CEECs close to the predicted levels at the end of the 1990s.

The literature on the SEECs is rather scarce compared to the literature on new EU member states. To our knowledge, the only studies that analyse trade potentials for the entire South-East European region are Christie (2002 and 2004). His results show significant differences of the actual trade from the potential values. The lack of transportation infrastructure is identified as a major obstacle to trade both within the region and with the developed countries. Vujčić and Šošić (2004) estimate gravity models for Croatia. However, these studies do not employ fully the panel dimensions of their datasets. Furthermore, they do not present a broader comparison with other regions. Such comparison would bolster the results and put them in perspective.

Nevertheless, Christie (2002) and Vujčić and Šošić (2004) identify some trade potentials for SEECs especially with developed countries. This reflects partially tariff and non-tariff trade barriers introduced during the 1990s. Croatia, for example, only recently joined the WTO, and free trade agreements between the SEECs are not yet implemented. It follows that the EU is especially likely to play an important role for the countries that liberalized trade with the Western Balkan region (Albania, Bosnia and Herzegovina, Croatia, FYR of Macedonia, and Serbia and Montenegro) by an autonomous trade concession in 2000. Furthermore, several countries of the region aim to join the EU as soon as possible.[6] The regional market is less attractive for the regional neighbours due to new trade barriers and income declines during the 1990s.

3.1 Econometric Issues

Estimating the gravity model and assessing trade patterns on the basis of the empirical results is subject to several econometric challenges. In the recent literature on gravity models, most papers have focused on the impact of policy variables (such as common borders, free trade areas or the participation in a currency union) instead of the structure of trade per se.[7] Many papers using the gravity approach still employ either a cross-section or a pooled ordinary least squares (OLS) specification, and often ignore heterogeneous characteristics of analysed countries. Other authors employed averaged data over longer periods (see Hamilton and Winters, 1992) or repeated cross-section regressions (see Fidrmuc and Fidrmuc, 2003) to account for structural changes in the trade of newly independent countries.

Failing to account for unobserved country heterogeneity can lead to distorted estimates. Serlenga and Shin (2004) as well as Cheng and Wall (2004) demonstrated that ignoring heterogeneity translates into biased estimates of bilateral trade relationships. Furthermore, Anderson and van Wincoop (2003) extended the standard theoretical framework of the gravity model by the so-called multilateral trade resistance term, which may be covered by country dummies (see also Feenstra, 2002). Similarly, Mátyás (1997, 1998) extended a standard gravity model with two sets of country dummies (for exporting and importing countries).[8] Subsequent research on panel estimators (see Egger and Pfaffermayr, 2003) showed, however, that instead of using one dummy variable per country, individual country pair dummies (fixed effects) should be included to get efficient estimators. For instance, the euro area may trade with two other countries in different amounts, even though the two partner countries have the same economic size, are equidistant from the euro area and share many other characteristics. These specifications, which usually include time dummies as well, fully utilize panel dimensions of trade flows between countries.

Another potential caveat of standard estimation techniques is that it cannot be ruled out that some of the right-hand side variables have some endogenous characteristics. For instance, the establishment of free trade areas may also depend on the initial level of bilateral trade between two countries. In the context of discussions about the trade effect of EMU, for instance, Micco et al. (2003) suggest that countries constitute a common club if they have already been engaged in a great deal of trade with each other. In short, unusually high trade flows may lead to the establishment of a free trade arrangement rather than vice versa.

Against this background, the following analysis is based on panel data econometrics that take country-specific effects into account, which – as emphasized by Micco et al. (2003) and Cheng and Wall (2004) – should reduce both the heterogeneity bias and the endogeneity bias (the intuition being that fixed effects take into account whether two countries have traditionally traded a great deal).

Taking the time series dimension into account by pooling the data is, however, still subject to several drawbacks. First, the inclusion of fixed effects normally does not allow estimating the coefficients of the time-invariant variables (such as distance) which are covered by the fixed effects. Second, the variables entering the gravity model may contain a unit root, requiring cointegration analysis instead of standard panel estimation techniques (see Faruqee, 2004). The first point is taken into account by using the two-step procedure presented below. In order to account for possible non-stationarity in the data, the results of the fixed effects estimator are compared with the results of the dynamic OLS specification (see Kao and Chiang, 2000).

In more formal terms, the gravity equation we estimate can be expressed as follows:

$$T_{ijt} = \alpha_{ij} + \theta_t + \beta_1 Y_{it} + \beta_2 Y_{jt} + \beta_3 D_{ij} + \beta_4 Q_{it} + \beta_5 Q_{jt} + \beta_6 \sigma_{ij} + \sum_{k=1}^{5} \gamma_k Z_k + \varepsilon_{ijt} \quad (15.1)$$

where T_{ijt} corresponds to the size of bilateral trade between country i and country j at time t, Y_{it} and Y_{jt} stand for the (real) GDP in the source country i and in the host country j, respectively, at time t, D_{ij} is the distance variable, Z_k reflects cultural, historical and political factors affecting bilateral trade between two countries. Consistent with the arguments made before, β_1 and β_2 are expected to be positive while β_3 should be negative. As standard in the literature, trade is defined as the average of exports and imports (in logs) and distance is measured in terms of great circle distances between the capitals of country i and country j (in logs). Obviously, this measure is not without problems as it implicitly assumes that land transport costs are comparable to sea transport costs. Moreover, it assumes that the capital city is the only economic centre of a country, which is probably more appropriate for small than for large countries. Following Micco et al. (2003), we also include the real exchange rate Q of each country against the USD, mainly to control for valuation effects as all trade data are expressed in US dollar terms. As real depreciation of a country's currency against the US dollar would tend to lower the US dollar value of its trade, the sign of β_4 and β_5 should be positive. Moreover, we include the standard deviation of the month-on-month log changes in the bilateral nominal exchange rate within a year (σ) as a proxy for exchange rate volatility and expect a negative sign for β_6. As discussed above, four additional factors possibly affecting bilateral trade were considered by including dummy variables for country-pairs: (1) a common language, (2) a common border, (3) being a part of the same country or multinational federation in the past, and (4) membership of free trade areas. Accordingly, all γ_k are expected to have a positive sign.

The terms α_{ij} are the country-pair individual effects covering all unobservable factors related to trade resistance including tariff and non-tariff trade barriers, geographical position, and openness to trade in general, as Z_k is unlikely to encompass all cultural, historical and political factors, which are intrinsically difficult to measure in practice. To a large extent, it should also account for the drawbacks of the distance variable discussed above and for any other non-observable characteristics. Accordingly, Cheng and Wall (2004) label the fixed effects a 'result of ignorance', although – as argued below – they may still entail useful information. θ_t are the time-specific effects – controlling for common shocks or the general trend towards 'globalization'– and ε_{ij} is the error term. In more general terms, these time dummies account for any time-varying non-observable factors affecting bilateral trade which are equally important for all trading pairs.

In terms of econometric methodology, we first estimate the regression using the standard fixed effects estimator. As the time-invariant variables are collinear with the country-pair individual effect, which precludes the estimation of coefficients for D_{ij} and Z_k (except the dummies for the free trade areas being created or expanded during the analysed period) we follow Cheng and Wall (2004) and estimate an additional regression of the estimated country-pair effects on the time-invariant variables in order to filter out the importance of these variables in the fixed effects,

$$\hat{\alpha}_{ij} = \beta_1 + \beta_2 D_{ij} + \sum_{k=1}^{k} \gamma_k Z_k + \mu_{ij}. \tag{15.2}$$

4. DATA AND ESTIMATION RESULTS

4.1 Data

The dataset includes annual data from 1980 to 2002. By the end of the sample period, it comprises 61 countries as some countries – particularly the economies in transition – entered the dataset only in the 1990s after the fall of the Iron Curtain, followed by the foundation of several new countries. This amounts to more than 50 000 observations and more than 3500 bilateral trade relationships. Trade data are mostly compiled from the IMF Direction of Trade Statistics; they are expressed in US dollars and deflated by US producer prices. GDP data come from the IMF International Financial Statistics and are deflated by US consumer prices. Missing data for some SEECs have been included from the Vienna Institute for International Economic Studies (WIIW) and EBRD Transition Reports. Exchange rate volatility is defined as the standard deviation of the month-on-month log changes in the bilateral nominal exchange rate within a year. The distance term reflects the aerial distance between the capital of the two countries under consideration and comes from Fidrmuc and Fidrmuc (2003) and the MS Encarta World Atlas software.

The dummy variable for common territory includes countries which constituted a common country at some point in the past 20 years. More specifically, they include the former Czechoslovakia (the Czech Republic and the Slovak Republic), countries of the former Soviet Union (Belarus, Estonia, Latvia, Lithuania, Moldova, Russia, and the Ukraine), and countries of Former Yugoslavia (Bosnia and Herzegovina, Croatia, FYR of Macedonia, and Slovenia). Overall, there are 56 country pairs which were part of the same nation state at some point in recent history. For the common language dummy, the variable was equal to one if in both countries a significant part of the population speaks the same language (English, French, Spanish, Portuguese, German, Swedish, Dutch, Chinese, Malay, Russian, Greek, Arabic, Serbo-Croatian or Albanian). Some countries enter several language groupings, such as Canada, where both English and French are native idioms, or Singapore, where English, Chinese and Malay are commonly used languages. Overall, there are 274 country pairs in which the same language is spoken. The dummy variable for having a common border refers to 179 land borders shared by the countries included in the sample. Finally, dummy variables have been included for the most important free trade arrangements, namely the EU, ASEAN, NAFTA, MERCOSUR and CEFTA.

4.2 Estimation Results

Table 15.2 presents the estimation results. The first column shows the results following the fixed effects (FE) formulation, which is suggested by Cheng and Wall (2004). In the first step, a regression excluding all time-invariant variables was run including as many country pairs as possible. The exchange rate volatility variable was excluded, because it was insignificant and inconsistently signed. The free trade areas were introduced or expanded during the analysed period; hence, they were already included in this step. The results suggest that all variables included in the specification (except the EU dummy) have the expected sign and are statistically significant.

As an alternative to the FE specification, the coefficients for the time-invariant variables can be estimated by the random effect (RE) model, which assumes that explanatory variables are uncorrelated with random effects. However, the Hausman test ($\chi^2(31) = 1775.7$) strongly suggests that this assumption is violated in gravity models, yielding inconsistent estimates. Correspondingly, the coefficient estimates of the RE model also diverge notably from the fixed effects specification.

The fixed effects model confirms that both domestic and foreign real GDP have a highly significant and less-than-proportional impact on bilateral trade. The magnitude of the coefficients suggests that a 1 per cent

Table 15.2 Estimation of gravity models

	FE (Step 1)	FE (Step 2)	RE	OLS	DOLS (Step 1)	DOLS (Step 2)	FE (Step 1)	FE (Step 2)
	full sample	full sample	full sample	full sample	full sample	full sample	OECD	OECD
Y_i	0.592**		0.869**	0.935**	0.635**		0.578**	
Y_j	0.532**		0.842**	0.921**	0.504**		0.600**	
Distance		−0.696**	−0.862**	−0.834**		−0.689**		−0.594**
Territory		0.09	1.324**	1.934**		0.126		
Border		1.016**	0.576**	0.345**		1.010**		0.724**
Language		1.298**	1.093**	0.828**		1.288**		0.354**
EU	−0.014		0.028	0.170**	−0.043		0.219**	
ASEAN	0.450**		0.408**	2.094**	0.406**			
MERCOSUR	0.244*		0.191**	0.713**	0.206*			
CEFTA	0.218**		0.228**	0.832**	0.231**			
NAFTA	0.450**		0.529**	0.270*	0.446**		0.201**	
Q_i	0.039**		0.077**	−0.017	0.104**		0.198**	
Q_j	0.052**		0.095**	0.004	0.037**		0.291**	
R^2	0.63	0.33	0.80	0.81	0.64	0.33	0.67	0.60
N	52683	3462	52614	52614	43976	3352	10034	458

Notes: *, ** denote significance at the 5% (1%) level. FE – fixed effects, RE – random effects, OLS – ordinary least squares, DOLS – dynamic OLS, Step 1 – first-step regression, Step 2 – second-step regression.

Source: Own estimations.

increase in economic activity at home or abroad should raise bilateral trade by about 0.55 to 0.60 per cent. The real exchange rate variables also enter the regression significantly – consistent with our concerns about valuation effects – but their coefficients are fairly small. The dummies for free trade arrangements enter significantly and with the right sign, with the exception of the EU dummy, which is not significant in this specification.[9]

The overall R^2 of the FE regression amounts to 0.63 – reflecting a 'within' R^2 of 0.43 and a 'between' R^2 of 0.63 – suggesting that even such a fairly simple specification is able to explain a significant part of the variation in international trade. However, there is still sizeable variation in the fixed effects and in the error term. The latter amounts to 0.51, implying that at the one standard error band trade may be 65 per cent higher or lower than the central estimate. The time dummies (not reported) are increasing over time, thereby encompassing the rise in international trade owing to globalization over the past 25 years. In the second stage of the regression, the distance term is strongly negative, implying that trade between two countries is almost 70 per cent higher if the country is half as distant as another otherwise identical market. Similarly, having a common border roughly doubles trade between the two countries and speaking the same language raises trade by another 130 per cent. The adjusted R^2 in the second-stage regression is 0.33, implying that these factors explain roughly one-third of the distribution of the country-specific factors.

Comparing these results with the pooled OLS estimator (which excludes country-specific effects), as employed in the earlier papers in the literature surveyed in the previous sections, also suggests that trade flows between the countries and the variables are correctly signed and highly significant. Adjacency, common language or a common history increase bilateral trade. Similarly, free trade areas are found to increase trade between the members. By contrast, other variables (including exchange rates) remain insignificant in this standard specification. However, the magnitudes of the coefficients are notably different from those in the FE estimation, suggesting that the bias introduced by neglecting country-pair specific factors is not negligible.

The robustness of the coefficient estimates is broadly confirmed by our sensitivity analysis: first, in order to account for possible non-stationarity in and cointegration among the variables of the gravity model – as suggested by Faruqee (2004) – panel dynamic OLS (DOLS) have been estimated. In this context, Kao and Chiang (2000) show that the FE estimator, while being asymptotically normal, may be asymptotically biased. Moreover, panel DOLS take into account the potential endogeneity of the variables as well as the presence of serial correlation by including leads and lags of the differenced explanatory variables as additional regressors. The DOLS results in Table 15.2 are very close to the results of the FE estimator, suggesting that the potential bias from the FE specification should be small.[10]

As a second robustness check, the sample was reduced to include only the OECD countries in the FE estimation. In this specification, several variables used in the full sample drop out owing to missing observations. In more detail, there are obviously no trade relationships simultaneously within MERCOSUR or CEFTA and the OECD. The number of observations used in this model drops to about 10 000, that is by roughly 80 per cent. Nonetheless, the coefficients retain their signs and significance. Domestic and foreign GDP are still highly significant and the coefficients are close to those estimated in the full sample. The dummy for NAFTA remains positive and significant but is smaller compared to the previous specification; the EU is now significant and positive in this specification. In the second-step regression, the coefficients of the time-invariant variables are somewhat smaller in absolute terms. In particular the language dummy seems to be less relevant, possibly reflecting the exclusion of former colonies in this sample. While the standard errors of this regression are generally somewhat larger, the fit of the model is even better than for the broader model, suggesting that the extension of the database also introduces a significant amount of noise.

Finally, we considered adding FDI flows as an additional regressor in the robustness analysis, but we decided not to keep it in the final estimation due to a number of caveats. First, FDI data are very volatile, thus considerably complicating estimation. Second, the endogeneity issue is particularly acute for FDI flows. As noted in section 2, Germany invested a great deal in CEECs, consistent with its high weight in the total trade of these countries. However, it is not clear whether FDI is driving trade or the reverse, while FDI is at the same time considered as a substitute for trade (see Markusen and Venables, 1998; and Egger and Pfaffermayr, 2004). Tentative results indicate that FDI enters the regression significantly and with a positive sign, but a low coefficient. Clearly, more research on this issue is needed before a better picture can be drawn.

4.3 Interpretation of Predicted Values

It is convenient to analyse the ratios of predicted and actual trade, which indicate the goodness of fit of the model. Yet, the evolution of this ratio also provides some information on the trade potential of a given country. This should not be interpreted as a forecast, however. First, the model is not set up for forecasting purposes (some of the variables being endogenous), and second, the predicted values are conditional on the values of the right-hand side variables taken at a certain time as well as the time effects. Above all, another complication arises due to the difficulty to interpret the fixed effects (the following section will return to this issue). Therefore, one should not read too much into the actual level of the comparison ratio, but focus rather on its evolution over time.

With a view to comparing the integration degrees for the CEECs and the SEECs with the euro area, we discuss trade flows[11] of the three largest euro area countries (France, Germany and Italy) to three groups of countries: (1) other large industrialized countries (for comparison purposes), (2) the largest CEECs, and (3) the SEECs. The results are as follows. First, the bilateral trade relationships of France, Germany and Italy with the other large industrialized countries are close to the model predictions, the ratios being most of the time close to one. This may suggest that the model does a relatively good job in explaining trade flows for the advanced economies. Second, for most of the CEECs, the ratios are downward sloping: they decrease from values around two (sometimes above) in the early 1990s to values close to or below one. This pattern is common to all three large euro area countries, but tends to be more pronounced in the case of France than in the case of Germany, and less so in the case of Italy. The high values of the ratio observed in the early 1990s could suggest that at the time, the CEECs were trading below potential with Germany, France and Italy. The subsequent decline in the ratio could indicate that this gap might have decreased over time.[12]

In the case of the SEECs, we observe very different patterns. Bosnia and Herzegovina seems to fluctuate without a clear trend in recent years vis-à-vis all three large euro area countries, while Albania and FYR of Macedonia actually have increasing ratios, suggesting that these countries' trade developed less dynamically than the fundamentals would have suggested.

4.4 Extracting Information from Country Heterogeneity

The country-specific effects estimated in this model still include valuable information for analysing integration of these countries into the world economy. Following broadly Anderson and van Wincoop's (2003) interpretation of fixed effects as multilateral resistance terms, we propose a measure of trade integration which is derived from country-specific effects after controlling for the levels of the time-invariant variables. Overall, a high fixed effect for a country pair corresponds to high bilateral trade openness, while a low or negative fixed effect indicates relatively close economies. Accordingly, aggregating the country-specific effects for a country over all partner countries provides an indication of the country's overall degree of integration into the world economy. More formally, from equation (15.2), the residuals denoted by $\hat{\mu}_{hj}$ are aggregated for a country h into a simple 'trade condition indicator', tci_h:

$$tci_h = \frac{1}{2(N-1)}\left(\sum_{i=1}^{N-1} \hat{\mu}_{ih} + \sum_{j=1}^{N-1} \hat{\mu}_{hj}\right) \tag{15.3}$$

Figure 15.4 ranks the trade condition indicator for all countries in descending order. This shows the average degree of trade integration as measured by country-specific effects for all country pairs, revealing several interesting insights for the CEECs and the SEECs. First, there remains a significant degree of heterogeneity as signified by the variance of the indicators. Second, the industrialized countries tend to display an above-average trade openness. For example, Germany and the USA trade four times more than an average country in our sample after controlling for the relevant fundamentals. Exceptions are Luxembourg and Greece, which appear to face a somewhat higher level of overall trade resistance, which in the case of Luxembourg may be due to the specific structure of the economy. Third, among emerging market economies mainly South-East Asian countries show high average fixed effects and, thus, low overall trade

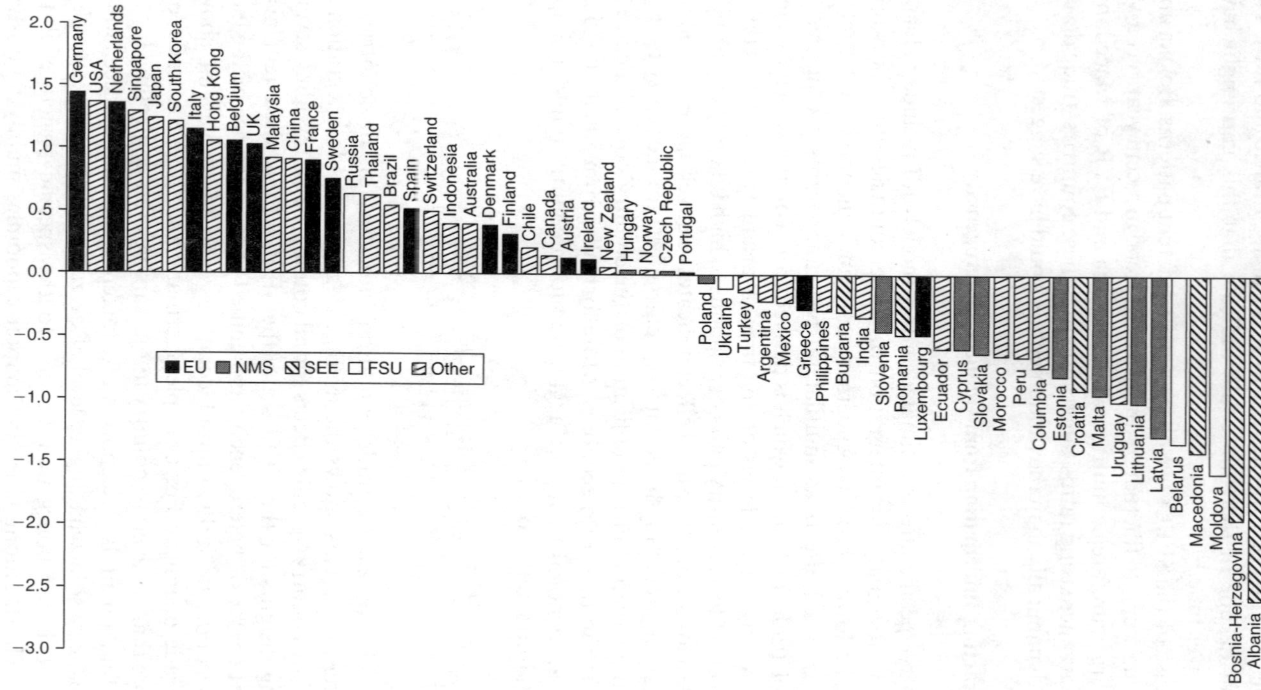

Source: Own estimations.

Figure 15.4 Trade conditions (average fixed effects) by countries, integration in world markets

resistance. For instance, Singapore and South Korea trade about 3.5 times above the average. Fourthly, the new member states are mostly found in the right-hand side spectrum of the chart. Only the Czech Republic, Hungary and Poland show trade openness measures that are fairly close to the sample average, while Slovenia trades 40 per cent less than an average country; the Slovak Republic, Cyprus and Estonia about 50 per cent below the average; and Lithuania and Latvia about 70 per cent below the average. Finally, to the far right-hand side of the spectrum are the SEECs. Bosnia and Herzegovina reaches only 15 per cent, and Albania only 8 per cent of the average trade level, suggesting that these countries still have a significant potential to integrate more into the world economy.[13]

While this analysis provided some assessment about the depth of the integration of the CEECs and the SEECs into the global economy, it would also be interesting to know whether there are countries which show particularly high or low degrees of integration with these countries, to identify which trade relationships should deepen disproportionately. This can be assessed by using the same indicator computed only for trade with the new member states or trade with the SEECs. These measures are again ranked for both country groups in descending order in Figures 15.5 and 15.6.

The trade orientation indicators are above the sample average only with very few countries, thereby broadly confirming the above result that both regions do still have significant potentials to integrate into the world economy. However, it also shows that these countries are already fairly well integrated with main countries of the EU such as Germany, Italy, France and the Netherlands. The CEECs are also fairly well integrated with the USA and some countries of the former Soviet Union. The latter is likely to reflect historical ties which are not sufficiently captured by the dummy variables included. The new member states also show a fairly high level of regional trade integration, especially with respect to the core former CEFTA countries (Czech Republic, Hungary and Poland). In turn, trade orientation of the SEECs to their regional neighbours is rather low, although it is higher than in the sample average. Most importantly, there seems to be significant scope for increasing SEECs' trade with the smaller OECD countries (including several EU countries) and many emerging markets.

5. CONCLUSIONS

This chapter analysed the rapid trade integration which took place in the past decade between Central and South-East European countries and the euro area. Estimations from gravity models augmented with a set of additional variables show that this rapid integration is not necessarily

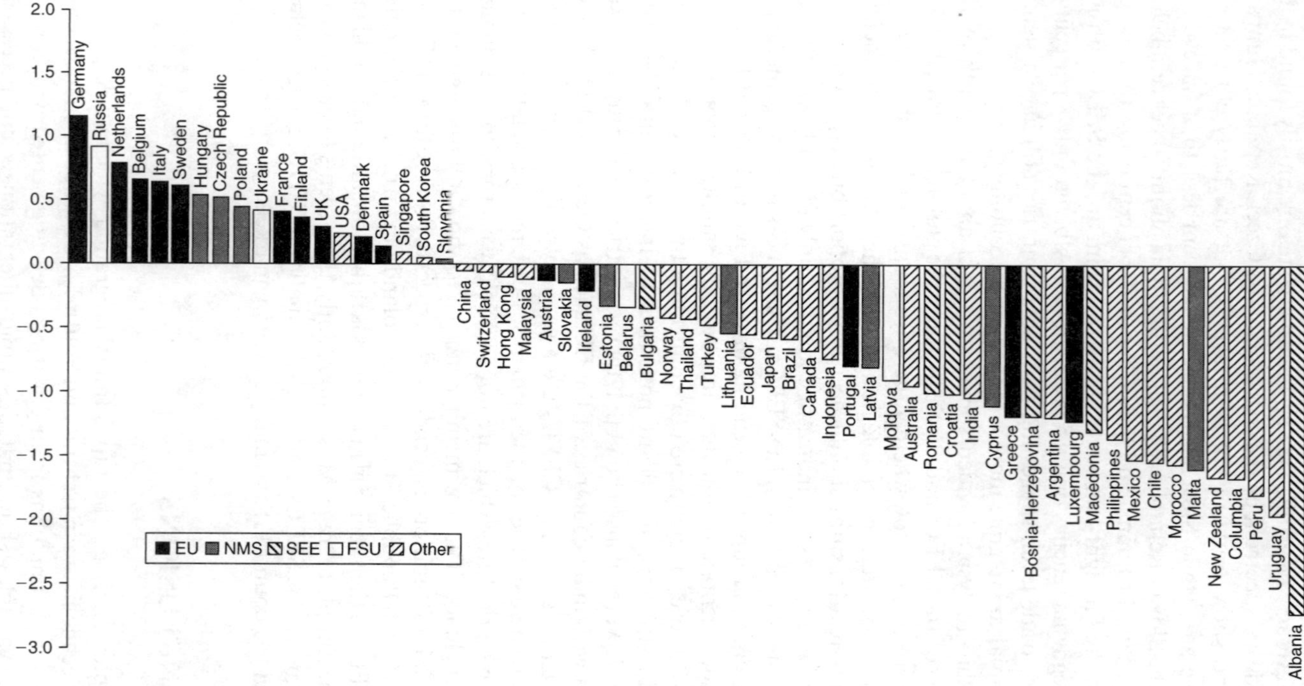

Source: Own estimations.

Figure 15.5 Trade conditions (average fixed effects) by countries, integration of the CEECs

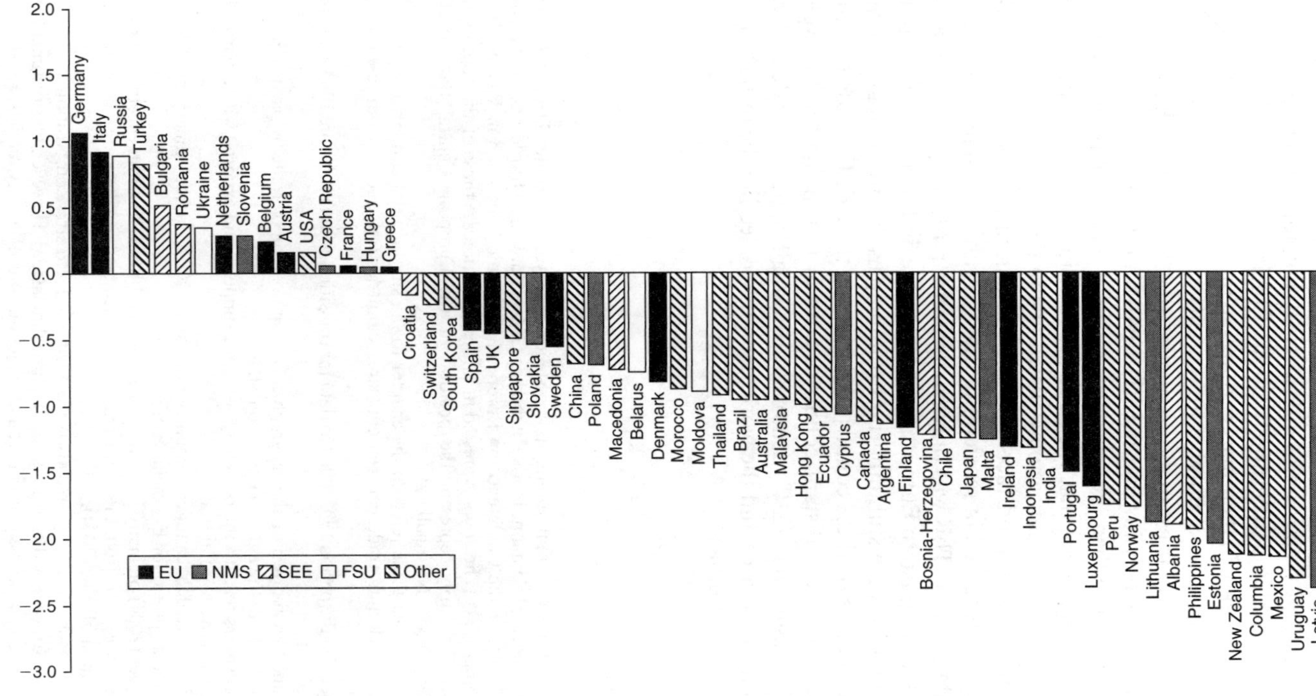

Source: Own estimations.

Figure 15.6 Trade conditions (average fixed effects) by countries, integration of the SEECs

inconsistent with fundamentals. Due to their geographical proximity with the euro area and their rising GDP levels, the natural evolution of these countries is to exchange a certain fraction of their goods with the euro area, implying an increase in their market shares in the euro area. Although these results are subject to a number of caveats related to the econometric methodology, current estimations suggest that trade of CEECs and the SEECs was artificially low in the early 1990s and that this gap has gradually narrowed since then. For the large CEECs, this gap has levelled off in recent years, suggesting that the pace of trade integration of these countries with euro area countries may slow down in the coming years.

Thus, both the stylized facts and the estimation results show that the CEECs have succeeded in reorienting trade towards the main countries in the world economy. This was only partly accomplished by a reorientation from the former Eastern European markets as we find that Russia, Ukraine and some CEECs are still important trading partners in the region (given the economic size of these countries). However, the CEECs trade too little with smaller or more distant countries both in Europe and in the world economy. Finally, the SEECs demonstrate a small degree of trade integration with the euro area and the world economy reflecting the overall closeness of their economies.

NOTES

1. We have benefited from comments by Stelios Makrydakis, Gunter Deuber, Carolyn Evans, Robert Holzmann, Doris Ritzberger-Grünwald, Peter Mooslechner and further participants of the Conference on European Economic Integration in Vienna, 28–30 November, 2004. The views expressed in this contribution are those of the authors and do not necessarily represent the position of the European Central Bank or the Oesterreichische Nationalbank.
2. Extra-euro area trade refers in the chapter to the sum of total euro area exports and imports, excluding trade between euro area countries (referred to as intra-euro area trade).
3. We focus on the period 1993–2003 as data for transition countries before 1993 are scarce and volatile.
4. A detailed breakdown of the geographical decomposition of trade by partner country is available from the authors upon request.
5. Market shares refer to the percentage of trade (imports and exports) with a particular country relative to total trade.
6. Croatia received a candidate country statute in 2004. In the same year, FYR of Macedonia applied for EU membership.
7. See Egger (2004) on analysis of free trade areas and Rose (2000) on effects of currency unions. Exceptions from this mainstream of applied trade analysis are Cheng and Wall (2004) and Fidrmuc (2004).
8. This approach is being referred also to as a triple indexed error composition model (that is, using two country dimensions and the time dimension). However, these estimates are still based on pooled versions instead of panel versions of gravity models.

9. The marginal effect of the dummy variables can be calculated by taking the exponential of the estimated coefficient minus one: a coefficient of 0.5 means that when the dummy is equal to one, trade increases – *ceteris paribus* – by 65 per cent ($e^{0.5} - 1 = 0.6487$) and a coefficient of 0.25 implies a 28 per cent increase.
10. Based on the Akaike Information Criterion, one lead and one lag were selected.
11. Detailed trade shares are available from authors upon request.
12. Unfortunately, one can not assess exactly how far from 'potential' these countries currently are as the fixed effects for the CEECs are affected by the transition process during the 1990s. Therefore, the methodology we are using allows us to analyse with precision only the evolution of the ratio over time.
13. As these economies were in a transition process in the estimation period, it cannot be ruled out that the intercept terms for these countries, which are estimated over a longer time span, have a downward bias suggesting a cautious interpretation of the magnitudes discussed. Nevertheless, our sensitivity analysis including the estimation of repeated regressions during the 1990s confirmed the overall robustness of gravity models (including the effects of country dummies). For a similar discussion of the effect of the transition process on the estimation of equilibrium exchange rates for these countries, see Maeso-Fernandez et al. (2004).

REFERENCES

Anderson, J.E. (1979), 'A theoretical foundation for the gravity equation', *American Economic Review*, **69** (1), 106–16.

Anderson, J.E. and E. van Wincoop (2003), 'Gravity with gravitas: a solution to the border puzzle', *American Economic Review*, **93** (1), 170–92.

Baldwin, Richard E. (1994), *Towards an Integrated Europe*, London: CEPR.

Cheng, I.-H. and H.J. Wall (2004), 'Controlling for heterogeneity in gravity models of trade and integration', *Working Paper* No. 1999-010E (Revised July 2004), St. Louis: Federal Reserve Bank of St. Louis.

Christie, E. (2002), 'Potential trade in South-East Europe: a gravity model approach', *Working Paper* No. 21, Vienna: The Vienna Institute for International Economic Studies (WIIW).

Christie, E. (2004), 'Trade flows in South-East Europe', mimeo, Vienna: The Vienna Institute for International Economic Studies (WIIW).

Deardorff, A.V. (1995), 'Determinants of bilateral trade: does gravity work in a neoclassical world?', *Working Paper* No. 5377, Cambridge: NBER.

Djankov, S. and B. Hoekman (1997), 'Determinants of the export structure of countries in Central and Eastern Europe', *World Bank Economic Review*, **11** (3), 471–87.

Egger, P. (2003), 'An econometric view on the estimation of gravity models and the calculation of trade potentials', *The World Economy*, **25** (2), 297–312.

Egger, P. (2004), 'Estimating regional trading bloc effects with panel data', *Weltwirtschaftliches Archiv*, **140** (1), 151–66.

Egger, P. and M. Pfaffermayr (2003), 'The proper panel econometric specification of the gravity equation: a three-way model with bilateral interaction effects', *Empirical Economics*, **28** (3), 571–80.

Egger, P. and M. Pfaffermayr (2004), 'Distance, trade and FDI: a Hausman–Taylor SUR approach', *Journal of Applied Econometrics*, **19** (2), 227–46.

Faruqee, H. (2004), 'Measuring the trade effects of EMU', *Working Paper* No. 04/154, Washington, DC: International Monetary Fund.

Feenstra, R.C. (2002), 'Border effect and the gravity equation: consistent method for estimation', *Scottish Journal of Political Economy*, **49** (5), 491–506.

Fidrmuc, J. (2004), 'The core and the periphery of the world economy', *Journal of International Trade & Economic Development*, **13** (1), 89–106.

Fidrmuc, J. and J. Fidrmuc (2003), 'Disintegration and trade', *Review of International Economics*, **11** (5), 811–29.

Hamilton, C.B. and A.L. Winters (1992), 'Opening up international trade with Eastern Europe', *Economic Policy*, April, 78–115.

Hausman, J.A. and W.E. Taylor (1981), 'Panel data and unobservable individual effects', *Econometrica*, **49** (6), 1377–98.

Havrylyshyn, O. and H.M. Al-Atrash (1998), 'Opening up and geographic diversification of trade in transition economies', *Working Paper* No. 98/22, Washington DC: International Monetary Fund.

Jakab, Z., M.A. Kovács and A. Oszlay (2001), 'How far has trade integration advanced? An analysis of the actual and potential trade of three Central and Eastern European countries', *Journal of Comparative Economics*, **29** (2), 276–92.

Kaminski, B., Z.K. Wang and L.A. Winters (1996), 'Export performance in transition economies', *Economic Policy*, October, 421–42.

Kao, C. and M.-H. Chiang (2000), 'On the estimation and inference of cointegrated regression in panel data', *Advances in Econometrics*, **15**, 179–222.

Linder, S. (1961), *An Essay on Trade and Transformation*, Uppsala: Almqvist and Wiksells.

Linnemann, H. (1966), *An Econometric Study of International Trade Flows*, Amsterdam: North Holland.

Maeso-Fernandez, F., C. Osbat and B. Schnatz (2004), 'Towards the estimation of equilibrium exchange rates for CEE acceding countries: methodological issues and a panel cointegration perspective', *Working Paper* No. 353, Frankfurt am Main: European Central Bank.

Markusen, J.R. and A.J. Venables (1998), 'Multinational firms and the new trade theory', *Journal of International Economics*, **46** (2), 183–203.

Mátyás, L. (1997), 'Proper econometric specification of the gravity model', *The World Economy*, **20** (3), 363–8.

Mátyás, L. (1998), 'The gravity model: some econometric considerations', *The World Economy*, **21** (3), 397–401.

Micco, A., E. Stein and G. Ordoñez (2003), 'The currency union effect on trade: early evidence from EMU', *Economic Policy*, October, 315–56.

Rose, A.K. (2000), 'One money, one market: estimating the effect of common currencies on trade, *Economic Policy*, April, 7–45.

Serlenga, L. and Y. Shin (2004), 'Gravity models of the intra-EU trade: application of the Hausman–Taylor estimation in heterogeneous panels with common time-specific factors', mimeo, Edinburgh: University of Edinburgh.

Vujčić, B. and V. Šošić (2004), 'Trade integration in South-East Europe and the trade potential of Croatia', in K. Liebscher, J. Christl, P. Mooslechner and D. Ritzberger-Grünwald (eds), *The Economic Potential of a Larger Europe*, Cheltenham, UK and Northampton, MA, USA: Edward Elgar, 127–44.

16. Foreign direct investment and trade as pivotal elements for catching up and competitiveness in CEE

Boris Nemsic

INTRODUCTION

Mobilkom austria is the leading mobile service operator in Austria. Our subsidiaries in Croatia (VIPnet), Slovenia (Si.mobil) and Liechtenstein (mobilkom liechtenstein) form the mobilkom austria group and serve more than 4.9 million customers in the heart of Europe. Our experience in Central Eastern Europe on foreign direct investment (FDI) and trade as pivotal elements for catching up and competitiveness in Central and Eastern Europe (CEE) is shared in this chapter.

Romano Prodi, when still the President of the European Commission, very aptly remarked: 'Europe's unification involving enlargement to embrace ten new members, a clear timetable for the other candidate countries and real prospects of full membership for all countries in the Balkans is the greatest contribution the Union could make to developing the whole continent – politically, economically and culturally.'[1]

The Western Balkans – or Central Eastern Europe, as many would prefer the area to be called – is a key target region of the mobilkom austria group, as are the ten new EU member states, a market of 75 million people. At the same time, the enlargement of the EU was the decisive step to finally overcome the historically grown divide between Eastern and Western Europe. Referring to Western Europe on the one hand and to Eastern Europe on the other hand already seems like an anachronism – the traditional connotations of Eastern Europe are definitely diminishing. I think that our company, mobilkom austria, exemplifies this breakdown of barriers. For full political unification to happen, it is of course necessary that other countries of the region, first of all Croatia, Bulgaria and Romania, also join the EU as soon as possible. I am quite sure that this will happen. There are many good reasons why this should be so, and there are almost no or only very poor reasons that might even slow down or stop this process – especially with regard to Croatia.

From an investor and business point of view, we are always at the vanguard of politics – and we should be. We open up markets before the rules of the EU are applied, before the league of systems is there and before everything has been settled. Our business, mobile communications, is the ultimate basis for trade that allows very fast investments in other countries. We invest abroad because our infrastructure can definitely contribute to the development of other industries. Mobile communications is a reliable infrastructure with a high level of service, and if you have this kind of infrastructure, other investors join in and follow you.

THE MAJORITY OF EUROPEAN CEOS PLAN TO INCREASE THEIR INVESTMENT IN THE ENLARGED EU TERRITORY

The investment climate is a key factor. In 2004 the public relations agency Pleon in Düsseldorf asked 100 top corporate leaders in Europe in which country they prefer to invest (see Figure 16.1). Ninety-two per cent of them said that they want to invest in an enlarged Europe, compared with only 68 per cent in a really booming Asian market. By comparison, the readiness to invest in North America was rather low, at 50 per cent. What this means is clear: it lays the foundation of a truly European perspective.

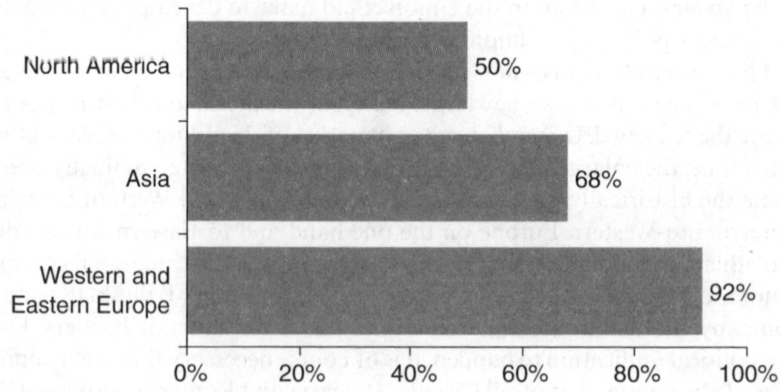

Source: Pleon (2004).

Figure 16.1 92% of Europe's top CEOs want to invest in the enlarged Europe

At any rate, corporate decision-makers are clearly focused on this region. A second major factor is of course the growth potential: I think that mobilkom austria is investing in the right countries.

GROWTH POTENTIAL IN THE ENLARGED EUROPE

The new EU member states (EU-10) generate a GDP of EUR 437 billion (according to Eurostat, 2004), and what is more important, their GDP growth (UN Report) is at about 4.5 per cent, compared with the very optimistic 2.5 per cent for the old member states (EU-15). So there is a growth potential for us. The consumer goods sector is not yet saturated. In the last decade, industrial business dominated investment in the EU-10. Investment in this decade, I think, will go more into services – which is again our business. Then, there is the infrastructure sector and transportation, but the focus will be on IT and telecommunications. If you have a good telecommunications infrastructure, then you can develop any business.

AUSTRIA'S POSITION IN CEE

What is Austria's position in CEE? Let me answer this question with regard to the five countries that are most important for mobilkom austria, bearing in mind that we are more focused on direct investments than exports and imports (see Table 16.1). Austria is a very interesting country. Given its small size, it is comparable with the target countries. Whatever criteria you look at here, we are really in the first row. Usually, we follow Germany and Italy, countries which are six times or ten times larger than Austria. We easily match other big industrial countries, concerning FDI in these countries. You can see that Austria with an FDI of 30.9 per cent in Slovenia, 25 per cent in Bulgaria and 16 per cent in Croatia is one of the biggest investors in the region and this will increase. Following our successful expansion strategy, the core target markets of mobilkom austria will be Bulgaria, Serbia and Montenegro as well as Bosnia and Herzegovina.

MOBILKOM AUSTRIA GROUP CONTRIBUTES TO CEE

What have we done already? Two examples: we founded VIPnet in Croatia and took over Si.mobil in Slovenia. And again, we did it long before the political integration happened. VIPnet was founded in 1998 and

Table 16.1 Austria's position in CEE in 2003

		Slovenia	Croatia	Bosnia Herzegovina	Serbia and Montenegro	Bulgaria
Exports	EUR million	11 288	5 468	n.a.	2 341	6 668
To Austria	%	7.33	7.75	3.68	3.32	2.02
To Austria	Rank	4	5	6	9	13
Imports	EUR million	12 239	12 546	n.a.	6 985	9 611
From Austria	%	8.61	6.60	4.43	3.22	2.23
From Austria	Rank	4	4	7	6	12
FDI incoming	EUR million	299	1 733	338	1 197	1 254
From Austria	%	30.9	15.9	n.a.	10.8	25.0
FDI incoming 1990–2003	EUR million	3 791	9 225	1 138	2 799	6 300
FDI incoming of GNP	%	1.1	6.0	4.8	5.8	6.3
FDI incoming of GNP 1990–2003	%	13.7	32.0	16.3	13.5	31.7

Source: Mobilkom austria research; BA-CA Konzernvolkswirtschaft; national central banks (balance of payments statistics); national statistics institutes.

started operations in July 1999. We built up the first private GSM network in Croatia, investing around EUR 580 million in Croatia until year end 2003 – an amount that was not easy to set aside given the cut-throat competition we face in the Austrian market.The second example is Slovenia, where we took over the second GSM operator in 2001. Again, this was long before the European rules applied in Slovenia, and they still do not apply – except formally. In Slovenia we invested around EUR 330 million until year end 2003.

Telekom Austria, our parent company, is listed on the stock exchange in Vienna, Austria and New York, USA and it is really a strong sign that a comparatively small operator in a small country, like mobilkom austria, has made such a major investment in countries like Croatia and Slovenia.

TARGET COUNTRIES

Beyond Croatia and Slovenia, other countries of South-East Europe are obvious targets for us. This includes Bulgaria, Serbia and Montenegro and Bosnia and Herzegovina. Others, like Hungary and the Czech Republic act more as benchmarks for us. Benchmarks, because we cannot invest everywhere. Figure 16.2 shows those markets in which mobilkom austria is interested in investing (the countries coloured in dark grey represent our existing markets; our target markets for further expansion are shown in mid-grey; the countries shaded in light grey serve as benchmarks for the region). From my point of view, the telecommunications industry of Austria missed the right moment to enter markets like the Czech Republic, Slovakia and Hungary; the right moment would have been ten years ago – at least.

Furthermore, the mobile penetration in South-Eastern Europe is on average still significantly lower compared to Central Eastern Europe. So the competition there is mainly limited to a duopoly. With our subsidiaries VIPnet and Si.mobil we are among the top mobile communications operators in the South-Eastern European market. With a total of about 1.5 million customers in those two countries we are really well positioned, competing in the area of expansion with, for example, Deutsche Telekom's T-Mobile, Vodafone and France Telecom's Orange. In addition, one way for Austria – a country of about 8 million people – to grow economically is to enter new markets.

MOBILE PENETRATION IN RELATION TO GNI

Figure 16.3 shows the mobile penetration in relation to gross national income (GNI) – there is a statistical correlation between a country's wealth

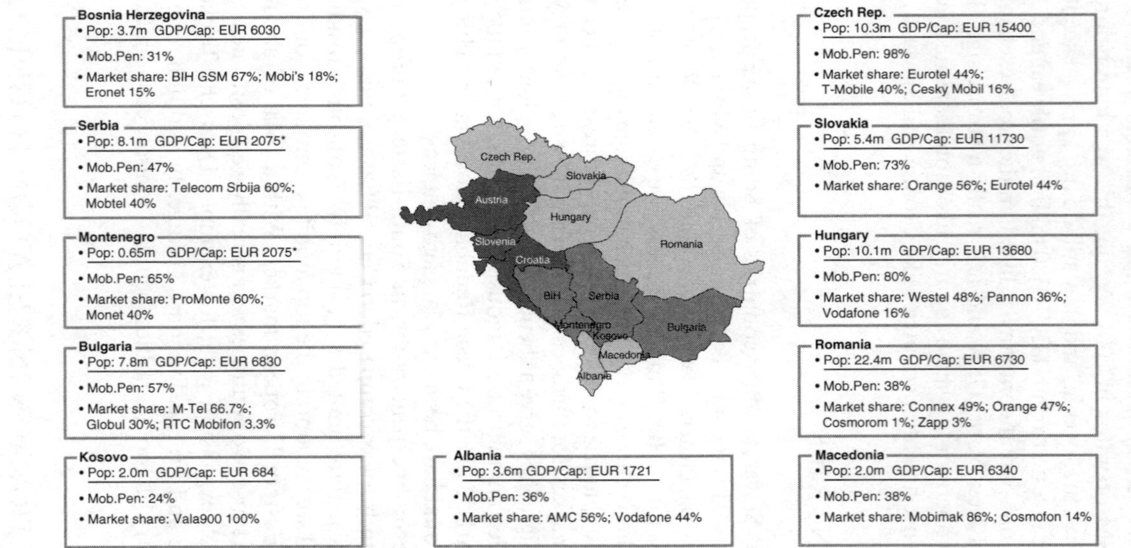

Notes: *EUR at exchange rate. GDP/Cap: refers to purchasing power corrected figures.

Source: Mobilkom austria research.

Figure 16.2 Target countries

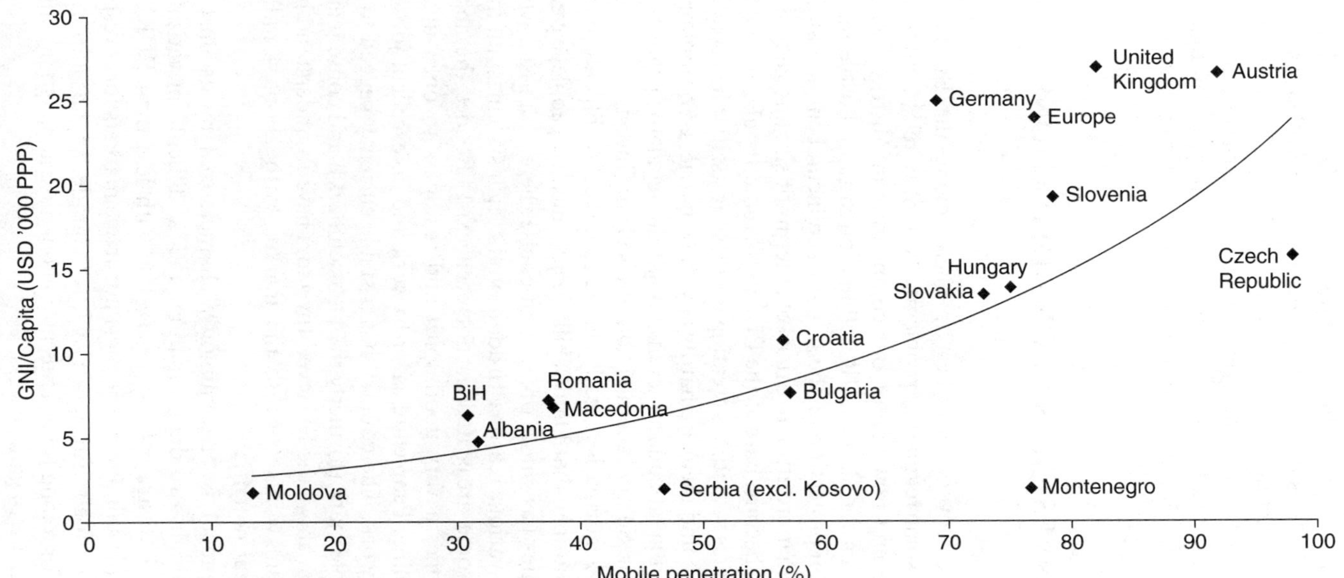

Note: Mobile penetration in relation to GNI.

Source: Worldbank YE 2003; Eastern Europe Wireless Analyst 1H 2004.

Figure 16.3 Mobile penetration in relation to gross national income

and the usage of telecommunications. It is not proved whether, for example, the GNI per capital drives the mobile penetration or the other way round or whether both statistics depend on other more influential factors. But the fact is that the more people use telecommunication, the richer a country is, or vice versa. In the context of mobile communication the development of the past few years shows that if mobile penetration rises the economy of the particular country will benefit.

SELECTED INVESTMENT CONSIDERATIONS IN CEE

In our experience, Slovenia was best in class among the EU-10, but Slovenia still faces some regulatory problems. Western Wireless, our former partner in Croatia and now one of our competitors in Austria, sued the Republic of Slovenia for about EUR 350 million arguing hostile market conditions based on protection of the state-owned incumbent operator.

Croatia is an even more attractive market in terms of size and geography. Croatia is about to become part of the EU but this country also faces some legal issues. Croatia is sometimes creating hurdles for itself; it has excellent conditions for FDI, and there are hardly any trade barriers. For mobilkom austria Croatia is a great country, even though the regulator protects the incumbent operator. So our recommendation is clear: 'Invest!'

Bosnia and Herzegovina is a really difficult market. A difficult market in the sense, for example, that highly skilled and educated people leave the country because they have more opportunities elsewhere – almost a whole generation left for various reasons. In addition the legal system is not independent, and in some areas it does not even exist. Besides the abovementioned challenges a very good spirit and readiness to open up the barriers are prevailing. People are eager to work and do excellent jobs – if you set the framework. The country has a stable currency pegged to the euro, the convertible mark (formerly the Deutschmark), and consequently there is no inflation above the EU level. Investors have to understand how the political system works because the market, with about 4 million people, reflects great potential.

Serbia's development is predominantly characterized by its unstable political system, high two-digit inflation and a difficult privatization process in several industries. FDI is very low with less than EUR 400 million, but Serbia is still one of the most attractive markets for investors. The market is definitely European, with Belgrade as an important European capital for a long time. Thus mobilkom austria has to use all its strengths and expertise to gain success.

Bulgaria is our top target country. There has been excellent development in the last four years: stable government, high investment grade and a rate of comparably low unemployment. Furthermore education is excellent, resulting in highly qualified employees. With the Bulgarian lev being pegged to the euro the inflation rate is quite low, and if corporate tax rates are reduced to 15 per cent Bulgaria will be highly attractive for investors.

NOTE

1. Speech: 'Five years later: What have been our targets, what are our results?', European Parliament, Brussels, 13 October 2004.

PART V

Confronting Serious Challenges: High Unemployment, Poverty, Brain Drain

17. Poverty, migration and employment in South-East Europe: what can the data tell us?

Robert Holzmann

INTRODUCTION AND SUMMARY[1]

The purpose of this chapter is to provide the empirical foundations of the development in poverty, migration and employment in the countries of South-East Europe (SEE, consisting of Albania, Bosnia and Herzegovina, Bulgaria, Croatia, Macedonia, Romania and Serbia and Montenegro). While the availability of these important but sensitive data in the countries of this region has improved, data coverage across these countries and over time is still lagging behind that of other (former) transition economies in the north.

Nevertheless, the available data and fragmented evidence suggest the following broad conclusions: first, the region was hit by two largely parallel shocks – transition crisis and the conflicts around the dissolution of the former Yugoslavia – the impact of which is visible in the development of GDP and other indicators. Compared to their peers to the north, who are by now all members of the EU, the fall was deeper and the recovery thus far weaker. Only since 2001 has the real GDP growth rate of SEE exceeded the growth rate of Central and Eastern Europe and the Baltics (CEB). Within SEE, only Albania was able to surpass its early-1990s GDP level, although it began from a low (per capita) level. Second, poverty has increased during the long years of transition largely due to the fall in output as there is little evidence for a major increase in income inequality. Since the late 1990s, however, poverty seems to have decreased in parallel to the recovery in output, and in synch with other transition economies. Third, as a reaction to the fall in output and increase in poverty, but also in reaction to armed conflicts and strong ethnic tensions, migration has increased in the region, with seeming differences between the countries with regard to level and flows of migration, but also regarding remittance behaviour. But data in this area are very patchy: the 12 per cent fall in population that the population statistics indicate for Bulgaria in the period from the late 1980s to early 2000 is much larger than the available flow data of migrants suggest. Fourth, the situation on the labour market mirrors that in other areas: it is, on average, worse than in other transition countries, and with some variation across the countries, unemployment is high and often increasing. The persistent high level of unemployment suggests main structural problems around firm and job creation. As in most other transition countries, the percentage of jobs in the informal sector is high and well above 30 per cent of total employment. While migration would be expected to have relieved the pressure on the labour market, unemployment has not gone down visibly.

Empirical cross-country studies by the World Bank for this sub-region and the (former) transition economies in Central and Eastern Europe and Central Asia (Europe and Central Asia, or ECA, in World Bank terminology) are en route but not yet finished. The most advanced study is on labour markets in the ECA region of which the first draft was presented at a cross-regional labour market conference in mid-November 2004.[2] The study on poverty for ECA is under preparation and is scheduled for presentation by mid-2005. Finally, a regional study on migration is planned with delivery envisaged for 2006.

DEVELOPMENT OF OUTPUT

The countries in Central, Eastern, Southern and Northern Europe and the new independent countries of the former USSR experienced a variety of differing developments during the transition from centrally planned economies to free market economies. The first group of countries experienced a more rapid transition, with a strong decline in GDP from 1989 to 1993, when recovery gradually set in. The countries of the former Soviet Union (excepting the three Baltic countries) initially experienced a slower decline than Eastern Europe, but from 1991 onwards GDP collapsed rapidly and continued to fall until well after 1993.

The countries of South-East Europe (SEE, consisting of Albania, Bosnia and Herzegovina, Bulgaria, Croatia, Macedonia, Romania and Serbia and Montenegro) were not able to keep up with their regional peers in Central and Eastern Europe and the Baltics (CEB) which are by now all members of the EU (Czech Republic, Hungary, Poland, Slovakia, Slovenia, Estonia, Latvia and Lithuania). Only since 2001 has the real GDP growth rate of SEE exceeded the growth rate of CEB (Table 17.1). Within SEE, only Albania was able to surpass its early-1990s GDP level, although it began from a low (per capita) level.

Table 17.1 Relative real GDP growth in SE Europe (1995 = 100)

	1992	1993	1994	1995	1996	1997	1998	1999	2000	2001	2002	2003
Albania	89.9	83.4	91.4	100.0	109.1	97.9	110.3	121.4	130.3	140.2	146.8	155.6
Bosnia and Herzegovina				100.0	185.9	253.9	293.6	321.7	339.8	355.0	368.9	381.8
Bulgaria	107.5	99.7	98.2	100.0	90.6	85.5	88.8	90.9	95.8	99.7	104.6	109.1
Croatia	116.3	102.7	94.5	100.0	105.9	113.1	116.0	115.0	118.2	123.4	129.9	135.5
Macedonia, FYR	117.7	110.0	101.8	100.0	101.2	102.6	106.1	110.7	115.7	110.5	111.4	114.9
Romania	103.9	94.7	96.2	100.0	104.0	97.7	93.0	91.9	92.4	97.3	101.5	109.2
Serbia and Montenegro				100.0	105.9	113.7	116.5	95.4	100.3	105.8	110.0	113.3
SEE Average	108.1	98.3	96.3	100.0	104.4	105.1	106.0	103.6	106.8	111.6	116.5	122.5
CEB Average	99.035	96.251	96.377	100.0	104.68	109.77	114.91	118.91	123.77	128.576	131.46	136.164

Source: WDI August 2004.

The same divide between CEB and SEE can also be observed in terms of per capita GDP. While the CEB average per capita income exceeds its 1991 level by more than 50 per cent by now, the SEE average was barely above its 1991 level by 2003 (Table 17.2). Since 1999, all SEE countries have experienced a strong increase in GDP per capita, with the exception of Macedonia. Among the SEE countries, Croatia has by far the highest per capita income, even exceeding the CEB average income and that of countries such as Poland and the Slovak Republic. Albania once again has displayed the highest growth rate among all SEE countries since 1993, with the obvious exception of Bosnia during the mid-1990s.

The same observations largely hold when analysing GDP per capita in purchasing power parities (PPP), with three interesting differences. The increase in income since 1995 is even more pronounced; the income dispersion between countries is weaker; and the ranking of a few countries is different (Table 17.3). The distance of Croatia's per capita income from that of other SEE countries is now much less pronounced and is closer to that of its peer countries to the north. And measured in PPP, the per capita GDP of Bulgaria comes second in the region.

Comparing the per capita income of the countries of the former Yugoslavia shows a clear North–South divide. Slovenia's per capita income was and still is more than twice as much as Croatia's, with the other republics lagging even further behind (Table 17.4). This reflects an insufficient income convergence process in former Yugoslavia and differences in fate and capacity to converge toward the European peers after the break-up in the early 1990s.

POVERTY

For the time being the availability of data on the scale and persistence of poverty in the region is limited. Comparable data on poverty are typically obtained through special household surveys, which are conducted only once every few years. A World Bank report on poverty in Europe and Central Asia (ECA) to be finalized and launched in summer 2005 will make available more data and fresh insights.

The change in income poverty is determined by the change in income level and in income distribution. The available data are consistent with the casual observation that poverty incidence measured as the share of population living below the re-valued USD 2 or USD 4 per day poverty line was essentially determined by output development (Table 17.5). It increased up to the late 1990s and has been falling ever since. The change in income distribution seems to have had little impact. The available data suggest that

Table 17.2 Real GDP per capita in SE Europe (constant 1995 US dollar)

	1992	1993	1994	1995	1996	1997	1998	1999	2000	2001	2002	2003
Albania	563	621	687	761	842	761	862	950	1015	1085	1130	1190
Bosnia and Herzegovina			425	546	981	1298	1455	1551	1595	1633	1675	1721
Bulgaria	1487	1477	1509	1559	1420	1349	1410	1450	1536	1651	1742	1827
Croatia	3783	3481	3686	4059	4398	4770	4932	4895	5003	5204	5473	5720
Macedonia, FYR	2571	2369	2311	2263	2270	2286	2351	2441	2541	2415	2432	2494
Romania	1376	1399	1456	1564	1632	1536	1466	1451	1461	1541	1615	1745
Serbia and Montenegro				1286	1358	1455	1489	1218	1280	1348	1830	1898
SEE Average	1668	1640	1602	1636	1711	1723	1740	1699	1749	1832	2006	2116
CEB Average	3284	3433	3562	3754	3934	4131	4330	4487	4679	4858	5002	5189

Source: WDI August 2004.

Table 17.3 *GDP, PPP per capita in SE Europe (constant 1995 int'l$)*

	1992	1993	1994	1995	1996	1997	1998	1999	2000	2001	2002	2003
Albania	2016	2154	2354	2554	2824	2558	2881	3193	3389	3603	3782	3975
Bosnia and Herzegovina			1560	2001	3406	4427	4313	4677	4849	4965	5117	5243
Bulgaria	5479	5449	5583	5840	5355	5057	5228	5332	5714	6121	6424	6789
Croatia	6263	5730	6070	6618	7185	7776	8091	8115	8329	8700	9110	9687
Macedonia, FYR	6213	5674	5486	5346	5378	5432	5574	5782	6026	5723	5742	5881
Romania	4915	5008	5208	5608	5860	5520	5274	5226	5243	5523	5806	6280
Serbia and Montenegro		n.a.	n.a.	n.a.	n.a.	n.a.	n.a.	n.a.	n.a.	n.a.	n.a.	n.a.
SEE Total (ex SaM)	5017	4987	4880	5248	5466	5357	5311	5370	5510	5774	6040	6434
CEB Average	7331	7406	7686	8090	8458	8931	9367	9700	10121	10529	10903	11315

Source: WDI August 2004.

Table 17.4 Real GDP per capita in former Yugoslavia (constant 1995 US dollar)

	1992	1993	1994	1995	1996	1997	1998	1999	2000	2001	2002	2003
Bosnia and Herzegovina			425	546	981	1298	1455	1551	1595	1633	1675	1721
Croatia	3783	3481	3686	4059	4398	4770	4932	4895	5003	5204	5473	5720
Macedonia, FYR	2571	2369	2311	2263	2270	2286	2351	2441	2541	2415	2432	2494
Serbia and Montenegro				1286	1358	1455	1489	1218	1280	1348	1830	1898
Slovenia		8710	9061	9419	9763	10 228	10 630	11 152	11 640	12 045	12 483	12 765

Source: WDI August 2004.

Table 17.5 Percentage of population under poverty line (PPP, 1996 int'l$), 1995–2003

	2000	2001	2002	2003
Poverty line = USD 2.15				
Albania			14.2%	
Belarus	18.5%	10.9%	8.2%	
Bulgaria		14.2%		7.0%
Georgia	31.5%	31.9%	27.6%	
Hungary	0.8%	0.6%	0.2%	
Kazakhstan		22.9%	20.2%	14.7%
Kyrgyz Republic	40.9%	35.6%	34.9%	
Moldova	60.2%	50.6%	35.9%	
Poland	1.7%	1.8%	2.1%	
Romania	15.0%	12.1%	11.6%	
Russia	11.1%	7.2%	5.3%	
Serbia			11.3%	10.0%
Tajikistan				46.1%
Turkey			5.9%	
Poverty line = USD 4.3				
Albania			60.8%	
Belarus	74.7%	62.0%	54.2%	
Bulgaria		46.1%		41.1%
Georgia	97.6%	98.1%	97.4%	
Hungary	15.3%	10.9%	10.0%	
Kazakhstan		66.1%	62.4%	55.4%
Kyrgyz Republic	85.0%	82.6%	82.1%	
Moldova	89.7%	85.4%	77.1%	
Poland	22.4%	22.5%	23.5%	
Romania	63.9%	56.0%	53.6%	
Russia	43.5%	36.0%	31.2%	
Serbia			62.2%	57.2%
Tajikistan				86.0%
Turkey			28.2%	

Source: World Bank Household Surveys, various years.

income of those captured in the household surveys has little changed, but the available data are very restricted in the time and scope of countries covered (Table 17.6).

According to recent World Bank household surveys, in Romania the percentage of people living on less than USD 2 a day rose from 9.2 per cent in

Table 17.6 Gini index

	2000	2001	2002	2003
Albania			0.323	
Bulgaria		0.338		0.278
Romania	0.281	0.284	0.291	
SaM			0.327	0.315

Source: World Bank Household Surveys, various years.

1998 to 12.1 per cent in 2001 and then decreased to 11.6 per cent in 2002; 53.6 per cent of the Romanian population lived on less than USD 4 a day in 2002. Extreme poverty is apparently higher in Albania (14.2 per cent living on less than USD 2 a day in 2002). In Serbia and Montenegro 10 per cent of the population fell under the USD 2 poverty line in 2003 (57.2 per cent for the USD 4 poverty line), and 7 per cent in Bulgaria (41.1 per cent under USD 4). Croatia seems to be doing much better with less than 1 per cent of the population living on less than USD 2 a day according to the World Development Indicators (World Bank, 2004a). The same source places 4 per cent of the Macedonian population under the USD 2 poverty line in 1998.

This regional experience replicates the global experience of an elasticity of income/consumption poverty and economic growth of broadly (minus) 1. This strong link of poverty reduction and economic growth has contributed to the drastic decrease in the share of people living on USD 1 a day or less in East Asia and Pacific from 472 (1990) to 217 (2001) as a result of output growth. However, economic growth alone is not sufficient to achieve the other millennium development goals such as those for health, education and youth employment.

MIGRATION

The temporary major decline in output, the widening income gap with the countries in Western Europe, the increase in unemployment and the armed conflicts in some parts of the region prompted significant outward migration from all countries in the region. Migration is not an unknown phenomenon in the region: from the early 1880s to the Second World War, and then again from 1945 to 1989, the region experienced substantial outward migration, strong return migration and major government-negotiated ethnic swaps both between the Ottoman Empire and the newly established or liberated countries of the region as well as among the latter countries (Hatton and Williamson, 1998; Sarris et al., 2004).

The perception of strong outward migration from the region is also prevalent in the neighbouring countries as well as in the traditional migrant-receiving countries in the old and new world. But data on migration, in particular on bilateral migration flows, are not easily available and largely incomplete and often inconsistent in stocks or even in flows. Additionally, it can be assumed that a considerable part of migration flows from SEE into the EU consists of illegal migration, making the scarcely available official data unreliable.

Since a significant fraction of migration from SEE was driven by armed conflict in the former Yugoslavia, a reliable source to track the movement of persons across international borders is the statistics of refugees and other persons of concern to the UNHCR (United Nations High Commissioner for Refugees). According to the UNHCR, the largest refugee population from the region in industrialized countries is Bosnian. The stock of Bosnian refugees peaked in 1996 at 1 million and has since fallen to 400 000. Likewise, the stock of Croatian refugees increased until 1997 but since then has remained relatively stable at around 350 000. Only in 2000 did the stock fall below 300 000. The third significant refugee population comes from Serbia and Montenegro, which constantly increased during the 1990s to around 150 000 in 2001, when it surged to more than 300 000 in 2002 (Table 17.7).

This development is also reflected in the UNHCR's statistics on asylum applications in the EU. Most applicants since 1993 came from Serbia and Montenegro, peaking in 1999 with more than 80 000 applications. The number of applicants from other SEE countries fell significantly between 1993 and 1995 and stayed below 10 000 annual applicants per country of origin from 1996 onwards (Table 17.8).

The available data on bilateral migration flows, mainly coming from the OECD's SOPEMI report and national statistical agencies, give a very incomplete picture. Table 17.9 summarizes the available data of annual migrant inflows into selected Western European countries by countries of origin. It has to be emphasized that the numbers represent annual minimum estimates and are not comparable over time as every year contains data from differing destination countries.[3] The numbers are fairly comparable for the years from 1999 to 2001 which show an inflow of migrants from SEE at a magnitude of 191 000 in 1999 and around 131 000 for 2000 and 2001.

One way to cross-check these numbers is to compare them with the annual change in total population, which should theoretically yield the net migration flow by subtracting the natural population change (birth minus

Table 17.7 *Refugee populations in industrialized countries by origin (thousands)*

	1993	1994	1995	1996	1997	1998	1999	2000	2001	2002
Albania	4.7	5.0	5.8	5.8	5.4	5.4	6.3	6.8	7.6	10.6
Bosnia and Herzegovina	618.4	776.1	769.8	993.9	849.2	640.1	598.2	505.0	447.3	406.8
Croatia	151.7	76.3	245.6	310.1	349.3	338.1	353.7	335.2	290.3	274.8
Macedonia, FYR	1.9	0.3	12.9	13.0	12.7	1.9	2.1	2.2	12.2	8.1
Romania	23.6	22.3	17.0	11.9	9.0	10.9	8.6	7.3	6.1	8.8
Serbia and Montenegro	58.3	55.0	86.1	104.0	106.7	115.3	172.5	146.7	144.2	327.4
SEE Total	858.6	935.0	1137.2	1438.7	1332.3	1111.7	1141.4	1003.2	907.7	1036.5

Source: UNHCR 2002.

Table 17.8 *Asylum applicants in the EU by origin (thousands)*

	1993	1994	1995	1996	1997	1998	1999	2000	2001	2002
Albania	4.4	1.9	1.3	1.1	4.7	2.9	3.9	5.8	3.4	3.3
Bosnia and Herzegovina	62.0	20.7	13.5	5.1	6.1	8.0	4.6	9.7	8.5	5.7
Croatia	25.1	5.2	3.5	2.9	3.1	1.3	1.3	2.1	1.2	2.5
Macedonia, FYR	1.8	2.4	4.1	2.3	2.1	1.0	1.0	0.8	4.8	3.1
Romania	87.1	21.4	13.9	9.0	10.3	8.5	7.8	7.0	4.9	5.5
Serbia and Montenegro	88.2	47.7	46.1	32.0	41.0	71.2	83.4	36.6	22.9	26.3
SEE Total	268.7	99.3	82.4	52.4	67.3	92.8	102.1	61.8	45.7	46.4

Source: UNHCR 2002.

Table 17.9 Inflows of migrants into selected Western European countries by origin

	1992	1993	1994	1995	1996	1997	1998	1999	2000	2001	2002
Albania	27	33	62	1853	1637	2528	2138	2592	1823	2006	1778
Bosnia and Herzegovina	12	20679	25697	76297	18444	13009	12599	15713	16192	20272	10735
Bulgaria	493	252	230	8463	7395	7670	6599	9627	12044	15078	13788
Croatia	67	218	959	15717	16926	15185	14840	18302	20760	21240	13082
Macedonia, FYR		31	348	4163	3795	4128	4169	4525	4695	6980	4062
Romania	964	621	578	25828	19692	16786	19756	22051	27852	24427	24882
Serbia and Montenegro	1760	3294	15809	58863	52358	42847	73699	118409	47986	41934	26662
SEE Total	3323	25128	43683	191184	120247	102153	133800	191219	131352	131937	94989

Source: Migration Policy Institute 2004.

death) from the total measured population change. In practice this method is also problem-laden as annual total population changes are rough estimates and are only verified by a decennial population census. This is most apparent in the case of Bulgaria, which apparently lost more than 1 million people between 1989 and 2003 or nearly 12 per cent of its 1989 total population (Table 17.10). This compares to an accumulated inflow of Bulgarians into Western Europe of only roughly 80 000 according to the available statistics, and a stock of Bulgarians in Western Europe of around 40 000 in 2002. Even when taking into account migration to other regions (like the US), illegal migration and naturalization, the numbers seem much too low. But even taken at face value the results have little credibility for some countries. The method suggests essentially no change in the population of Albania, while it is estimated that some 500 000 Albanians are in living in Greece, and another 200 000 or so in Italy.

The problem of incomplete data is even worse when considering the stock of migrant populations in Western Europe, as even countries like Austria do not publish annual data. For 2001, the year for which the data are most complete, statistics put the total number of migrants from SEE in Western Europe at 2.2 million. In summary, reliable data on migration in source as well as receiving countries are essentially missing for the region. This makes well founded economic and social analysis virtually impossible for the time being.

Table 17.10 Total population in SE Europe (thousands)

	1989	1996	2003	Change 1989–2003	Change in %
Albania	3 238	3 143	3 169	−69	−2.1
Bosnia and Herzegovina	4 440	3 538	4 140	−300	−6.8
Bulgaria	8 877	8 363	7 824	−1 053	−11.9
Croatia	4 767	4 530	4 456	−311	−6.5
Macedonia, FYR	1 998	1 983	2 049	51	2.6
Romania	23 152	22 608	22 200	−952	−4.1
Serbia and Montenegro	10 473	10 581	8 104	−2 369	−22.6
SEE Total	56 945	54 746	51 942	−5 003	−8.8

Source: WDI August 2004.

Remittances have attracted a lot of attention recently as a major and stable means of development finance. Officially registered remittances to SEE have been steadily increasing throughout the 1990s, with the exception of Bosnia and Herzegovina (Table 17.11). Serbia and Montenegro is the main remittance-receiving country in the region with USD 2.7 billion in 2003, followed by Bosnia and Herzegovina (USD 1.2 billion), Croatia (USD 1 billion) and Albania (900 million). Altogether the region received USD 6.2 billion in official remittances in 2003. But these official data often conflict with individual country estimates, which are typically much higher. For example, the data in Table 17.11 for Romania suggest a mere 124 million remittances in 2003 while a recent local estimate reported in the *Financial Times* alludes to some EUR 2 billion (or USD 2.6 billion), that is, 20 times more.

Despite the likely major underestimation of the level of remittances, presented as a share of GDP (Table 17.12), they play a major role in Bosnia and Herzegovina (17 per cent of GDP in 2003), Albania (15 per cent) and Serbia and Montenegro (14 per cent). In Croatia and Macedonia the share is 4 per cent, while for Romania and Bulgaria the numbers are insignificant. Taken at face value, the data would suggest that the Bulgarian and Romanian diasporas are loosening their ties with their countries of origin, also implying that the migrant communities of these countries consider themselves as permanent rather than temporary migrants, without the intention to return.

EMPLOYMENT

Unemployment is a persistent problem not only of SEE but of the whole Eastern European region (and also in most countries in the West). Unemployment is not only high, but still increasing. The average unemployment rate of SEE countries increased from 12.4 per cent in 1989 to 17.6 per cent in 2003, parallel to the CEB average, yet at a higher level (the CEB average in 2003 was 10.3 per cent). The problem is worst in Macedonia with an unemployment rate of over 30 per cent since 1995. Most other SEE countries display rates around 15 per cent. Romania seems to perform best with a rate of only 7 per cent in 2003 (Table 17.13). But the low rate for Romania may simply reflect low incentives to register for unemployment benefits and/or an income level too low to stay unemployed.

These high unemployment rates hint at a structural unemployment problem. As in most other countries of the ECA region, the percentage of estimated employment in the informal sector of the total employment is high (Macedonia: 45 per cent, Croatia: 32 per cent, Serbia and Montenegro: 39 per cent, Bulgaria: 36 per cent, Romania: 33 per cent for 2000/01; see Figure 17.1). The high level of informal employment is seemingly little

Table 17.11 Received remittances in SE Europe (US dollar, millions)

	1992	1993	1994	1995	1996	1997	1998	1999	2000	2001	2002	2003
Albania	152	332	307	427	551	300	504	407	598	699	734	889
Bosnia and Herzegovina							1 542	1 386	1 147	1 072	1 049	1 178
Bulgaria					42	51	51	43	58	71	72	67
Croatia		230	376	544	668	617	625	557	644	728	870	1 069
Macedonia, FYR					68	78	63	77	81	73	106	171
Romania			11	9	18	16	49	96	96	116	143	124
Serbia and Montenegro					1 295	662	1 033	948	1 132	1 698	2 089	2 707
SEE Total	152	562	694	981	2 641	1 724	3 867	3 513	3 755	4 458	5 062	6 205

Source: BOP 2004; WDI August 2004.

Table 17.12 Remittances as share of GDP (%)

	1992	1993	1994	1995	1996	1997	1998	1999	2000	2001	2002	2003
Albania	21.4	27.0	15.5	17.6	18.3	13.9	18.4	11.8	16.2	16.4	15.2	14.5
Bosnia and Herzegovina							35.9	29.5	25.2	21.4	18.7	16.9
Bulgaria					0.4	0.5	0.4	0.3	0.5	0.5	0.5	0.3
Croatia		2.1	2.6	2.9	3.4	3.1	2.9	2.8	3.5	3.7	3.8	3.8
Macedonia, FYR					1.5	2.1	1.8	2.1	2.3	2.1	2.8	3.6
Romania					0.1	0.0	0.1	0.3	0.3	0.3	0.3	0.2
Serbia and Montenegro					9.6	4.3	7.6	9.6	13.2	14.7	13.3	14.1

Source: BOP 2004; WDI August 2004.

Table 17.13 Unemployment rate (% of total labour force)

	1992	1993	1994	1995	1996	1997	1998	1999	2000	2001	2002	2003
Albania	26.5	22.3	18.4	12.9	12.3	14.9	17.7	18.4	16.8	16.4	15.8	15.0
Bosnia and Herzegovina	n.a.	n.a.	n.a.	n.a.	n.a.	n.a.	n.a.	n.a.	n.a.	n.a.	n.a.	n.a.
Bulgaria	15.3	16.4	12.8	11.1	12.5	13.7	12.2	16.0	17.9	17.3	16.3	n.a.
Croatia	15.3	14.8	14.5	14.5	10.0	9.9	11.4	13.5	16.1	15.8	14.8	14.3
Macedonia, FYR	26.3	27.7	30.0	35.6	31.9	36.0	34.5	32.4	32.2	30.5	31.9	36.7
Romania	8.2	10.4	8.2	8.0	6.7	6.0	6.3	6.8	7.1	6.6	8.4	7.0
Serbia and Montenegro	n.a.	n.a.	n.a.	13.4	13.2	13.8	13.7	13.7	21.6	12.8	13.8	15.2
SEE Average	18.3	18.3	16.8	15.9	14.4	15.7	16.0	16.8	18.6	16.6	16.8	17.6
CEB Average	7.3	8.5	10.4	11.7	11.4	10.3	10.3	11.8	12.7	12.5	11.7	10.3

Source: ILO 2004.

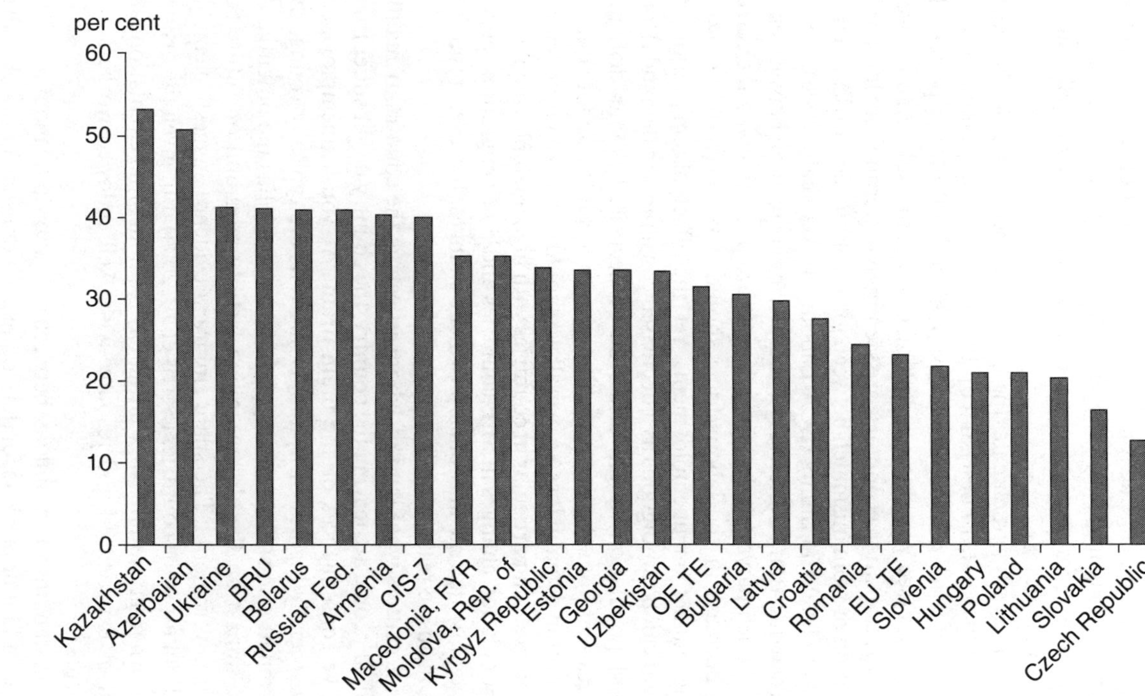

Source: Schneider (2002); Schneider and Klinglmair (2004).

Figure 17.1 Employment in the informal sector, 1998/99

related to tight labour market regulations. Only 23 per cent of firms in SEE report labour regulations as a moderate or major constraint (Figure 17.2). This is one of the lowest complaint levels registered among the regions in the world. (The complaint list is led by Latin America with 53 per cent.) On the other hand, senior management is spending 10 per cent of its time dealing with regulations (Figure 17.3). And the costs of providing security (equipment and personnel for security services) are particularly high in SEE at 2.7 per cent of total sales.

In terms of investment climate, the SEE region scores 5.2 on the start-up-cost index (0 worst, 10 best), 6.0 on the access-to-finance index, 6.1 on the market-regulations index, and a disappointing 2.0 on the perceived-corruption index (see World Bank, 2004b). Overall, this sub-region as well as many of the transition economies are seemingly suffering from low levels of job creation or from mismatch between job creation and job destruction with regard to level and timing (ECA Labour Market Team, 2004).

The special question of interest is if there is any correlation between emigration and unemployment. In principle outward migration and the corresponding decrease in the labour force should have – *ceteris paribus* – a reducing impact on unemployment. Yet the effect of emigration on employment can be ambiguous as a decreased consumption demand (from a decreased population) might also lead to decreased labour demand. Remittances sent home by migrants, though, could substitute for some of the consumption demand loss, so overall we should expect an improvement in labour markets, in particular in countries with high unemployment rates. Plotting population changes in SEE countries and other migration-related variables against income and unemployment changes, however, results in rather inconclusive results (no figures).

Clearly, it matters what kind of labour is leaving the country. If mainly highly skilled people are leaving the country, the country might suffer from the negative consequences of the brain drain. As youth unemployment rates are especially high in SEE, and as migrants are typically young, the countries might also suffer from a youth drain, which has the potential of a negative impact on the already falling fertility rates and on future tax returns for governments. The spare empirical evidence suggests elements of brain drain for some countries (Sarris et al., 2004). But given the history of high return migration this may ultimately result in brain circulation and the return of experienced and resource-wise, well endowed workers and entrepreneurs.

Our understanding of the linkage between migration and labour markets, and the role of labour markets for development, is only beginning. As other international and national institutions, the World Bank has started to work on migration issues, including the role of migration for development, and

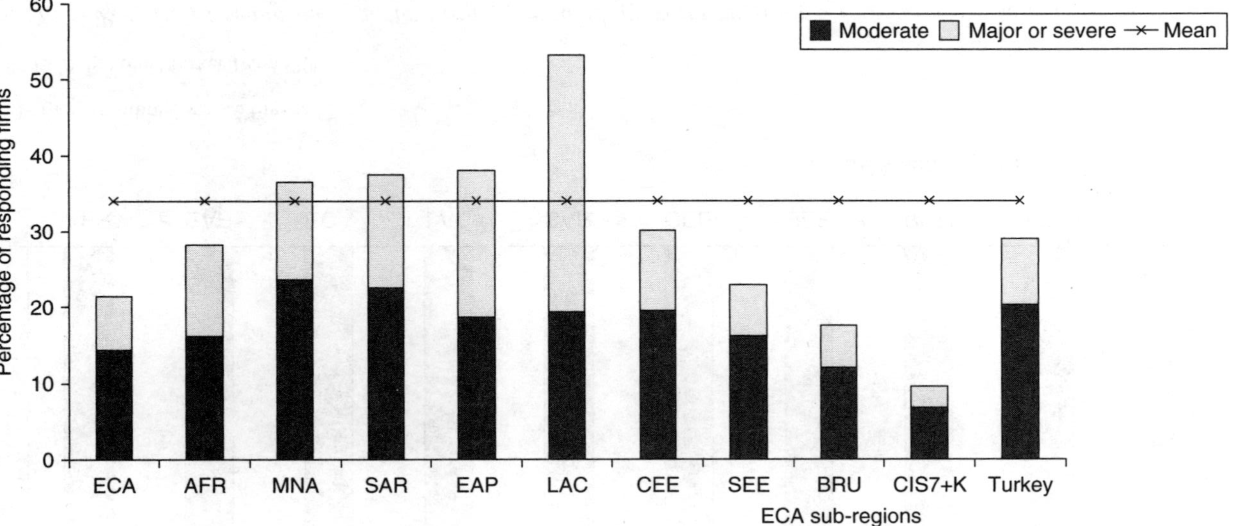

Note: Key to sub-region labels used in Figures 17.2–17.3: ECA: Europe and Central Asia; AFR: Sub-Saharan Africa; MNA: Middle-East and Northern Africa; SAR: South Asia Region; EAP: East Asia and Pacific; LAC: Latin America and Caribbean; CEE: Central and Eastern Europe; SEE: South Eastern Europe; BRU: Belarus, Russia and Ukraine; CIS7+K: Commonwealth of Independent States and Kazakhstan.

Source: ECA Labour Market Team (2004).

Figure 17.2 Labour regulations as an obstacle

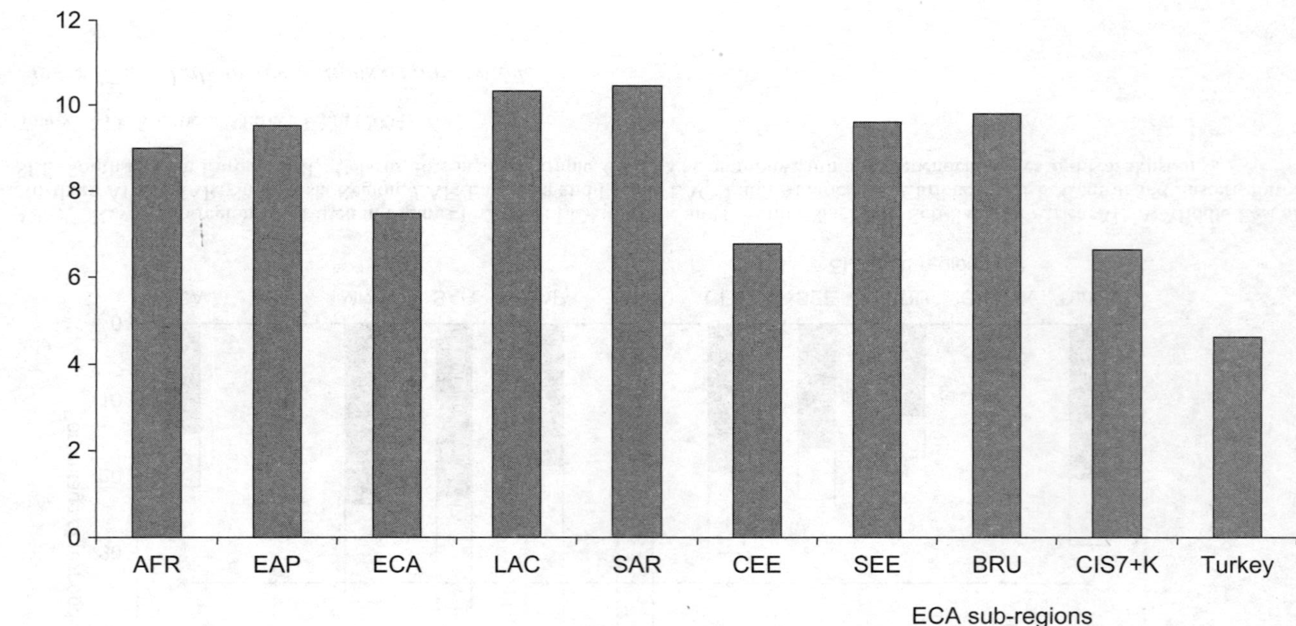

Note: For key to subregions see Figure 17.2.

Source: ECA Labour Market Team (2004).

Figure 17.3 Per cent of senior management time spent dealing with regulations

more specifically the challenges and opportunities of migration for the EU and its neighbouring countries (Holzmann and Muenz, 2004). The role of labour markets for development, including the impact of migration, is part of a labour market research programme recently launched by the World Bank. A regional stocktaking conference in November 2004 presented the regional labour market experiences (including for ECA), served to identify broad commonalities and differences between the regions (and sub-regions), and helped determine priorities for the multi-year research programme (for details, see www.worldbank.org/sp/labor).

NOTES

1. The findings, interpretations, and conclusions expressed herein are those of the author and do not necessarily reflect the views of the World Bank and its affiliated organizations, or those of the Executive Directors of The World Bank or the governments they represent. Excellent research support by Johannes Koettl from the Social Protection team is gratefully acknowledged.
2. ECA Labour Market Team (2004).
3. Not all Western European countries report data for every year. Data from France and Italy, for example, are largely absent, while the UK reports for some, but not all countries of origin. The problem is aggravated by varying definitions of migrants, as some countries report migrants by country of birth while others report migrants by country of citizenship, which mainly affects statistics on stocks of migrants.

REFERENCES

ECA Labour Market Team (2004), *Labor Markets in Europe and Central Asia: Towards Creating More and Better Jobs*, preliminary draft, November, Washington, DC: World Bank.

ECA Migration Team (2004), *Enhancing Gains through International Labor Flows in Europe and Central Asia*, project under preparation, Washington, DC: World Bank.

Hatton, J. Timothy and Jeffrey G. Williamson (1998), *The Age of Mass Migration – Causes and Economic Impact*, New York: Oxford University Press.

Holzmann, Robert and Rainer Muenz (2004), *Challenges and Opportunities of International Migration for the EU, its Member States, Neighboring Countries and Regions*, Stockholm: Institute for Futures Studies.

Migration Policy Institute (2004), *Migration Information Source, Global Data Center*, available at http://migrationinformation.org. Last accessed on 3 January, 2005.

OECD (2004), *Trends in International Migration* (annual publication), SOPEMI, Paris: OECD.

Sarris, Alexander, Etleva Germenji and Evgenia Markova (2004), *Balkan Migration: An Assessment of Past Trends and Policies and the Way Ahead*, Rome: Agriculture Organization of the United Nations.

Schneider, Friedrich (2002), *The Size and Development of Shadow Economies of 22 Transition and 21 OECD Countries*, Bonn, Germany: IZA (Institute for the Study of Labour), Discussion Paper 514.
Schneider, Friedrich and Robert Klinglmair (2004), *Shadow Economies Around the World: What Do We Know?*, Bonn, Germany: IZA (Institute for the Study of Labour), Discussion Paper 1043.
United Nations High Commissioner for Refugees (UNHCR) (2002), *Statistical Yearbook 2002: Trends in Displacement, Protection and Solutions*, Geneva, Switzerland: UNHCR.
World Bank (2004a), *World Development Indicators*, Washington, DC: World Bank.
World Bank (2004b), *World Development Report 2005: A Better Investment Climate for Everyone*, Washington, DC: World Bank.

18. Jobless growth in South-East Europe, migration and the role of the EU

Tito Boeri

1. INTRODUCTION

On 1 May 2004, ten new countries formally joined the European Union (EU). The new members are small economically – they have significantly lower income per capita levels than the EU-15 – but large demographically. By 2007 the second phase of the Eastern enlargement, involving two key countries of South-East Europe, namely Bulgaria and Romania, should take place. By then, the number of EU citizens will have grown by more than 100 million.

The Eastern part of Europe is growing fast but, especially in its Southern components, failing to generate jobs. In some of the high-unemployment areas of the EU-15, such as Andalusia or the Italian Mezzogiorno, an opposite phenomenon is observed: low growth but decreasing unemployment. These developments add to income inequalities between old and new members of the EU another potential source of East–West migration, namely unemployment differences.

Concerned about this migration potential and under the pressure of public opinion, governments in the EU-15 are de facto closing their doors to workers from the new member states (NMS). This is a by-product of a lack of coordination at the EU level. As there is no agreement at the EU level on a common set of rules to be applied to the new citizens during the seven-year transition period, each of the old members has decided to establish its own rules. In general, these rules substantially tighten migration or introduce other restrictions for the newcomers.

Supra-national authorities in the EU are also taking a rather negative stance vis-à-vis early euro adoption by the NMS. The standard argument is that early EMU participation would prevent the NMS from using the exchange rate and interest rates as absorbers of asymmetric shocks. Furthermore, it is stressed that the NMS economies are too 'weak' to be subjected to the rigours of the single currency and the Stability and Growth Pact (SGP), and hence that nominal convergence to the EMU rules may delay real convergence, that is, the convergence in incomes per capita.

Many of these concerns are ill-founded. More importantly, they seem to ignore the interactions between macroeconomic stability, growth and migration. A stable macroeconomic framework for these countries is essential to foster growth and increase job creation, thereby reducing migration pressures, which will not be lower in seven to ten years' time, at the end of the transitional periods for migration. Euro adoption could provide such a stable macroeconomic framework, reducing the risk of emerging markets contagions and bringing down interest rates on public debt in these countries which are harmful to job creation. Foreign direct investment (FDI) attracted by the elimination of currency risk and macro-stability would also promote stronger employment growth, increasing the job content of growth and hence moving the NMS away from the current jobless recovery.

The remainder of this chapter is organized as follows. Section 2 characterizes jobless growth in South-East Europe. Section 3 discusses migration restrictions vis-à-vis the NMS. Section 4 analyses the interactions between euro adoption, employment growth and migration. Section 5 concludes.

2. JOBLESS GROWTH

Employment growth in Eastern European countries, notably in the South East, has been to date only weakly correlated to output growth: since the start of economic transition these countries never experienced two consecutive years of net job creation and also displayed remarkable large job losses in the 1998–2000 period.

It was the mid-1990s that marked a change in the responsiveness of employment to output changes in the NMS. Before that date formerly planned economies in this region displayed significantly larger employment-to-output elasticities than the Commonwealth of Independent States (CIS). Employment ceased to be responsive to output variations in 1997, and in the most recent years the correlation between output and employment growth has been flat.

The same regime change was also observed in the unemployment-to-output elasticity: from being strongly negative at early stages of transition, the correlation between unemployment and GDP growth became statistically insignificant in the last few years.

Figure 18.1 offers a key characterization of jobless growth, namely the output and employment dynamics within each country grouping. The horizontal line in each panel denotes a GDP growth rate of 3 per cent while

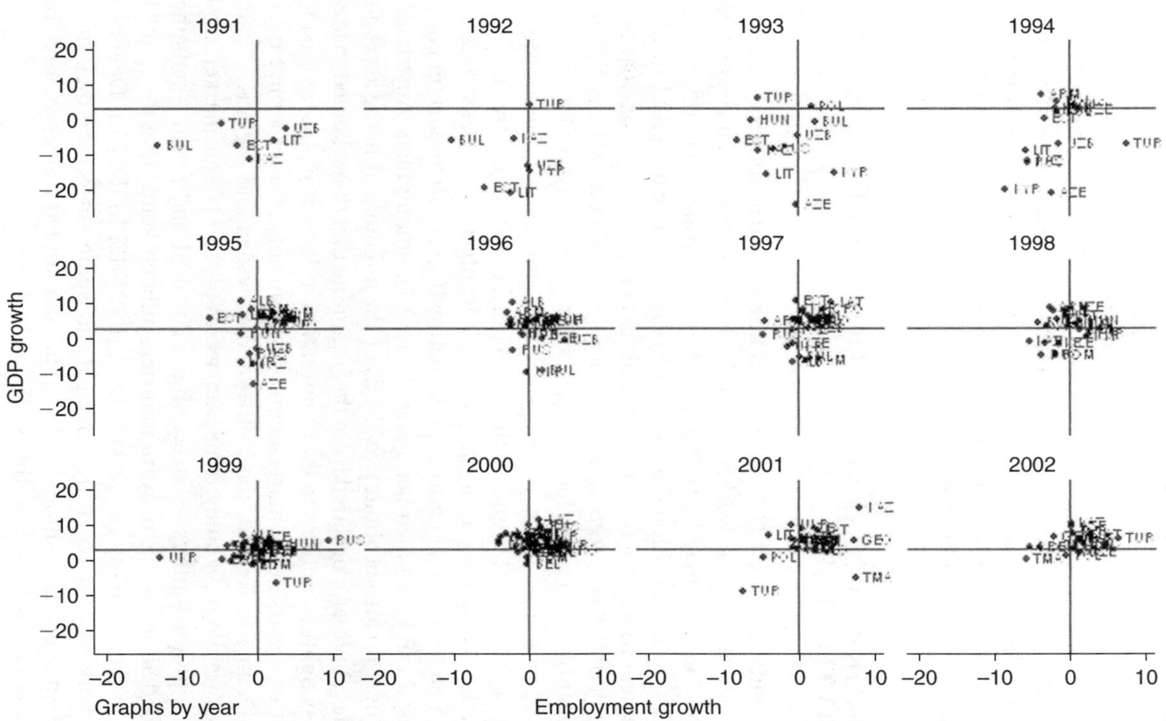

Figure 18.1 Jobless growth in recent years

the vertical line corresponds to zero employment growth. The points in the North-East and South-West region of each panel correspond to countries and years in which employment and GDP growth are positively correlated, both in booms and in recessions. Conversely, the presence of points in the North-West and South-East regions of the diagrams reflects the break-up of the negative relationship between growth and unemployment. Significantly, a lack of correlation between employment growth and GDP growth is observed mainly in the recent years and in the North-West portions of the diagram, pointing to jobless growth rather than positive job creation during output recession.

3. MIGRATION RESTRICTIONS: A RACE TO THE TOP

Most countries of the EU-15 introduced transitional arrangements for the free labour mobility of workers from the NMS, under which the opening of labour markets may be postponed up to a maximum period of seven years.[1] Similar transitional arrangements had also been agreed in other enlargement rounds: in the case of the accession of Greece a six-year transitional period was agreed, and, at the accession of Portugal and Spain, a seven-year transitional period was introduced, later on reduced to six years. However, what makes the present rules different from those adopted in previous enlargement rounds is that individual countries are free to decide on whether or not to apply transitional arrangements. Delegating the decision on transitional periods to the national level had important consequences: 7 out of 15 member states of the EU, among them Austria and Germany, who attract about two-thirds of the migrants from the accession countries at present, declared from the beginning that they planned to leave relatively tight restrictions to the immigration of labour in place at least for the first two years after enlargement.[2] Governments of another five countries – Denmark, Ireland, the Netherlands, Sweden and the UK – stated that they were not planning to restrict access to their labour market, while the remaining countries – Greece, Italy, Portugal and Spain – remained undecided although the relevant ministers publicly stated that they were in favour of free mobility of workers from the NMS. In the end, Denmark, the Netherlands, Greece, Italy, Portugal and Spain reneged on their initial plan to open up their labour markets and all adopted transitional restrictions vis-à-vis workers from the NMS.

Italy, Portugal and Spain in particular opted for restrictive provisions. Italy, in particular introduced a quota of 20 000 work permits for workers from the NMS, well below projected immigration flows to this country while Greece, Spain and Portugal decided to leave their immigration restrictions in place at least for the first two years.

From a political economy standpoint, this tightening of restrictions is a reaction to the mounting concerns of the public in the established EU members (the EU-15) about migration issues. According to a 2002 survey by Eurobarometer, one in two EU citizens believes that migrants, wherever they come from, are already abusing the welfare state, and two out of three consider that the EU should only open up to countries at comparable living standards.

Closing the door to the new citizens will hurt EU growth and inflate the ranks of shadow employment among workers from the NMS.

From the allocative standpoint, the new restrictions will alter the geographical orientation of migration, preventing migrants from the NMS going to the countries where they can be most productive. In labour markets with low mobility, migrants play an important role by increasing average productivity, contributing not only to stronger growth but also to higher incomes per capita.

A better way to deal with concerns of citizens would have been to adopt a common transitional quota set by the EU as a whole – enabling the realization of at least part of the potential welfare gains in the form of higher growth while providing information on migration pressures. The quota could have been established at a level based on past migration episodes, perhaps accommodating an annual inflow of some 400 000 people, in line with the 'consensus forecasts' on the migration potential associated with enlargement (Boeri and Bruecker, 2001).

While transitional restrictions are in place, reforms that tackle concerns about the future viability of the welfare system need to be carried out. In seven to ten years' time, when the 'transitional period' is over, differences in incomes between the old and new members will still exist, and will be sizeable.

4. THE EMU TRACK

While Western Europe is temporarily closing borders to workers from the NMS, current members of EMU are making it more and more difficult for the new members to enter monetary union. Tight requirements are imposed on this track. In particular, the requirement of spending two years in the exchange rate mechanism (ERM) II has been kept in place in spite of the fact that some countries come from currency unions and have a longstanding experience of fixed parities with the euro. Moreover, the text elaborated by the Convention on the Future of Europe was amended by the inter-governmental conference (IGC), introducing new procedural obstacles to nominal convergence.

These additional hurdles being put on the NMS' path to EMU are inspired by the view that nominal convergence (convergence to EMU) would delay real convergence (convergence in GDP per capita). But this view is wrong for a number of reasons.

First, possession of an independent currency for the NMS can be more of a shock generator than a shock absorber for middle-income countries, exposed to turbulence in emerging markets. Indeed, an important determinant of exchange rate and real interest rate movements in the region would seem to have been changes in the risk premium. These changes were due to increases in the premium required of emerging markets, an effect which would very largely disappear after EMU accession.

Second, under a stable and low-inflation macroeconomic environment, acceding countries can be expected to generate labour productivity improvements much faster than current EU members, and EMU participation would provide such an environment.

Third, euro adoption would promote FDI, contributing significantly to reducing capital shortages in the region and exerting positive knowledge spillovers on firms in the NMS, which badly need better human capital.

All of this also means that labour market conditions are bound to improve in the convergence to the euro. There is, indeed, evidence that in the NMS there is a strong complementarity between capital and labour. Moreover, employment growth in the region has been found to be negatively affected by high real interest rates (Boeri and Garibaldi, 2004), and real interest rates in the euro area are much lower than those experienced by most Central and Eastern European economies. Hence, adopting a common currency would provide a low interest rate environment in the years to come, and would probably help these countries to increase the job content of growth. If growth were to continue, low real interest rates would also lead to a reduction in unemployment. Keynesian arguments are often used to argue that fiscal consolidation required to accommodate euro adoption could hamper growth and job creation in the NMS. However, evidence on the recessionary effects of fiscal consolidation packages is far from uncontroversial: in a number of cases fiscal consolidation packages involving public expenditure cum tax cuts indeed strengthened macroeconomic performance even in the short run. Concerning employment growth, if fiscal consolidation involves a reduction in wages being paid to civil servants, it may avoid the crowding out of private employment in many low productivity (for example in the retail trade) jobs. Thus, the adjustment required for euro adoption is also far from negative from the employment standpoint.

5. CONCLUSIONS

Strong economic growth in the new EU member states and South-East Europe is generating many new jobs. Rather than imposing its conditionality to stimulate more structural reforms in the East, Western Europe is welcoming its new members by shutting the doors in the face of the workers coming from the East and making it more difficult for NMS to join EMU. As shown in this chapter, these restrictions are not justified by migration pressures and rely on ill-founded concerns that nominal convergence could delay real convergence. Moreover, they are mutually inconsistent: delaying EMU convergence would just worsen labour market conditions with respect to a scenario of relatively quick convergence to the euro, by increasing real interest rates and negatively affecting FDI directed to the NMS. This ultimately means that delaying EMU convergence may backfire in terms of stronger East–West migration pressures.

NOTES

1. Free movement is granted to the citizens from the new member states in principle, but the EU countries can restrict the access to their labour markets during the transitional periods.
2. Beyond Austria and Germany this was Belgium, Finland, France, Greece and Luxembourg.

REFERENCES

Boeri, T. and H. Bruecker (2001), 'Eastern enlargement and EU-labour markets: perceptions, challenges and opportunities', *World Economics*, **2** (1), 49–67, March.

Boeri, T. and P. Garibaldi (2004), 'Are labour markets in the new member states sufficiently flexible for EMU?', *Journal of Banking and Finance*, forthcoming.

19. Unemployment in the Western Balkans: a synoptic diagnosis

Kalman Mizsei and Nicholas Maddock

INTRODUCTION

This chapter examines the level and characteristics of unemployment in the Western Balkan.[1] The hypotheses as to why unemployment in the region is so high are reviewed and gaps in the analysis of, and data on, unemployment and related matters in the Western Balkans are identified.

All the Western Balkan countries have aspirations to membership of the European Union (EU), with Croatia likely to be the first to accede. Having formally applied for membership in February 2003, it became a candidate country in April 2004.[2] Macedonia also applied for membership (in March 2004), while the other Western Balkan countries are participating in the so-called Stabilisation and Association Process.[3] This is analogous to the preparatory process for membership pursued by the European Commission in the formerly socialist countries of Central and Eastern Europe (CEE) which joined the EU in 2004, as well as in Romania and Bulgaria (which are expected to accede in 2007).[4] In broad terms, it involves a contractual process which is tailor-made to each country and based on agreed criteria and goals which aim to ensure that prospective candidate countries pursue EU-compatible practices in political, economic and sectoral reform.[5] As such, it is a precursor to a detailed review of compliance with the *acquis communautaire* and the ensuing design and implementation of a programme of actions necessary for accession (which, in total, comprise the so-called negotiations for membership).

Prospective candidate countries are required, as part of the Stabilisation and Association Process, to comply with the overarching criteria established at the 1993 Copenhagen European Council.[6] These criteria, which have become widely known as the Copenhagen criteria, specify that three conditions must be met, of which the second[7] is 'the existence of a functioning market economy, as well as the ability to cope with competitive pressures and market forces within the Union'. Further, one of the conditions for the start of negotiations for a Stabilisation and Association

Agreement (SAA), which is in effect the contract between the EU and the country concerned under the Stabilisation and Association Process, is 'substantial results in the field of political/economic reforms (stable economic environment, liberalization of prices, regulatory framework, competitive banking sector, etc)'.[8] High unemployment in the countries of the Western Balkans is thus of concern in respect both of compliance with the Copenhagen criteria and the requirements for an SAA and thereby seen as potentially impeding and delaying the region's future within Europe.

More generally unemployment is, or may form, a barrier to the successful completion of the transition from socialist to market economies in the region partly because of the threats it poses to political and social stability. In a region that has recently seen several wars (which themselves significantly delayed the start of the transition) and where occasional localized conflict still occurs, this is obviously of concern. Some observers have suggested that the civil disturbance in Kosovo in March 2004 can be partially attributed to extraordinary levels of unemployment. Similar concerns are voiced about the potential effects of unemployment in parts of Macedonia and Serbia.

It also raises the question of whether approaches to economic transition in the Western Balkans should differ from those adopted in the first wave of Central and Eastern European transitional countries (that is, those that acceded to the EU in 2004 and those expected to accede in 2007). The approach to date in the Western Balkans has been strongly similar to that in this first wave but, in terms of unemployment, outcomes to date have differed. Thus, while the experience of Central and Eastern Europe in transition should in principle provide valuable guidance for the Western Balkans in their transition and development strategy, it is reasonable in view of the chronic unemployment to question the validity of replicating the approach wholesale.

LEVELS AND CHARACTERISTICS OF UNEMPLOYMENT IN THE WESTERN BALKANS

Official unemployment rates in the Western Balkans are very high and, in some cases, increasing (Table 19.1). This is despite economic growth in the region in recent years (Table 19.2), which has not (in the formal sector) resulted in the increase in demand for labour that might have been expected.

Unemployment is currently at much higher levels in the Western Balkans than in the CEE countries that joined the EU in 2004, and in Bulgaria (Table 19.3). Clearly, however, the usefulness of this comparison is limited

Table 19.1 Unemployment (%) in the Western Balkans 1999–2004

Country	1999	2000	2001	2002	2003	2004[1]
Albania	18	17.1	13.5	15.8	15.2	14.5
Bosnia and Herzegovina	38.9	39.7	40.1	41	42	n.a.
Croatia	13.6	16.1	15.8	14.8	14.1	n.a.
Macedonia	32.4	32.2	30.5	31.9	36.7	n.a.
Serbia and Montenegro	27	27	28	29	30	34
Kosovo	n.a.	n.a.	n.a.	47	50	n.a.

Note: 1. Data for 2004 are based on projections.

Sources: European Commission (2004a); European Commission (2004b); World Bank (2004).

Table 19.2 Real GDP growth (%) in the Western Balkans 1999–2004

Country	1999	2000	2001	2002	2003	2004[1]
Albania	10.1	7.3	7.2	3.4	6.0	6.0
Bosnia and Herzegovina	10.0	5.6	4.5	5.5	3.5	5.0
Croatia	−0.9	2.9	3.8	5.2	5.0	–
Macedonia	4.3	4.6	−4.5	0.9	3.2	2.0
Serbia and Montenegro	−18.0	5.0	5.5	4.0	3.0	5.0
Kosovo	–	–	21.2	1.2	3.1	3.2
Western Balkans	1.1	5.1	6.3	3.4	4.0	4.2

Note: 1. Preliminary projections.

Source: European Commission (2004a); European Commission (2004b).

since the CEE countries are at a more advanced stage in transition than the Western Balkans and indeed, by virtue of accession to the EU, they can be considered to have met the Copenhagen criteria and thus to be functioning market economies. In contrast, and with the exceptions of Albania and Macedonia, transition in the Western Balkans region has been delayed and impeded by recent wars (and even in Macedonia civil conflict in 2001, subsequent to the start of the transition, is also likely to have delayed and

Table 19.3 Unemployment rates (%) in selected Central and Eastern European countries, 1996, 2001 and 2003

Country	1996	2001	2003
Bulgaria	12.5	18	13.5
Estonia	9	12.4	5.5
Czech Republic	3.5	9.8	10.5
Lithuania	7	12.5	10.7
Poland	13.2	18	18
Slovakia	12.8	17.2	15
Slovenia	14.4	11	11.2
Hungary	11.4	5.8	6.1

Source: Vienna Institute for International Economic Studies (2004).

impeded reforms). Nonetheless a similar picture emerges if a comparison is made between unemployment rates in the Western Balkans in 2003 and those in CEE and Bulgaria in 1996 (when, as in the Western Balkans now, some 4–5 years had elapsed since the start of the transition).

Disaggregation of unemployment in the region (Table 19.4) shows that it is predominantly long-term (that is mainly people who have been unemployed for more that one year). Indeed, with the exception of Croatia (where the long-term unemployed are still a majority), over 70 per cent of the unemployed are long-term unemployed. Young people are disproportionately affected (Kosovo is an exception), as are women in Croatia and Kosovo and, to a lesser extent, in Albania.

Unemployment rates appear highest amongst vulnerable groups and the less educated (although data are patchy and comprehensive information covering the Western Balkans is not available). Thus, in Macedonia, whereas the national unemployment rate in 2002 was 32 per cent, unemployment amongst ethnic Albanians was 61 per cent, Roma 79 per cent and Turks 58 per cent.[9] In Montenegro, the rate for Roma in 2002 was 43 per cent.[10] The unemployment rate in Kosovo for those with only elementary education in 2003 was 66 per cent, compared to a national rate of 47–50 per cent.[11]

Estimating unemployment levels in the Western Balkans is, however, complicated by the size of the informal sector. There is a general supposition that official unemployment rates overestimate unemployment since, it is suggested, a significant proportion of the registered unemployed are in fact employed in the informal sector. Estimates from Kosovo suggest that adjusting for informal sector employment may lower effective

Table 19.4 *Labour market characteristics*

Country	Unemployment rate	Male unemployment rate (% of male labour force)	Female unemployment rate (% of female labour force)	Youth (<24 years) unemployment (% of total unemployed)	Long-term unemployment (>1 year) (% of total unemployed)
Albania (2003)[1]	15.2	12.9	18.2	28.4[2]	91.8[3]
Bosnia and Herzegovina (2003)[1]	41	n.a.	n.a.	n.a.	n.a.
Croatia (2003)[1]	14.8	15.5	23.2	41.7[2]	56.4[3]
Macedonia (2002)[4]	31.9	31.7	32.3	58.4	84.5[3]
Serbia and Montenegro (2003)[1]	29	14.4	16.4	59.1[2]	74.8[3]
Kosovo (2002)[5]	47	37	69	41	73

Notes:
1. International Labour Organization, ILO LABORSTA database, http://laborsta.ilo.org/.
2. UNICEF Innocenti Research Centre, TransMONEE Database 2003.
3. International Labour Organization, http://www.ilo.org/public/english/region/eurpro/budapest/info/bul/04-1/2004_02.htm.
4. World Bank (2003b).
5. World Bank (2004).

unemployment rates by 15–17 percentage points.[12] Similarly, studies in Bosnia and Herzegovina in 2001 estimated that 362 000 workers were employed in the informal sector compared to formal sector employment of 638 000.[13] However, while the informal sector in the Western Balkans does appear substantial, some countries of CEE have equally large informal sectors, although the informal sector (when expressed as a percentage of gross national income) is generally lower (Table 19.5). In these terms, the size of the informal sector in Bulgaria and Romania is comparable to those in the Western Balkans.

Low absolute poverty levels in the Western Balkans may provide a proxy indicator of the importance of the informal sector in providing employment and income. Unemployment and poverty are closely correlated[14] and the high levels of unemployment coupled with the shallow social safety nets characteristic of the region might be expected to lead to higher absolute poverty levels than is the case (Table 19.6). Yet, except in Kosovo, there is little or no extreme absolute poverty (insufficient income to meet a minimum food basket), while levels of absolute poverty (based on a basket of food and non-food items) are also below levels that might be expected given the high unemployment rates.[15]

Table 19.5 Informal economy (2003)

Country	Value of the informal economy as % of gross national income
Albania	34
Bosnia and Herzegovina	34
Croatia	33
Serbia and Montenegro	29
Bulgaria	37
Romania	34
Hungary	25
Latvia	40
Poland	28
Slovenia	27
Slovakia	19

Source: International Finance Corporation. 'Doing business: benchmarking business regulations'. Database available at http://rru. worldbank.org/DoingBusiness/.

Table 19.6 Percentage of population suffering absolute poverty in the Western Balkans (2003 figures unless stated)[1]

	Extreme poverty			Poverty	
	Calorific value (calories/day) of minimum food basket	Cost (euro equivalent/day)	% of population below extreme poverty line	Cost of total basket (food and non-food) (euro equivalent/day)	% of population below poverty line
Serbia	2288	0.81	0	2.4	10
Montenegro	Not known	1.37	5[2]	3.87	12
Bosnia and Herzegovina	2240	1.04	0	3.01	20[4]
Macedonia	Not defined in Macedonia's interim Poverty Reduction Strategy (2000)				
Croatia	No poverty assessment since 2001 (which was based on 1998 figures)				
Kosovo (2001 figures)	2100	0.93	12[3]	1.74	50
Albania	2288	0.8	5	1.28	25

Notes:

1. Data originally obtained from national Living Standards Measurement Surveys (or similar). For information on the methodology and coverage of Living Standards Measurement Surveys, see http://www.worldbank.org/lsms.
2. Surveys did not include Roma or people living in collective centres for refugees.
3. The rate for Roma, Ashkaelia and Egyptian minorities is 23 per cent and for refugees 17 per cent.
4. The percentage of the population below the poverty line in the Republika Srpska is 25 per cent, whereas it is 16 per cent in the Federation BiH. Poverty in urban areas is suffered by 14 per cent of the population, whereas the rate is 20 per cent in rural areas and 24 per cent in rural areas where ethnic communities are mixed.

CAUSES OF UNEMPLOYMENT IN THE WESTERN BALKANS

In addition to the supposition that official unemployment is overstated because of widespread employment in the informal sector, there are a number of hypotheses as to why rates in the Western Balkans are so high. These are the effects of recent wars; economic underperformance; low levels of foreign direct investment; labour market rigidities; underperformance of the small and medium-sized enterprises (SME) sector; and labour force participation rates. It is recognized that the break-up of former Yugoslavia into separate independent states and the continuing uncertain status of Kosovo may also be contributory factors. However, no attempt is made in this chapter to analyse their effects on unemployment.

The evidence related to these hypotheses is examined below on the basis of published data. It is recognized that inter-linkage between these factors is possible and hence that there may be compound causal effects. No attempt is made to assess these compound effects and this methodological limitation is acknowledged.

THE EFFECTS OF RECENT WARS

While there are no detailed studies of the economic effects of the recent wars in former Yugoslavia, estimates of the effects of civil war in Kosovo suggest that output there fell by 20 per cent more than it would have done in the 'normal' recession characteristic of the early stages of the transition.[16] Empirical studies of the economic consequences of civil wars elsewhere (Collier, 1999) show much lower reductions in GDP and indeed very much lower than the falls in GDP experienced in Bosnia and Herzegovina during the war years.[17] As a result, there is little basis for judging the validity of this estimate.

However, while the likelihood of loss of output due to war is intuitively obvious (through depleting human and capital stock and loss of confidence), the dynamic post-war economic effects are harder to evaluate. It is of course likely that the very high growth rates in the immediate post-war period in Bosnia and Herzegovina (21 per cent in 1995, 86 per cent in 1996, 37 per cent in 1997, and 10 per cent in 1998[18]) reflect recovery from the pronounced falls in GDP during the war. It may, however, also reflect the installation of new capital stock[19] and 'enforced' technological improvement (that is, where new technology has replaced that destroyed by the war) which may in turn result in higher labour productivity.

As a result, the effects of wars on employment in the region are hard to assess beyond the facile conclusion that a war-affected transitional country is likely to be in a worse economic condition for a period after the war than one where the transition took place in conditions of peace. In practice, however, the tail-off in growth rates in the region since 2001 suggests that both the negative consequences of war in the Western Balkans and pronounced post-war bounce may now have largely been felt, except perhaps more nebulously in respect of confidence. The recent conflicts in the region therefore probably cannot be cited as a principal explanator for unemployment levels.

ECONOMIC UNDERPERFORMANCE

Comparison of cumulative GDP growth (Table 19.7) suggests that economic performance in this respect in the Western Balkans was, over the six-year period from 1998 to 2003, broadly comparable with that achieved by Bulgaria and Romania, but slightly poorer than that in Estonia, Latvia and Lithuania. Performance in these terms was, however, markedly poorer than in the Russian Federation and the Ukraine and, while this comparison is obviously complicated by the effects of oil revenues in the Russian Federation, the contribution of the Ukraine to this trend is notable.

If, however, similar comparisons are made instead for the four-year period from 2000 to 2003, thereby removing the influence of very high growth rates in the immediate post-war period in the Western Balkans, the picture is different and suggests poorer performance in the Western Balkans than in all other comparator areas. The reason for this tail-off in growth rates is not clear, but seems likely to be associated in part with reduced foreign assistance and failure to compensate through higher foreign direct investment (FDI) levels (see below).

FOREIGN DIRECT INVESTMENT

FDI levels in the Western Balkans show considerable variation between years (Table 19.8) and between the countries of the region,[20] thereby complicating conclusions about performance in this respect. Thus, while in recent years, FDI in the Western Balkans has generally been lower than in the CEE countries that joined the EU in 2004, increases in 2003 led to roughly comparable levels. In addition, the level of FDI for the region as a whole has consistently exceeded or matched that for Bulgaria and Romania.

The recent increases in FDI in the Western Balkans appear to be largely due to progress in privatization programmes,[21] although there are no data available for the region which convincingly demonstrate this through a division of FDI into *greenfield* and privatization-related investments. However, of the USD 95 million FDI in Macedonia in 2003, 70 per cent was

Table 19.7 Gross domestic product (constant 1990 prices USD million)

Country	1998	1999	2000	2001	2002	2003
Bosnia and Herzegovina	5479	6005	6341	6627	6885	6963
Serbia and Montenegro	16893	12765	13582	14329	14873	15022
Macedonia	3739	3900	4076	3892	3927	4049
Croatia	20822	20643	21232	22033	23185	24274
Total GDP	41454	43313	45231	46881	48870	50308
Index (1998=100)	100	104	109	113	118	121
Index (2000=100)			100	104	108	111
Estonia	9692	9631	10334	11002	11660	12185
Latvia	10947	11258	12028	12983	13770	14734
Lithuania	14035	13780	14328	15261	16299	17750
Total GDP	34674	34669	36690	39246	41729	44669
Index (1998=100)	100	100	106	113	120	129
Index (2000=100)			100	107	114	122
Russian Federation	555491	590771	650117	683217	715084	767462
Ukraine	100861	100698	106630	116476	120724	130986
Total GDP	656352	691469	756747	799693	835808	898448
Index (1998=100)	100	105	115	122	127	137
Index (2000=100)			100	106	110	119
Bulgaria	15821	16185	17058	17752	18596	19489
Romania	31927	31560	32238	34087	35741	37438
Total GDP	47748	47745	49296	51839	54337	56927
Index (1998=100)	100	100	103	109	114	119
Index (2000=100)			100	105	110	115

Source: United Nations Common Database, UNSTATS, 2004, http://unstats.un.org/unsd/cdb/.

from privatization receipts.[22] In contrast, by 2002, virtually all FDI in CEE was for greenfield and reinvestments.[23] This is not surprising given that the countries of CEE – Hungary included – started the transition process, and made substantial progress in privatization, earlier than the Western Balkans. It may also suggest that, while most FDI in CEE is now greenfield and hence likely to be predominantly job-creating, FDI in the Western Balkans is likely to involve job losses in the short term as state- and socially-owned enterprises are restructured and privatized (since, as Svejnar, 2004, shows, many privatized firms reduce employment immediately after privatization).

Table 19.8 Foreign direct investment as percentage of GDP

Country	1999	2000	2001	2002	2003
Western Balkans	4.3	4.1	5.7	3.9	5.4
Western Balkans excluding Croatia	1.5	2.4	3.9	3.4	3.0
2004 accession countries (excluding Cyprus and Malta)	5.5	6.1	4.9	5.2	2.2
Bulgaria and Romania	3.9	4.1	3.7	2.6	4.8

Sources: Centre for European Policy Studies (2004); European Bank for Reconstruction and Development (2004).

LABOUR MARKET RIGIDITIES

The assessment of the influence of labour market rigidities on unemployment is complicated by the number of possible influencing factors. Indeed, for comprehensive analysis, there is also the need to take into account so-called *off-setting flexibilities*, which represent a potentially countervailing influence.[24]

Nevertheless, analysis of wage rates (Table 19.9) in the Western Balkans relative to those in CEE, Bulgaria and Romania, and in the Russian Federation and the Ukraine provides prima facie evidence of labour market rigidities. Thus, despite comparatively poorer economic performance since 2000 (see above), wage rates in all the Western Balkan countries for which data are available are above those for Bulgaria, Russia and the Ukraine.[25] Wage rates for Croatia and Macedonia exceed those for Romania, while wages in Croatia are also much higher than those in countries that acceded to the EU in 2004. Overall, this suggests that there are factors which are causing stickiness in labour costs and so preventing wages falling closer to market clearing rates.

Garibaldi and Mauro (2002) and Svejnar (2004) have shown that payroll taxes impact negatively on unemployment rates. However, evidence suggests this is unlikely to be a contributory factor in the Western Balkans since they are levied there at a similar rate to those in some CEE countries and at a lower rate than in Romania (Table 19.10).

Micevksa (2004) has sought to analyse the effects of employment protection legislation on unemployment in South-East Europe and has compiled Employment Protection Legislation (EPL) indices[26] for countries of the region (Table 19.11). While the limitations of this approach are

Table 19.9 Monthly wages (2002)

Country	Average gross monthly wage (euro equivalent)
Croatia	724
Macedonia	185
Serbia and Montenegro	150
Bulgaria	132
Romania	174
Poland	544
Hungary	504
Czech Republic	515
Estonia	416
Latvia	301
Lithuania	331
Russian Federation	147
Ukraine	75

Source: Vienna Institute for International Economic Studies (2004).

Table 19.10 Payroll taxes in the Western Balkans, South-East Europe and selected Central and Eastern European countries (2002)

Country	Payroll taxes % of base salary
Croatia	41.2
Macedonia	31.5
Serbia and Montenegro	53.2
Bosnia and Herzegovina	46.9
Bulgaria	45.0
Romania	60.5
Poland	48.2
Hungary	44.0
Czech Republic	47.5
Slovakia	50.0
Estonia	33.0
Slovenia	38.0

Source: Micevska (2004) and Riboud et al. (2002).

Table 19.11 Employment protection legislation (EPL) indices

	Year	Regular employment	Temporary employment	Collective dismissals	EPL index
Western Balkans					
Albania	1995	2.1	3	2.8	2.6
Bosnia and Herzegovina	2003	1.8	3.1	3.3	2.6
Croatia	2003	2.6	1.9	4.3	2.6
Macedonia	2003	2.0	3.1	4.0	2.8
Serbia and Montenegro	2001	2.2	3.1	3.8	2.9
SEE					
Bulgaria	2003	2.2	3.4	3.6	2.7
Romania	2003	1.7	3.0	4.8	2.8
Western Balkans and SEE average	2001–2003	2.1	2.9	3.7	2.7
CEE average	2000	2.7	1.2	4.1	2.4
EU average	2000	2.4	2.3	3.2	2.5

Source: Micevska (2004).

recognized (that is legal protection of workers in formerly socialist countries is often only partially respected or not at all, and there are in practice opportunities informally to hire-and-fire workers), it does have the virtue of capturing the many regulations affecting employment. EPL indices take values from 1 to 6, with the higher the value of the index, the stricter the employment protection legislation.

While there has been some weakening of employment protection legislation in the Western Balkans in recent years (World Bank, 2002), the EPL for all types of employment is still stronger than in CEE countries and in the 'old' EU of 15 member states (although results need to be treated with some caution given different periods of comparison). The stronger overall EPL, however, reflects stricter EPL on temporary employment[27] and collective dismissals,[28] since EPL on regular employment[29] is weaker than in CEE and the EU 15.

Micevska (2004) shows that the EPL for temporary employment[30] and, less strongly, collective dismissals[31] is correlated with levels of unemployment in the region (and, conversely, that the EPL for regular employment is not). The evidence of comparatively strong EPL for temporary work and collective dismissals may also help explain the high levels of unemployment amongst young people and women noted above.[32] Thus, if as might be supposed, women and young people have a higher propensity to access temporary labour markets than other groups, the stricter EPL for this type of work is thus likely to have a disproportionate effect. Micevska (2004) also shows that the EPL index and the size of the informal economy are highly correlated.[33]

UNDERPERFORMANCE OF THE SME SECTOR

As in the formerly socialist countries of CEE, private sector development in general, and SME development in particular, is seen as a key element in stimulating growth and employment in the Western Balkans. But the existence of apparently jobless growth (see above) in the Western Balkans may suggest that the private sector's contribution to date has been below expectations.

If this is true, it begs the question of whether SMEs in the Western Balkans have the potential to contribute as expected and, further, whether reliance on SME development as a cornerstone of private sector development is still merited. Indeed, and following this logic, if the rates of formation and the absolute numbers of SMEs were lower, and the rate of mortality higher, in the Western Balkans than in the formerly socialist countries of CEE (either now or at a similar stage in the transition), then the possible contribution from SMEs may be constrained relative to that which was achieved in CEE. The same applies if SMEs in the Western Balkans were predominantly engaged in low-barriers-to-entry and low value-added activities with limited potential to mature into high value-added SMEs offering significant employment.

Unfortunately, however, evidence related to both these contentions is inconclusive, with no clear trends apparent. This partly reflects the restricted data availability for the Western Balkan countries and probable discrepancies.

LABOUR FORCE PARTICIPATION RATES

No clear explanation of higher unemployment emerges from the analysis of labour force participation rates, which are broadly comparable or lower than in CEE (Table 19.12). Indeed, paradoxically, despite very low levels of labour force participation by women in Kosovo, female unemployment there remains high.

Table 19.12 Labour force participation rates (% of those aged 15+), 2002

	2002		
	Men		Women
Albania	52.3		35.6
Bosnia and Herzegovina	n.a.		35
Croatia	50.8		37.7
Macedonia	63.7		41.5
Serbia and Montenegro	n.a.		n.a.
Kosovo	56		27
Hungary		53	
Poland		55	
Czech Republic		50	
Slovakia		49	

Source: Vienna Institute for International Economic Studies (2004).

CONCLUSIONS

The published information summarized in this chapter suggests that the most likely causes of the high official rates of unemployment in the Western Balkans are relatively poor economic performance in the last four to five years and labour market rigidities associated with employment protection legislation. It is of course likely that economic performance and levels of FDI are linked and hence the failure to attract levels of FDI comparable to the countries of CEE and, in particular, the likelihood of low levels of greenfield FDI, are contributory (and argue for increased efforts to create an investment-friendly environment). In addition, there is clear evidence that, because of the size of the informal sector, official unemployment rates in the Western Balkans overstate the problem and that relatively high employment legislation is a cause of this phenomenon.

The stricter employment protection legislation on temporary employment in the Western Balkans seems likely also to explain the disproportionate incidence of unemployment amongst young people and women. But there is no empirical explanation of the predominance of long-term unemployment. It might be supposed that stronger employment protection legislation leaves the unemployment pool more stagnant and hence unemployment durations tend to be longer. It is also possible that there is a sub-set of the labour force with unsuitable skills which cannot easily re-enter labour markets, perhaps because of inability to access retraining. However, these remain hypotheses.

These conclusions do not pose a challenge to the prevailing economic orthodoxy in respect of solutions to unemployment in the Western Balkans, which comprise *inter alia* sound macroeconomic management, establishing a conducive environment for FDI, and reducing labour market rigidities. Unfortunately, however, the data available on SME development in the Western Balkans mean that conclusions in respect of continued adherence to this approach as a cornerstone of economic strategy cannot be derived.

If labour market rigidities are indeed an important determinant of unemployment in the region (as the evidence on the effects if employment protection legislation suggests) then further analysis of the most influential rigidities is merited. This clearly has policy implications and may also reveal, and determine the effect of, rigidities which were not felt as strongly in the formerly socialist countries of Central and Eastern Europe (including, for example, the contingent employment liabilities associated with socially owned enterprises in former Yugoslavia). In these cases, and unlike the general model for economic recovery and development in transitional countries, there is no tailor-made policy response available which can be transferred from the countries of Central and Eastern Europe. As a result, new policies in respect of these novel rigidities may be required.

NOTES

1. The 'Western Balkans' are defined as comprising Croatia, Serbia and Montenegro, Bosnia and Herzegovina, the former Yugoslav Republic of Macedonia (hereinafter referred to as 'Macedonia'), Kosovo and Albania.
2. See Commission of the European Communities (2004), 'Croatia: Opinion on the application of Croatia for membership of the EU', Brussels: 20 April 2000 COM (2004)-257 final.
3. In May 1999, the European Commission set out a vision for the region's development. This was based on (a) recognition that the main motivator for reform – including the establishment of a dependable rule of law, democratic and stable institutions and a free economy – was a relationship with the EU based on a credible prospect of membership once the relevant conditions had been met (this prospect was offered explicitly at the Feira European Council in June 2000); (b) the need for the countries to establish bilateral relationships between themselves which would allow greater economic and political stability in the region to develop; and (c) the need for a more flexible approach which, although anchored to a common set of political and economic conditions, allowed each country to move ahead at its own pace. In November 2000 the Zagreb Summit formally established the Stabilisation and Association process by gaining the region's agreement to a set of objectives and conditions. In return for the EU's offer of a prospect of accession on the basis of the Treaty on European Union and the 1993 Copenhagen criteria and an assistance programme to support that ambition, the countries of the region undertook to abide by the EU's conditionality and use the Stabilisation and Association

process, and in particular the Stabilisation and Association Agreements when signed, as the means to begin to prepare themselves for the demands of accession to the EU.

4. The formerly socialist countries which acceded to the EU in 2004 (Estonia, Latvia, Lithuania, Poland, the Czech Republic, the Slovak Republic, Slovenia and Hungary) and Romania and Bulgaria all concluded Association Agreements with the EU prior to the start of negotiations for membership.
5. Only Croatia (October 2001) and Macedonia (April 2004) have signed Stabilisation and Association Agreements with the EU. In the other countries, feasibility studies have either been conducted (Albania, completed January 2003; and Bosnia and Herzegovina, completed November 2003) or are underway (as in Serbia and Montenegro). A similar approach is in process in Kosovo under the Stabilisation and Association Process Tracking Mechanism.
6. Under the Thessaloniki Agenda for the Western Balkans adopted by the European Council of June 2003, it is stated that – 'the pace of further movement of the Western Balkans countries towards the EU lies in their own hands and will depend on each country's performance in implementing reforms, thus respecting the criteria set by the Copenhagen European Council of 1993 and the Stabilisation and Association Process conditionality.'
7. The two other criteria are 'stability of institutions guaranteeing democracy, the rule of law, human rights and respect for and protection of minorities' and 'the ability to take on the obligations of membership, including adherence to the aims of political, economic and monetary union'.
8. See Council Conclusions of 29 April 1997.
9. Government of the Republic of Macedonia (2002).
10. World Bank (2003a).
11. World Bank (2001).
12. World Bank (2004).
13. See World Bank (2002). The study also showed that employment in the informal sector is disproportionately amongst those with limited formal education (303 000 out of 362 000 or 84 per cent of those employed in the informal had only vocational, elementary or uncompleted elementary education), while 64 per cent or 230 400 were working in agriculture or construction. Those working in agriculture had little choice but to work in the informal sector since most agricultural enterprises are not registered.
14. Government of the Republic of Macedonia (2002). See also Japan Bank for International Cooperation (2003).
15. Further possible evidence of the effect of the informal sector is provided by the Human Development Index. Compiled by the United Nations Development Programme, this is a composite index, which combines economic aspects with indicators of health and education. The index shows general increases throughout the region since 1996.
16. World Bank (2004).
17. GDP in Bosnia and Herzegovina fell sharply between 1990 and 1994, with falls of 23 per cent in 1990, 12 per cent in 1991, 30 per cent in 1992, 40 per cent in 1993 and 40 per cent in 1994. See European Bank for Reconstruction and Development (2002).
18. See Bulletins of the BiH Statistics Agency for the years concerned.
19. An example is housing and infrastructure reconstruction in Bosnia and Herzegovina where, since 1996, the EU has provided over EUR 500 million for this purpose.
20. Foreign direct investment levels as expressed as a percentage of GDP in 2003 were as follows: Albania 2.7 per cent, Bosnia and Herzegovina 4.9 per cent, Croatia 6.2 per cent, Macedonia 1.1 per cent, and Serbia and Montenegro 6.3 per cent (Centre for European Policy Studies, 2004).
21. Centre for European Policy Studies (2004).
22. Macedonian Privatisation Agency, mimeo.
23. Ministry of Economy and Privatization (undated). Foreign direct investment in Hungary, http://www.gkm.hu/dokk/main/gkmeng/investments/econ_dev/fdi_en.html.
24. The option of early retirement in circumstances when the dismissal of older workers is costly is an example of an off-setting flexibility.

25. In contradiction, Svejnar (2004) has pointed out that the relatively poor economic performance of formerly socialist economies in Central Asia has occurred with less rather than more labour market regulation and institutionalization.
26. Employment Protection Legislation refers to regulations which restrict employers' freedom to dismiss workers. Indices involve a weighting of 22 indicators, some of which are quantitative (that is notice period and mandatory severance payment), while others are constructed on the basis of qualitative information (that is difficulty of dismissal, willingness of courts to allow law suits on employment-related matters, interpretation of the notion of 'just cause' for dismissal).
27. Temporary employment legislation regulates the use of fixed-term contracts, their renewal, and maximum duration. It also affects the functioning of temporary work agencies.
28. The definition of collective dismissal varies, and while in many countries it involves more than five workers, labour codes in Albania and Croatia refer to the dismissal of at least 20 workers. The legislation stipulates requirements and payments associated with such dismissals.
29. Regular employment legislation establishes rules for hiring and firing procedures concerning permanent workers, including notification requirements and severance payments.
30. Correlation coefficient of 0.474 significant at 1 per cent.
31. Correlation coefficient of 0.287 significant at 10 per cent.
32. Scarpetta et al. (1996) show that young workers are the most adversely affected by labour market rigidities.
33. Correlation co-efficient of 0.689 significant at 1 per cent.

REFERENCES

Centre for European Policy Studies (2004), *Europa South-East Monitor*, Issue 51, January.

Collier, Paul (1999), 'On the economic consequences of Civil War', *Oxford Economic Paper*, **51**, 168–83.

European Bank for Reconstruction and Development (2002), *Transition Report 2002*, November, London.

European Bank for Reconstruction and Development (2004), *Transition Report – Update*, London, April.

European Commission (2004a), 'The Western Balkans in transition', Occasional Paper No. 5, Directorate General for Economic and Financial Affairs, Brussels, January.

European Commission (2004b), 'The Western Balkans in transition', Enlargement Paper No. 23, Directorate General for Economic and Financial Affairs, Brussels, December.

Garibaldi, Pietro and Paolo Mauro (2002), 'Anatomy of employment growth', *Economic Policy*, **17** (34), 67–114.

Government of the Republic of Macedonia (2002), 'National strategy for poverty reduction in the Republic of Macedonia', Skopje, August.

International Finance Corporation, 'Doing business: benchmarking business regulations', database available at http://rru.worldbank.org/DoingBusiness/.

International Labour Organization, ILO LABORSTA database, http://laborsta.ilo.org/.

International Labour Organization, http://www.ilo.org/public/english/region/eurpro/budapest/info/bul/04-1/2004_02.htm.

Japan Bank for International Cooperation (2003), 'Poverty profile: Former Yugoslav Republic of Macedonia', March.

Micevska, Maja (2004), *Unemployment and Labour Market Rigidities in South-East Europe*, Global Development Network South-East Europe and Vienna Institute for International Economic Studies, June.

Riboud, Michelle, Carolina Sánchez-Páramo and Carlos Silva-Jáuregui (2002), 'Does eurosclerosis matter? Institutional reform and labor market performance in Central and Eastern European Countries in the 1990s', World Bank, *Social Protection Discussion Paper* No. 0202, March.

Scarpetta, Stefano (1996), 'Assessing the role of labour market policies and institutional settings on unemployment: a cross-country study', *OECD Economic Studies* No. 26, pp. 43–98.

Svejnar, Jan (2004), 'Labour market flexibility in Central and East Europe', in Marek Dabrowski, Ben Slay and Jaroslaw Neneman (eds), *Beyond Transition: Development Perspectives and Dilemmas*, Aldershot, UK: Ashgate.

UNICEF Innocenti Research Centre, TransMONEE Database 2003.

United Nations Common Database, UNSTATS (2004), http://unstats.un.org/unsd/cdb/.

Vienna Institute for International Economic Studies (2004), *Handbook of Statistics: Countries in Transition*, Vienna.

World Bank (2001), 'Kosovo Poverty Assessment, December, Report No. 23390-KOS, Washington, DC.

World Bank (2002), 'Bosnia and Herzegovina: Labor market in postwar Bosnia and Herzegovina (How to encourage businesses to create jobs and increase worker mobility)', Report No. 24889-BIH. November, Washington, DC.

World Bank (2003a), 'Serbia and Montenegro Poverty Assessment', Report No. 26011-YU. Washington, DC, November.

World Bank (2003b), 'Country Economic Memorandum: Tackling unemployment', September, Washington, DC.

World Bank (2004), 'Kosovo Economic Memorandum', Report No. 28023-KOS, May, Washington, DC.

20. Unemployment, poverty and brain drain: summing up

Thomas Wieser

We know that the starting conditions for transformation in South-East Europe have been considerably more difficult than anywhere else in Europe because of the combination of three challenges: First, the transformation from a market social system as in former Yugoslavia appears to be even more difficult than from a truly centrally planned economy. Second, we simultaneously had in this region the problem of state building, which most other transformation countries (despite the drifting apart of a former Czechoslovakia) did not have. Third, the problems of conflict and war.

The results have been a widespread combination of huge poverty, unemployment, organized crime and a surging informal sector. All of that is underpinned by weak institutions. By way of illustration, GDP per capita in Serbia at the time of writing is just slightly more than half of what it was one and a half decades ago.

What are the causes for high unemployment? What are the consequences? Do we have possible remedies? How did we get here? Where are we going? What are the chances for reforms from within? And what can we, from outside, do to help, apart from giving good advice? These are questions to which we expected some answers from the preceding contributions by Robert Holzmann (Chapter 17), Tito Boeri (Chapter 18) and Kalman Mizsei and Nicholas Maddock (Chapter 19).

Basically the contributions of Holzmann, Boeri, and Mizsei and Maddock, despite all their differences in approach and analysis, suggest the following: poverty is indeed a problem, but things are getting better; high unemployment is a problem, but things are not getting better; brain drain is a fact of life that in the very long run is not as problematical as it may look today.

We have seen that output is down; growth is jobless, poverty indices are getting better but are still worrisome. Large external imbalances are financed to an astonishing degree by remittances by migrants abroad. Of these migrants, we are told that the well-educated have left, but that the majority of them come back. When they immigrated to their new countries of residence they met differing, but high restrictions. We saw that such restrictions buy time, but do not solve problems. This makes it very clear why they are attractive to politicians.

In general, we know that the economics of migration are inherently difficult to model, and we are better at *ex post* explanations than at forecasting migration movements. If you look at migration figures in the EU of the EU-15, it is quite astonishing where people gravitated to over the last 40 years – and from where they have re-migrated and from where they have not re-migrated. There are huge and economically inexplicable differences that go right down to the city level of, for example, German regions.

While all three contributors emphasized that they had further questions, but no definite answers for solving the problems of the region, I think that a few answers or attempted answers do indeed emerge.

One finding is that of low FDI. Mizsei and Maddock (Chapter 19), however, find that FDI is actually astonishingly high given relative wages compared to other countries in the wider region. Second, framework conditions for starting up and running businesses are extremely detrimental to doing so. Third, there is obviously a need to foster employment in the official sector, given very high employment shares in the unofficial sector. And lastly, we need to invest more in fostering professional and transparent institutions, and to overcome the negative effects of the fragmentation of markets.

The building up of markets is key to another important question, that of European integration: Tito Boeri (Chapter 18) suggests that the *expectation* of accession to the EU is the main reform driver, but that the effects wear off rapidly upon accession. If this hypothesis is right, we should see accession to the EU as the carrot, which may need to remain equidistant from the donkey's mouth if reforms are to succeed. But this is not a politically palatable way of moving forward.

Obviously, following from Boeri, all the assistance programmes of the EU – which should supplement programmes by the international financial institutions, not overlap or contradict them – should have built in a considerably higher structural conditionality than is contained at present. This is a task for the EU member states. And in order to get that task right they need to reflect more carefully on what the policy problems in the region are, and where they stem from. At present, policy prescriptions look more as if they had been photocopied than thought through. The findings of Boeri, Holzmann and Mizsei and Maddock could be a fruitful input for such policy change in present member states.

PART VI

Banking in South-East Europe and the Leading Role of Austrian Banks

21. Estimating the gap in banking efficiency between Eastern and Western European economies

Laurent Weill

1. INTRODUCTION

There is a commonly accepted view that Eastern European banks are suffering from lower cost efficiency than Western European banks. Indeed Scholtens (2000) and Riess et al. (2002) notably argued that the current situation of banking sectors in transition countries of Eastern Europe lags behind the banking sectors of developed countries of Western Europe. The main reason underlying this rationale is that, in spite of the major transformation of the banking sectors in the transition economies of Eastern Europe during the 1990s, it is difficult to modify the habits and behaviours inherited from the old regime within such a short period.

The existence of a gap in banking efficiency between Eastern European and Western European countries is a very important question for two reasons. First, bank credit is by far the largest source of external finance for companies in the Eastern European countries (Caviglia et al., 2002). Indeed, the financial markets are underdeveloped in transition countries, resulting in a high dependence on bank credit for financing. Consequently, investment is particularly sensitive to the changes in banking performance in these countries. Indeed, an improvement of banking performance means a reduction of loan rates, but also a better allocation of financial resources, and therefore an increase in investment that favours growth.

Second, the upcoming EU membership of several transition countries renders the question of companies' microeconomic performances more pertinent, and therefore also the performance convergence of banks. Indeed, the major point is to establish whether these countries will function normally as market economies in the coming years.

It is therefore of utmost interest to assess the performance of banks of transition countries of Eastern Europe in comparison to the banks of developed countries of Western Europe.[1] We aim to provide evidence on this topic by estimating cost efficiency using a large sample of banks from Western and Eastern countries, with a stochastic frontier approach. Eastern countries include six EU countries and also two South-East European countries (Croatia, Romania), which allows us to compare cost efficiency between the two latter groups.

Why use a stochastic frontier approach to measure performance rather than more usual performance indicators? Several advantages can be argued in favour of this approach. First, it provides synthetic measures of performance. Indeed, unlike basic productivity measures (for example output per employee), the efficiency scores computed with the stochastic frontier approach allow several input and output dimensions to be included in the evaluation of performances. Second, it computes relative measures of performance. Specifically, a cost frontier is estimated, which allows each bank to be compared with the best-practice banks. As a result, the cost efficiency score assesses how close a bank's cost is to what a bank's optimal cost would be for producing the same bundle of output. It then directly provides a relative measure of performance.

Third, efficiency frontiers take the scale effects into account. Indeed, with standard cost ratios, the existence of scale economies may be a benefit for large banks in terms of performance. With cost efficiency scores, the scale effects are disentangled from the 'pure' performance measures. Fourth, frontier efficiency techniques allow environment effects to be disentangled from the pure performance measures. Indeed, to assess managerial performance in a relevant way requires the effects of the environment to be separated from the pure performance indicators. Frontier efficiency techniques provide tools to take economic environment into account, while standard measures of performance do not.

We answer two questions in this chapter. Question 1: do Eastern banks have lower efficiency levels than Western banks in Europe? Evidence is needed to assess the level of backwardness in the performance of Eastern banks: does it really exist? And if the answer is affirmative, how far are Eastern banks from Western banks? We estimate cost efficiency scores for both categories of banks to provide an answer. We conclude in favour of a significant advantage in efficiency for Western banks in comparison to Eastern banks.

Question 2: is the efficiency gap between the two groups of banks the result of the economic environment? Indeed, even if banks are less efficient in transition countries, this efficiency gap may not be the result of a lower managerial performance, but may rather reflect a less favourable economic environment for Eastern banks. For instance, Eastern countries have lower levels of per capita income and intermediation ratios[2] than Western countries, which makes the work of banks harder. It is therefore of utmost interest to assess the role of the environment in the efficiency gap. We proceed to this analysis by estimating a cost frontier that includes environmental variables.

The structure of the chapter is as follows. Section 2 outlines the methodology used for the cost efficiency measures. Section 3 describes the data and variables, and section 4 develops the empirical results. Finally, we provide some concluding remarks in Section 5.

2. METHODOLOGY

Several techniques have been proposed in the literature to measure efficiency with frontier approaches (stochastic frontier approach, distribution-free approach, data envelopment analysis). They mainly differ in the distributional assumptions used to disentangle inefficiency differences from random errors. We choose here the stochastic frontier approach, which disentangles inefficiency from random error by assuming a normal distribution for the random error and a one-sided distribution for the inefficiency term (Aigner et al., 1977). This approach has been widely used to measure estimated banking efficiency in the literature (Allen and Rai, 1996; Weill, 2001, among others).

We estimate cost efficiency, which measures how close a bank's cost is to what a best-practice bank's cost would be for producing the same bundle of outputs. It then provides information on waste in the production process and on the optimality of the chosen mix of inputs.

The basic model assumes that total cost deviates from the optimal cost by a random disturbance, v, and an inefficiency term, u. Thus the cost function is $TC = f(Y, P) + \varepsilon$ where TC represents total cost, Y is the vector of outputs, P the vector of input prices and ε the error term, which is the sum of u and v. In more detail, u is a one-sided component representing cost inefficiencies, meaning the degree of weakness of managerial performance, whereas v is a two-sided component representing random disturbances, reflecting bad (good) luck or measurement errors. Both u and v are independently distributed. While v is assumed to have a normal distribution, we assume a gamma distribution for the inefficiency term, following Greene (1990). Following Jondrow et al. (1982), bank-specific estimates of inefficiency terms can be calculated by using the distribution of the inefficiency term conditional to the estimate of the composite error term. Greene (1990) provided the estimate of the cost inefficiency term with a gamma distribution.

We estimate a system of equations composed of a Fourier-flexible cost function and its associated input cost share equations, derived using Shepard's lemma. We choose the Fourier-flexible form, as it has been found to dominate the translog form (McAllister and McManus, 1993). The specification of the Fourier-flexible cost function includes only Fourier terms for the output quantities following, notably, Altunbas et al. (2001). Estimation of this system adds degrees of freedom and results in more efficient estimates than just the single-equation cost function. Since the share equations sum to unity, we solve the problem of singularity of the disturbance covariance matrix of the share equations by omitting one input cost share equation from the estimated system of equations. Standard symmetry constraints are imposed. Homogeneity conditions are imposed by normalizing total costs, price of labour and price of physical capital by the price of borrowed funds. The system of equations is estimated using the Iterative Seemingly Unrelated Regression (ITSUR) estimation technique.[3]

3. DATA AND VARIABLES

Data were gathered from the 'Bankscope' database of BVD-IBCA. We use unconsolidated accounting data for 692 banks in 2000. There are 535 banks from 11 Western countries (Austria, Belgium, Denmark, France, Germany, Greece, Italy, the Netherlands, Portugal, Spain, the United Kingdom), and 157 banks from 8 Eastern countries (Croatia, the Czech Republic, Hungary, Latvia, Poland, Romania, Slovenia, Slovakia).

The sample of Western countries provides a satisfactory benchmark for the Eastern countries, as it includes major EU countries such as France and Germany, and catching-up countries such as Greece or Portugal. We can then compare the bank performance of Eastern countries with various categories of EU countries. Eastern countries include six EU member countries from the membership wave in 2004, but they also include two South Eastern European countries (Croatia, Romania).

We consider only commercial banks for Western countries. The reason is twofold. First, almost all banks selected for Eastern countries are commercial banks. It is consequently more relevant for our comparison to consider only the same category of banks in Western countries. Second, to keep all cooperative and savings banks in Western countries would have resulted in a sample largely dominated by German banks, as Germany has a very developed network of cooperative and savings banks. Therefore, a frontier including all these banks would have been a less representative European efficiency frontier than the one estimated here with only commercial banks for Germany.

We proceed to a different treatment of outliers on Western and Eastern banks, because of the different size of the samples. We adopt the Tukey box-plot, based on the use of the interquartile range, to clean the data for

Western countries: banks with observations out of the range defined by the first and third quartiles greater or less than one-and-a-half the interquartile range were excluded for each mean input price over the period. For the set of banks from Eastern countries, which is clearly smaller than the one for Western countries, we do not adopt the Tukey box-plot, but only eliminate outliers for Eastern countries.

We adopt the intermediation approach for the definition of inputs and outputs: This assumes that the bank collects deposits to transform them, using labour and capital, into loans. Two outputs are included: loans and investment assets. The inputs, whose prices are used to estimate the cost frontier, include labour, physical capital and borrowed funds.

As data on the number of employees are not available, the price of labour is measured by the ratio of personnel expenses to total assets, notably following Altunbas et al. (2001). The price of physical capital is defined as the ratio of other non-interest expenses to fixed assets. The price of borrowed funds is measured by the ratio of paid interests to all funding. Total costs are the sum of personnel expenses, other non-interest expenses and paid interest. Table 21.1 reports summary statistics for outputs, inputs, input prices, total cost, and total assets by geographic zone.

4. RESULTS

This section is organized so as to answer each of the two questions presented in the introduction in turn. Namely, the first subsection describes cost efficiency scores obtained with a common cost frontier on the whole set of banks to assess the gap in bank efficiency between both zones. The second sub-section displays the results obtained when environmental variables are included in the cost frontier.

4.1 Are Eastern Banks Less Efficient than Western Banks?

We compare the efficiency of Eastern and Western banks by estimating a cost frontier on the whole set of banks. Main descriptive statistics for the cost efficiency scores are presented in Tables 21.2 and 21.3, and displayed in Figure 21.1. We observe that Western banks are more cost-efficient than Eastern banks: the median cost efficiency score is 66.79 per cent for Western banks, while it is 54.07 per cent for Eastern banks. The cross-country analysis shows in fact that Western countries have efficiency score medians ranging from 57.41 per cent for Portugal to 74.05 per cent for the United Kingdom, while the medians for Eastern countries range from 36.35 per cent for Romania to 72.29 per cent for the Czech Republic.

Table 21.1 Descriptive statistics

	East		West	
	Mean	Standard deviation	Mean	Standard deviation
Outputs				
Loans	440 224.4	976 365.6	3 848 452.1	13 984 360.0
Investment assets	462 863.5	1 114 757.1	3 598 711.4	16 658 466.9
Inputs				
Personnel expenses	16 839.4	42 164.5	81 934.3	297 369.3
Other non interest expenses	20 748.5	46 265.9	64 598.8	214 132.0
Interest paid	67 649.0	174 024.0	322 136.3	1 524 427.2
Input prices				
Price of labour	0.0207	0.0137	0.0156	0.0090
Price of physical capital	1.2647	1.2878	2.0727	1.9569
Price of borrowed funds	0.0792	0.0573	0.0404	0.0173
Other characteristics				
Total assets	1 000 237.2	2 282 810.1	8 381 665.9	35 802 928.9
Total costs	105 236.9	260 002.5	468 669.3	1 993 749.1

Note: All values are in thousands of dollars, except input prices.

Source: Own calculations.

In both zones, we then observe large differences in banking efficiency. But the range of efficiency medians is clearly higher for Eastern countries than for Western countries. Among Western countries, Greece and Portugal have the least efficient banking sectors. It is noticeable that these countries are also the EU catching-up economies with the lowest per capita income among Western countries.

Figure 21.1 presents a clear description of the ranking of countries in terms of banking efficiency. Among Eastern countries, Czech banks are as cost efficient as the most efficient EU banks, while Hungarian banks outperform the banks of the least efficient EU banks, namely Greek and Portuguese banks. Otherwise, the banks originating from the six other

Table 21.2 Efficiency scores by zone

Zone	N	Median	Standard deviation
East	157	54.07	14.38
West	535	66.79	9.88

Note: All figures are in percentage.

Source: Own calculations.

Table 21.3 Efficiency scores by country

Country	N	Median	Standard deviation
Croatia	33	55.91	11.94
Czech Republic	15	72.29	10.92
Hungary	11	61.34	10.18
Latvia	18	56.89	8.59
Poland	32	50.05	12.41
Romania	19	36.35	19.42
Slovakia	16	46.87	13.20
Slovenia	11	55.56	11.14
Austria	30	63.73	9.76
Belgium	20	66.37	6.11
Denmark	42	61.96	5.36
France	115	68.88	12.44
Germany	142	70.54	9.29
Greece	10	59.27	10.73
Italy	75	65.62	6.74
Netherlands	10	70.29	16.10
Portugal	13	57.41	7.20
Spain	56	63.17	8.16
UK	22	74.05	7.39

Note: All figures are in percentage.

Source: Own calculations.

Eastern countries clearly underperform compared to the banks of Western countries. Romanian banks, incidentally, are by far the least efficient banks of our sample. Furthermore, we can observe that there are no groups of Eastern countries using geographic criteria, as the South-East European countries (Croatia and Romania) do not form a specific group which would be different from other Eastern countries.

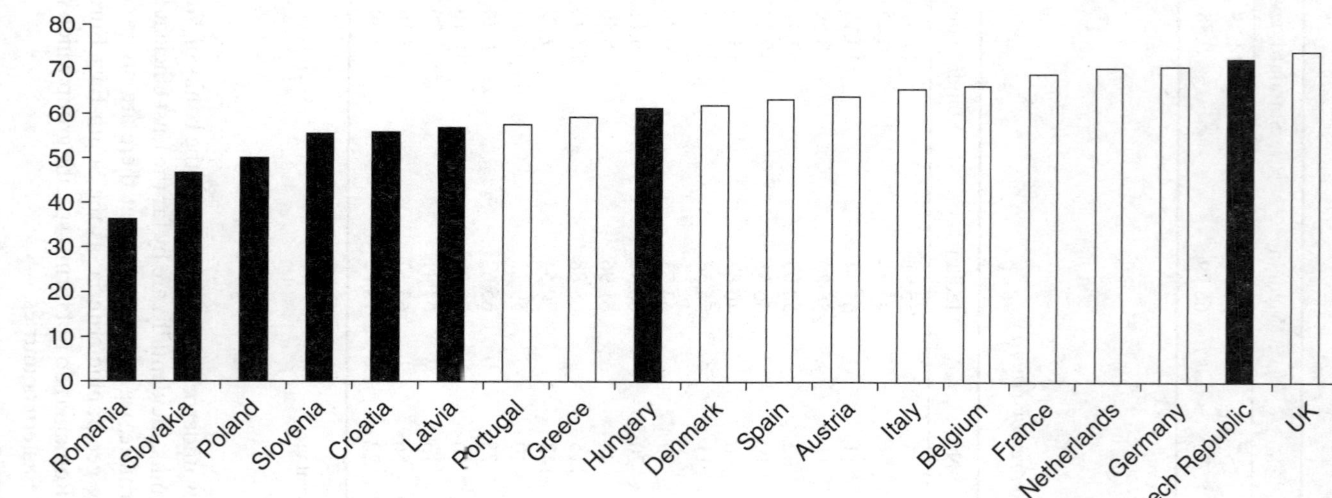

Note: Black boxes represent Eastern countries, white boxes represent Western countries.

Source: Own calculations.

Figure 21.1 *Efficiency scores by country*

Our results then support the existence of an efficiency gap between Eastern banks and Western banks. We consequently provide a positive answer to question 1. Therefore, we have now to investigate the reasons for this gap. A first answer would be to accuse the managers of Eastern banks: the lower efficiency may result from their weaker performance. Furthermore, the commonly accepted view is that Eastern banks suffer from weak managerial expertise, resulting from lack of experience of banking in a market economy.

Nevertheless, an alternative explanation can be advanced. Indeed, the environments in which banks operate are undoubtedly different in the two zones. The macroeconomic environments are not comparable, as Eastern countries suffer from a backwardness in economic development. Furthermore, the banking structure features are very different, notably because of the lack of maturity of banking markets in Eastern countries. Consequently, the differences in environment might explain the efficiency gap: Eastern banks may be less efficient only because of more difficult environmental conditions. Therefore, before accusing weak managerial performance, a satisfactory conclusion on the sources of the weaker efficiency for Eastern banks needs an analysis of the impact of environment on efficiency scores.

4.2 Does Environment Matter in the Efficiency Gap?

We now test the role of environment on the efficiency gap between Eastern and Western banks. Indeed it might happen that the differences in efficiency between the two groups may result only from dissimilar environments. In an application on French and Spanish banks, Dietsch and Lozano-Vivas (2000) have notably demonstrated that the efficiency gap between both groups of banks was reduced when environmental variables taking macroeconomic and banking structure variables into account were introduced in the cost frontier.

Environments are particularly different between the two parts of Europe for obvious reasons. The transition started just a decade ago, making the macroeconomic environment still underperforming in Eastern countries, as emphasized by the comparison of per capita income or rate of inflation, even if there are substantial differences among these countries. Furthermore, the banking structure is very different between Eastern and Western countries, notably because Eastern countries were still endowed with planned banking industries one decade ago.

The study of Grigorian and Manole (2002) provides some support on the potential influence of macroeconomic environment on bank efficiency in transition countries. These authors regress technical efficiency scores for banks of 16 transition countries on a set of variables including firm-specific variables, but also country-specific variables such as per capita income, rate of inflation, and the ratio of broad money to GDP. Their conclusion from these macroeconomic variables is that only per capita income has a significant influence on bank efficiency, which is positive.

We estimate a cost frontier that includes environmental variables. We test seven environmental variables, categorized into two groups. The first group is called 'macroeconomic conditions', including per capita income, rate of inflation, and population density. Per capita income is obtained by dividing GDP by the number of inhabitants. This factor is expected to affect the demand and supply of deposits and loans in numerous ways. In particular, the countries with higher per capita income may have clients consuming more banking products.

Inflation might increase inefficiency, as excessive branch networks are often associated with high inflationary environments, as suggested by Grigorian and Manole (2002). The density of population is measured by the ratio of inhabitants per square kilometre. We assume that banks in low density countries will face higher costs than banks in high density countries, consequently the density of population is supposed to have a positive influence on efficiency.

The second group is called 'banking conditions', including the density of demand, the accessibility of banking services, the intermediation ratio, and banking competition. Those variables reflect the features of the structure of the European banking markets. The density of demand is measured by the ratio of total deposits per capita. This variable is expected to have a positive influence on bank efficiency, as banks which operate in markets with a lower density of demand would likely incur higher expenses. The accessibility of banking services is obtained by dividing the number of branches by the number of square kilometres. A higher banking density may favour bank efficiency by making the access to banking products easier for customers. The intermediation ratio is obtained by dividing the total of loans by the total of deposits. This ratio is assumed to have a positive influence on efficiency, because the higher the ratio, the lower the quantity of deposits needed to produce loans will be, and consequently the cost of the production of loans.

Banking competition is measured with the Rosse-Panzar test of competition (Rosse and Panzar, 1977). It is a non-structural test, meaning that it takes the actual behaviour of banks into account without using information on the structure of the banking market. It is based upon the estimation of the H-statistic, which aggregates the elasticities of total revenues to the input prices. The H-statistic determines the nature of market structure: it is equal to 0 in monopoly, between 0 and 1 in monopolistic competition, and 1 in perfect competition.

The test is performed on our sample which was described above in section 3. Our aim is to have a measure of competition for each country. We then need to have country-specific estimates of the coefficients of input prices to analyse banking competition for each country. To obtain these, we include interactive terms for each input price, joining the variable with a dummy variable for each country. We also include two variables, total assets and the ratio of equity to total assets, to take differences in size and risk into account respectively, as in Bikker and Haaf (2002) and Weill (2004).

Several effects of banking competition on bank efficiency may be expected, with, notably, a positive influence resulting from the competitive pressures. But we might also expect a negative link based on the 'efficient-structure' hypothesis from Demsetz (1973), according to which the best-managed firms have the lowest costs and consequently the largest market shares, which leads to a higher level of concentration.

The environmental variables used in this chapter describe country-specific conditions in terms of wealth, structure of the banking market, and regulation. Data come from the European Banking Federation and OECD. They are displayed by zone in Table 21.4.

We observe large differences in environmental variables between the two zones that can explain the efficiency gap. Most variables are significantly higher on average in the West than in the East with two exceptions: the rate of inflation, which is higher in the East, and banking competition, which is rather similar in both zones. Thus, Western levels of environmental variables can favour bank efficiency, as they are associated with higher bank

Table 21.4 Mean values of environmental variables for Western and Eastern banks

	East	West
Macroeconomic conditions		
Per capita income (GDP/number of inhabitants)	4 807.89	22 835.34
Rate of inflation	12.40	2.49
Population density (number of inhabitants/km^2)	0.097	0.181
Banking conditions		
Density of demand (deposits/number of inhabitants)	2 371.01	23 795.08
Accessibility of banking services (branches/km^2)	0.015	0.090
Intermediation ratio (loans/deposits)	0.751	1.065
Banking competition (Rosse–Panzar H-Statistic)	0.489	0.526

Source: European Banking Federation; Main Economic Indicators, OECD.

efficiency. It is therefore relevant to test their influence on the efficiency gap between Eastern and Western banks.

The estimation of the cost frontier with environmental variables shows that only three of the tested environmental variables are significant. Indeed the ordinary least squares (OLS) estimation of the cost function displays significant and negative signs for per capita income and intermediation ratio, and a significant and positive sign for the rate of inflation. The results of the estimation of the cost frontier with environmental variables are reported in Tables 21.5 and 21.6. We observe that the efficiency gap is hardly reduced: the medians of cost efficiency scores are 54.34 per cent for Eastern banks and 67.57 per cent for Western banks.

However, the cross-country analysis of Eastern countries provides interesting observations. Efficiency of Eastern banks is clearly influenced by environmental variables, as six of the eight Eastern countries have a variation in efficiency above 1 point. Nevertheless, these countries do not have similar variations: Polish (+1.88 points), Romanian (+4.90), Slovak (+1.50) and Slovenian (+3.23) banks improve their efficiency, but Croatian (−1.03) and Latvian (−3.46) banks are then less efficient. Thus, these opposite modifications of efficiency for Eastern banks lead to the conclusion that the inclusion of environmental variables does not reduce the efficiency gap between the two zones. It can, however, be argued that this inclusion reduces the substantial differences in efficiency between Eastern countries. Indeed, as the efficiency of the least efficient banking sector (in Romania) was increased, while the efficiency of the most efficient banking sector (the Czech one) remained stable, the range of cost efficiency medians among Eastern countries is smaller when environmental variables are taken into account.

Nevertheless, the differences in macroeconomic and banking environments do not provide a satisfactory explanation to the efficiency gap between Western and Eastern banks. Thus, the answer to question 2 is rather negative.

Table 21.5 Efficiency scores with environmental variables by zone

Zone	N	Median	Standard deviation
East	157	54.34	14.03
West	535	67.57	9.62

Note: All figures are in percentage.

Source: Own calculations.

Table 21.6 Efficiency scores with environmental variables by country

Country	Median without environment	Median with environment	Change
Croatia	55.91	54.88	−1.03
Czech Republic	72.29	72.22	−0.07
Hungary	61.34	53.43	+0.80
Latvia	56.89	53.43	−3.46
Poland	50.05	51.93	+1.88
Romania	36.35	41.25	+4.90
Slovakia	46.87	48.37	+1.50
Slovenia	55.56	58.79	+3.23
Austria	63.73	64.99	+1.26
Belgium	66.37	67.00	+0.63
Denmark	61.96	62.18	+0.22
France	68.88	70.62	+1.74
Germany	70.54	70.64	+0.10
Greece	59.27	62.58	+3.31
Italy	65.62	66.48	+0.86
Netherlands	70.29	74.72	+4.43
Portugal	57.41	62.11	+4.70
Spain	63.17	64.02	+0.85
UK	74.05	75.08	+1.03

Note: All figures are in percentage.

Source: Own calculations.

5. CONCLUSION

This work has provided evidence on the efficiency gap between Eastern banks and Western banks in Europe. We have investigated this question by answering two questions about this possible efficiency gap. (1) *An efficiency gap exists between banks in Eastern countries and those in Western countries.* However, there are very different levels of banking efficiency among Eastern countries, with, notably, the high degree of efficiency of Czech banks. Furthermore, it is of utmost interest to observe that the two South-East European countries (Croatia, Romania) do not constitute a separate group from the other Eastern countries. (2) *The efficiency gap is not explained by differences in environmental variables.* Indeed, the estimation of the cost frontier for the whole set of banks with the inclusion of environmental variables does not significantly reduce the differences between the efficiency medians of banks of both groups of countries. Therefore, we tend to support the hypothesis of a lower managerial performance in Eastern countries than in Western countries.

In summary, our work has provided evidence on the existence of an efficiency gap between Western and Eastern banks, mainly caused by differences in managerial performance. Our results should, however, be considered with care. Indeed, further research is needed on the comparison of Western and Eastern banks in terms of efficiency. This work should be considered as an exploratory approach on this issue.

NOTES

1. To simplify notation in the chapter, the banks of transition countries of Eastern Europe and the banks of developed countries of Western Europe are respectively called 'Eastern banks' and 'Western banks'. Similarly, Eastern and Western European countries are respectively called 'Eastern countries' and 'Western countries'.
2. Caviglia et al. (2002) observe that the ratios of domestic credit to GDP and of deposits to GDP in the transition countries acceding to the EU in 2004 represent only one-third of the EU countries' levels.
3. Kmenta and Gilbert (1968) proved that this procedure generates maximum likelihood estimates.

REFERENCES

Aigner, Dennis, C.A. Knox Lovell and Peter Schmidt (1977), 'Formulation and estimation of stochastic frontier production function models', *Journal of Econometrics*, **6**, 21–37.

Allen, Linda and Anoop Rai (1996), 'Operational efficiency in banking: An international comparison', *Journal of Banking and Finance*, **20**, 655–72.

Altunbas, Yener, Lynne Evans and Philip Molyneux (2001), 'Bank ownership and efficiency', *Journal of Money, Credit and Banking*, **33** (4), 926–54.

Berger, Allen, Robert De Young, Hesna Genay and Gregory Udell (2000), 'Globalization of financial institutions: Evidence from cross-border banking performance', *Brookings–Wharton Papers on Financial Services*, **3**, 23–125.

Bikker, Jakob and Katharina Haaf (2002), 'Competition, concentration and their relationship: An empirical analysis of the banking industry', *Journal of Banking and Finance*, **26**, 2191–214.

Caviglia, G., G. Krause and C. Thimann (2002), 'Key features of the financial sectors in EU accession countries', in C. Thimann (ed.), *Financial Sectors in Transition Countries*, Frankfurt: European Central Bank.

Demsetz, Harold (1973), 'Industry structure, market rivalry and public policy', *Journal of Law and Economics*, **16**, 1–9.

Dietsch, Michel and Ana Lozano-Vivas (2000), 'How the environment determines the efficiency of banks: A comparison between French and Spanish banking industry', *Journal of Banking and Finance*, **24** (6), 985–1004.

Greene, William (1990), 'A gamma-distributed stochastic frontier model', *Journal of Econometrics*, **46**, 141–63.

Grigorian, David and Vlad Manole (2002), 'Determinants of commercial bank performance in transition: An application of data envelopment analysis', *IMF Working Papers*, No. 02/146.

Jondrow, James, C.A. Knox Lovell, Ivan Materov and Peter Schmidt (1982), 'On the estimation of technical inefficiency in the stochastic frontier production function model', *Journal of Econometrics*, **19**, 233–38.

Kmenta, Jan and Roy Gilbert (1968), 'Small sample properties of alternative estimators of seemingly unrelated regressions', *Journal of the American Statistical Association*, **63**, 1180–200.

McAllister, Patrick and Douglas McManus (1993), 'Resolving the scale efficiency in banking', *Journal of Banking and Finance*, **17** (2–3), 389–405.

Riess, Armin, Rien Wagenvoort and Peter Zajc (2002), 'Practice makes perfect: A review of banking in Central and Eastern Europe', *EIB Papers*, European Investment Bank, **7** (1), 31–54.

Rosse, James and John Panzar (1977), 'Chamberlin vs Robinson: An empirical study for monopoly rents', *Bell Laboratories Economic Discussion Paper*.

Scholtens, Bert (2000), 'Financial regulation and financial system architecture in Central Europe', *Journal of Banking and Finance*, **24**, 525–53.

Weill, Laurent (2001), 'Does restructuring improve banking efficiency in a transition economy?', *Applied Economics Letters*, **9** (5), 279–81.

Weill, Laurent (2004), 'On the relationship between competition and efficiency in the EU banking sectors', *Kredit und Kapital*, **37** (3), 329–32.

22. Banking reform in South-East Europe: accomplishments and challenges

Evan Kraft[1]

1. INTRODUCTION

The transformation of the banking industry in transition countries has been one of the most dramatic and far-reaching aspects of the quite dramatic and far-reaching process of transition. For example, while in 1995 foreign bank penetration in the former Communist countries of Central and Eastern Europe (CEE) and South-East Europe (SEE) was minimal, by 2002 foreign banks held majority shares, and often overwhelmingly large shares, in 13 of the 15 countries of CEE and SEE. In SEE, Albania, Bosnia and Herzegovina, Bulgaria, Croatia and Romania had foreign majority ownership (measured by capital), with Macedonia very close to 50 per cent and Serbia and Montenegro somewhat behind as of end-2004.

Such a transformation from a banking system dominated by either state-owned banks of questionable quality or newly formed and untested private banks, to one dominated generally by reputable (but by no means first-tier quality) EU banks would have been difficult to imagine ten years ago, particularly in some of the poorer and politically less stable SEE countries. The transformation of the banking industry has turned one of the most vulnerable and unstable parts of the economies of the transition countries into one of the most advanced sectors, one which at times seems so far ahead of other sectors as to cause certain problems.

Nonetheless, policy makers and regulators continue to face important, if somewhat less daunting challenges in SEE countries. Many of these challenges come from the underdevelopment of key institutional supports for the growth of banking. Above all one must point to weak legal infrastructure, which does not protect creditor rights in a timely, predictable and effective manner. This is one of the causes of a growing retail bias in banking, which, if allowed to continue too long, could ultimately impair the banking system itself. This retail bias also aggravates current account problems, and creates prudential and macroeconomic policy dilemmas.

Other problems include inadequately developed securities markets and securities market regulation, and generally underdeveloped non-bank financial institutions. These also threaten to limit the growth of the financial system and the quality of economic growth in general.

Furthermore, foreign bank entry has often been accompanied by a consolidation process that has increased concentration in banking markets. This may actually increase effective competition, as a small number of strong banks are able to contest markets effectively, as opposed to a large number of very small banks competing against one (or a small number of) large bank(s) held over from socialism. Consolidation may also enhance financial stability, by creating franchise value that limits risk taking (Beck et al., 2003). Still, there are threats to competition from concentration, most obviously the threat of merger between the foreign banks (or their parent companies) and the greater opportunities for tacit collusion with a small number of players.

In addition, the entrance of foreign banks, while resolving many of the most burning issues facing bank supervisors, creates new challenges in this area as well. Even though most foreign banks have taken the form of subsidiaries, and thus are clearly under the regulatory purview of SEE supervisors, there are important issues regarding information sharing and coordination between SEE supervisors and the EU supervisors of the parent banks. In addition, while crisis management responsibilities are relatively clearly defined (more clearly than within the EU in some respects), there are some grey areas regarding the legal reach of third-country courts if the parent bank's subsidiaries have problems, and major challenges in crisis management for countries with currency boards (and hence no lender of last resort in the conventional sense) and for all countries with weak fiscal positions.

A final set of problems includes operational risk and reputation issues. Several major operational risk incidents have occurred at the overseas subsidiaries of foreign banks. This creates reputational as well as financial risk. In addition, the popular image of foreign banks is often poor, even though customers trust foreign banks. Thus, reputation and image may be problems for the foreign banks in SEE.

The rest of this chapter is structured as follows: section 2 briefly reviews the main benefits of foreign bank entry. In section 3, legal infrastructure problems and the retail bias issue are discussed. Section 4 deals with some of the competition policy issues created by the foreign-bank led consolidation, and section 5 looks at supervisory challenges. Section 6 offers some brief conclusions.

2. BENEFITS OF FOREIGN BANK ENTRY

In the early phases of transition, attempts were made to privatize and restructure the banking systems inherited from socialism. However, the transition countries were beset with banking and financial crises, and the fiscal burden of recapitalizing failed banks rapidly became problematic in many countries. In addition, it was difficult to find private bank owners who were not the banks' main customers, and who possessed any experience and know-how in banking.

These were the main reasons why most countries in CEE and later in SEE decided to sell their banks to strategic foreign partners. Looking back, several benefits of this decision can be seen.[2]

First and foremost, stability has been dramatically enhanced. Failures of banks sold to reputable foreign partners have been almost unknown. Some exit has occurred in cases where the foreigners changed their business strategy, or where the CEE/SEE ventures proved disappointing. But overall, the overwhelming majority of foreign banks have earned substantial profits, grown solidly, and, quite simply, provided stability. In addition, in CEE and SEE, as in Latin America, foreign banks have been willing to lend in cyclical downturns, thus playing an important role in dampening macroeconomic fluctuations during the entry and expansion period.[3]

Second, the foreign banks have brought with them rapid improvements in many areas of the banking business. Foreign banks' expertise in marketing and risk management is apparent. Investments in information technology have also been evident in many cases. While it is true that some of this expertise is available on the market through consulting services and the like, it remains true that the foreign banks have engaged in substantial technology transfer. One suspects that such transfers would not have been so substantial if the banks had remained in domestic hands, first because much of the knowledge is very likely proprietary to the foreign banks and probably cannot be fully replicated even by consultants, and second because the large investment needs in areas such as IT could not have been met due to the limited resources of domestic banks.

Third, related to the previous point, foreign banks have been very active in the introduction of new products and services, some of which were standardized products already offered in the foreign banks' home markets. Again, it is true that strong domestic banks were able to innovate (see Galac and Kraft, 2000, for examples from Croatia), but nonetheless foreign banks seem to have been more innovative in terms of the number and range of new products offered.

Fourth, the arrival of foreign banks brought fresh capital into the transition countries, both in the form of equity investment, and later in the form of lending both from the parent banks to the subsidiaries and from the international markets to the subsidiaries.

Fifth, the arrival of foreign banks has helped consolidate CEE and SEE banking systems, producing waves of mergers and acquisitions that have decreased the number of banks. Later in this chapter, I will argue that this consolidation has mainly increased competition, but I will also offer some caveats.

Another way to get a feeling for the transformation in banking is to look at the transition progress indices published by the EBRD. Table 22.1 compares progress in banking with progress in two related areas – securities markets and non-bank financial institutions (NBFIs) – and competition policy.

Several observations can be made. First, progress in banking is substantially greater than in the other areas. The difference of almost a full point in 2004 is huge, since total progress on all three indicators together only barely exceeds one point in most of the countries. Second, two of the SEE countries, Croatia and Bulgaria, are now considered by the EBRD to have banking systems almost meeting minimal EU standards. This is an enormous achievement for countries that suffered significant banking crises in the second half of the 1990s. Third, although progress has been substantial in the last five years, SEE countries still lag far behind the CEE average, with the new EU member states a bit less further ahead in banking than in the other two areas covered here.

A different way to illustrate the significance of the progress made in banking reform is shown in Figure 22.1, which plots the difference between real lending interest rates and real deposit interest rates against the EBRD Banking Reform Indicator. The steeper line represents a trend calculated using all the observations, and the flatter line excludes Serbia and Montenegro, and Romania, both of which have much higher inflation and seem to be outliers.

Whichever way one calculates the trend, it is clear that banking reform does lead to narrow spreads. In other words, the fruits of banking reform are being passed on to customers.

Table 22.2 provides some further information about the development of the banking sector. Again, there are impressive gains in many areas, most of all in privatization. In fact, the figures understate privatization accomplishments, since the sale of the Savings Bank in Albania in early 2004, and further privatizations in Romania in late 2003 are not reflected in the data. These transactions bring the level of state ownership below 10 per cent in each country.

Also, growth in M2/GDP in Bosnia and Herzegovina, Bulgaria, Croatia and Macedonia was very rapid in the 1998–2003 period. Domestic credit to

Table 22.1 EBRD transition indicators for SEE

SEE	Banking sector reform		Securities markets and NBFIs		Competition policy		Total progress
	1999	2004	1999	2004	1999	2004	1999–2004
Albania	2.0	2.7	1.7	1.7	1.7	2.0	1.0
Bosnia and Herzegovina	2.3	2.7	1.0	1.7	1.0	1.0	1.1
Bulgaria	2.7	3.7	2.0	2.3	2.3	2.3	1.3
Croatia	3.0	4.0	2.3	2.7	2.3	2.3	1.4
Macedonia	2.7	2.7	1.7	2.0	1.0	2.0	1.3
Romania	2.7	3.0	2.0	2.0	2.3	2.3	0.3
Serbia and Montenegro	1.0	2.3	1.0	2.0	1.0	2.3	3.6
SEE Average	2.3	3.0	1.7	2.1	1.7	2.0	1.4
CEE Average	3.3	3.6	2.8	3.2	2.7	2.9	0.8

Source: EBRD Transition Report 2004.

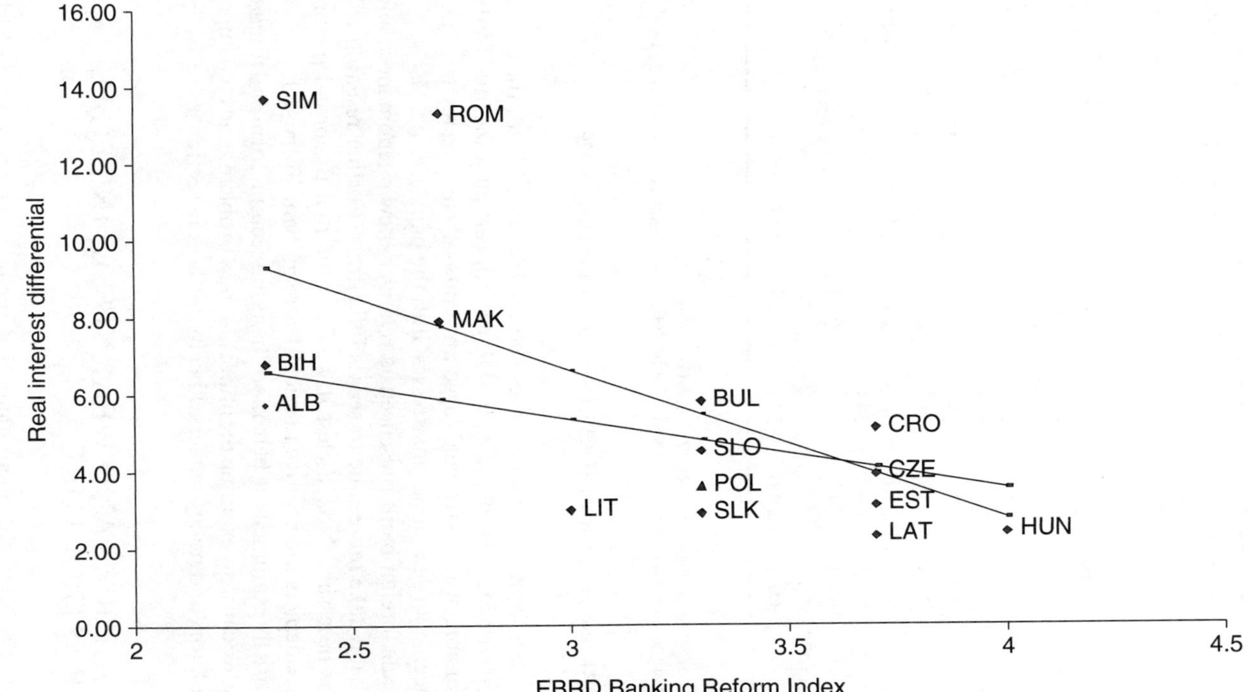

Source: Author's calculations based on EBRD Transition Report 2004.

Figure 22.1 Banking reform and interest differentials

Table 22.2 Indicators of banking sector development

	Asset share of state-owned banks		M2/GDP		Domestic credit to private sector		Capital share of foreign banks
	1998	2003	1998	2003	1998	2003	2002
Albania	85.6	51.9	48.3	47.1	2.2	5.1	73.6
Bosnia and Herzegovina*	75.9	5.2	20.5	45.6	8.9	14.6	66.8
Bulgaria	56.4	0.4	28.5	47.8	12.2	25.8	66.6
Croatia	37.5	3.4	41.7	66.8	26.6	48.5	78.3
Macedonia	1.4	1.8	13.3	29.9	17.7	14.9	44.6
Romania	75.3	40.6	24.8	24.4	11.6	9.5	64.9
Serbia and Montenegro**	90.0	34.1	16.6	20.2	11.2	5.6	n.a.
SEE average	60.3	19.6	27.7	40.3	12.9	17.7	65.8

Notes:
* Asset share of state-owned banks 1999 instead of 1998.
** Domestic credit to private sector for Serbia only, 2002. Asset share of state-owned banks Serbia only.

Source: EBRD, except for foreign bank shares, which are from BSCEE (2003).

the private sector grew strongly in these countries as well, with the exception of Macedonia. Part of the M2/GDP growth certainly was due to the euro conversion, which attracted large amounts of euro legacy currency that had been hoarded 'under mattresses' into the banks.

Large-scale foreign bank presence is a relatively new phenomenon, and it will probably take more time to see its full effects. Further research will certainly be necessary. Nonetheless, I would argue that the broad picture painted here depicts the positive impact of foreign bank entry so far.

Having briefly examined the benefits of banking sector reform and foreign bank entry, we can now examine the important new problems and challenges facing regulators and policy makers. I begin this task in section 3.

3. RETAIL BIAS AND WEAKNESSES IN LEGAL INFRASTRUCTURE

One of the very apparent phenomena that seems to be universal in SEE (and quite widespread in CEE as well) has been the rapid growth of

Table 22.3 Ratio of household loans to total loans (per cent)

	Albania	Bosnia	Bulgaria	Croatia	Macedonia	Romania
1997	–	5.2	10.3	28.9	6.5	4.4
1998	5.1	8.8	20.1	32.5	7.3	4.9
1999	48.1	9.8	18.2	37.9	9.9	4.5
2000	36.2	12.9	17.6	42.3	7.6	4.7
2001	14.3	20.6	19.4	43.8	7.4	5.6
2002	18.3	34.5	19.4	47.5	10.7	8.5
2003	23.1	38.2	22.6	52.7	20.7	17.2

Source: National central banks.

consumer credit. This growth certainly has a rational explanation: if households expect their incomes to rise in the future, it makes sense to borrow in the present and thereby smooth consumption. In addition, the initial stock of consumer credit, and the share of consumer lending in total lending, was quite low in all SEE countries (see Table 22.3); hence an expansion of consumer credit seems natural from this perspective as well.[4]

Despite this, there are two main concerns about the flowering of consumer lending. The first is macroeconomic. All of the SEE countries are struggling with substantial current account deficits. Rapid growth in consumer lending contributes to current account deficits via increased demand for imported consumer goods and via the currency appreciation generated by the foreign funding sources often used to underwrite it.[5]

The second concern is institutional. There is some reason to believe that one of the reasons for the intensity of the consumer lending boom is the relative unattractiveness of wholesale lending due to institutional weaknesses, above all the poor functioning of the legal system. Wholesale lending relies much more than retail on a strong legal system to enforce contracts, seize collateral and provide smooth and effective bankruptcy procedures. While it is true that home mortgage lending does rely heavily on the legal system, repayment rates on home mortgages are almost universally substantially higher than on corporate loans, so that the legal system risk is somewhat compensated for by lower repayment risk. Also, corruption, a major issue in many SEE countries, impacts wholesale lending much more than retail. Furthermore, as the World Bank (2003) points out, high barriers to business start-up and wind-up, weaknesses in corporate governance, unreliable implementation of accounting standards and poor financial disclosure present important hurdles to future business development. Finally, legal instability and legal uncertainty are major problems. If agents are not sure whether current laws will be in place in the future, or if they are unsure whether laws will be enforced, they cannot plan their actions so as to behave in a legal manner (Schönfelder, 2004).

Perhaps the rapid growth in retail lending would have occurred irrespective of the problems facing wholesale lending. It is not entirely clear whether foreign banks' country budgets are constrained by the supply of funds the banks are willing to commit or by estimates of the growth of demand. That is, it is not clear whether foreign banks' budgets for retail lending were larger at the expense of their budgets for wholesale lending, or whether better conditions for wholesale lending would have resulted in higher overall budgets and thus the same retail lending growth plus higher wholesale loan growth.

Also, it should be emphasized that there is no particular evidence that foreign banks are more retail-biased than domestic ones; many banks, both foreign and domestic, have particular business strategies that emphasize one or the other segment.

In conclusion, I can only echo the point made by the World Bank (2003) that development of wholesale lending and of more sophisticated banking and financial products in general will be stunted if these institutional factors are not sorted out in the near future.

4. COMPETITION AND COMPETITION POLICY

The entry of foreign banks has been part of a general consolidation of the banking sectors of SEE. After a period of very easy entry in the early 1990s, failures and acquisitions during and after banking crises brought substantial decreases in numbers of banks. For example, Croatia had 61 banks and 36 savings banks in 1997, but by 2003 it had a mere 40 banks and no savings banks at all. Bosnia and Herzegovina had 61 banks in 1999, and only 37 in 2003.

Although this consolidation process has certainly increased conventional measures of market concentration, it can be argued that banking markets have often become more competitive rather than less competitive. Allen and Gale (2001) provide a rigorous model of how this could take place. They consider competition between large numbers of unit banks, each operating only one office, as compared to competition between two bank networks. Under very general conditions, they find that the two bank networks provide a more competitive outcome, with prices closer to marginal cost, than the large numbers of unit banks.

While this argument was designed to describe the reform process in the United States, which actually legally enforced unit banking in many states prior to the 1980s, it would seem to apply to SEE countries as well. In most SEE countries, many of the new entrants of the 1990s were in fact unit banks or at least banks with a very small number of branches, operating in very restricted local markets. While some of these banks did grow rapidly and form more extensive networks, there is reason to be sceptical about the degree of competition that such banks were capable of providing to the large banks inherited from socialism. That is, outside of former Yugoslavia, each country had a near-monopolist Savings Bank, usually still in state ownership, against which the new private banks were Lilliputian in size. In former Yugoslavia, there were also dominant state-owned banks such as Stopanska Banka in Macedonia, Jubanka in Serbia, Zagrebačka and Privredna Banka in Croatia, but these were not quite as dominant as their Savings Bank counterparts in the other SEE countries.

Privatization of these large players to foreign owners created formidable market leaders in SEE. Still, foreign banks' purchase of smaller players, which was often followed by further acquisitions, and rapid growth of greenfield foreign banks, also provided substantial competition. Thus, banking systems such as those of Croatia, Bosnia and Herzegovina, and Bulgaria as of 2004, characterized by 5–10 fairly strong foreign-owned players, may well be more competitive than systems with large numbers of smaller banks seen in these countries 5–10 years before.

Indeed, Claessens and Laeven (2003) estimate the levels of competition in a large sample of countries using the Panzar–Rosse methodology. They find that neither the conventional Herfindahl–Hirschman Index (HHI) nor CR5 measures are significant predictors of the degree of competition, but that foreign bank presence is, with a positive correlation (greater foreign bank presence correlated with greater competition).

In the same vein, the link shown above between banking reform and real lending–deposit interest rate differentials also suggests that concentration has not impeded competition in transition countries. The Croatian case provides some further evidence in this regard. Figure 22.2 plots the HHI along with the author's estimates of the Lerner competition index (Kraft, 2004b). The Lerner index is essentially a mark-up over marginal cost estimated via a cost-function and accompanying factor-price equations (see Angelini and Cetorelli, 2003, for an application to Italian data). Thus, a decrease in the Lerner index indicates more competitive conditions.

What we see is a substantial increase in concentration after 1998, with the HHI increasing roughly 300 points. This increase occurs due to a number of failures during 1999; foreign banks entered en masse during that year and the following year, but, with one exception, the foreign banks did not make multiple acquisitions, so that their entry by and large had no effect on concentration.

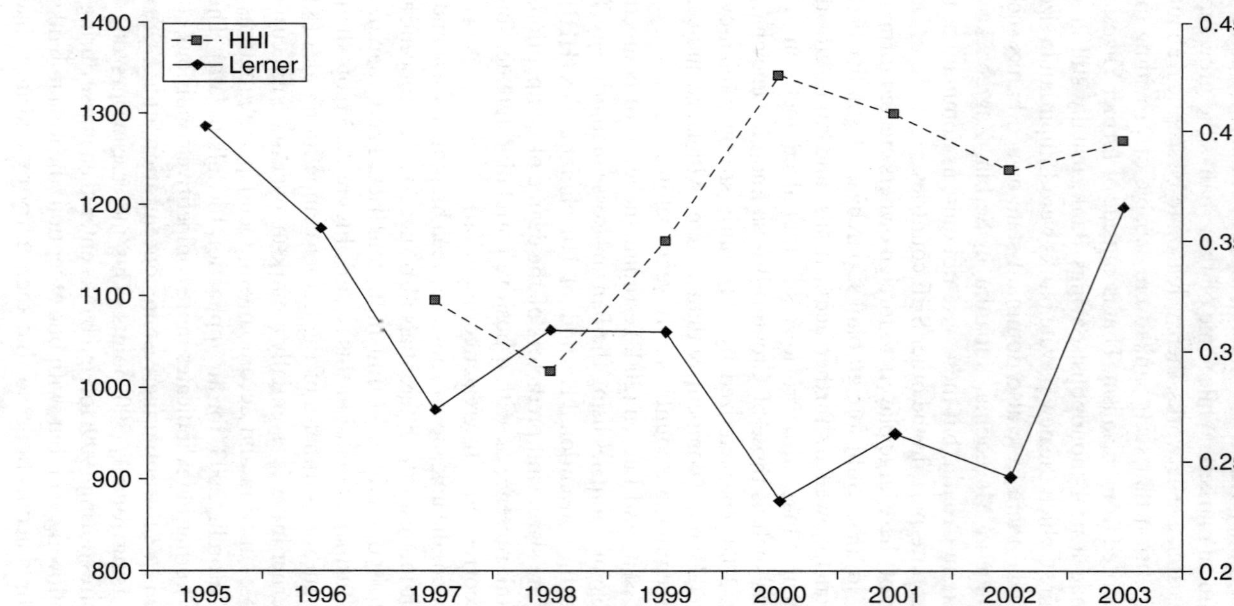

Source: Kraft (2004b).

Figure 22.2 Herfindahl–Hirschman Index vs. Lerner index for Croatia

At the same time, we see that the Lerner index falls in 2000, indicating an increase in competitive conditions. However, we also see that the Lerner index had increased in 1998 and later was to increase in 2003. The increase in 1998 was probably due to the beginning of the banking crisis, in which a number of aggressive banks that had offered very high deposit interest rates failed. Most banks lowered deposit interest rates to distance themselves from the failed risk-takers, and thus the mark-up rose.

The situation in 2003 was rather different. In that year, the central bank imposed a sort of penalty on rapid loan growth. Banks whose loan portfolio grew faster than 4 per cent per quarter were required to buy low-yield central bank securities. Banks responded by limiting lending, cutting back on wholesale loans and focusing on more profitable retail business. This portfolio shift also seems to have resulted in increased mark-ups.

Looking beyond these particulars, there does seem to be evidence from the Croatian case that competition increased after consolidation and foreign bank entry. But the picture is not entirely unambiguous.

This suggests to me that, while the initial entry of foreign banks and the formation of a number of strong competitors may have raised competition, it cannot be taken for granted that a high level of competition will be maintained. Clearly, with fewer banks, the opportunities for tacit collusion will be greater. Also, foreign banks are becoming accustomed to high profits in SEE, and they may not be willing to undermine this with aggressive competition. This is particularly troubling if one believes that the development of the wholesale business, which is closely related to medium-term growth prospects, requires greater risk-taking than the foreign banks have been willing to take so far. Indeed, a study commissioned by USAID criticizes Croatian banks for putting as much risk as possible on clients and failing to develop many business lines that are taken for granted in advanced countries (Porter, Chilsen and Company, 2003).

Two other problems deserve mention in the competition field. The first is the danger that, through mergers between mother banks, SEE countries could find themselves faced with unacceptably high levels of concentration. In principle, this problem can be handled through close cooperation between regulatory authorities in the home countries and SEE, and by the licensing mechanism. That is, if a merger occurred between two parent banks in the EU that owned large banks A and B in an SEE country, the licensing authority in SEE would receive a request for a change in ownership in either bank A or B. If it were properly informed, the licensing authority could simply deny the merged parent bank the right to become owner of both bank A and B, and order the sale of all or part of one of the banks. There could be political pressures placed on the licensing authority, but in principle the divestiture option should be adequate to prevent excessive concentration.

Another, perhaps more difficult, issue lies in the enforcement of anti-trust legislation in the more mundane daily business of banks. In some cases, SEE central banks have taken over anti-trust issues in banking from a competition authority. This seems appropriate and relatively straightforward for the issues posed in merger and acquisition cases, but may be trickier in cases of abuse of dominant position and anti-competitive practices. These latter kinds of cases are more typical of the work of competition authorities, and require legal and microeconomic analysis that central banks may not possess. In the context of poor anti-trust regulation in general in SEE, this area may turn out to be the most difficult in practice, especially with complex network externality issues such as ATM fees coming more and more to the fore.

It is clear that the small size of the SEE markets is an important hindrance to the development of competition. The EU accession process should help accelerate competition, both by encouraging cross-border financial flows that may compete with domestic banks and limit anti-competitive behaviour, and by encouraging further entries by EU banks into SEE markets. In the longer-term, participation in the Single European Market – even if it is not as unified as we might like – certainly should increase banking and financial sector competition. Still, even in this somewhat distant future, local authorities will continue to be responsible for maintaining competition in their local markets, in the same way that local authorities in large countries like the United States must work to maintain competitive conditions in local markets. Learning to analyse local competitive conditions and to devise regulatory remedies, including divestitures, should be high on the agenda of competitive authorities in SEE countries.

5. SUPERVISORY CHALLENGES

At the European level, central banks and financial service regulators are facing a very new and daunting set of challenges. The rise of cross-border and cross-industry financial groups has rendered the supervisory structures in place outmoded, and triggered a heated debate on the optimal structure for financial regulation. Numerous countries have responded by unifying financial supervision into a single authority, starting with Norway in 1986. With the establishment of the UK Financial Services Authority in 1997, this movement gained momentum, and now single regulators can be found in some ten EU member states (Masciandaro and Porta, 2004).

The creation of single regulators is meant to address the cross-industry nature of financial integration. The cross-border issues have so far been addressed through the designation of responsibility for bank branches with the home country supervisors, and responsibility for bank subsidiaries with the host country supervisors. This division of labour has been reinforced by a series of Memoranda of Understanding (MOU), which specify the forms of cooperation applicable during normal supervisory processes and during crises.

There is some doubt, however, whether this system is robust enough, especially in the face of large-scale financial disturbances. Lender-of-last-resort functions, like supervisory functions, are still at the member-state level in the EU. This raises some doubts as to whether the existing system would be able to handle a situation where one or several large cross-border institutions had problems in multiple jurisdictions. Furthermore, the Memoranda of Understanding (MOUs) do not have legal force, and have yet to be tested in practice. Conflicts in approach or interest between supervisors in different countries could lead to deviations from the MOUs, which could in turn complicate or slow down crisis management.[6]

How will these problems affect SEE countries? Probably not very much in the immediate future. For one thing, with relatively undeveloped capital markets, SEE countries do not really have to deal with financial conglomerates and the supervisory challenges they entail. Even if such firms enter SEE markets, they will mainly be providing banking services in the upcoming years.

For another thing, almost all the foreign banks operating in SEE are operating as subsidiaries. This means that any problems affecting the foreign banks in SEE will be squarely the problem of SEE supervisors, central banks and ministries of finance. While this makes matters simpler, it is not necessarily a source of great comfort. For it means that SEE countries could be faced with problems at systemically important banks. In two cases (Bulgaria and Bosnia and Herzegovina), currency board arrangements preclude conventional lender-of-last-resort operations. In all cases, relatively weak fiscal positions would make any large bank failures a serious problem for all concerned.

The good news, of course, is that these banks have strong foreign parents who should be able to stand by them in a crisis. However, even here one must be cautious. The case of Riječka Banka, which experienced foreign exchange trading losses due to a rogue trader, shows that foreign owners may not be willing to recapitalize their subsidiaries. In the Riječka Banka case in 2002, the majority owner, Bayerische Landesbank, walked away from the bank, and returned ownership to the Croatian government. The government then succeeded in very quickly organizing a sale to Erste Bank, thus stabilizing the situation. Although the ending was happy, this tale is a sobering one for SEE policy makers.

A more immediate set of problems relates to information sharing between SEE supervisors and home country supervisors. The SEE operations of most foreign banks account for very small fractions of the banks' total business. Thus it is unlikely that home country supervisors will worry too much about these subsidiaries. At the same time, any information about the parent banks' operations could have substantial market value, so that home country supervisors may be reluctant to risk giving too much information to SEE host country supervisors. This is problematic for the SEE supervisors, who would like to know as much as possible about the parent banks' financial status and plans. Building confidence and improving incentives for information sharing between supervisors remains a significant practical problem.

Furthermore, there are some ambiguities about cross-border implications of bankruptcy procedures. For example, if bank A, incorporated in an EU country, has subsidiaries in the United States and an SEE country, and if the US subsidiary fails, could the US courts try to seize assets from the SEE subsidiary to meet claims of US creditors? Questions like these are currently unanswered, and it is not too far-fetched to think that they will become relevant in the near future.

A final point about foreign banks and banking supervision in SEE is that the pace of Basel II implementation in SEE is not yet clear. For those SEE countries about to join the EU, Basel II implementation will begin shortly after accession. This requires that supervisors make decisions about which of the many menu options in the new Accord they will enforce. There will no doubt be pressure from the foreign banks to allow the use of risk models employed by the banks in their EU home countries in SEE. One can be sceptical about whether enough data exist on SEE risks to make the use of such models advisable in the near future. In another work (Kraft, 2005), I have suggested that SEE supervisors avoid any rush to implement advanced risk-based capital standards in Basel II, thereby putting aside possible pressure from banks and from international financial institutions or ratings agencies that may view more sophisticated practices as better. On the contrary, I believe that simpler techniques should be maintained as long as necessary.

6. CONCLUDING THOUGHTS

SEE countries have accomplished a great deal in the area of bank reform. Entrance of reputable foreign banks, along with improved supervision and macroeconomic stability, has produced major advances in the banking area. At the same time, however, development of non-bank financial institutions and capital markets continues to lag behind, as does anti-trust regulation and securities regulation. Weaknesses in the legal framework, continued poor corporate governance, inadequate accounting and disclosure, and barriers to firm entrance and exit hinder the business environment and dampen growth prospects.

The banking sector cannot get too far ahead of the rest of the economy. Only a continuation of the broad-ranging reforms undertaken so far can lead to more balanced and sustainable growth. Strong banking sectors can contribute to such growth, but they cannot be the sole motor. Policy makers in SEE still have much work to do.

NOTES

1. The views expressed in this chapter are those of the author and do not necessarily represent the views of the Croatian National Bank.
2. The studies on which this section is based include Konopielko (1999); Papi and Revoltella (1999); Storf (2000); Galac and Kraft (2000); de Haas and van Lelyveld (2002); Kraft (2004a); de Haan and Naaborg (2004); Mero and Valentinyi (2003) and Fries and Taci (2002).
3. See Clarke et al. (1999); Crystal et al. (2001) and Dages et al. (2000), for analysis of the Latin American experience.
4. Even Croatia, which stands out in Table 22.3, started with a ratio of consumer credit to GDP of 6 per cent in 1995, far below the 50 per cent average in the EU.
5. For a detailed discussion of the link between lending booms and macroeconomic instability, as well as policy responses, see Kraft and Jankov (2005).
6. For a more optimistic view of the current situation, see Lanoo (2004); Eisenbeis (2004) and Aglietta (2004) are more sceptical.

BIBLIOGRAPHY

Aglietta, M. (2004), 'Comments on Lanoo', paper presented at the conference 'New Architectures of Financial Supervision in Europe', Bocconi University, November.

Allen, F. and D. Gale (2001), *Comparing Financial Systems*, Cambridge, MA: MIT Press.

Angelini, P. and N. Cetorelli (2003), 'The effects of regulatory reform on competition in the banking industry', *Journal of Money, Credit and Banking*, **33** (5), 663–84.

BSCEE – Banking Supervisors of Central and Eastern Europe (2003), *BSCEE Review*.

Beck, T., A. Demirguc-Kunt and R. Levine (2003), 'Bank concentration and crises', NBER Working Paper W9921.

Claessens, S. and L. Laeven (2003), 'What drives bank competition? Some international evidence', paper presented at World Bank Conference on Bank Concentration and Competition, 3–4 April, Washington.

Clarke, G., R. Cull, L. D'Amato and A. Molinari (1999), 'The effect of foreign bank entry on Argentina's domestic banking sector', *World Bank Working Paper* 849, World Bank.

Crystal, J.S., B.G. Dages and L. Goldberg (2001), 'Does foreign ownership contribute to sounder banks in emerging markets? The Latin American experience', *Current Issues in Economics and Finance*, **8**, 1–6.

Dages, B.G., L. Goldberg and D. Kinney (2000), 'Foreign and domestic bank participation in emerging markets: Lessons from Mexico and Argentina', *New York Federal Reserve Bank Economic Policy Review*, **6** (3).

De Haan, J. and I. Naaborg (2004), 'Financial intermediation in accession countries: The role of foreign banks', in D. Masciandaro (ed.), *Financial Intermediation in the New Europe: Banks, Markets and Regulation in EU Accession Countries*, Cheltenham, UK and Lyme, US: Edward Elgar.

De Haas, R.T.A. and I.P.P. van Lelyveld (2002), 'Foreign bank penetration and private sector credit in Central and Eastern Europe' SSRN FEN website, July.

Eisenbeis, R. (2004), 'Agency problems in the design of bank regulatory and supervisory structures', paper presented at the conference 'The Structure of Financial Regulation', Bank of Finland, September.

European Bank for Reconstruction and Development (2004), *Transition Report 2004*, EBRD.

Fries, S. and A. Taci (2002), 'Banking reform and development in transition economies', *EBRD Working Paper*, No. 71, June.

Galac, T. and E. Kraft (2000), 'What has been the impact of foreign banks in Croatia?', *Croatian National Bank Survey*, S-4.

Green, C.J., V. Murinde and I. Nikolov (2004), 'Are foreign banks in Central and Eastern Europe more efficient than domestic banks?', *Journal of Emerging Market Finance*, **3** (2), 175–206.

Hermes, N. and R. Lensink (2004), 'Foreign bank presence, domestic bank performance and financial development', *Journal of Emerging Markets Finance*, **3** (2), 207–29.

Koivu, T. (2002), 'Do efficient banking sectors accelerate economic growth in transition countries?', Bank of Finland, *BOFIT Discussion Papers*, No. 14.

Konopielko, L. (1999), 'Foreign banks entry into Central and East European markets: Motives and activities', *Post-Communist Economies*, **11** (4), 463–85.

Kraft, E. (2004a), 'Foreign banks in Croatia: Reasons for entry, performance, and impacts', *Journal of Emerging Markets Finance*, **3** (2), 153–74.

Kraft, E. (2004b), 'Measuring competition in the Croatian banking system', manuscript, Croatian National Bank.

Kraft, E. (2005), 'Financial sector development in Southeast Europe: Requirements of and responses to EU Accession and Basel II', forthcoming in I. Mattaeus-Maier and J.D. von Pischke (eds), *Financial Sector Development in South-East Europe: Opportunities and Challenges of EU Accession*, Berlin: Springer Verlag.

Kraft, E. and L. Jankov (2005), 'Does speed kill? Lending booms and their consequences in Croatia', *Journal of Banking and Finance*, **29** (1), 105–21.

Lanoo, K. (2004), 'The transformation of financial regulation and supervision in the EU', paper presented at the conference 'New Architectures of Financial Supervision in Europe', Bocconi University, November.

Lensink, R. and N. Hermes (2004), 'The short-term effects of foreign bank entry on domestic bank behaviour: Does economic development matter?', *Journal of Banking and Finance*, **28** (3), 553–68.

Majnoni, G., R. Shankar and E. Varhegyi (2003), 'The dynamics of foreign bank ownership: Evidence from Hungary', *World Bank Policy Research Paper* No. 3114, August.

Masciandaro, D. and A. Porta (2004), 'Single financial authorities and central banks in Europe: Recent trends', paper presented at the conference 'New Architectures of Financial Supervision in Europe', Bocconi University, November.

Mero, K. and M.E. Valentinyi (2003), 'The role of foreign banks in five Central and Eastern European countries', *Magyar Nemzeti Bank Working Paper*, No. 2003/10.

Naaborg, I., B. Scholtens, J. de Haan, H. Bol and R. de Haas (2004), 'How important are foreign banks in the financial development of European transition countries?', *Journal of Emerging Market Finance*, **3** (2), 99–124.

Papi, L. and D. Revoltella (1999), 'Foreign direct investment in the banking sector: A transitional economy perspective', *Development Studies Working Papers*, No. 133, Bocconi University, November.

Porter, Chilsen and Company (2003), 'SME access to finance in Croatia: Is there a problem?' study for US AID, July, available at http://www.dec.org/pdf_docs/PNACY901.pdf.

Schönfelder, B. (2004), 'Post-communist legal systems: the deep-rooted difficulty of overcoming communist legacies. With special regard to Croatia', paper presented at the 65th anniversary conference of the Economics Institute of Zagreb, November.

Storf, O. (2000), 'Foreign banks in the transformation process – Hungary and Poland', *Deutsche Bank Research* special report, 3 January.

World Bank (2003), 'Croatia Country Memorandum: A Strategy for Growth through European Integration', World Bank, Washington.

23. Banking in South-East Europe: *status quo* and the way forward

Norbert Walter

1. BANKING IN SOUTH-EAST EUROPE (SEE)

The banking sectors of the South-East European countries have made remarkable progress in the last couple of years. However, they still have quite a long way to go to match their counterparts in the euro area in terms of efficiency.

To start off, I will sketch some important lines of development. It is useful at the outset to compare the banking sector in SEE with that in the rest of Europe. Some tables will show in which aspects SEE has closed the gap with former EU countries and in which fields reforms are required.

After the description of the banking sector, I will argue why it is important for an economy to have sound financial markets. For the transition economies in SEE, especially, it is very important to move forward in creating a mature banking sector to nurture the process toward economic prosperity.

Before closing with an outlook for the banking sector in SEE, I will describe Romania in somewhat greater detail as a good example of a banking sector evolving amid the changes from a centrally planned economy to a market economy. I am sure that the fast and substantive changes in the banking sector and in financial market regulation, not only in Romania but in all of SEE, will continue in the next few years.

2. DESCRIPTION OF THE BANKING SECTOR IN SOUTH-EAST EUROPE

2.1 Banking Sectors are Still Relatively Small

The banking sectors in the South-East European economies are still relatively small. This is shown by the total assets/GDP ratio, which in South-East Europe was only about two-thirds that of the Eastern

European EU countries in 2002, and no more than one-fifth that of the euro area (see Table 23.1 and Figure 23.1). These empirical findings indicate the large potential for the banking sector in SEE. Even in cases where SEE is merely closing the gap to Eastern European EU countries, the

Table 23.1 Market size

	Total number of banks (foreign-owned)	Total assets (% of GDP)
Albania	13 (12)	49
Bosnia and Herzegovina	40 (21)	51
Bulgaria	34 (26)	46
Croatia	46 (23)	99
FYR of Macedonia	20 (7)	39
Moldova	16 (10)	32
Romania	31 (24)	27
Serbia and Montenegro	50 (12)	32
South-East Europe	**250 (135)**	**47**

Source: EBRD; IMF; DB Research calculations.

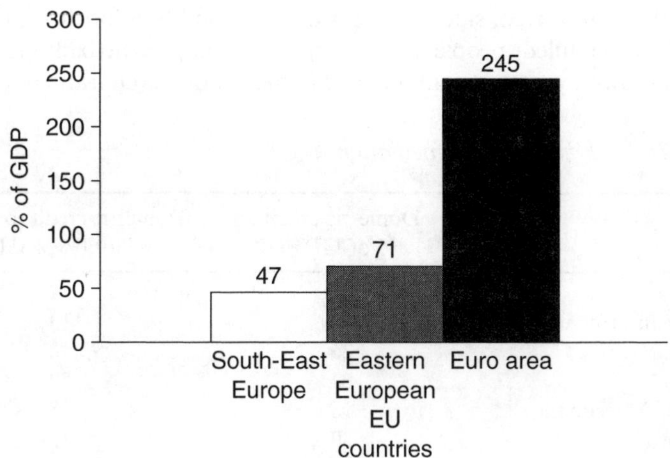

Note: All figures given here and in the tables and figures below refer to 2002.

Source: EBRD, IMF.

Figure 23.1 Total assets

total asset/GDP ratio will rise by half. Croatia is the leading country in SEE in terms of development of the financial sector. Croatia has not only the highest assets/GDP ratio at 99 per cent, but also the highest grade of all countries in SEE in the EBRD's 'Financial sector reform indicators, 2003'.

2.2 The Degree of Financial Intermediation is Still Low

This can be seen from the ratio of domestic credit/GDP as well as of domestic credit to private sector/GDP (see Table 23.2 and Figure 23.2). Here, the ratios are quite similar to those for market size. Similar to the total asset/GDP ratio, domestic credit to the private sector as a percentage of GDP will go up by two-thirds if SEE catches up with the EU countries of Eastern Europe. If the domestic credit/GDP ratio is interpreted as the degree of financial intermediation, one has to be aware of non-performing loans, which are quite high in some SEE countries. For example, 36 per cent of total loans were bad loans in FYR of Macedonia in 2002. In Serbia and Montenegro the share was 29 per cent (European Bank for Reconstruction and Development, 2004).

2.3 People are Gaining Confidence in the Banking Sector

Prospects for an accelerated development of the banking sectors in the region have improved, since an important precondition for this is increasingly being fulfilled: people are gaining confidence in the banking sector. This is shown by a significant increase in the deposit/GDP ratio during the

Table 23.2 Financial intermediation

	Domestic credit (% of GDP)	Domestic credit to private sector (% of GDP)
Albania	45	7
Bosnia and Herzegovina	12	13
Bulgaria	25	18
Croatia	64	52
FYR of Macedonia	18	18
Moldova	30	18
Romania	13	8
Serbia and Montenegro	14	16
South-East Europe	**27**	**20**

Source: EBRD, IMF.

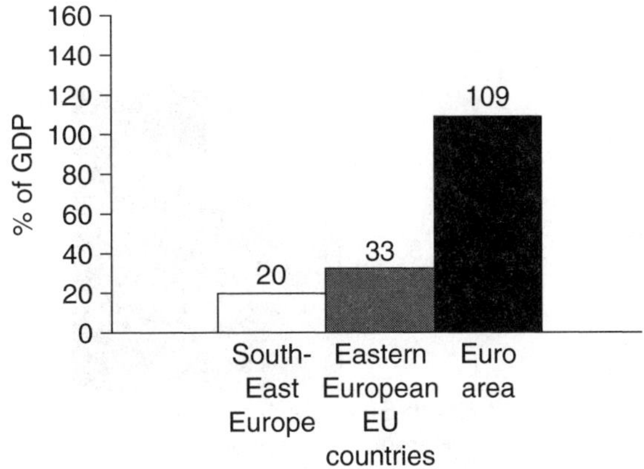

Source: EBRD, IMF.

Figure 23.2 Domestic credit to private sector

Table 23.3 Confidence of public

	Total deposits (% of GDP)
Albania	41
Bosnia and Herzegovina	38
Bulgaria	36
Croatia	65
FYR of Macedonia	23
Moldova	18
Romania	21
Serbia and Montenegro	17
South-East Europe	**33**

Source: EBRD, IMF.

previous two to three years. It showed up across the region, although the ratio rose from different levels and to a different extent, depending on the country (see Table 23.3 and Figure 23.3). The countries in SEE can be divided in three groups based on their total deposits as a percentage of GDP. FYR of Macedonia, Moldova, Romania, and Serbia and Montenegro enjoy little public confidence, with the result that deposit ratios total between 17 per cent and 23 per cent of GDP. The second group has deposit ratios that are slightly higher than the SEE average, which is 33 per cent.

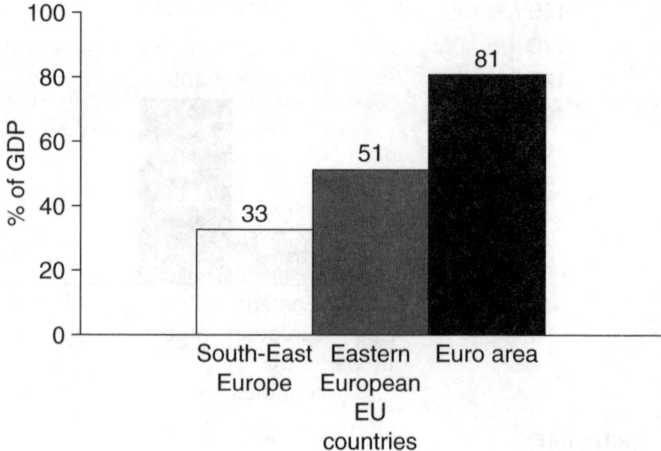

Source: EBRD, IMF.

Figure 23.3 Total deposits

This is true for Albania, Bosnia and Herzegovina, and Bulgaria, which have values between 36 per cent and 41 per cent. Croatia is undisputed leader in terms of public confidence in the banking sector with a deposit/GDP ratio of 65 per cent. True, the uptrend in the deposits/GDP ratio in many South-East European countries was supported by the fact that large amounts of hoarded cash have been channelled into the banking system (European Bank for Reconstruction and Development, 2004). This factor is, however, not the only – and probably not even the major – cause for the marked increase in deposits.

2.4 Presence of Foreign Banks has Increased Significantly

As privatization has progressed, the presence of foreign banks has increased significantly across the region. At the end of 2002, the asset share of foreign banks in South-East Europe was somewhat more than half of total assets, with the share varying widely across countries (see Table 23.4). The smallest share of assets owned by foreign banks can be found in Serbia and Montenegro, where only 27 per cent of the assets are owned by foreign banks. The situation is completely different in Croatia, where foreign banks own 90 per cent of total assets, which is an extraordinarily high number relative to the average of 55 per cent in South-East Europe. In addition to the figures mentioned above, merely 4 per cent of shares are owned by state-owned banks in Croatia, which indicates that the processes of

Table 23.4 Ownership structure

	Asset share of foreign banks (% of total assets)	Asset share of state-owned banks (% of total assets)
Albania	46	54
Bosnia and Herzegovina	77	6
Bulgaria	75	14
Croatia	90	4
FYR of Macedonia	44	2
Moldova	37	13
Romania	53	44
Serbia and Montenegro	27	36
South-East Europe	**55**	**6**

Source: EBRD.

consolidation and privatization in the Croatian banking sector are nearly over. In Bosnia and Herzegovina and in the FYR of Macedonia the privatization of the banking sector is almost finished, with the share of assets held by state-owned banks at 6 per cent and 2 per cent, respectively. Looking at all countries in SEE, the share of assets owned by foreign banks should be markedly higher today, if one takes into account the notable changes in ownership structure that havc occurred in several countries of the region since the beginning of 2003. The number of banks in the region amounted to 250 at the end of 2002, with somewhat more than half in foreign ownership (see Table 23.1). Since then, the number of banks has probably continued to fall as the consolidation process in the sector has not yet come to an end.

2.5 There are Good Reasons for a Strong Presence of Foreign Banks

There are good reasons for the strong presence of foreign banks in the region. For the host countries, they bring important know-how to the banking sector combined with the capital strength of their parent companies, and they offer a wide range of banking services. For foreign banks, investments in the region open attractive earnings prospects, compared with their home markets. For example, in 2002, the average interest margin in South-East Europe was 50 per cent higher than that in the Eastern European EU countries and three times that of the euro area, partially as a consequence of the still low competition in the host countries' banking sector (see Table 23.5 and Figure 23.4). Another incentive for

Table 23.5 Profitability

	Interest rate margin (percentage points)
Albania	6.0
Bosnia and Herzegovina	8.2
Bulgaria	6.6
Croatia	9.4
FYR of Macedonia	8.5
Moldova	9.1
Romania	16.1
Serbia and Montenegro	16.6
South-East Europe	**10.8**

Source: EBRD.

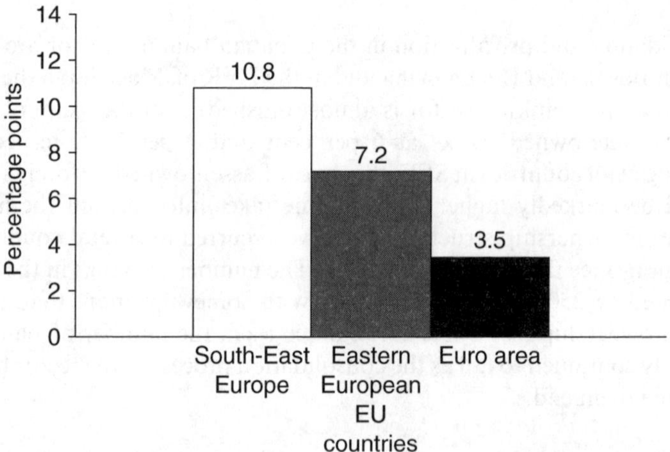

Source: EBRD.

Figure 23.4 Interest rate margin

foreign banks to expand into South-East Europe is the sizeable growth potential.

2.6 Foreign Currency Plays an Important Role in the Banking Sector

Foreign currency plays an important role in the banking sector in South-East Europe, with regard to both deposits and loans. This is particularly true for the major countries in the region. For example, in Romania and Bulgaria the share of foreign exchange deposits amounted to almost half of total deposits at the end of last year, and on the loan side the respective shares were at a similar level. Business in foreign exchange harbours a currency risk in addition to credit risk, which renders the banking sector vulnerable to sharp depreciation of the domestic currency.

2.7 Organizing Efficient Banking Supervision is Still a Must

Virtually all countries in the region have a need for action in this respect. This partly reflects the necessity of adapting an already existing regulatory framework to new structural developments in the banking sector; for example, the growing importance of consumer and mortgage lending (Romania is a case in point). In other cases it is necessary to establish the relevant institutions and the basic legal framework for banking supervision (for example in Serbia and Montenegro). In almost all countries, banking supervision is gradually improving.

2.8 Asset Share of both Foreign Banks and Private Banks is Higher than in the Eastern European EU Countries

Most of the Eastern European EU countries suffered a more or less serious banking crisis during their transformation to a market economy. Experience has shown that the earlier the crisis occurred, the less intense it was; moreover, countries which quickly turned to privatizing their banking sector also fared better (Bank Austria Creditanstalt, 2004). Some of the South-East European countries seem to have drawn their conclusions from this fact: at a relatively early stage, they reduced the asset share of state-owned banks in the banking sector through privatization to a minimal residual amount (Bosnia and Herzegovina, Bulgaria, Croatia, Macedonia). In other countries of the region, bank privatization proceeded at a slower pace (Albania, Romania, Serbia and Montenegro), but since 2003 it has gathered speed even here (see Table 23.4). The asset share of both foreign banks and private banks is higher in South-East Europe than in the Eastern European EU countries (see Figures 23.5a and 23.5b). Of course, the South-East European countries also have to cope with the legacy of the past – bad loans, for example – but with a few exceptions (Macedonia, Serbia and Montenegro) their share of non-performing loans in total loans should meanwhile be in single digits. My impression is that the cost of consolidation of the banking sectors, measured as a percentage of GDP, is lower on average in the South-East European economies than it has been for the Eastern European EU countries.

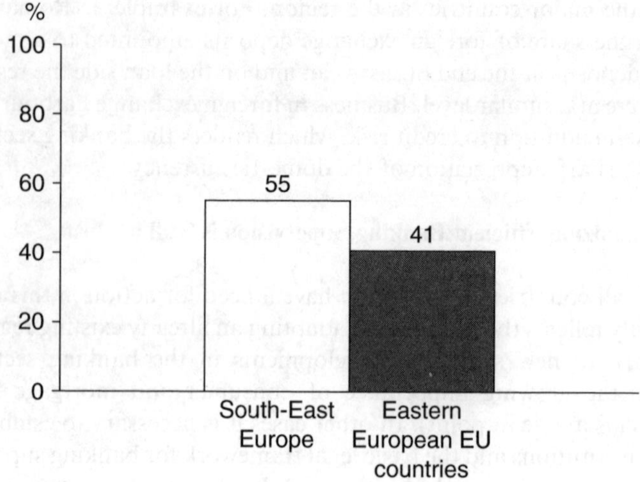

Source: EBRD.

Figure 23.5a Asset share of foreign banks (% of total assets)

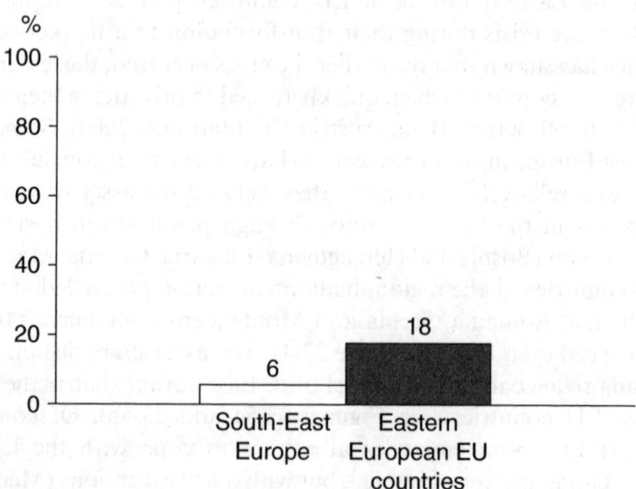

Source: EBRD.

Figure 23.5b Asset share of state-owned banks (% of total assets)

2.9 Inflation, Interest Rates and Earnings Prospects will Converge in Eastern European EU and in SEE

All countries in South-East Europe are striving to bring down inflation or to keep it at its current low level, respectively. This holds particularly true for the countries which are seen as candidates for the next one or two EU enlargement rounds (Bulgaria, Romania, Croatia). As a consequence, the average inflation rate in the region is likely to fall in the next couple of years. In close connection with this, there will be an alignment of the interest rate level to that in the Eastern European EU countries and later on to that of the euro area. In the short term and probably also in the medium term there will be a good opportunity to compensate or even over-compensate the negative effect of this development on bank earnings in South-East Europe by raising the share of higher-margin lending business – an option rendered possible by the improvement of risk management – and by tapping banks' productivity reserves (assets per employee, staff costs as a percentage of assets; see also Bank Austria Creditanstalt, 2004). In the long run, however, earnings prospects in the three regions should converge.

3. TO MAKE HIGH GROWTH RATES SUSTAINABLE, SOUTH-EAST EUROPE NEEDS ROBUST FINANCIAL MARKETS

Why is it important from a macroeconomic point of view for countries in SEE to improve the efficiency of the banking sector and the financial markets? To enhance the living standard in South-East Europe in the medium and long term it is crucial to make investments more attractive for foreign and domestic sources of capital. With a higher level of investment, the growth potential in the countries of SEE will rise. Unemployment and poverty can be reduced as a consequence of stronger economic growth. To realize investment opportunities it is necessary to have an effective banking sector. Only then will the allocation of risk and capital in the economy be optimal, even in periods of economic and financial distress. To reach this ambitious goal it is necessary for economies in SEE to establish well-designed financial market regulation and supervision. This includes the development of institutions and of a legal framework for banking supervision. It is important especially for the fast growing economies in SEE – with plenty of profitable investment opportunities – to avoid financial market instability, since instability will have the effect of curbing GDP growth by a substantial amount in subsequent years.

Financial instability has a negative impact on the real economy. Financial distress in the banking sector reduces the level of output in the economy as it causes a misallocation of capital and risk. If bankrupt financial institutions have to be bailed out by the public sector, financial instability will cause additional fiscal costs. The instability may be triggered by macroeconomic shocks which can include a rapid movement in interest rates, exchange rates or asset prices. A main reason for the high vulnerability of financial institutions to macroeconomic shocks is similar and positively correlated exposures of financial market participants. Tremendous recessionary pressure and a shrinking potential output may be the consequences of macroeconomic shocks if the mentioned correlation of exposures between individual market participants is high.

The last few decades saw a typical pattern of financial crises. A crisis is triggered, for example, by a rapid fall in asset prices or the end of an investment boom. Most financial crises occur after an overheating of the economy. It is thus crucial for countries in SEE to establish effective financial market regulation in order to achieve sustainable economic growth.

Interactions between the behaviour of financial market participants and financial risks mirror the demand for regulation and good policy design. Capital adequacy is widely regarded as one of the main tools in dealing with financial stability. In this sense Basel II is an effective way to avoid financial instability.

Sound financial regulation improves macroeconomic conditions for economies, especially in transition economies. However, during the period of turning from a government-owned to a market-based financial system the banking sector as well as the financial markets will be under stress.

4. ROMANIA'S BANKING SECTOR EMBRACING MARKET ECONOMICS

Romania has already made progress in the transition to a market economy. But in comparison to other candidates for EU entry, Romania has to accelerate the pace of implementing reforms. Particularly with regard to privatization, corporate governance, competition policy and financial sector development, Romania is still behind other EU accession candidates. On top of this, Romania has to deal with a severe corruption problem before it addresses other reforms in politics and economics. Resolution of the corruption problem will enhance Romania's economic potential. Improved law enforcement and better overall governance will make Romania more attractive to foreign investors and facilitate domestic investment. In other words, to make high economic growth sustainable, Romania has to concentrate on institutional reforms.

The Romanian banking sector provides a good example of how a banking system develops in a transformation economy. Changes in the banking system over the past few years have been accompanied by fast economic growth. The Romanian economy is growing at one of the highest rates in SEE and therefore offers great investment opportunities. In addition to the potential in corporate banking, Romania may emerge as an attractive market for retail banking with its population of 22 million. The reform of the Romanian banking sector goes hand in hand with the need for sound financial market regulation and supervision. With Romania aiming for membership of the EU in 2007, the country has already improved its banking sector and financial regulation. But to achieve the banking and financial standards reached by the current EU members, Romania still has a long way to go.

The Romanian banking system experienced several years of crisis in the 1990s during which efficiency and also profitability declined. The return to efficiency and profitability therefore started at a low level. Privatization and restructuring of the banking sector made progress. The most important consequence of the consolidation process was the reduction of the share of non-performing loans in the total loan portfolio, from 59 per cent in 1998 to 2 per cent in 2002 (Bank Austria Creditanstalt, 2004). In addition, the privatization of the banking sector has improved its efficiency. The gains were won by a steady decline in the number of credit institutions in the last few years. As a consequence, the five largest banks managed 63 per cent of total assets in the market in September 2003. The pattern was quite similar in terms of deposits (64 per cent). In recent years foreign banks have become more and more successful in establishing business in Romania. The share of total banking sector assets managed by foreign banks rose to 58 per cent by the third quarter of 2003. In 1998 this figure was merely 20 per cent.

Despite the progress, Romania has a long way to go to catch up with other financial markets in Europe. The degree of financial intermediation in Romania, measured as the total assets of the banking sector relative to GDP, is really low at 33 per cent. The value for Poland is 65 per cent, and for the Czech Republic 107 per cent. In recent years the growth of the overall economy has always outstripped the expansion of the banking sector. This shows that financial market regulation must be pushed through in order to foster the Romanian banking sector. In December 2003, to improve financial stability, the Romanian parliament adopted a new Banking Act, which is a financial market regulation in line with EU standards and Basel Committee recommendations. For example, the capital adequacy ratio is 12 per cent for credit institutions. In addition, a bank is not allowed to lend more than 20 per cent of its own funds to related parties or to clients with large exposures.

In addition to the reforms already implemented, further reforms are required because the Romanian banking sector faces numerous challenges. Besides the weak judiciary and the low level of financial intermediation already mentioned above, there is a strong need to reform the insurance and pension systems. Private pension legislation should enable private pension fund companies to provide quality services for future retirees. Romania's insurance market is very small, so the requirements for improving the legal framework and supervision in the insurance sector are even greater than in the banking sector. The creation of a pension fund sector is important for the real economy, too. Pension savings have a long time horizon and therefore are suitable for long-term investments. Financial instruments like corporate bonds and mortgages used in a sound legislative framework reduce a firm's cost of capital and therefore provide a basis for a higher growth potential in the economy.

5. OUTLOOK FOR SEE'S BANKING SECTOR

To summarize, I consider the following to be interesting and important. The South-East European countries started restructuring their banking sectors later than the Eastern European EU countries. This means that virtually all countries of the region learned from the experience of the frontrunners of reform in Eastern Europe, like, for example, the Czech Republic. This seems to be particularly true for Bosnia and Herzegovina, Bulgaria and Croatia, where the banking sectors today are to a very high degree in private foreign hands. Customers appreciate the services of foreign banks across the region. This has resulted in a major increase in confidence in the banking sector. Provided the South-East European countries remain committed to transition, they will be able to utilize the considerable potential for growth of their economies. This in turn will boost the development of the national banking sectors. Of course, risks to banks in the region have increased due to the rising complexity of banking activities. But thanks to the modern methods of risk management introduced by foreign banks and thanks to improving banking supervision, it should be possible to control these risks. Since competition in the Eastern European EU countries such as the Czech Republic, Hungary and Poland has already become rather strong and earnings margins have narrowed accordingly, the banking sectors in South-East Europe with their still high margins and large productivity reserves are increasingly attracting the interest of Western banks.

REFERENCES

Bank Austria Creditanstalt (2004), *Banking in CEE*, Extra Report.

Christl, J. (2004), *Macroeconomic Consequences of Financial Regulation*, 25th SUERF Colloquium, Keynote Speech.

European Bank for Reconstruction and Development (2003), *Strategy for Romania*.

European Bank for Reconstruction and Development (2004), *Spotlight on South-Eastern Europe, An Overview of Private Sector Activity and Investment*.

International Monetary Fund (2004a), *International Financial Statistics*.

International Monetary Fund (2004b), diverse *Country Reports*.

24. Banking in South-East Europe: the case of the Raiffeisen Group

Heinz Wiedner

This chapter describes, first, where the Raiffeisen group operates in the region of South-East Europe, what businesses we run, and what overall approach we have pursued in opening up these markets. Then some general economic and financial indicators for the region are provided. Finally the chapter focuses on banking concentration and market shares in the regional banking sectors.

Throughout the region, the Raiffeisen Group has basically adhered to the principle of entering the markets at an early stage. We have typically set up greenfield operations and, in some countries, have later moved on to acquisitions when wanting to expand our portfolio, or when the opportunity came up. Our most recent acquisition in South-East Europe was the Savings Bank of Albania, which we bought at the beginning of 2004.

With regard to the question of either using local management and know-how or bringing in foreign expertise, we do in principle rely on local management. We obviously provide external support, help, coaching and certain tools and instruments that we have available, but it is one of our governing principles to have local management there to run the bank as much as possible. This is because it is still more important to know the environment, to know your local customers than it is to only know Western practices. Obviously, that has to be complemented by group know-how and knowledge of best practice. Finally, we pursue a universal banking approach rather than concentrating on specific customer or market segments. We consider most of these markets to be too small to support niche players, and focusing only on one niche is risky and does not produce adequate scale effects.

The above indicates that Raiffeisen ventured East really very early in the process of transition. The establishment of the first Raiffeisen bank in the whole region of Central and Eastern Europe, in Hungary, dates back to 1987, before the fall of the Iron Curtain. We have since added practically one country per year so that to date we operate in 15 countries in the region. The only countries in South-East Europe where we have no presence are

Macedonia and Moldova. These two countries are still at a very, very early stage of development, and while we have not ruled out going there in principle, these countries are not our top priority at this stage. Especially in South-East Europe, we are very well positioned in the individual markets in terms of competition. For instance, we moved up to the top rank in Serbia in 2004. Yet the number by itself is not even that meaningful, what really counts is the overall importance compared to the rest of the markets. Obviously in very large markets like Russia, even a number twelve bank can be quite significant, because none of the foreign banks has a larger share in that huge market.

The key interim figures for 2004 indicate that South-East Europe accounts for nearly half of Raiffeisenbank's total assets in the overall region of Central and Eastern Europe. But in terms of business outlets, in terms of branches, South-East Europe already accounts for more than half – not least because of our presence in Romania, the largest country in that region, where we have over 200 outlets. The same holds true for employees – we have about 9000 employees in that area, compared to 20 000 in the overall region. This, if you look at Raiffeisen Zentralbank as the parent company, is 20 000 out of 22 000 employees. So we have a staff of 20 000 in Central and Eastern Europe but only close to 2000 in Austria. That also shows that we see ourselves clearly as a Central and Eastern European bank, and not only as an Austrian bank with ownership interests in these countries.

With regard to general GDP growth data, growth rates in the region are much better than in the rest of the euro area. Recently, the Russian-speaking areas posted the highest growth rates. But what we call the second wave of EU countries – Romania, Bulgaria and Croatia – are obviously now picking up a lot of speed. Romania has been reported to have reached 8 per cent growth of GDP in 2004. The economies of these countries have accelerated in recent years, and the outlook is very, very promising.

Another indicator of future potential is the volume of domestic credits in relation to GDP. Here a volume of 110 per cent of GDP for the euro area compares with levels of 20 per cent to 35 per cent in South-East Europe. This also shows clearly why, at the same time, there is increasing pressure to expand banking assets, and to expand loans at a faster pace than GDP growth. I think that is quite natural, but we also understand the concerns of the central bank to limit such growth to manageable dimensions. Obviously, if you look at loans to households, you see a similar high gap, with a very positive development in 2002 and 2003; 2004 was even stronger in some areas. But you see South-East Europe and the second wave of accession countries – Romania, Bulgaria and Croatia – moving uphill very, very fast, but still having reached only 10 per cent of GDP, far from the 49 or 50 per cent levels in the euro area.

In terms of deposits, the picture is somewhat different – which is quite understandable, as money is put into consumption, with people purchasing cars, renovating their homes and buying TVs and refrigerators. That money is to a certain degree taken out of the deposits side. So the deposit growth is clearly no longer as strong as it used to be, and in some areas it is even shrinking.

Banking concentration in Central and Eastern Europe (in terms of the market shares of the five largest banks) continues to be lowest in Russia and the Ukraine. In Serbia things are changing, but concentration is still relatively low. In most of the countries the top five banks account for around 60 per cent, a level that one can consider a good level of concentration. I still see some movement in that respect, but maybe not that much any more. There are still some privatizations going on. At the time of writing, Romania had two large banks which are to be privatized, the largest one being Banca Commerciale, which will probably be privatized towards the latter part of 2005, and CEC, the local savings bank coming up for privatization soon. That will also still have an impact on the banking landscape in that market. Privatization in the EU countries of Central and Eastern Europe has largely been completed; this is also true for Croatia.

Regarding the banking sector in the second-wave countries, you can clearly see that there are two countries that have been predominant in moving into these markets, namely Italian and Austrian banks. Between them, they have a share of more than 50 per cent in the South-East European banking market. Among the Italian banks, Banca Intesa and Unicredito moved quite successfully into these markets in recent years. German banks, in contrast, are not significant players in that area. That is somewhat surprising, but it is a fact today, and I think that to enter the region now would be very late and quite expensive.

If we analyse the market share in what we still call transition markets – Albania, Serbia and Bosnia – then you still see a more fragmented picture. But again the Austrian banks are quite active, for instance Hypo-Alpe Adria has made quite an aggressive move into these markets.

As a final point, what are the main functions that international banks actually have? I would say, to create trust and confidence among the population. I think that has happened in Central and Eastern Europe. As mentioned in other sections in this book, in the changeover period to the euro, when in some of the countries the Deutsche mark was still a very predominant currency, people tended to keep a lot of cash in their homes. I think that a great deal of that money has since been brought to the banks and converted into euros. That was money that previously was not part of the economy, which now has become available as working capital in the economy. Obviously, the transfer of know-how and technology, the introduction of new products and services made this possible. And also, even contrary to popular belief, support is being lent to the small and medium-sized enterprise (SME) sector. Raiffeisen banks have focused very much on that segment in recent years, and is the fastest growing area in our whole portfolio. It is, however, an area that one has to understand. Clearly, before you move into that sector, you have to understand the environment and you have to know on what criteria to base your lending decisions. Otherwise you venture into unknown and risky territory. My personal experience in Romania has been that in the past, some of the smaller companies with access to state-owned banks used to treat loans more like subsidies rather than real loans. Here, a change in culture has occurred. Therefore, the SMEs constitute a segment one has to be quite careful with, but it is definitely a very promising one – both for banks and for the respective countries.

We also see that there is a role in introducing and helping local companies to get access to international markets – into the EU but also into other areas of the region. That is something that we at Raiffeisen are promoting actively. And at the same time, by being there and by creating a banking infrastructure, we are also attracting other foreign direct investors into those countries. We also provide sponsorships of conferences on specific countries, in Austria and elsewhere, where we actually join forces with the individual countries to present their values to a business community.

In summary let me say that we at Raiffeisen are extremely pleased and proud to be active in South-East Europe. We believe that we are still at the beginning in fact; the potential for future growth is clearly there, and together with other partners we can provide sustainable growth in the future. We are not so naive to believe that growth will continue at the current pace every year over the next ten years; I would love to see that, but it is not something one could count on. So you have to make sure that you can weather storms when they happen. However, overall we are convinced that this region is a very attractive one indeed for many years to come.

25. Banking in South-East Europe: the case of Erste Bank

Manfred Wimmer

I would like to react to some of the terms – and their counterparts – used in the other contributions to this section. One of those counterpart pairs is foreign banks versus domestic banks. I do not share that thinking. That is not a category for Erste Bank as a group. We very much like to think about our operations in, presently, Central Europe and Croatia, as domestic banks. These banks of course happen to have a foreign owner in the same way as the majority of our shareholders are non-Austrians. Yet we define markets as our home markets and this is what we mean; we feel at home there and this is where we see our faith and destiny. We are a company listed on the Vienna stock exchange which has a market value at present of roughly EUR 9 billion. If you look at the distribution of this market value, 50 per cent of our market value is represented by our business in the Czech Republic, a further 15 per cent by our business in Slovakia, a further 15 per cent by our businesses in Hungary and Croatia and a mere 20 per cent of our total enterprise value is represented by our business in Austria. Now guess where we feel at home? I do not think that in attitude and perception there is a huge difference between a bank with foreign owners and a bank with domestic owners. If you look at where we allocate our capital and what we do with the profits, we pay a dividend which is less than 25 per cent of our net profit on a regular basis. The rest is being reinvested into the business. Presently, about 30 per cent of our capital is allocated to the Central and South-East European businesses, and 70 per cent is still allocated to Austrian and international business, and the group-wide treasury business. This capital allocation is shifting at a dramatic speed and I would assume that within the next three years, probably, the capital allocation will be split in equal portions between Central and South-East Europe on the one hand, and the mature markets and international markets on the other hand.

Second, while the approach to comparing efficiency between Western banks and domestic banks presented by Laurent Weill (see Chapter 21) may have its merits, at Erste Bank we believe in simply measuring efficiency by way of the cost–income ratio, which compares our cost to our operating income. On that basis any one of our Central and South-East European businesses is more efficient than the Austrian business. This has to do with a number of factors. I am not surprised about the relatively high efficiency level in our Central European markets because the cost-to-income ratios there are on a sustainable basis in the range of 55 or 54 per cent of operating income, whereas in Austria it is roughly 67 per cent. This still is, compared to German banks, a quite attractive ratio. However, there are certain limitations in the Austrian environment that prevent us from dramatically increasing our efficiency levels. First of all, it is an extremely competitive and saturated market in which margins are thin. Second, we have very high labour costs. Third, we have the most inflexible labour statute that you can imagine. A substantial proportion of our staff in Austria enjoys life-time employment, which takes away some flexibility. But I think that is not even the point. Measuring efficiency by way of the cost–income ratio also implies that you can turn two screws to improve this ratio. One is to improve on the cost side and the other is to improve on the revenue side and basically promote growth. That is what Central and Eastern Europe and South-East Europe is about. We go there because of the growth prospects. Growth and expansion of our operations is the clear priority compared to fine-tuning the efficiency of the operations.

Third, there is always the topic of greenfield investment versus acquisitions. In my opinion, this view does not reflect the reality of investment decisions. You do not look at a market and just think: 'Should we go for a greenfield investment or for an acquisition?' I think the reasons for deciding one way or the other go much deeper. This has to do with the very fundamental strategy you pursue. For instance, there is a huge difference in strategy between RZB and Erste Bank. Both approaches are perfectly legitimate. Both approaches are extremely successful in their own right. But they are just fundamentally different. The contribution by Heinz Wiedner (see Chapter 24) gives you a perception of the breadth and depth of the RZB network. Our most important priority, in contrast, is focus – concentration on our core business: we are a retail bank. So we focus and concentrate on the retail business. We would not opportunistically divert into a wholesale business as the driving business, just because there is an attractive investment opportunity in that business in a particular country.

Moreover, we focus on a small number of markets. That is why we now have operations only in four countries outside Austria, namely the Czech Republic, Slovakia, Hungary and Croatia. We focus on a small number of markets because in retail banking it is important to have country-wide coverage and a significant market share, which means that you have to have a large organization in a market in order to command market share. And you cannot build a large organization (that is, a branch network) with a greenfield operation within any reasonable period of time, which is why we only acquire. That is why we regularly enter markets later than other people, because we have to wait until the right targets come to the market. Our favourite acquisitions are savings banks. Savings banks are usually the last pieces of the banking industry which come to the market because they are usually perceived as a national treasure. There is always an element of national pride and an element of social responsibility, and therefore it is always very difficult for a country to privatize its savings banks. But these are our favourites, and as every single one of these investments is a major investment, we cannot purchase a large number of them. So we have to focus and concentrate.

Fourth, that sort of principal policy determines how you build your asset base. I think it was Mr Kraft who came to the conclusion in his analyses that foreign banks 'prefer' retail assets to wholesale assets. That is not a matter of preferring retail assets to wholesale assets because you can foreclose more easily. It goes much deeper than that. This results from the fundamental business model. We are a retail bank. That is why we prefer retail assets. In most markets it is actually much more difficult to foreclose on retail collateral assets than on corporate collateral assets. For instance, mortgages on residential housing collateral are incredibly difficult to foreclose. So it is not easy, but at least until now the payment behaviour and the performance of the Eastern European retail portfolios is more stable and is better than the performance on the corporate side.

Fifth, so where do we go from there? I need to say a few words on South-East Europe versus Central Europe, because our current emphasis clearly is in Central Europe. Now, what is different? In Central Europe we had the chance to buy large retail banks in big chunks in a few transactions and occupy a substantial market share there. In the only South-East European market where we are present, which is Croatia, we had to follow a different pattern because South-East Europe is different. South-East Europe is typically made up of fairly small markets in fairly small economies. Usually, the banking industry is more fragmented. The Croatian banking scene was extremely fragmented until serious crises hit. It still is pretty much fragmented. I guess the same holds true for Serbia and for some of the other countries of former Yugoslavia. In South-East Europe, probably only Romania and Bulgaria are different cases. There you have large bulge-bracket banks, which can give you a large market share in one go. But I think the degree of fragmentation of the market is a differentiating factor.

What else is different? It is sort of a differentiation in accession perspectives. We believe in the geographical coherence of our markets, so we try to expand in an organic way across the geography of Europe. We like to invest in countries neighbouring those where we already are, and we also like to invest in markets that have a defined and clear EU accession perspective and time line. This was not the case for South-East European countries until pretty recently, with the exception of Slovenia, but it is now the case at least for Romania, Bulgaria and Croatia. And because we like geographical coherence we now consider Serbia as an essential bridging market. Therefore, we develop an interest in the region as a whole, as long as the individual markets have a minimum size and are at a minimum stage of development, which permits us as a retail bank to develop and prosper.

What do we need as a retail bank in terms of ingredients? Of course we like under-penetrated markets, which create a huge upside potential. But still, we need a middle class – we are a middle class bank. Therefore, a market has to have a middle class or at least a developing middle class. A middle class requires a degree of political and social stability to prosper, which is why we need a degree of political and social stability to prosper. In addition, we need a prospect of sustainable superior growth, triggered by that EU accession schedule.

These are the cornerstones of attractive target markets for us. From these you can conclude why South-East Europe is now becoming the most promising target market for Erste Bank Group.

Index

Aglietta, M. 365
Aguado, S. 174
Aigner, Dennis 337
Aizenman, Joshua 152
Al-Atrash, H.M. 253
Albania
  currency regime 111
  migration data problems 294
  poverty 289
  remittances 295
  SAP progress 43
  unemployment 315
Albu, Lucian 142
Alfaro, L. 209
Allen, F. 358
Allen, Linda 337
Altunbas, Yener 338, 339
Anderson, J.E. 249, 254, 261
Angelini, P. 359
Angeloni, I. 93
anti-trust legislation 362
Antohi, Dorina 130, 142
Aoki, Kosuke 126
Argy, Victor 152
armies, *see* military forces
asylum seekers, *see* refugees
Austrian banks xi, 4–5; *see also* banking sector; Erste Bank; OeNB
Avramovic, D. 93

Backé, P. 84, 93, 116
Bairoch, Paul 145
Balassa–Samuelson effect 106, 133
Baldwin, Richard E. 252
Baliño, T. 93
Balkans 31; *see also* Western Balkans
banking sector
  asset share of state-owned banks 375–6
  competition 358–62
  confidence 370–72, 384
  cost efficiency 347–8
    compared to Western Banks 339–43, 386–7
    and environment 343–7
    measuring 337–9
    significance 335–7
  foreign banks presence 352–6, 361, 372–4, 384–5, 386
  and foreign currency 374–5
  institutional concerns 357–8
  reforms 350–51
  retail bias 356–8, 388
  significance 377–8
  size 370
  stability 352
  supervisory challenges 362–4
  see also central banks; Erste Bank; Raiffeisen Group
banks, local, confidence in 54–5
Barisitz, S. 101, 111, 113, 117
Barrel, R. 212, 214
Barro, R.J. 78
Beck, T. 351
Berend, Ivan T. 145
Berg, A. 77, 93
Berger, Helge 152
Bernanke, Ben S. 127
Bevan, A. 212, 214
Bikker, Jakob 345
Blanchard, Olivier 126
Boeri, Tito 305–11, 332
Bogetić, Z. 174
Borensztein, E. 74, 77, 93, 209, 210
Bosnia, refugees 290
Bosnia and Herzegovina
  banking sector 358
  currency regime 110–11
  investment considerations 276
  remittances 295
  SAP progress 43–4
Braconier, B.H. 213
brain drain 300, 331

Brainard, L.S. 212
Braumann, B. 107
Brenton, P. 212
Breuss, F. 211
bribery tax 224, 236; *see also* corruption
Broda, Christian 74
Bruecker, H. 309
Bruno, Michael 148, 152
Bulgaria
  1991 floating exchange rate programme 177–9
  1991 unsuitability for currency board 179–81
  1992–1996 policies 181–7
  1997 onwards, currency board 187–93
  banking systems 353
  investment considerations 277
  migration data problems 294
  prospects 193
  recent approaches to macroeconomic stabilization 176–7
  relations between central and commercial banks 196
  remittances 295
Bulgarian lev 112, 188, 189, 194, 197
Bulir, A. 115
Busek, Erhard 30–38
business environment 51–3
Bussière, Matthieu 242–68

Calvo, Guillermo A. 77, 130, 151
Campos, N.F. 214
Carstensen, K. 212
Caviglia, G. 335, 348
CEB (Czech Republic, Estonia, Hungary, Latvia, Lithuania, Poland, Slovak Republic, Slovenia) 47, 282
CEE, *see* Central and Eastern Europe
CEE-5 (Czech Republic, Hungary, Poland, Slovakia, Slovenia) 21
Central and Eastern Europe (CEE)
  and Austria 271
  relationship with euro 65–6
Central and Eastern Europe and the Baltics (CEB), *see* CEB
central banks
  Bulgaria 196
  net debtors 124
  see also banking sector; NBR; NBY; OeNB
Central Europe and the Baltics (CEB), *see* CEB
Cetorelli, N. 359
Chang, Roberto 135
Cheng, I.-H. 252, 254, 256, 257, 266
Chiang, M.-H. 255, 259
Christiano, Lawrence J. 126
Christie, E. 214, 238, 253
Christl, Josef xi–xiv, 65–8
Claessens, S. 212, 359
Collier, Paul 319
confidence, in banks 54–5, 370–72, 384
corruption
  Albania 43
  burden on business 224, 236
  expropriation laws affecting 205
  impacting wholesale 357
  Macedonia 44
  ongoing problem 41, 53
  Romania 378
  see also crime, organized
cost efficiency, *see* banking sector, cost efficiency
crime, organized 31, 32, 41; *see also* corruption
Croatia
  banking sector 353, 358, 372
  currency regime 111
  investment considerations 276
  mobilkom austria 271–3
  poverty 289
  refugees 290
  remittances 295
  SAP progress 44
  unemployment 315
Crystal, J.S. 365
currency boards 179–81, 187–93; *see also* exchange rate regimes
current account deficits 8, 25

Daianu, Daniel 119–44
Dallas, H. 82
data availability 28, 50, 281–2, 294
de Haan, J. 365
de Haas, R.T.A. 365

De la Torre, Augusto 74
Deardorff, A.V. 249
Deichmann, J.I. 214
deindustrialization 24
Demekas, Dimitri G. 209–41
democratization 30
Demsetz, Harold 345
development gap 145–7
Di Mauro, F. 211
Dietsch, Michel 343
Djankov, S. 245
dollarization
  abandoning 168
  definitions 69, 157–8
  effects 158–61
  South-East Europe 79–81
  sustained 82–92
  tourism 85–6
  trade-offs 70–72, 78–9
  unilateral 81, 91–2
  see also euroization
dollarization, de facto/unofficial 72, 157–8
dollarized economies 170
Dooley, Michael P. 149
Dornbusch, Rudiger 147, 152
Duisenberg, W.F. 81
Dvorsky, S. 115

Eastern Adriatic region 31; *see also* Western Balkans
ECOFIN (Council for Economic and Financial Affairs), position on unilateral euroization 81
Edwards, Sebastian 71, 77, 84, 85, 149, 152, 160
Egert, B. 106
Egger, P. 211, 253, 254, 260, 266
Eichengreen, B. 105
Eisenbeis, R. 365
Ekholm, K. 213
electricity, *see* power shortages
emigration, *see* migration
employment, *see* unemployment
employment protection legislation (EPL), *see* labour markets, rigidities
EMU (Economic and Monetary Union) 2, 13–16, 309–10
EPL (employment protection legislation), *see* labour markets, rigidities
Erste Bank 386–9
Estrin, S. 146, 212, 214
EU, *see* European Union
euro
  attitudes in Central and Eastern Europe 65–6
  role in South-East Europe 10, 67–8
euro deposits 108–10
euroization
  definitions 69, 77
  extent 108–10
  Montenegro 165–9
  risks 67
  trade-offs 72–4
  see also dollarization
European integration 1–5, 9, 12–18
European investment plans 270–71
European Union (EU)
  financial assistance programmes 42–3
  interest limited in Western Balkans 30
  migration concerns and restrictions 305–6, 308–9
  trade integration model 242–4, 256–63
  trade with South-East Europe 58, 244–9
  trade with Western Balkans 40–41
exchange rate regimes
  approaches 147–8
  CEE experiences 150–51
  challenges in selecting 115–16
  and growth 148–9
  pegged 69–70
  in place xii, 110–14
  as policy tool 107–8
  Romania 137–8
  South-East Europe 151–2
  types 155–8
  see also currency boards
export-led growth 201–3
exports 24–5, 50–51

Falcetti, Elisabetta 47–61
Faruqee, H. 255, 259
FDI, *see* foreign direct investment
Feenstra, R.C. 211, 254

Feige, E. 109
Fidrmuc, Ján 245, 253, 254, 256
Fidrmuc, Jarko 99, 242–68
finance, access to 53–5
financial markets 106–7, 114
Fischer, S. 74, 78, 152
Fontaine, Pascal 18
foreign banks 352–6, 361, 372–4, 384–5, 386
foreign currency
 and banking sector 374–5
 see also exchange rate regimes
foreign direct investment (FDI)
 bribery tax 224, 236
  see also corruption
 case for 209–11
 determinants 211–14, 224–30
 distribution of 33, 215
 greenfield investment 387
 in infrastructure 207
 policy environment 222
 potential 230–31
 and privatizations 205–7
 recent growth in 9, 31, 203–5
 South-East Europe 55, 58, 104
 threshold effects 231–6
 and unemployment 320–21
 Western Balkans 320–21
 see also banking sector, foreign banks presence; mobilkom austria group
Frankel, Jeffrey A. 74, 82, 93, 107, 210
Fratianni, Michele 152
French, R. 142
Frenkel, Jacob A. 152
Frieden, Jeffrey 75
Fry, M. 155, 156
fundamentals 100–104

Galac, T. 352, 365
Gale, D. 358
Garibaldi, P. 214, 310, 322
GDP growth 7–9, 282–4, 320
Gerschenkron, Alexander 146
Ghosh, Atish R. 74, 149
Giavazzi, F. 152
Gilbert, Roy 348
Giovannini, Alberto 152
Glick, R. 93
Gligorov, V. 117
Goldfajn, I. 77, 78
Gordon, D. 78
Graham, E. 209
gravity models 249–56
 of trade integration with EU 256–63
Greene, William 337
Greenspan, Alan 142
Grigorian, David 343, 344
Gruber, T. 108
Grubert, H. 212
Gueorguiev, Nikolay 141

Haaf, Katharina 345
Halpern, L. 106
Hamilton, C.B. 252, 254
Handler, H. 110
Hanke, S. 165, 174, 177, 180
Hansen, B.E. 233
Hanson, G. 211
Hassett, K.A. 212
Hatton, J. Timothy 290
Hausmann, Ricardo 74
Havrylyshyn, O. 253
Heller, Robert 152
Herzegovina, *see* Bosnia and Herzegovina
Hines, J.R., Jr 212
Hoekman, B. 245
Holland, D. 214
Holzmann, Robert 281–304, 332
Horváth, Balázs 209–41
Horvath, Julius 145–54
hub and spoke 29
Hubbard, R.G. 212
Hunya, G. 214, 223

Iara, Anna 133
IFIs (international financial institutions) 48, 54
immigration, *see* migration
inflation 7–9, 377
inflation targeting (IT) 125–8
 in Romania 128–35, 136–7
infrastructure 35, 207; *see also* mobile communications; power shortages
international trade 40, 58
intra-regional trade 29, 40
investment climate 300
Investment Compact 33, 36, 223
investment plans 270–71

Isarescu, Mugur 142
Issing, Otmar 138
IT, *see* inflation targeting
Ize, Alain 74

Jakab, Z. 253
Janicki, P.H. 212
Jankov, L. 365
Javorcik, B.S. 209
Jeanne, Olivier 141
Jonas, Jiri 127
Jondrow, James 337
Jun, K. 212

Kaiser, M.C. 152
Kallai, Ella 119–44
Kaminski, B. 253
Kao, C. 255, 259
Kenen, Peter 74
Kinoshita, Y. 214
Klinglmair, Robert 299
Kmenta, Jan 348
Konopielko, L. 365
Korhonen, I. 99
Kose, M.A. 94
Kosovo
  currency regime 110
  unemployment 315–17
Kraft, Evan 350–67
Krgović, Ljubiša 155–75

labour markets
  and EMU 310
  regulations 300
  rigidities 322–5
Laeven, L. 359
Lafrance, Robert 152
Lahiri, A.K. 93
Landes, David S. 146, 152
Landesmann, Michael A. 21–9
Lankes, H.-P. 211, 214
Lanoo, K. 365
Lehman, A. 238
Levin, Andrew T. 126, 142
Levy Yeyati, Eduardo 69–76, 109, 148
Liebscher, Klaus xi–xiv, 1–5
Lim, E.-G. 209, 211
Linder, S. 249
Linnemann, H. 249
Lipschitz, L. 209
Liviatan, Nissan 181, 197
Lozano-Vivas, Ana 343
Lungu, Laurian 128

Macedonia, former Yugoslav Republic of
  currency regime 111
  poverty 289
  SAP progress 44
  unemployment 295
macroeconomic performance 48–51
Maddock, Nicholas 312–30, 332
Maeso-Fernandez, F. 267
Magendzo, I.I. 84, 85
Manole, Vlad 343, 344
Marin, D. 214
Markusen, J.R. 211, 212, 260
Masciandaro, D. 362
Maskus, K.E. 211, 212
Masson, P. 93
Mátyás, L. 254
Mauro, P. 93, 322
Mazzaferro, F. 93
McAllister, Patrick 338
McKinnon, Ronald 70
McManus, Douglas 338
Melvin, Michael 152
Mero, K. 365
Micco, Alejandro 71, 254, 255
Micevska, Maja 322, 323, 324, 325
migration 289–95
  EU concerns and restrictions 305–6, 308–9
  and unemployment 300–303
military forces 31; *see also* wars, recent
Mishkin, Frederic S. 127, 134, 151
Mizsei, Kalman 312–30, 332
Moalla-Fetini, R. 110
mobile communications 269–70, 273–6
mobilkom austria group 269–70, 271–3
Mody, A. 238
Moldova 32
monetary policy 104–8, 115; *see also* inflation targeting
Mongelli, F.P. 78
Montenegro
  currency regime 110
  euroization 165–9

monetary system history 161–4
see also Serbia and Montenegro
Mooslechner, Peter xi–xiv, 99–118
Muenz, Rainer 303
Mundell, Robert 18, 74, 78
Mutti, J. 212

Naaborg, I. 365
Navaretti, G.B. 211
NBR (National Bank of Romania) 119–20, 123–5, 132, 136
NBY (National Bank of Yugoslavia) 161–4
Nemsic, Boris 269–77
Nenova, Mariella 176–98
Nerlich, Carolin 151
Nitsch, V. 93
NMS-8 (EU new member states from CEE) 24, 25, 26–7
Nowotny, Ewald 201–8

Obstfeld, M. 93, 105
OCA (Optimal Currency Area) theory 70–71, 72–3, 82, 85
OeNB (Oesterreichische Nationalbank) 3, 4–5, 6
OeNB East–West conferences xi–xiv, 1, 3–4
Ohrid Framework Agreement 44
Olivares, G. 77, 78

Padoa-Schioppa, T. 86
Pagano, M. 152
Pain, N. 212, 214
Panzar, John 344
Papl, L. 365
Persson, T. 93
Pfaffermayr, M. 254, 260
policy environment 222
and FDI 212–14, 230–31
Poole, William 152
Porta, A. 362
poverty 284–9, 317
Powell, Andrew 72
power shortages 201–3
Prasad, E.S. 94
pre-accession programmes 29
Priebe, Reinhard 39–46
privatization 40, 384
public administration reform 41–2

Quah, D. 93

Radice, E.A. 152
Rai, Anoop 337
Raiffeisen Group 382–5
Ranki, Gyorgy 145
reform, *see* banking sector, reforms; public administration reform; structural reforms
refugees 290
regional cooperation 32–5
Reinhart, Carmen M. 109, 131, 141, 149
remittances 295
Resmini, L. 212
Revoltella, D. 365
Ribakova, Elina 209–41
Riboud, Michelle 323
Riess, Armin 335
Riječka Banka 363
Ritzberger-Grünwald, Doris xi–xiv, 99–118
Rogoff, Kenneth S. 109, 149
ROL (Romanian leu) 123–4
Romania
banking sector 341, 378–80, 384
central bank position 123–5
corruption 378
currency regime 111
inflation history 119–23
inflation targeting implementation 128–35
monetary and exchange rate policy choices 135–8
poverty 288–9
remittances 295
unemployment 295
Rose, Andrew K. 70, 74, 82, 93, 107, 110, 210, 266
Rosse, James 344

SAA, *see* Stabilisation and Association Agreements
Saint-Amant, Pierre, *see* St-Amant, Pierre
Sanfey, Peter 47–61
SAP, *see* Stabilisation and Association Process
Sarris, Alexander 290, 300
Savić, N. 174

Scandinavian model of inflation 106
Scarpetta, Stefano 329
Schnatz, Bernd 242–68
Schneider, Friedrich 299
Scholtens, Bert 335
Schönfelder, B. 358
Schuler, K. 174, 177, 180
SDK (Social Bookkeeping Department) 162
SEE, *see* South-East Europe
Serbia
  currency regime 111
  investment considerations 276
Serbia and Montenegro
  poverty 289
  refugees 290
  remittances 295
  SAP progress 44–5
Serlenga, L. 254
SFRY (former Socialist Federal Republic of Yugoslavia) 58, 100–101
SGP (Stability and Growth Pact) 2–3
Shin, Y. 254
Singh, H. 212
Slovenia
  investment considerations 276
  mobilkom austria 271–3
SME sector, and unemployment 325–7
Smidkova, K. 116
SOPEMI report 290
Šošić, V. 253
South-Central Europe 31; *see also* Western Balkans
South-East Europe (SEE) xi
St-Amant, Pierre 152
Stabilisation and Association Agreements (SAA) 43
Stabilisation and Association Process (SAP) 42–6
Stability and Growth Pact (SGP) 2–3
Stability Pact for South Eastern Europe 30, 35–8
state expenditure 28
state-owned banks, *see* banking sector, asset share of state-owned banks
Stix, H. 109
Storf, O. 365
structural reforms 51
  and FDI 213–14
Sturzenegger, Federico 71, 72, 74, 109, 148
Svejnar, Jan 321, 322, 329
Svensson, Lars E.O. 125

Taci, A. 60
Tavlas, G.S. 82
taxation regimes 102
  and FDI 212–13
  and unemployment 322
Tepic, Sladjana 47–61
Tieman, Alexander 124, 142
Toubal, F. 212
trade, *see* international trade; intra-regional trade
Traistaru, Iulia 133
Transnistria 32
Trichet, Jean-Claude 6–11
trilemma, monetary policy 105

unemployment 331–2
  correlation to growth 306–8
  data reliability 28, 50
  and EMU 309–10
  levels 28, 33, 50, 295–303
  and poverty 317
  Western Balkans 313–17, 319–27
Urga, Giovanni 146

Valentinyi, M.E. 365
van Lelyveld, Iman 365
van Wincoop, E. 74, 249, 254, 261
Velasco, Andrés 135
Venables, A.J. 211, 214, 260
Vernon, R. 211
von Hagen, Jürgen 148, 152
Vranceanu, Radu 132, 141
Vujčić, B. 253

Wall, H.J. 252, 254, 256, 257, 266
Walter, Norbert 368–81
wars, recent 319–20; *see also* military forces
Weber, Axel A. 12–18
Wei, S. 213
Weill, Laurent 335–49
Western Balkans 31, 39
  economic development 39–42
  EU accession 312–13
  mobilkom austria group 269–70

Stabilisation and Association Process 42–6
unemployment 313–17
Wiedner, Heinz 382–5
Wieser, Thomas 331–2
Williamson, Jeffrey G. 290
Williamson, John 152
Wimmer, Manfred 386–9
Winkler, Adalbert 77–96, 115, 161
Winters, A.L. 252, 254
Wójcik, C. 84, 116
Woodford, Michael 126
Wu, Yi 209–41
Wunnava, P.V. 212
Wyplosz, C. 106

Yugoslavia, *see* SFRY

Zettelmeyer, Jeromin 141
Zhou, Jizhong 148, 152